Y0-CFS-834

Princeton Theological Monograph Series

K. C. Hanson, Charles M. Collier, D. Christopher Spinks, and Robin Parry, Series Editors

Recent volumes in the series:

William A. Tooman
Transforming Visions: Transformations of Text, Tradition, and Theology in Ezekiel

L. Paul Jensen
Subversive Spirituality: Transforming Mission through the Collapse of Space and Time

Roger A. Johnson
Peacemaking and Religious Violence: From Thomas Aquinas to Thomas Jefferson

Joel Burnell
Poetry, Providence, and Patriotism: Polish Messianism in Dialogue with Dietrich Bonhoeffer

William J. Meyer
Metaphysics and the Future of Theology: The Voice of Theology in Public Life

Christopher L. Fisher
Human Significance in Theology and the Natural Sciences: An Ecumenical Perspective with Reference to Pannenberg, Rahner, and Zizioulas

Randall W. Reed
A Clash of Ideologies: Marxism, Liberation Theology, and Apocalypticism in New Testament Studies

Nikolaus Ludwig von Zinzendorf
Christian Life and Witness: Count Zinzendorf's 1738 Berlin Speeches

Thriving in Babylon

Thriving in Babylon

Essays in Honor of A. J. Conyers

Edited by
DAVID B. CAPES
and
J. DARYL CHARLES

◆PICKWICK Publications • Eugene, Oregon

THRIVING IN BABYLON
Essays in Honor of A. J. Conyers

Princeton Theological Monograph Series 152

Copyright © 2011 Wipf and Stock Publishers. All rights reserved. Except for brief quotations in critical publications or reviews, no part of this book may be reproduced in any manner without prior written permission from the publisher. Write: Permissions, Wipf and Stock Publishers, 199 W. 8th Ave., Suite 3, Eugene, OR 97401.

Pickwick Publications
An Imprint of Wipf and Stock Publishers
199 W. 8th Ave., Suite 3
Eugene, OR 97401

www.wipfandstock.com

ISBN 13: 978-1-60608-956-9

Cataloging-in-Publication data:

Thriving in Babylon : essays in honor of A. J. Conyers / edited by David B. Capes and J. Daryl Charles.

Princeton Theological Monograph Series 152

xxxix + 382 p. ; 23 cm. Includes bibliographical references.

ISBN 13: 978-1-60608-956-9

1. Conyers, A. J., 1944–2004. 2. Christianity and culture. I. Capes, David B. II. Charles, J. Daryl, 1950–. III. Title. IV. Series.

BR115 C8 T49 2011

Manufactured in the U.S.A.

Contents

List of Contributors / vii

Foreword by Jürgen Moltmann / xi

Introduction / xiii

Biography of A. J. "Chip" Conyers
— *Deborah A. Conyers & James C. Conyers* / xix

Eulogy for Abda Johnson "Chip" Conyers
—*John W. Shouse* / xxxix

PART ONE: Faith

1. The Unfinished Agenda of Evangelical Theology
—*Millard J. Erickson* / 3

2. "Center," "Horizon," and Rhetorical Focus in Ignatius of Antioch—*Robert B. Sloan* / 19

3. Reading Scripture as a Christian—*Randy Hatchett* / 54

4. The Reformed Objection to Natural Theology: A Catholic Response to G. C. Berkouwer—*Eduardo J. Echeveria* / 69

5. On the Liturgical Consummation of a Christian Worldview: Worldview, Worship, and Way of Life
—*David K. Naugle* / 101

6. Share in the Joy: The Eschatology of A. J. Conyers
—*William D. Shiell* / 126

7. Speaking about Transcendence: Three Medieval Theologians—*Phuc Luu* / 147

8. "These Are the Masks of God": Martin Luther and the Protestant Life of Vocation—*Brian C. Brewer* / 178

PART TWO: Culture

9   Here I Stand . . . or Do I?—*Jean Bethke Elshtain* / 207

10   Reclaiming Tolerance: A. J. Conyers and Fethullah Gülen
—*David B. Capes* / 223

11   Fyodor Dostoevsky's *The Brothers Karamazov*: Resisting Pernicious Tolerance by Living the Iconic Life
—*Ralph C. Wood* / 240

12   Post-Consensus Ethics, the Natural Law, and Civil Society—*J. Daryl Charles* / 263

13   What Sort of Community? The Catholic Vision of the Church after Toleration—*Coleman Fannin* / 297

14   Passing It On: Biblical Wisdom as an Act of Love
—*David Lyle Jeffrey* / 327

15   Richard Weaver, the Gospel, and the Restoration of Culture—*Bradley G. Green* / 338

16   Preserving the Church's Story—*D. H. Williams* / 365

Selected Bibliography of A. J. Conyers / 381

Contributors

Brian C. Brewer
Assistant Professor of Christian Theology
George W. Truett Theological Seminary, Baylor University

David B. Capes
Dean of the Graduate School
Director of the School of Theology
Houston Baptist University

J. Daryl Charles
Director and Senior Fellow of the Bryan Institute for Critical Thought & Practice
Bryan College

Deborah A. Conyers
Waco, Texas

James C. Conyers
Lewisburg, West Virginia

Eduardo J. Echeverria
Professor of Philosophy at the Graduate School of Theology
Sacred Heart Major Seminary

Jean Bethke Elshtain
Laura Spelman Rockefeller Professor of Social and Political Ethics
University of Chicago Divinity School

Millard J. Erickson
Distinguished Professor of Theology
*The Kairos Institute
Port of Spain, Trinidad and Tobago*

COLEMAN FANNIN
PhD Candidate
University of Dayton

BRADLEY G. GREEN
Associate Professor of Christian Studies
Union University

RANDY HATCHETT
Professor of Theology
Chair of Philosophy
Houston Baptist University

DAVID LYLE JEFFREY
Distinguished Professor of Literature and the Humanities
Baylor University

PHUC LUU
Adjunct Instructor
Houston Baptist University

JÜRGEN MOLTMANN
Professor Emeritus of Systematic Theology
University of Tübingen

DAVID K. NAUGLE
Distinguished University Professor and Professor of Philosophy
Dallas Baptist University

WILLIAM D. SHIELL
Senior Pastor
First Baptist Church of Knoxville

JOHN W. SHOUSE
Professor of Christian Theology
Golden Gate Baptist Theological Seminary

Robert B. Sloan
President
Houston Baptist University

D. H. Williams
Professor of Religion in Patristics and Historical Theology
Baylor University

Ralph C. Wood
University Professor of Theology and Literature
Baylor University

Foreword

It is with deep gratitude that I take the opportunity to write a few words for this volume of essays in honor of A. J. Conyers—widely known as "Chip" Conyers—for we were connected both in friendship and mutual respect. He was one of the best scholars to write a dissertation on my theology in large measure because he was one of the most original in his own theological thinking. If I remember correctly, we first met at the Southern Baptist Theological Seminary in Louisville in 1983. He had already written his dissertation on the Christian concept of history and wanted to discuss this with me. Our conversation went late into the night. His dissertation became his first book: *God, Hope and History: Jürgen Moltmann and the Christian Concept of History* (1988).

We met over the years that followed at conferences, mostly in the States. Whenever he published a new book, he would send me a copy. I recall receiving *The Long Truce* and *The Eclipse of Heaven: Rediscovering the Hope of a World Beyond*. I liked to follow his ways of thinking and learned from his insights. Our last meeting took place when he invited me to give the second Parchman Lectures at George W. Truett Theological Seminary in Waco, Texas, where he had recently moved with his family. Looking again at the photos taken on that occasion, I can see on his face already the signs of his sufferings. I spoke on "Is There Life after Death?" and "Perichoresis: An Old Magical Word for a New Trinitarian Thinking." Chip had organized everything perfectly. The responses to my lectures were given by excellent theologians. Gloriana and Leo Parchman were present, and Chip proved to be a wonderful host and guide in his new life in Waco, Texas. This was our last meeting face to face.

Thriving in Babylon is a critical title for the global situation where we are seeking God and trying to reflect on our God-experiences. These essays demonstrate the breadth and depth of Chip Conyers' interests and thoughts. He was a most fruitful theologian, a stimulating thinker, and a great and beloved teacher. I am proud to have been of some help in developing his spirit and I deplore his too-early death. This volume of essays will prove that A. J. Conyers is not forgotten but present in the minds and hearts of his friends and colleagues and students.

Jürgen Moltmann
Tübingen
October 4, 2009

Introduction

THIS VOLUME, MULTIFACETED IN ITS SCOPE, FLOWS OUT OF THE WELLspring of deeply-held convictions shared by its coeditors. It is a mirror of our belief that the intersection of religion and culture, of theology and public life, is both critically important and vastly misunderstood—when not neglected—among people of faith. At the same time, the volume reflects our deepest appreciation for a friend, colleague, mentor, and theologian who, over the last two decades, provided astute cultural commentary and thereby embodied the intersection of theology and public life in the healthiest of ways. A premature death in 2004 prevented this remarkable friend and cultural "warrior" from exerting even greater influence. Though confessionally Baptist, A. J. (Chip) Conyers had a unique ability, through his gracious ecumenical spirit and extraordinary intellectual breadth, to think, teach, and write for the benefit of those who were outside of his own confessional boundaries. Chip was a champion of the "permanent things," to use the language of T. S. Elliot, and as a result he spoke to wider Christendom.

Anyone who knew Chip marveled at his intellectual dexterity. In a day of increasing hyper-specialization, Chip crossed interdisciplinary boundaries with grace and fluidity. He was comfortable discussing church life or christological controversy, Heidegger and Hegel or human dignity, trinitarianism or religious tolerance, faith and the Enlightenment or the fatherhood of God. With a wondrous combination of fatherly wisdom and reasoned passion, he could speak quite elegantly to the matters of democratic pluralism or human depravity, *Veritatis Splendor* or Wittgensteinian language games, the "linguistic turn" or liturgical reform. And this he did seemingly with the greatest of ease.

Those who were fortunate to encounter Chip were astonished at the sheer girth of his scholarship. His repertoire included historical and systematic theology, Christian history, political philosophy, philosophical hermeneutics and linguistics, and philosophical theology. More than anything, however, Chip understood the culture, discerning the historical and sociological roots of ideas, which made him a first-rate social critic with penetrating cultural analysis. Resisting the tendency of many who, sensing the theological currency of the times, permit themselves to become "children of the times," Chip addressed cultural trends through the lens of historic Christian orthodoxy, and he did so with philosophical robustness. Thereby he showed himself to be a student of the culture without being coopted by the forces and currents of the culture that he understood so well. Like Ambrose and Augustine, Chip confessed and took seriously the Christian's dual citizenship in this world; and like them he thought long and hard about the nexus of religious faith and cultural involvement. Like Aquinas, he was equally comfortable probing the philosophical meaning of human existence as well as exploring the majestic heights of Christian theology.

Against the sectarian Tertullian spirit, he answered the perennial question "What does Athens have to do with Jerusalem?" with an informed theological perspective that blended cultural engagement with eschatological hope. Chip, we need to emphasize, was not content either to retreat into pious devotionalism or to become a theologically unreflective activist.

In noting that Chip eschewed the sectarianism of Tertullian's thinking, we grant that qualification is in order. In posing the well-worn question of what Athens and Jerusalem have to do with one another, Tertullian was waxing rhetorical. After all, for him, the former represented intellectual culture and the life of the mind, while the latter represented our spiritual heritage through Christ. And, after all, he reasoned, we will *not* be judged on the basis of how much worldly wisdom and cultural refinement we have assimilated. At bottom, then, he was asking about the relative worth of those things which comprise the present life. Is not, therefore, intellectual pursuit, cultivation of the life of the mind, and the realization that "ideas have consequences" in the end an unnecessary luxury? Or, in the words of one commentator, by cultivating the life of the mind are we are not simply "fiddling while Rome is burning?"[1]

It is not at all difficult to understand how Tertullian draws certain conclusions. In his famous treatise *On Idolatry*, we learn much of

1. See in this regard the wonderfully prescient essay by John F. Crosby, "Education and the Mind Redeemed," *First Things* (December 1991) 23–28.

his rationale. The Christian, he writes, may not serve in the military, just as one may definitely not work for the state as a civil servant or a magistrate. But equally idolatrous, he argues, are educational ventures. So, for example, the Christian must not aspire to be either a teacher or a student, since both require the study of Greek and Roman classics. But danger lurks among the practical trades as well. Thus, the Christian may be neither a goldsmith, nor a silversmith, nor a woodcutter, since all of these vocations require the faithful to fashion idols for their pagan clients. And, of course, certain types of dress as well as a host of public places are grounds for idolatry and therefore must be avoided at all costs. Alas, one cannot be too careful, for the danger of idolatry is ubiquitous.

The difficulty, of course, is that the Tertullian mindset—at least that of the later sectarian Tertullian—is escapist in character. Its focus is "eschatological" to the extent that it severs, at least in meaningful ways, any allegiances to the temporal order in the interest of remaining faithful to the heavenly. But as Augustine painstakingly sought to demonstrate in *The City of God*, even when the culture is literally collapsing around us, as it was for Augustine, this will not do. Our dual citizenship requires that we engage culture, and that we do so meaningfully.

In this regard, Chip was decidedly anti-Tertullian, for he understood the necessity of occupying faithfully. His eschatological perspective held the temporal and the future in proper tension. And this in turn allowed him neither to fear cultural engagement nor to flirt with or succumb to its subtle entrapments. As a pilgrim and exile, whose true home was heavenly, Chip nevertheless lived with gusto, anchored in the awareness that the Lord Almighty was sovereign, and that this Sovereign Lord places us in particular cultural contexts for a purpose. Which brings us to the theme of this volume.

We chose "Thriving in Babylon" for several reasons. As a biblical metaphor, Babylon is richly suggestive (fully apart from its usage in the apocalyptic genre). For example, the author of 1 Peter employs it to complement the theme of being sojourners and resident aliens in a strange culture, hostile to God (5:13). This strangeness, however, in Peter's view should not give rise to an attitude of contempt toward others (or, for that matter, toward the social institutions that comprise culture). Rather, Christians are to be winsome and engaging in their manner, even while they are called to be circumspect and discerning. This, surely, was one of Chip's great virtues. He was as winsome an individual as you will ever care to meet; and he was as discerning an individual as you will ever want to meet. He neither lived with an attitude of contempt barely beneath the skin—as both religious fundamentalists and post-liberal religious activists smugly tend to do—nor did he capitulate to the cultural *Zeitgeist*, as is the temptation with every generation and in virtually every social location.

In addition, we are struck by the model of Daniel and his Hebrew friends as they acclimated to Babylonian culture. And a severe acclimation it was. It is easy for us to forget the thundering words of the prophet Jeremiah, who, very much *against the religious tide* of his day, exhorted the faithful who were exiled in Babylon in no uncertain words. Recall his admonition: "This is what the Lord Almighty declares, 'I have carried you there, and thus it is in accordance with my purpose that you are there. You are to build houses, settle down, plant crops and gardens, marry, have children and grandchildren. You are to increase, and while you are doing so, you are to seek the peace and welfare of the city in which you are living.'"[2] In the end, Daniel and his friends acclimated well to Babylonian culture, despite the fact that in their studies and in their lifestyles they were continually brushing against cultural influences that potentially could undermine their faith. Yet, they did not merely survive; rather, their God permitted them to *thrive*.

But recall the context. God's purpose, as announced through Jeremiah, was clear and unambiguous—even as it was theologically unpopular. This lack of ambiguity was important in light of conflicting theological voices that claimed religious authority—voices that doubtless were shouting, "Do *not* settle down!" "Do *not* pray for Babylon!" "Do *not* work for that culture's peace and welfare!" To the contrary: "Live with contempt for Babylon and the surrounding culture, and expect soon-coming 'deliverance' (a rapture from responsibility, as it were)!" Or perhaps Jeremiah's religious opponents were shouting to the exiles, "Stand on the sidelines and make 'prophetic' denunciations while building your own little isolated, counter-cultural communities!"

In putting together this volume, we are struck by the fact that whether one's political proclivities lean toward the religious left or right, both justifications for contempt toward the culture and withdrawal from (or non-participation in) the social institutions of the culture are

2. Our paraphrase of Jer 29:4–7.

wrong-headed and, in fact, an abdication of the church's responsibility to the world. This needs to be said, and Chip Conyers would have it no other way.

Of course, the opposite danger—being coopted by and absorbed into the surrounding culture, whereby the church is scarcely distinct—is ever with us, as it has been from the beginning. This tendency we also readily acknowledge. Here, Chip's orientation, i.e., avoiding the twin errors of withdrawal and accommodation, made him shine like the sun, an orientation that is worthy of emulation. Hence, a collection of essays by thoughtful thinkers and writers—individuals representing diverse backgrounds, commitments, and academic disciplines who nevertheless admired Chip's work—is but the least that might be offered as a tribute.

Surely Chip's students—and those of us who were fortunate enough to know him—are better people as a result. He helped us in being reconciled to fruitful endeavors within culture without capitulation. Because of this we are profoundly grateful. A *festschrift* in his memory is therefore one small but tangible means by which to honor him and his important legacy.

John Henry Newman expressed well, in *The Idea of a University*, the unity and integrity of being that Chip Conyers embodied. We think it worth repeating: "I wish the intellect to range with the utmost freedom, and religion to enjoy an equal freedom; but what I am stipulating for is, that they should be found in one and the same place, and exemplified in the same persons.... I wish the same spots and the same individuals to be at once oracles of philosophy and shrines of devotion.... I want the intellectual layman to be religious, and the devout ecclesiastic to be intellectual." This, we dare say, Chip was.

• • •

We wish to express our appreciation to those who contributed to this volume. When we shared the idea of a *festschrift* honoring Chip Conyers among his family, former colleagues, and students, all were eager to participate and worked diligently—despite the demands of busy schedules—to meet our deadlines. We are pleased with both the quality and scope of the essays because they exhibit the breadth and depth of Chip's own work.

We wish also to express our gratitude to Chris Spinks and the staff at Wipf and Stock for embracing the project; their guidance was extremely valuable as we moved through the process together. We were pleased to discover early in our relationship that Chris had been Conyers' student, so he shared our desire to honor his former teacher.

Special thanks to Houston Baptist University for its financial assistance with this project. We wish to thank Dr. Evan Getz as well for proofreading parts of the manuscript. Chris Fresch, Dr. Capes' graduate assistant, helped with a variety of tasks as we brought this volume to publication. When we think of Chris and students like him, we remember why teaching is such an important vocation.

Biography of A. J. "Chip" Conyers

Deborah A. Conyers and James C. Conyers

VOCATION SEEMS THE APT SUBJECT FOR HIS LAST BOOK, FOR HIS LIFE began and ended with God's calling. God chose him for His gracious purpose and showed evidence of that choice throughout his life. As God chose Moses for His divine purpose, He gave the ineffable explanation, "*I will be gracious to whom I will be gracious*" (Exod 33:19, NRSV). St. Paul echoes this notion in his letter to the Romans; it is God's gracious will to have mercy, to choose those through whom He will show His power and purpose. Just so, God's calling to this servant was a lifelong witness that "*it depends not on human will or exertion, but on God who shows mercy*" (Rom 9:16).

His roots as a Southerner powerfully shaped Chip's life. His father and his family were deeply rooted in Georgia history, and his mother, Iva McCall, was from Morgantown, North Carolina. He was named Abda Johnson Conyers III after his father and was the third in a line with that improbable name. His grandfather was named for Abda Johnson, a Confederate colonel and commander of the 40th Regiment Georgia Volunteers, who served with distinction until the end of that troubling and bloody conflict. His father, who often had to explain or spell his name, had the good sense to call him "Chip"—the metaphorical "chip off the old block."

The first details of his life, however, ran distinctly counter to those Southern roots. Chip was born in San Bernardino, California. Although both parents had called Atlanta, Georgia, their home, World War II had set in place other demands and circumstances. His father, a logistics officer in the Army Air Corps, was stationed at the San Bernardino Army Air Field at the time of Chip's birth, May 29, 1944. After the war the Conyers family welcomed another son and returned to Georgia, to start a business and raise a family in Decatur.

In 1950 Chip entered first grade at Fifth Avenue Elementary School in Decatur. School was not much of a challenge for him in those days so he created a few more challenges for himself. At age nine he began to compose short stories, and he continued to write on various topics, a habit he would continue for the rest of his life. He wrote a series called "Pioneer Boy," inspired by the legend of Davey Crockett, which was popular at that time. He founded "The Conyers Family Newspaper," circulation of four. He organized a Civil War museum on his front porch complete with collectables such as Confederate money, miniballs, Indian arrowheads, and fossils of various kinds. This enterprise attracted the attention of the local paper.

One evening in 1952 the Conyers family gathered around a new television set to watch a Billy Graham Evangelistic Crusade. Even in those early years of television, all the furniture had been oriented toward the glowing screen. They watched and listened as a massive choir sang "This Is My Story" and other hymns. George Beverly Shea stepped forward to sing his signature song, "How Great Thou Art." Then, in the midst of a stadium full of people, a young, energetic Billy Graham came to the podium, read Holy Scripture, and preached in a soft Southern accent. It was for the Conyers a recognizable voice shaped in the mountains of western North Carolina where their mother grew up, and where they occasionally visited family. He was sincere, earnest, inviting, yet powerful, and full of certainty and assurance. After the sermon Graham gave the invitation, as the choir sang the song that would be repeated many times in these crusades, "Just As I Am." From the comfort of their living room the family watched as hundreds of people moved slowly down the steps of the stadium and walked out onto the field in order to receive God's love and forgiveness. Then that handsome, square-jawed, rugged and sincere face of Billy Graham filled the television screen, and he addressed the television audience personally. He invited all who were watching—in living rooms, hotel rooms, and bars—to come as these people in the stadium were coming to give their lives to Christ. This was all new and its meaning was uncertain, but not to Chip. To the surprise of the rest of the family, Chip, without prompting, got up from his cross-legged position onto his knees, put his hands together, bowed his head and prayed silently. "What is he doing?" his younger brother asked. His mother said, "He is giving his life to Christ," and it seemed like a dividing line in his life. Chip was called by Christ.

Leaving the comfort of his local elementary school, Chip entered eighth grade at Decatur High School. This was a much larger school, a place where a child could easily get lost. Chip arrived as an unknown among many other unknown children. It was a high school that in 1957 was known for its football team and its potential drug problem. At least for Chip, it was a decidedly unfriendly and unhappy place.

In October of that year, however, his father made a surprise announcement: the family was moving to a farm in rural Georgia. At the point of an unpromising future, a whole new possibility opened up for Chip. It was an opportunity that he did not squander. Instead of a large, impersonal high school, he found himself in a small school, grades first through twelfth, among the rural folks of Georgia, who placed a high value upon relationships with their neighbors. They were no longer occasional attendees of large churches in the Atlanta area, but members of a small rural church that was the center and focus of community life. Sports were no longer the make-or-break, life-or-death issue that it was for boys in the city schools. Other organizations and pursuits, such as church and the Future Farmers of America (FFA), were just as important or more so in that rural community.

This new setting provided Chip with the opportunities of leadership, expression of his creativity, and a community that recognized and encouraged his particular gifts. In church he was a Sunday School teacher, and at the age of sixteen the superintendent of the Sunday School. He led the morning assembly before Sunday School every week. In school he was an honor student and president of the local chapter of FFA. He also won the FFA public speaking award for the county and was recognized by county public schools for his academic achievements. Some of the friends he made in high school would become lifelong friends. This tightly knit rural community welcomed the Conyers family into their midst.

Once again it was not school that offered the challenges, but his own reading in the areas of philosophy and political theory. One summer after his junior year in high school, Chip read *Marx and Engels: Basic Writings on Politics and Philosophy*. This book introduced him to dialectic materialism and the thoughts that were shaping the social and political realities of the West. Later, as he continued to read works in philosophy and politics, he would begin to see the connection between the cultural decline of the West, the easy acceptance of materialism, and the rejection of its Christian foundation.

In his senior year, as Chip accumulated more academic honors, his principal, P. B. Ritch, saw him as an especially promising student. But he knew the family's financial situation was strained and there was no money to send him to school. So Ritch stepped in and took Chip's situation in hand. He learned of a scholarship that provided full funding to study at a junior college in the mountains of North Georgia. He provided the application for the scholarship and a valuable endorsement to the scholarship committee. With Chip's academic achievements and a high SAT score, he was accepted by the school and funded fully by the scholarship committee.

Young Harris College was for Chip, like most college freshmen, a first step into a wider world. He became active in the social and political organizations on campus, becoming president of the student body and joining the school's only social fraternity for men. He became a member of the debate team and proved a tough opponent in competitions with other college debaters around the state. His achievements qualified him for membership in an on-campus honor society. Membership in this society, however, was accompanied with various humiliating initiation rituals, such as having his head shaved—which was very unfashionable at the time—and wearing a large onion on a rope around his neck like an odiferous talisman.

It was in this unfortunate condition that Chip met Debby Anderson, a beautiful and intelligent coed at Young Harris. She was from Murphy, North Carolina, a small town just across the Georgia-North Carolina border. He met her one evening when his family was eating at a popular family-style restaurant where Debby was working as a waitress to earn money for college. This seemingly inauspicious meeting, from Chip's perspective, became a blossoming romance. In their second year at the junior college they started dating regularly. After graduating from Young Harris Junior College in 1964, they both moved to Athens, Georgia to attend the University of Georgia. It wasn't long until they made plans to be married.

On the rainy afternoon of December 26, 1964, with umbrella in hand, Chip met Debby in the muddy parking lot of the Belleview Methodist Church, and then walked her down the aisle as a small number of family and friends witnessed their marriage and listened as traditional vows were spoken. They were but twenty years old, an age Chip's mother was certain was too young for marriage. But the marriage lasted forty faithful and loving years, until Chip's death in 2004.

The University of Georgia was the traditional family college for the Conyers family for generations stretching back to the early nineteenth century. Chip studied political science there and became a student and later a friend of Dr. Albert Saye, a noted historian, professor of law, and distinguished professor of political science. Under the tutelage of Dr. Saye, Chip was introduced to the political theory that underlay the Georgia and United States Constitutions and the political freedoms that are derived from such a form of government. As his studies progressed in political science and constitutional law, he became more familiar with the political movements of the late 1960s that threatened freedom under law through anarchistic philosophies. The stable influence of Dr. Saye served him well in these turbulent years.

At UGA Chip became a part of the Demosthenian Literary Society, a debate society for the politically minded. He became president of that society in his senior year as he honed his skills in critical thinking, rhetoric, and debate. That year he also campaigned successfully as a member of student senate representing the School of Arts and Sciences. These were exciting times for both Chip and Debby. They made many friends, and Chip was earning a reputation for success in areas that could lead to a career in public office, law, or any number of other avenues. As graduation loomed ahead, they wondered what the future held and where the call of God would take them.

At this time Chip and Debby moved out of Athens into a real house—with two bedrooms!—in the small community of nearby Hull, Georgia. It was a small hosue, but apartment living had grown tiresome. Though they had begun their marriage by joining a Methodist church—which was the denomination of the Conyers family—Chip became more and more disenchanted with that denomination as he saw the extremes to which students were being led in the campus Methodist student organization. Debby grew up Baptist, and with the move to Hull, they started attending a local Baptist church. There they met a number of young, thoughtful couples with whom they had many late-night discussions on topics of religion and politics. As was Chip's usual experience in relationships of this kind, he became the unofficial leader of the group. Whenever he heard of some especially interesting event, the whole group was off to attend it whenever possible.

One such event was a lecture by Thomas J. J. Altizer, a theologian from Emory University in Atlanta, who had recently gained worldwide notoriety due to an article published in *Time Magazine* entitled "Is God Dead?" Chip began to understand from this lecture and many other cultural indicators that politics and, more importantly, the church, were sliding into leftist ideologies based in Marxist thought. He became convinced that it was the church and the eternal truths of God that would change hearts and minds, not the leadership or actions in the temporal arena of politics. He spoke with their pastor, Rev. Joe Wingfield, about his interest in the ministry, and Rev. Wingfield began to find him opportunities to speak in area churches.

After graduation from the university, Chip taught in a Madison County School not far from Athens. It was during that year of teaching that he began the soul-searching that conclusively led him to seminary rather than law school. At the same time Debby was experiencing her own call to ministry. Both felt that their lives needed to represent something more than temporal, personal successes. But unlike many who make the choice to attend seminary, Chip and Debby did not have family or friends to give them advice on which seminary to attend. Southeastern Baptist Theological Seminary in Wake Forest, North Carolina, was the closest to Athens of the six Southern Baptist seminaries, so that is where they decided to go. They moved to Wake Forest in August of 1967 to begin a journey that lasted a lifetime. It was a journey that led Chip against the tide of modernism and liberal theology, which seemed to be overwhelming politics and the church at that time. They did not know what to expect at Southeastern. A short visit there earlier in the spring had given them no clue as to the nature of the people they would meet there. Their first thought, that they might be among Bible-toting fundamentalists, was completely wrong. This was at the height of the Vietnam War, and many of the students had come there to avoid the draft. Southeastern was also—much to their surprise and chagrin—the most liberal seminary in the Southern Baptist Convention at that time. However the decision to attend there had been made; and God was in it. The atmosphere of the place drove him to study, research, and think about theology and its connection to myriad philosophies and worldviews. Had he been in a more traditional setting, he may not have worked so hard or taken his studies as seriously. By the grace of God, he had found the right place and, more importantly, the right calling.

Early in his seminary career Chip went to speak in a small, rural Christian church. Soon he was contacted by another Christian congregation, and he and Debby were alternating Sundays with the two churches. It was a critical time in the life of these two congregations. At that time they were independent congregations struggling with the decision to enter the United Church of Christ denomination. Some members of both congregations looked favorably at this proposition, but most were uncertain. Chip supported these congregations by researching into denominational theology, beliefs, and practices. His report to them surprised the members of these congregations. The UCC held beliefs and practices so widely divergent from their own that they decided immediately not to join that denomination.

After earning his Master of Divinity degree in 1971, Chip and Debby returned to Hull Baptist Church for Chip's ordination into the ministry. He had been called to serve as pastor of Maple Spring Baptist Church in Louisburg, North Carolina, where he and Debby would serve for the next two years. His sermons there were engaging, solidly biblical, and lovingly faithful to Jesus Christ. They were also thoughtful and scholarly, perhaps a characteristic not fully appreciated by all of his congregants. On the whole, life in the local church was a good experience for Chip, but he missed the more academic and scholarly pursuits of seminary. Maple Springs was a small church and not able to pay their pastors very much, so Chip supplemented their income by teaching at a small private Christian school. Debby took this time to finish her undergraduate studies at Meredith College in nearby Raleigh, which was one of the reasons for remaining in that area. Chip also kept his hand in the more academic side of theology by writing and publishing.

Chip's first significant publication, an article entitled "God and Man in Dialogue with Marxism," appeared in *Christianity Today* on July 2, 1971. It was a short essay that sharply criticized theologians, denominational leaders, and ecumenical organizations that found much in common with Marxist ideals of social reform. The Communist objectives of a "world community, economic leveling, and a classless society" seemed to them acceptable, and a "socialized Christianity" reformed by the Marxist ideologies was an attractive "use" of the church. Chip pointed to the "man-centered" thinking of these theologians, for whom

"God is in a position of merely seconding the bold reforms man calls into being." The article examined those modern political movements that proclaim freedom and justice but end in tyranny and the loss of humanity. Therein Chip contrasted that end with a God-centered biblical view, which results in true freedom, true humanity, and peace. He would return to these themes in many of his writings.

In 1973 Debby graduated from Meredith College with a B.A. in English literature, and Chip wanted to move back to his home state of Georgia. He found a church in the small town of Ila that seemed a good fit for them. The move placed them in very familiar territory, only sixteen miles from Athens and the University of Georgia. It seemed like a good place for ministry, local culture, and possibly academic pursuits, but this was not to be. They would stay there for only two years; and although they gained some lifelong friends, they left only light footprints in Ila. One of Chip's accomplishments was, however, to establish an ongoing relationship with the Baptist Sunday School Board in Nashville, Tennessee. He continued to write Sunday School curricula for them for many years. He also wrote and published many book reviews in the Baptist publication *Home Missions* and in *Christianity Today*.

In these first years out of seminary, Chip's calling was growing in clarity and focus. It was becoming more obvious that he had God-given talents and desires for writing, teaching, and speaking. He also realized that opportunities to express these talents would be more available if he earned a doctorate in theology. The next step, therefore, was a significant one. Chip entered Southern Baptist Theological Seminary as a Garrett Fellow in Systematic Theology. This was the fulfillment of a prayer he had offered for several years, and it would open many doors for him.

In 1975 they packed their belongings and moved to Louisville, Kentucky. This move opened doors into work with several celebrated scholars in both theology and politics. More than reading the works of these scholars, he would learn from them directly, and his experience with these influential leaders became an important source of his growth as a scholar, a theologian, and a disciple of Jesus Christ.

The first of these was Dr. Dale Moody, distinguished professor of systematic theology, who at that time had taught at "Southern" for almost thirty years. As Chip's major professor, Dr. Moody had studied with two of the most outstanding theologians of the twentieth century, Emil Brunner and Karl Barth; and he, in turn, encouraged his students to study with the best and the brightest in the world. In their first conversation, Dr. Moody found that Chip was interested in theology, history, and politics. He immediately suggested that his dissertation focus on the writings of the German theologian Jürgen Moltmann. This insightful suggestion became the object of Chip's study, the subject of his dissertation, and the content of one of his first books. Chip found Dr. Moody's discussions and assistance to be constant helps through his seminary years, and the two maintained a friendship up until Dr. Moody's death in 1992.

The second scholar with whom Chip would study was the eminent political scientist, philosopher, historian, and theologian Gerhart Niemeyer, of the University of Notre Dame. During the spring of 1976 he had classes with Professor Niemeyer and spent many hours daily in the library. Niemeyer was a trusted advisor in foreign policy and was called upon at various times by presidents and the United States Congress. He was a significant part of the intellectual foundation for the rise in political conservatism, and he had an enduring friendship with William F. Buckley Jr. as well as others in that movement. Niemeyer was a philosopher, a theologian, and a prophet. As his obituary would later note, he was a traditionalist, which meant that he was concerned with the abiding truth of things. This gave Chip an opportunity to examine the ideologies that have developed in the last two centuries with such destructive force and to gain a deeper understanding of the gospel in the modern world.

The third scholar with whom Chip would study was the eminent German theologian Jürgen Moltmann. Blessed with some support and means of their own, Chip and Debby spent six months in Germany, primarily at the University of Tübingen. Conversations and study with Moltmann became the basis of his doctoral dissertation, which was later published as *God, Hope and History: Jürgen Moltmann and the Christian Concept of History*. This experience and the knowledge he gained from his study of Moltmann's concept of history helped Chip to solidify an intellectual foundation in which theology, politics, and history were bound together. This study also opened the way for his later incisive critiques of the modern world from a Christian perspective; and it furnished the means by which to formulate alternatives to the clearly destructive path of modernism. His intent was to show the way out of the darkness of a functional atheism and nihilism and into the light of Christ, based upon Holy Scripture and the philosophical traditions of Christian thought.

During their time overseas Chip and Debby learned much about the German language and culture; they visited many of the cities and villages in western Germany. They also took some time to spend a week with Francis and Edith Schaeffer at their L'Abri Community in Switzerland. They ended their European travels with a week in England, mostly London, enjoying the theater and other sites before their homeward journey in July 1978.

After they returned to the States, the news arrived that Debby's mother had passed away while they were en route; and other family matters had to be taken care of immediately. When they returned to Louisville, Kentucky, it was time for Chip to begin in earnest the work of completing his dissertation. Then in November the couple learned that they were expecting a child. So much had happened in so short a time, but this was exciting news indeed. After nearly fourteen years of marriage, they had all but given up hope that they would ever have a child. This was surely a special gift from God.

The blessed event would come the following summer with the most remarkable timing. Emily McCall Conyers was born just after midnight on the morning of July 12, 1979, the very day—indeed the very morning—that Chip was scheduled to defend his dissertation. With a boundless joy to counter the lack of sleep, he made it through his defense flawlessly.

His doctoral degree was conferred in December 1979; by that time Chip had already completed a semester of teaching at Central Missouri State University (CMSU) in Warrensburg, Missouri. They had moved there in late summer when Emily was only four weeks old to fill a post funded by the Missouri Baptist Convention as Baptist Chair of Bible.

The Conyers' home in Warrensburg, only two blocks from the campus, became the center of life as the family grew, and as Debby turned the somewhat neglected old Victorian house into a home of beauty. Chip presided over Bible studies, meetings with colleagues, gatherings of students, and dinners for invited lecturers. They became active in a young and growing church, where among other jobs, Debby led a women's Bible study.

It was during this time that the trickle of publications during his seminary years became more of a steady stream of articles and books.

His first book, entitled *How to Read the Bible*, was based largely on his experience at CMSU in teaching Bible courses to undergraduate students. The second book, based on his dissertation, was published soon after they left Warrensburg.

Chip found that his position at CMSU afforded a considerable amount of freedom, and he used that time and freedom to organize a number of significant events on campus. One was a series of symposia on subjects such as bioethics, Christianity and the arts, and other topics that invited discussion and debate on campus. Each symposium featured well-known speakers and consisted of various events, lectures, and presentations over several days. These were often well attended, not only by students, but by the faculty and the community. One debate on evolution versus creationism filled the university auditorium and produced quite heated exchanges both in the debate and in classrooms for weeks following.

The big event of those years, however, was the birth of their son. The name that Chip inherited was passed on to another generation; they named him Abda Johnson Conyers IV and called him "John." When he grew up, he chose to be called "AJ" instead; but his family still calls him John. John and Emily—both intelligent, resourceful, strong-willed, and creative—immensely enriched the lives of their parents and their entire family.

In those days Chip was often invited to speak and lecture in Baptist circles around Missouri. He served as a visiting professor of theology at Midwestern Baptist Theological Seminary in Kansas City. Every Sunday and many weeknights were filled with Bible studies and preaching engagements in churches both large and small. This included a nearly year-long interim as pastor of their own large and busy Baptist church in Warrensburg.

As Chip sought a broader venue for academic endeavors, he was invited to teach at the Baptist College of Charleston. The family moved there in the summer of 1987, and he took the position as Chairman of the Department of Religion and Philosophy and Professor of Religion. He continued in Charleston what he started in Missouri, hosting symposia and making every effort to build a good academic environment. The college was relatively young and went through a number of changes while Chip was there, including a name change. The Baptist College at

Charleston became Charleston Southern University, a name suggested by Chip and soon accepted by the Board of Governors.

The seven years spent in South Carolina enriched the whole family. Debby found new friends and activities in the historically rich Charleston area, and the children found new friends at church and school. Despite heavy administrative duties at the university, Chip entered a productive period of writing and publishing as he began to find his voice in social, historical, and moral commentary on the modern world. This was particularly the case for his book *The Eclipse of Heaven: Rediscovering the Hope of a World Beyond*, published in 1992, which examined the loss of transcendence in the Western world.

While Chip was serving in South Carolina, many miles away in Waco, Texas, a new seminary was founded at Baylor University. The first organizational meeting of the seminary trustees was held on July 18, 1991. The name "George W. Truett Theological Seminary" was chosen by the regents of Baylor a year before. Years of conflict within the Southern Baptist Convention had brought about the creation of several new seminaries, but Baylor's seminary was to have a new vision that enthusiastically embraced the best of the Baptist faith, with intellectual integrity, academic excellence, and a high regard for the authority of Scripture.

Seminary representatives contacted Chip during this process, and by the time the seminary opened in fall 1994 he had become part of the founding faculty as Professor of Theology. When he arrived in Waco in the summer 1994, many decisions regarding curriculum, student life, and other matters of importance for the seminary were yet to be made. One of Chip's major contributions was his advocacy for the use of primary texts in the study of theology. His counsel on this and other matters during the early years set Truett Seminary on a track of study they still follow today.

On July 1, Chip was in Waco for the closing of their newly purchased house on Park Avenue. Chip stayed in the house with only a minimum of furniture, kitchen utensils, and clothes for the month as he took part in the effort to prepare for the opening of Truett Seminary in late August. Debby and the children remained behind to sell the South Carolina house and prepare for moving to Texas. Their new home was a very large Federalist style, three-story house that was a "grand dame" of the roaring twenties. It also had a sizable brick carriage house in back that they converted into a comfortable, single-story home for Chip's parents, who were then in their eighties and becoming less able to live on their own.

There could not have been a time of more intense disparity of emotion as events of that summer unfolded. On the one hand, there was the excitement of a new home, a new community, and the new position at the seminary. On the other hand, Chip was feeling exhausted and drained after completing his duties at Charleston and packing his office for the move. He made no time to visit a doctor even though he had a cough that lasted for weeks. He was run down and lacked his usual energy. Debby insisted that he see a doctor in Waco as soon as he could.

Reluctantly taking the time from his pressing duties, Chip visited a doctor recommended to him. This doctor's preliminary examination resulted in a tentative diagnosis of mononucleosis, but he suggested that a bone marrow biopsy should also be done. The word "biopsy" undoubtedly triggered concern, and Chip was alone in Waco, spending nights in an empty and unfamiliar house, with his beloved family more than eleven hundred miles away. He had the bone marrow biopsy done, and then waited days for the result, speculating about the diagnosis but telling no one as yet about his ordeal.

With his family still in South Carolina also awaiting the news, Chip's new colleagues at Truett accompanied him to receive the results of the biopsy. The news was not good. He was in the early stages of Chronic Lymphocytic Leukemia (CLL). If there was any good news that day, it was the doctor's suggestion that with close monitoring no treatment was necessary at that time. Still, this was a terrible blow, so it was decided that the family should be together, regardless of the cost. With the house in South Carolina not yet sold, the rest of the family made its way to Texas.

By August Chip was feeling much better and enthusiastic about the coming semester. He was surrounded by family, and the empty, echoing house on Park Avenue was finally filled with furniture, books, music—all the stuff of life.

Truett Seminary opened with a convocation on Sunday, August 28, 1994, and classes began the following Monday with fifty-one registered students. The seminary's first location was First Baptist Church in Waco, located a few blocks from the Baylor campus. The congregation graciously offered the use of their facility for the seminary's temporary home. The entire second floor of the expansive B. H. Carroll Education Building was given over for offices and classrooms along with other areas of the building that were shared by church and school.

As family life adjusted to the new environment, Chip was absorbed in the challenges of the new seminary and his writing. His health and energy level had returned, and classes were going well. He was asked to serve on the Faculty Senate and the Search Committee seeking a new dean for Truett when the founding dean, Robert Sloan, became President of Baylor University. Chip began to apply for grants and to write both books and articles. During these first years, he published two books: *Basic Christian Theology* and *The End: What Jesus Really Said about the Last Things*. For the latter book Chip preferred the title *Last Things*, which was used later when the book was re-released. This book focused on the Gospels, especially Mark 13, the "Little Apocalypse."

Chip's essays and articles in those years appeared in more diverse publications, some of which had higher public profiles and reached a more diverse readership. Among these periodicals were *Books and Culture*, *First Things*, and *Touchstone*. His writings were cited and reviewed with growing frequency, and increasingly he was called upon for interviews and commentary on the work of others. He continued to write for Baptist publications as well and served on the editorial boards of several academic journals.

Chip continued in good health for three years. In the summer of 1997, however, his oncologist noticed an elevation in the number of white blood cells and began to talk about chemotherapy. Not knowing how this might affect his work, he delayed telling anyone else the news. Though he hoped to make it to Christmas break that year, by mid-November his symptoms had returned—weakness and constant coughing—and his red blood cell count dropped significantly, killed off by his own white blood cells. One morning he awoke with dizziness and blurred vision, and he was too weak to stand. Shortly after Debby and Chip arrived at the Emergency Room at Hillcrest Hospital in Waco, he began to slip into a coma. He was moved immediately into the Intensive Care Unit and given blood transfusions. He continued to slip in and out of consciousness, and nothing the doctors and staff did seemed to increase his red blood cell count. His team of doctors in Waco decided it was time to move him to Baylor University Medical Center in Dallas. They were not sure that Chip would make it to Dallas alive, but his best chance of survival was in the equipment and treatments available in Dallas. Slowly, he began to respond to treatment, but he remained in Dallas through December and most of January.

The outpouring of love and assistance from their church and university was enormous. Whatever they needed was provided at the proper time. As one example of this, it was during this extended hospital stay in Dallas that their first grandchild was born. Debby was in Waco taking care of Emily and a deacon from their church, Joe McKinney, was asked to go and stay with Chip during this time. When he got there the nurses taking care of Chip got together and talked Joe (a distinguished professor of economics at Baylor) into sneaking him out of the hospital, taking him to Waco for his grandson's birth, but warning him that, like Cinderella, he must be back by midnight or the insurance would be stopped! This they did, and arrived in time to be with the family and a host of friends for the birth of Paul Bennett Conyers. Mother and son were fine, and true to his word, Dr. McKinney rushed Chip back to Dallas and to his hospital room before the midnight deadline. As soon as she could manage it, Debby returned to Dallas to be with Chip, where he remained for another two weeks.

Chip was finally released in late January to convalesce at home, but had to spend several more weeks in the local Waco hospital. John's sixteenth birthday was celebrated in a meeting room on the cancer ward of Hillcrest Hospital that year. John, who liked to be called "A.J." by his friends, must have felt isolated during these hectic and trying events. He had to remain in Waco to attend school while his dad was in Dallas and in the hospital in Waco. However, he had great school friends who supported him and stood by him during this time.

Chip was significantly weakened, and his health never completely recovered from this prolonged illness. From that time until the end of his life six years later, he was in and out of hospitals, periodically receiving blood transfusions, and regularly receiving chemotherapy. Much of his medical attention he received locally, but he also made occasional trips to Houston's M. D. Anderson Cancer Center. He saw a CCL specialist there who used several experimental drugs on Chip, but his leukemia never stayed in remission for more than a few months. In spite of all this, he was determined not to slow down but to continue to fulfill his duties at home and in the seminary.

Some students expressed amazement that he was suffering from a potentially fatal disease. Except for the obvious weight loss, he never seemed to be ill. He remained energetic, engaged, and interested in everything about his students and their work. He never mentioned the ordeal he was enduring at that time, but he gladly responded to any questions or expressions of sympathy. Often he would respond to inquiries, saying that he would use all the time God gave him to fulfill his calling. Despite his illness and hectic schedule he took time every week to meet for prayer with his fellow pro-life friends at an abortion clinic. He even fulfilled his duties as an elected member of the Baylor University Faculty Senate. But a most joyous part of his calling was that of "Papa." He doted on his new grandson, and as he had done with his daughter and son before him, he could often be seen holding the infant while sitting at his desk at home, absorbed in writing. This little domestic scene, rarely or never seen by his students or colleagues, was the full expression of his gifts and his calling, and he was never lacking in gratitude toward God for them all.

In 1999 St. Augustine Press republished his book *The Eclipse of Heaven*, and his next major publication bore the intriguing title of *The Long Truce: How Toleration Made the World Safe for Power and Profit*. The subject of this volume, published by Spence Press in 2001, was a description and critique of the modern project of "toleration." The book examined the history of the principle of toleration from Aristotle to Frederick Nietzsche. Whereas toleration was based in widely accepted moral principles that defined certain ends for human behavior, the modern age has fully embraced the philosophy of John Stuart Mill and others who have found individual happiness, with no moral parameters, to be acceptable and preferred. The shift, as he follows this history, has opened the possibility for a Lockean understanding of toleration with a basis in individual personal preference, whose end is a superficial peace and harmony. This in turn created the foundation for centralized power of the state and indifference to values. This pervasive attitude in the modern world does not recognize a *telos*, a final cause or ultimate end for human life. This was the crack in the foundation of modern life that he identified in this work; and as any house buyer learns, a crack in the foundation may not seem significant at first, but in time the result will be disastrous and costly. One might say, in this sense, this work is prophetic.

The alternative that he proposed was not to discard toleration, but to reclaim a traditional practice of toleration. He discussed the distinction as follows:

> What I am distinguishing as the practice of toleration, over against the doctrine that emerges from development of democratic liberalism, is the logical result of a recognition that our imperfections oblige us to listen to the insights of others. We are utterly dependent upon the gifts of society and traditio—even traditions other than our own. It is toleration that recognizes not the implied self-sufficiency of the individual or of various idiosyncratic groups in a supposed pluralistic world but the insufficiency of these limits and the ultimate need for a catholic vision. Even as the doctrine of toleration promotes isolation, the practice of toleration gently nudges us into community. Therefore, authentic toleration serves, and does not hinder, the forming and functional life of groups within society. It does not hinder in that it does not discourage the quest for ultimate meaning that is the inner light and life of any social group of any lasting importance. (*The Long Truce*, 242–43)

Toleration as it is presently practiced has banished all public discussions of ultimate meaning of human life for the sake of public peace. By doing so it ends all discussion about transcendent sources of morality. This is accompanied by secularization and the disappearance of a generally accepted morality. Hence, instead of a people living under heaven with an eye toward a gracious but demanding God, the state now functions in the place of God. Without a shared morality or purpose, and with all transcendent values suppressed in the public forum, the state exercises its growing need for laws, reaching into more areas of public and private life for the sake of public peace and unity.

As it turned out, this book created more of a stir than any of his earlier books. It spawned reviews both positive and negative, perhaps because he had struck a nerve with his political analysis. He was interviewed about the book by various media outlets, most significantly by Mars Hill Audio Journal. In the same year, he also published a major essay in *First Things* on the subject of toleration. All this brought considerable exposure to the book, and because the publisher, Spence Press, published conservative and often Catholic works, Chip's writing was extending his writings to a broader audience than his previous books had reached.

Following the publication of *The Long Truce*, Chip's reputation as a scholar and teacher continued to grow, even as his health grew worse. Dr. Keating, the specialist at M. D. Anderson, continued to try therapies that had been successful with other patients, but the leukemia refused to remain in remission. At this point, Chip was receiving various treatments and undergoing various procedures for a range of symptoms. By 2002 he had been diagnosed with an aggressive skin cancer that was treated at the local hospital, but it required more extensive surgery the next year at M. D. Anderson. Chip spent that summer enduring the most painful treatments and surgeries of his life, including extensive skin grafts.

Thinking the worst was behind them, Chip and Debby were back in Houston that autumn to prepare for a bone marrow transplant. It had been decided after an intensive round of chemotherapy that a bone marrow transplant would be his best chance of putting the CLL in a long-term remission. While in the hospital, a slip on a wet floor prompted some x-rays in search of any injuries that might have incurred. What the x-rays revealed, however, was completely unexpected. There was a small mass in Chip's right lung. Further investigation led to a diagnosis of small-cell carcinoma, a very aggressive, untreatable form of cancer. This placed all other possible therapies and procedures in a different light. Slowly they began to realize that there would be no bone marrow transplant, or any other treatments. Finally, they were told that Chip had only a few months to live.

Debby and Chip went back to Waco, but more trips would be made to Houston for collapsed lungs, chemotherapy, and blood transfusions in an attempt to prolong his life. However, in the spring semester Chip went back to teach his classes. To the amazement of his colleagues and friends, he remained quite cheerful even as his appearance became more skeletal. The seminary students, who now numbered almost four hundred, deeply appreciated his heroic efforts, although he would never think of himself as a hero. He was doing, he might say, just what he was called to do. For the second time in his career at Baylor, he was voted by the graduating class as "Professor of Choice" for 2004.

He also continued to write and to speak during this time. One article, which appeared in the Waco *Tribune-Herald* (July 24, 2004), concerned his experience of facing death. He wrote:

> Occasionally someone will ask me how I have been able to continue any kind of normal life during a time in which it was disclosed that I had leukemia, an aggressive skin cancer, and an incurable lung tumor. Their remarks, intended and taken as a kindness and a consolation, unfortunately also tempt me to want to believe that at least part of what they say is true. How I would like to be as brave and cheerful as they say! How I would like to be the victorious Christian who faces trials with light-heartedness, rather than self-pity or preoccupation with his own rescue. But the pain returns. In quiet moments the shadow of doubt makes itself known even on the sunniest of days. The interaction of these moods is fortunate. They cause me to reflect on my real reactions, not only as a human being who loves life passionately, but as a believer who has learned slowly and still inadequately to trust a kind and merciful God.... Troubled times have this virtue: They drive us "outside of ourselves." I asked very basic questions and got what I have taken to be answers. I was driven ever deeper into a desperate search for a place to stand. The "answers" were not a reasoned approach to my situation, or an answer to my troubles. It is more a sentiment that grew stronger with time.... It had nothing to do with my moving toward God; it was about God's moving toward us, making his presence known.

He also worked on two books during these years of his most severe illness. One was a collaborative work on the theology of baptism. This was an ecumenical effort that included a variety of traditions and perspectives, and Chip was asked to add a Baptist perspective to the volume. Although much of the writing was done, it would not be completed.

The second book was *The Listening Heart: Vocation and the Crisis of Modern Culture*. It was to this volume that he devoted himself in his limited time between bouts with his illness. The argument of the book followed two contrasting paths of "vocation": the calling of God in the life of a person or a community; and "choice," i.e., the exercise of the will of the autonomous individual. The first path is a calling that comes from outside and above us, to do that which we might not necessarily choose to do, and which may lead to suffering but ultimately to joy. The second is the act of the autonomous self in pursuit of that which is pleasing to the self as its principal criterion. The book ends with a stunning conclusion that calls for a decision. Echoing the words of Moses, he presents the alternatives of life or death, blessing or curse:

> Throughout this work I have returned to a central conviction. Perhaps at first it was a mere intuition, but in ways it has served as a vocation for this period of my life. The thought is essentially this: only when members of a community understand life as a response to a large and generous world, created by a merciful providence will the possibilities of a life together become more fully realized. Otherwise without this spirit infusing and animating a people, existence is reduced to competing forces clashing at twilight, groping for whatever is left of power, fame, and fortune before the darkness descends. For then while the isolation becomes rooted in every human domain, its end is necessarily found in the dust of death.
>
> However, with this spirit of vocation—this conviction that we are not after all our own, but we belong to Another, then the world opens up, becomes a place for others and is illuminated by a spreading and abiding hope.

This would be Chip's last book. He submitted the final draft to Spence Publishing, but much of the work that always remains between an editor, a publisher, and a writer was still not complete, and the date of its release was delayed. However, through the determination of the publisher, Tom Spence, to ensure that it would see the light of day, and the heroic effort of the editor-in-chief, Mitch Muncie, the work was finally completed three years after Chip's death. The result is a book that continues to shine like a beacon in dark times. The American Library Association named it to its list of the top ten religion books for 2007.

Chip's life began and ended with the theme of vocation, a calling from God. His life, like any life viewed from the perspective of the gospel, was not a symbol, an example, or a type. His was an irreplaceable life whose absence cannot be filled and whose uniqueness is beyond replication. He was, for those who knew him, and those who will come to know him, a prophet whose eye saw a bit more than most of us. Like Gandalf in Tolkien's *The Lord of the Rings* trilogy, he did play a certain role and he did leave a specific gift. In "The Last Debate" of *The Return of the King*, the last book of the trilogy, Gandalf gives perspective to the events unfolding in that final confrontation with evil. He says, "*It is not our part to master all the tides of the world, but to do what is in us for the succor of those years wherein we are set, uprooting the evil in the fields that we know, so that those who live after may have clean earth to till.*" We believe that this was the gift that Chip left for us and for generations to come.

Eulogy for Abda Johnson "Chip" Conyers

Delivered at the First Baptist Church of Waco, Texas

July 20, 2004

John Shouse

MY ASSIGNMENT IS TO GIVE TRIBUTE TO AND THANKS FOR THE LIFE of Chip Conyers—not as a family member or as a minister but as a colleague and friend. This is the relationship that many of you enjoyed with Chip.

Sometimes I come to moments like this hoping to add to the knowledge of the life we are celebrating. At this moment, however, I want nothing other than to be a faithful voice for what so many of you experienced through your friendship and association with Chip. Chip's life with us was not only rich and giving but remarkably consistent. The Chip I knew, I believe, you all knew. So, Debby, thank you for the privilege of voicing in this moment the experiences and thanksgiving of so many of us for your husband Chip.

C. S. Lewis wrote that friendship is forged on common interests. As fellow graduate students in theology, Chip and I certainly had that. We were students at the same school, navigating together through the same schedule, sharing the same interests, and being advocates of similar commitments; we were even fellows together of the same professor. If Lewis was right, we had all the natural ingredients for friendship, and a friendship we had.

But as I think of Chip, I find Lewis' explanation either too thin or Chip too large. To be with Chip was to be with a person who was not only intellectually curious but humanly interested. Chip was engrossed in ideas but he was committed to people. Chip put it succinctly himself in his later writing: "Reality is relationship—which is to say that God is love."

As a graduate student Chip was remarkably productive. However, he always made time for friends—sitting down over a cup of coffee, totally present and attentive in the moment. His ability to be present for others was a remarkable achievement of character and grace.

Chip's brother Jim spoke of Chip as an "organizer." He was also a "networker." To know him was both to benefit from his own undivided attention and also to be introduced to others. Chip was connected to people and he connected people to people. He loved to introduce friends to friends. When Chip wrote that reality was relationship, he was describing the charter of his own life. It was an open-hearted, graciously giving, intellectually committed, and elegantly expressed life of love.

If Robert Frost had a lover's quarrel with the world, Chip had a lover's engagement with it. Love has been defined as the determined decision to seek the best for the other. Chip was that kind of lover. In his memoir on Ludwig Wittgenstein, Cornell philosopher Norman Malcolm said that "to be Wittgenstein's friend was to have the very best summoned from you. It was to be called to be a better person yourself." Chip was that kind of friend.

In his luminous book *Eclipse of Heaven*, Chip speaks of values he lived. His argument is that modern life, in losing a sense of transcendence, has turned inward. "Non-transcendence is self-absorption" (p. 81). Or, put positively, "transcendence is when we look at one another. . . [and] attend to that outside ourselves." That was Chip. Chip, you were unfailingly "other-directed." You attended to things—and persons—outside of yourself and you made us all the better for it.

Alexis de Tocqueville observed that the end of life is only found beyond life. People of faith reflect this by being possessed of "great and lasting desires. While thinking of the other world, they (find) the great secret of success in this one." We are assembled here in large measure because Chip was a person of such great and lasting desires and because he had found and faithfully lived this great "secret of success."

Chip was a man who was deeply other-interested. He was describing his own life when he wrote: "The honesty and helpfulness of judgment—of anything, whether of art, literature, personal behavior—must first at least attempt to free itself of self-centeredness and self-interest. To the degree that it becomes sympathetic, it gains the power to be truthful."

Chip was other-directed because, in the words that were used a hundred years ago in the American South to describe Christian salvation, he was "grasped by the power of a great affection." He was, as Paul put it, by love compelled.

Chip's humor was more than just the capacity for twinkle in his grey-blue eyes. Real humor requires perspective. Chip described it as detachment—not from others but from the prison of self-importance. "Being a God, after all, is too serious a matter to leave room for laughter. G. K. Chesterton said 'angels can fly because they take themselves lightly.'"

In describing where the technological and scientific legacy of the twentieth century had left us, Chip told the story of the pilot who announced to his passengers news both good and bad. "First, the good news," he said. "We're making extremely good time. The bad news is, we're lost." Comparing the richly textured marriage vows from the *Book of Common Prayer* with more recent compositions, Chip commented that the difference was akin to that between "Mount Sinai and Madison Avenue" or between "the Ancient of Days and *Days of our Lives*."

Chip was gracious and graceful. Grace, he once wrote, means that "life is overshadowed by a benevolent mystery." Life is a response to this gift. "As children we receive the world, as adults our focus narrows to that we have constructed by our own effort. The huge gift is forgotten while our miniscule response becomes a source of obsession, pride, anxiety, envy, guilt and fear."

So Chip reminds us that life is a gift. In short, it is grace. I am not surprised to hear that Chip's last book—from which Jim read—is on vocation. I will read it and I will look forward to hearing again and learning again from my friend. To speak of vocation is to speak of a "calling." It is yet another recognition that the meaning of life is relationship. It is a consequence of his discovery of the secret that life is a gift. If life is a vocation, it is a calling and our lives are meant to be a response to it.

I have been asked to speak of Chip as a colleague and theologian. Chip's interests were wide-ranging. He had a renaissance mind. Chip was a scholar not out of pretension or elitism but out of an appetite for ideas and sense of service to others. He believed ideas have consequences and lives could be helped and set right by correcting them. In his last e-mail to me he wrote, "We have lived in decadent times but at least we have been asked to live in interesting times."

Chip's mind was broad-ranging and precise, catholic and evangelical, creative and confessional, classical and contemporary, theoretical and relevant. To me he was one of the most compelling Christian classicists since C. S. Lewis.

Much of Chip's writings are in the area of "public theology." While doing this, though, he never failed to understand that public sense is made only through immersing life in the particular story of God's redeeming purposes in Jesus Christ.

He wrote as he lived—with elegance, style, and beauty. It was a skill he earned by honing it and developing it. I don't think writing is simply the expression of thoughts we have antecedently to saying them. The articulation of a thought is of a piece with having it. Chip thought well, in part, because he wrote well.

My favorite contemporary playwright is Tom Stoppard. In one of his plays he has his central character—who happens also to be a playwright—say, "Writers aren't sacred, but words are—get the right ones in the right order and you can nudge the world a little, or write poems that children will speak after you when you are gone."

I believe, Chip, you left words that will nudge the world. On this occasion not just of remembering you but of thanking you I wish to be moved by your words one more time. And what better place might there be than to hear the words you used to draw a picture of that realm which we here still are viewing "through a glass darkly" but which you are now experiencing more fully and face to face? What is life like where heaven is no longer eclipsed but experienced? Chip writes:

> It is though our love of God and our love of other human beings—and even our proportionate love of the rest of creation—that heaven is realized. For heaven is God's created order in which love is realized and in which self-interest can be laid to rest. It is love of another—that is it is exchanging our self-centered life for an other-centered life. It is fulfilling life by loving God and loving one's neighbor.... The evidence of heaven ... comes by the steady turning of hearts toward Christ who is the way.

Thank you, Chip, for saying it. But thank you also for so consistently showing us.

Chip, you were right in the most important things of life. You lived your life here in light of that "benevolent mystery" that the New

Testament calls an open secret, but which remains unseen by so many. You understood that life is a gift, that grace means we are overshadowed by a benevolent Mystery, and that because God is Triune and God is love; life means relationship.

Because your interests were larger than your self, you grew larger and grander and closer to God.

You who are now experiencing it taught us: "The meaning of the resurrection is more than the assurance of personal survival. It means that life given to God can never be lost." Although I will miss regular access to your gracious spirit, twinkling eyes, acute mind, warm smile, and encouraging voice, I am grateful that because of the faithful giving of your life to God none of us will finally lose your friendship or your love.

Chip, you are as fine a friend as it is given a person to have and as fine a man as it is given in life to know. I am thankful to God that he grasped you so passionately, and I am thankful to you that you returned your life so robustly to life's Maker and life's Lord.

PART ONE

Faith

1

The Unfinished Agenda of Evangelical Theology

Millard J. Erickson

One of the highlights of my visits to Waco was always the opportunity to discuss theology with Chip Conyers. His keen mind, intellectual curiosity and warm personality made those discussions both enjoyable and beneficial. As everyone who knew Chip remembers, he was passionate about theology, and, as a churchman, especially about its relevance to the life of the church.

One topic we frequently discussed was evangelical theology's unfinished agenda. As long as evangelicals have been examining the doctrinal content of Scripture, one would expect that the major issues had been worked out, or at least that the major positions on each of these issues would have been defined. Yet despite this long and intensive effort, much remains to be done by way of theological reflection. Some issues pertinent to the evangelical theological endeavor have scarcely been addressed, while others, although explored, are in need of additional attention. This essay will not attempt to resolve those issues. Rather, it will be programmatic in nature, seeking to examine certain of these issues by identifying underlying issues, describing some of the positions taken on them, and in some cases, suggesting directions in which the discussion might profitably go.

The reasons for this task being still incomplete are several. It may be worthwhile to examine these reasons before investigating the actual topics, for unless we know why these have been neglected, that trend may continue.

One reason for this neglect is a failure to think through the logical implications of elements of one's theology. Thus, the need for certain questions does not arise. One theologian affirmed his belief in the bodily resurrection of Jesus but did not subscribe to the idea of his ascension. When asked, "What happened to the body of Jesus, then?" he replied, "I just don't think about that." For if there is any truth to logic, then one who holds an idea (or a combination of ideas) that implies another concept is logically committed to belief in the conclusion as well. One advantage of working out the implications of a particular tenet is that it may assist us in assessing the truth of that tenet. It may be that the tenet itself cannot be conclusively verified by appeal to our primary authority, being insufficiently addressed there. The logical implication, however, may be more clearly addressed in the primary authority, thus giving us clues to the veracity of the initial tenet. This will be a negative rather than a positive test of the truth of the antecedent. If the implication is positively taught by Scripture, that does not guarantee the truth of the tenet that forms the premise, being a case of affirming the consequent. If, however, the implication is disproved by Scripture, that would, by the valid argument of denying the consequent, establish that the premise (the antecedent) is also untrue.

The failure to see unexpected consequences of belief or action is, of course, not unique to theologians, or even to scholars in general. It is said that 95 percent of all new businesses fail within five years. There are many reasons for such failures, including inadequate capitalization, inexperienced leadership, and other factors, but a major cause is simply failure to anticipate the problems that may, and in many cases do, arise. Similarly, security lapses in software may not be discovered until a hacker exploits them. In the case of theology, it may be many years, even centuries, before someone takes a logical implication and extends it to its extreme. Often, the heretic is the best friend of the orthodox theologian, for the former forces the latter to think through his position more adequately.

Another reason is following what I term "customary consistency," over against logical consistency. In a given tradition, a certain idea may be held, not because it is clearly taught in Scripture, or because it follows by logical implication from other elements of that doctrinal position, but simply because it has always been held and taught by theologians in that tradition. It may be an attempt to sustain that position by taking the most extreme form thereof, thus making it as complete as possible. What happens is that the customary form in which the theological system is encountered includes this feature or this element of doctrine, so that there comes to be a psychological expectation that this is logically implied by the major tenets of the system. This being the case, if the major elements are considered to be demonstrably supported by Scripture, the supposed implication will be thought to be warranted as well. This will then close discussion, whereas in reality the issue has not been resolved. A closely related phenomenon is the tendency to cite all possible arguments for a position, even if there is contradiction among some of those arguments.

A third reason for failure to explore an issue may stem from inability to recognize the cultural or other factors that condition one's own view. Thus, no need is felt to formulate or revise the doctrinal expression in light of new developments bearing on the doctrine. Another way of putting this is that what has sometimes been thought to be biblical teaching was actually a widely held view of astronomy, physics, or metaphysics.

One instance of this now widely recognized by holders of a variety of positions was the geocentric view of the universe. For a long time this was thought to be taught by Scripture, and therefore any variant view had to be resisted. At some point the Copernican revolution succeeded, and was sufficiently established that it became apparent even to the theologians. They came to recognize that what they had been defending was not a teaching of the Scriptures at all, but rather a particular astronomical view that was so much a part of the general public's thinking that the Scriptures were read through the lens of that view. The same can be said of numerous philosophies.

Ironically, certain theologians have made much of the influence of certain ideologies on opposing theologies, yet either without an awareness or an admission of a similar conditioning effect of historical or cultural forces or of non-theological assumptions on their own theology. In the heyday of the biblical theology movement, it was almost a cliché to speak of Greek influences on theology. Yet those advancing these allegations often proceeded as if their own view was simply ideologically sterile, or free from any such influences. In a sense this could be overlooked on principle, since these theologians were not claiming that all theologies are under such influence. It was therefore necessary to demonstrate that what was true of the theologies they were criticizing was also true of their view, although the ideology infecting it was different. Such an omission is more damaging when made by a theology that maintains that all views are conditioned yet acts as if this universal statement did not include its own view, but without offering either exempting conditions or examples of exceptions.

Sometimes this inadequate treatment of a doctrine is the result of theologians being from one or a few select subgroups of the human race, or of the church. If all theologians are men, or Europeans or North Americans, for example, they may be unable to see even within Scripture insights that are there and that others may be able to see quite clearly. This type of shortcoming is becoming more evident, and, we trust, rarer, with the passage of time.

Another common cause of failure to explore a doctrinal issue sufficiently results from failure to interact with current factors. There is no scholarly necessity for a theologian to accept the latest position on an issue. Each theologian is, however, responsible to be aware of current positions. To assume that one has disposed of an alternative position because one has refuted a form in which it previously existed is hazardous, as well as to assume that one's own view is secure because one has rebutted old criticisms of it. But through ignorance of new challenges, it thus becomes vulnerable to them. Just as it is now impossible to evangelize persons who lived and died decades or even centuries ago, so it is also often ineffective to give one's interaction to obsolete views, or obsolete varieties of perennial views.

One failure to deal adequately with a doctrinal issue may stem from what I regularly term "chronocentrism." By that I mean at least as much as what C. S. Lewis meant by "chronological snobbery," the idea that the present is superior to any preceding time, and therefore has nothing to learn from it. My concern goes beyond that, to the idea that the present time will never be superseded. That is the idea that the final state has been achieved, and of such ideas are born doctrinal constructions that are often obsolescent when first promulgated. One sometimes gets the impression from some children of the Reformation that all that can be said on a given subject has now been said. Similarly, some postmodernists do not appear to consider the likelihood that postmodernism will also be replaced.

This is not to say that nothing can be gained from the study of historical theology. One additional cause of omission of doctrinal exploration is failure to recognize that in principle the underlying issue of a current discussion is the same as one that has been discussed in the past. For example, a discussion of contemporary Jehovah's Witness theology might well be simplified and enhanced by a study of fourth-century Arianism, on which it is based. While the contemporary Jehovah's Witness adds some unique variations to the ancient formulation, in some respects it is here unnecessary to reinvent the wheel.

Conceptual and linguistic ambiguity also contributes to doctrinal gaps. Sometimes discussion proceeds using well-known terminology, with both parties assuming that they mean the same thing by those terms. In some cases, this vagueness may have been deliberately cultivated by persons who do not wish to reveal their exact positions on important issues. When the differences become evident, effort is made to articulate more fully what is meant. In an increasingly pluralistic intellectual world, refined expressions of doctrine are important.

Let us now consider some of the unresolved issues. I will not here attempt to deal with the "big three:" divine sovereignty and human freedom; the three persons and one nature within the Trinity; or the two natures and one person of Christ. Those have been debated for a long time, and it is possible that we will not see a conclusion of the debate until the eschaton. They seem to so far exceed human comprehension that earthly discussion may not succeed until then. Rather, we will examine somewhat smaller issues, some of them of fairly recent debate, and in some cases, the proposed answers are not even recognized as insufficient.

I will contend in this essay that frequently when a problem has proven irresolvable, the real reason is that there is an underlying issue that has not received adequate attention. In each case I will try to identify that foundational question and suggest some directions from which alleviation might come. I will limit the discussion to six examples: the extent and nature of divine foreknowledge; the nature of divine transcendence; the destiny of the unevangelized; the status of those who die in infancy; the intermediate state of believers between death and resurrection; and the nature of the believer's resurrection body.

1. *Divine foreknowledge*. For much of the history of the church, there was basic agreement that God knows in advance all that will happen throughout history. While there were some who challenged this idea, they were often outside the mainstream of orthodoxy. In the past two

decades, however, controversy over this issue has arisen within evangelical theology. Some of the debate has been over how God knows the future. Three basic answers have been offered.[1] "Simple" foreknowledge is the view that God simply "sees" the future, often including the concept of an atemporal God, for whom past, present, and future are equally directly known. Calvinism holds that God knows the future because he has decreed it. "Middle" knowledge contends that God knows all the possibilities that may be, and chooses to bring into reality those that will eventuate in ways that he desires. The recent alternative to each of these has come from a movement known as "open theism," which asserts that while God knows some of the future, especially those matters involving physical or natural occurrences, he does not necessarily know in advance all the actions of free moral agents, particularly humans. Various biblical passages are cited in support of this view, some indicating God's surprise at what has occurred, while others express his repentance or change of mind.

Under criticism that their view denies God's omniscience, some open theists have made an interesting move. Just as God's inability to do the logically contradictory or what is contrary to his nature does not count against his omnipotence, so God's not knowing the future is in no sense a refutation of his omniscience, for the future is not something that can be known. It has no reality, or as it is sometimes put, it does not "exist."[2] In many aspects of the debate, the underlying issue is the nature of human freedom: whether it is compatible or incompatible with certainty about what will be done. Here, however, the issue is the nature of the future and its reality.

In one sense, of course, the future does not "exist," if by that we mean that its events are now present with us. But in that sense the past does not "exist," either. This is merely saying that neither the past nor the future is the present. Beyond that, however, the question is whether events that have not yet occurred have the ontological status necessary to be knowable.

It is here that modern physics may provide some potentially helpful ideas. What has emerged is a questioning of the reality not of the future, but of time itself. Albert Einstein's theory of relativity asserted that

---

1. For an overview of these alternatives, see Beilby and Eddy, *Divine Foreknowledge*.

2. Boyd, *God of the Possible*, 120–27.

both time and space, which in Newtonian physics were considered fixed realities, are actually relative. This included the paradox of simultaneity. An event may be perceived at different times by two observers, removed from the location of the event by different distances. Thus, what is a past event for one person may be future for another. Beyond that, quantum physicists have begun to entertain the idea of time travel. One particular form of that is described as "wormholes," interconnected black holes that enable direct travel not only from one place to another, but also from one time to another. While this is all hypothetical, it reveals that the idea of time usually involved in the discussions of foreknowledge is rather naïve. While some theologians are proclaiming the unreality of the future, some physicists apparently find no conceptual difficulty in the idea of persons from the future traveling back to us. Much more work needs to be done on the nature of time, but there may be help here for us in understanding this disputed doctrine.[3]

2. *The nature of divine transcendence.* In a sense, the relationship between immanence and transcendence is one of those perennial puzzles we mentioned earlier that probably will not be resolved within this life. I am concerned, however, that we have continued to think of divine transcendence largely in the conceptual form in which it is expressed in Scripture, i.e., that of spatial distance, and have taken this rather literally, rather than as the metaphor that I believe it is. In particular, we have tended to follow older models of physics in our thinking about God's relationship to the world, neglecting some potentially fruitful insights of recent scientific thought.

Søren Kierkegaard, the nineteenth-century Danish philosopher and theologian, introduced into the discussion the concept of dimensional beyondness. By this he meant not simply that God is far removed from our spatial dimensions, but that in some sense he is beyond usual dimensions. Kierkegaard gave relatively little content to this, however. Now quantum mechanics physicists are entertaining the idea that reality may not be limited to the four dimensions of which Einstein spoke—three of space, plus time. There may be as many as ten of these spatial dimensions. We cannot literally conceive of them or form a picture of what this would be like, being limited to and by our experience. Nonetheless, the mathematical calculations regarding such a scheme

---

3. Thorne, *Black Holes*, 483–522.

are workable and indeed resolve some of the puzzles of physics. When reality is thought of in terms of these additional dimensions, a number of issues become simpler to deal with, and a number of issues regarding the various forces in our universe are more easily related to each other. Just as a three-dimensional being would definitely transcend two-dimensional beings, so a four- or five-dimensional being would live beyond the three spatial dimensions with which we are familiar.[4]

I am not prepared to declare that this way of understanding reality is superior to the Newtonian, or more specifically, the Einsteinian scheme, or if it is, that this is somehow a final understanding of things. Even if it is superior to those earlier versions of physics, it also will be succeeded by other theories. I am, however, suggesting that theologians and philosophers might benefit from an investigation of this set of concepts. A number of other issues might be helped by thinking of them from such a vantage point. One is the question of miracles. These have usually been thought of either as instances of natural laws currently not known or understood by us, as violations of natural law, or as God working in such a way as to offset the effects of natural law, which continues to work nonetheless. If, however, God inhabits more than three spatial dimensions, then he can easily do what to us three-dimensional beings is inexplicable, as physicist Kaku has pointed out.[5] We have long puzzled over how Jesus could have appeared among his disciples who were in a room with the doors locked (John 20:26). For a being coming from additional dimensions, this would present no problem.

3. *The destiny of the unevangelized.* What happens to those who do not accept Jesus during their lifetime because they have never heard the gospel? One rather vocal position has been the exclusivist or restrictivist view that no one is saved apart from an explicit conscious faith in Jesus. An inclusivist position, on the contrary, may allow for a postmortem opportunity to hear and accept, but most frequently appeals to the concept of "implicit faith." This is the idea that through the general revelation one may come to a sufficient knowledge of God and of one's condition to commit oneself to at least the contours of the gospel: an abandonment of reliance on one's own works and a trust in a gracious God who forgives on the basis of his own provision of sacrifice for hu-

4. Kaku, *Hyperspace*, 45–54.
5. Ibid.

man sin. Although not knowing the details of the means of salvation, these people, like the Old Testament saints, are saved by the work of Jesus Christ. The restrictivist position contends that a major change took place with the incarnation and earthly work of the second person of the Trinity so that only a faith in him based on an explicit knowledge of his person and work will suffice. A third option, less common and less discussed, has been held by some throughout the church's history, and advocated by persons such as J. I. Packer.[6] This allows for the possibility of salvation for someone who places his faith in the provision and forgiveness by a gracious God, but without knowledge of the details of that provision.

One issue that underlies this is whether this radical change in the nature of saving faith was occasioned by the coming of Christ. John Piper in his *Let the Nations Rejoice!* repeatedly asserts that a "tremendous" change was made, but his argument rests on a number of unsupported assumptions and questionable biblical interpretations.[7] A second issue is the extent of the beliefs necessary for salvation. Frequently, in this context, there is a failure to distinguish between how much one must know, understand, and believe in order to be saved, and how much one may know and deny and still be saved. These two issues go beyond the scope of this investigation, however.

It appears to me that one crucial issue, frequently inadequately treated, is the nature and extent of the general revelation. This is especially significant for this matter, since Paul in Romans 1 and 2 seems to link condemnation of unbelievers to their failure to respond to the knowledge of God made known to all persons in the external creation and in their inward moral nature. In particular, his statement in 1:20, "so they are [or in order that they might be] without excuse," seems to indicate that there was the possibility of their being redemptively related to the true God through the general revelation. If not, the statement would make little sense, for they could offer as their excuse the fact that they could not possibly have met God's requirements.

This depreciation of general revelation has other serious consequences. There is the importance evangelistically of being able to relate the gospel to some aspect of the general experience of the unbeliever.

---

6. Packer, *God's Words*, 210. In recent years even Billy Graham has expressed a similar view.

7. Piper, *Let the Nations*, 125–33.

In a religiously pluralistic society, especially where there is legal separation of church and state, any arguments for particular ethical positions will need to be based on considerations accessible to persons of differing or no religious commitment.

Part of the neglect of the doctrine of general revelation by many evangelicals appears to me to stem from one or both of two concerns. One is that to the extent that we allow something to be known from the general revelation, special revelation will be neglected or will suffer. This was also a major concern of Karl Barth. If, however, the special revelation witnesses to the existence of a general revelation, then we do not honor the former by denying or ignoring the latter. The second fear is a practical one: that if we allow that apart from the special revelation it may be possible to know something about God, we have opened the door to persons being saved without explicit knowledge of Jesus Christ, and there will consequently be a diminution of evangelistic effort on the part of Christians. Apart from the issue of whether this is a valid inference, I question whether making doctrinal decisions on such pragmatic grounds is a wise course of action. If it is, then perhaps a bit of preaching of salvation by works would not be a bad idea, especially at times such as a major capital funds program.

I see some indications that perhaps not just a neglect of the doctrine of general revelation but an actual rejection of its authenticity is at work. For example, Piper considers the position that suggests that if someone were, subsequent to the life and ministry of Jesus to come, solely by general revelation, to a belief similar in outline to what the Old Testament believers held, he might be saved. Piper emphatically rejects this idea. Saving faith must come through special revelation. He says, "special revelation has always been the path to salvation, and this special relation was centered in Israel, the promise of a Redeemer, and the foreshadowings of this salvation in the sacrificial system of the Old Testament. Jesus is now the climax and fulfillment of that special revelation so that saving faith, which was always focused on special revelation, is now focused on him."[8] There has been no change in the means of saving knowledge from the Old Testament to the New: "Even before Christ, people were not saved apart from special revelation given by God. . . . It is not as though general revelation through nature was effective in producing faith before Christ but ceased to be effective

8. Ibid., 127 n. 24.

after Christ. According to Romans 1:18–23, general revelation through nature has always been sufficient to make people accountable to glorify and thank God, but not efficient to do so."[9] Later, however, Piper writes, "it was God's wisdom that determined that men would not know him through their wisdom ... Why? To make crystal clear that men on their own, by their own wisdom (religion!) will never truly know God."[10] The implication seems to be that any knowledge of God outside of special revelation is a human achievement, rather than a revelation from God. This view of general revelation shows some similarities to that of Karl Barth. There appears to be confusion over whether the problem lies with humans' refusal to accept what is plainly shown, the insufficiency of the content of the knowledge, or the means by which it comes. I would suggest that further work needs to be done on the biblical passages that speak of God's revelation in nature and human personality, such as Psalm 19 and Romans 1–2.

4. *The status of those who die in infancy.* Another issue that currently appears somewhat clouded concerns the fate of those who die in infancy, or even physically mature adults who never come to a sufficient stage of mental ability to be able to understand and believe the gospel. The question is what becomes of them after death. Are they condemned to eternal damnation, or are they somehow participants in salvation, so that they spend eternity with God?

In general, most Christians believe and assert that such infants somehow spend eternity in heaven. Various reasons for this are given. Some denominations that believe in infant baptism hold that although they may be guilty because of Adam's first sin, baptism effects regeneration of the corrupted nature, and thus also justification from the guilt of that sin. For most evangelicals, however, this is not an acceptable answer. In some way, the grace of Christ counters the effect of sin. Arminians hold that although all are affected by that sin, no culpability attaches to it.

Earlier Calvinists held that in some sense, everyone participated in that initial sin, with at least two consequences: corruption and guilt. Corruption meant that all persons are born with a natural inclination to do evil. Guilt meant that all were subject to punishment for sin, includ-

---

9. Ibid., 126–27 n. 24.
10. Ibid., 131.

ing the fact of death. So Louis Berkhof, for example, wrote, "The guilt of Adam's sin, committed by him as the federal head of the human race, is imputed to his descendents. This is evident from the fact that, as the Bible teaches, death as the punishment of sin passes on from Adam to all his descendants."[11] Charles Hodge makes a similar affirmation, explaining and arguing it at great length.[12] These Calvinists usually argued that just as Adam's sin was imputed to all, so Christ's righteousness is imputed to all, except for those who excluded themselves from it. Thus, based on Romans 5, just as Adam's sin was imputed to persons who had not committed the sin, so Christ's atoning sacrifice was imputed to them.

Recently, some self-identified Calvinists have modified the idea that persons will be judged for the original sin of Adam. Particularly in connection with the question of the fate of those who die in infancy or at least before attaining sufficient maturity to recognize right and wrong, they contend that persons will be judged only for the sins that they personally commit. Ronald Nash, for example, says, "original sin leaves all humans including infants and the mentally incapable both guilty and depraved."[13] Then, however, he goes on to say that "God's condemnation is based on the actual commission of sins," offering commentary on 2 Cor 5:10, "Note the clear statement that the final judgment is based on sins committed during our earthly existence. Note further that since infants are incapable of being moral agents, since they die before they are able to perform either good or evil acts, deceased infants cannot be judged on the criterion specified in this verse."[14] As elect, these infants are somehow regenerated prior to death. Nash, however, has stated so broadly the principle of responsibility only for sins personally committed that it extends beyond infants, thus modifying the traditional Calvinist view of original sin. It would appear that the underlying issue is the nature of imputation of guilt for original sin, and that more reflection is needed in that area.

I would suggest that a more fruitful possibility, which provides both for the reality of imputation of guilt and for those dying in infancy not being condemned, would be what I term "conditional imputation."

11. Berkhof, *Systematic Theology*, 246.
12. Hodge, *Systematic Theology*, 2:188–205.
13. Nash, *When a Baby Dies*, 59.
14. Ibid., 60–61.

On this scheme, at the point of reaching moral consciousness and accountability, persons become liable for the original sin of Adam, unless they consciously repudiate the sinful nature that they now realize they possess. While this is necessarily a construct as well, it does preserve the parallelism of Rom 5:19. Just as the righteousness of Christ is not imputed to persons without their acceptance of it, so the corruption and guilt resulting from Adam's sin is only imputed when acquiesced in by the individual.

5. *The intermediate state.* What transpires between the time a Christian dies and the general resurrection, in connection with the second coming? The traditional answer has been that the person exists in a conscious but incomplete, somehow disembodied state in God's presence. At the resurrection, the person's soul or spirit will be reunited with the resurrected and transformed body. One alternative was that of soul sleep, the idea that the person simply is in a state of unconsciousness, so that the next experience he/she has after death is that of the resurrection. The argument for the idea of personal, "disembodied" existence was based on biblical passages that seemed to refer to such. Among these were Jesus' promise to the repentant thief on the cross, "This day you will be with me in paradise" (Luke 23:43), Paul's statement about being "away from the body and at home with the Lord" (2 Cor 5:8), as well as Jesus' story, perhaps a parable, of the rich man and Lazarus (Luke 16:19–31). These seemed to present problems for the soul sleep view.

More recently, however, biblical scholars, including some evangelicals, have come to a view of the absolute unity of human nature that really does not allow for any sort of existence apart from the body. Based on study of the pertinent Hebrew and Greek terms, they believe that the Bible does not teach that the person has both a physical aspect (the body) and an immaterial aspect (the soul and/or spirit). Instead, these terms tend to be used rather interchangeably in referring to the person.[15] Thus, no such conscious intermediate state between death and resurrection is possible. This logically should lead to the question of just what that one nature is, but most do not ask that question. One who is willing to do so is Nancey Murphy, who unhesitatingly opts for what

---

15. Robinson, *The Body*.

she terms "non-reductive physicalism," as distinguished from the more controversial term, "materialism."[16]

If, however, there is no non-material aspect of the human that can exist independently of an embodied existence, there is difficulty in conceptualizing the intermediate state. One attempted solution is a version of the soul sleep doctrine, namely that the person really does not exist until again coming to life in an embodied or physical state. A more recent alternative is the idea of an immediate resurrection, following directly upon death. Finally, a number of evangelicals, including some whose primary work is in philosophy, are arguing for a contingent monism, or something of the type, in which the fullest form of human existence is in an embodied state, but according to which it is also possible for human existence to continue, at least temporarily and incompletely, without bodily form.[17]

Much of the debate will need to take place with respect to metaphysical assumptions. The monists' charge is that the dualists have approached Scripture and read it through the lens of Greek metaphysical dualism, while the latter contend that the monists are themselves working from presuppositions, such as behaviorism, and that this has led them to distort passages like Luke 16:19–31 and 2 Cor 5:6–10. More attention will need to be given to these discussions.

6. *The resurrection body.* Many have held that the believer's resurrection body will be in many ways of the same physical nature as the body possessed within this life, yet transformed in some way to preclude suffering, deterioration, and death, and controlled by the Spirit. In some cases this is taken so literally that there will be actual physical eating of meals in heaven; the marriage feast of the lamb will be a literal feast.[18]

The assumption in this discussion is often that the resurrection body that believers will possess in the future is of the same nature as the body that Jesus had after his resurrection, during his continued time on earth. The problem, however, is that Christ's body seemed to display contradictory characteristics. On the one hand, it could be touched, which Jesus invited Thomas to do to verify that it was indeed he (John 20:24–29). On the other hand, this body did not seem to have some of

---

16. Murphy, "Nonreductive Physicalism," 97.
17. Moreland and Rae, *Body & Soul*.
18. Geisler, *Battle for the Resurrection*, 121–22.

the limitations of a usual human body. For example, Jesus appeared in the midst of a group of disciples, with the doors to the room closed and locked.

This has led to considerable debate and some alternatives to the physical view above. One was propounded by George Ladd and also held and expounded by Murray Harris. On such a view, Jesus' resurrection body was a spiritual body, invisible and non-material, but at times he manifested himself to his followers in a physical form. Thus, Jesus materialized, as it were, within the room where the disciples were (John 20:19) and ate fish with them (Luke 24:41–43). Yet this was only a temporary manifestation of his resurrection body.[19]

It appears that the underlying problem may be a failure to develop a clear understanding of the nature of Christ's ascension, which in some traditional views serves very little purpose other than to transport a physical object from one place in the physical universe to another, and in rather Newtonian categories at that. On most views, it really has no doctrinal significance, since it did not affect any change in Jesus.

Another alternative, advanced by James Orr, has received relatively little attention in recent years. It is that the glorification of Jesus' body took place in two stages, the first at the resurrection, and the second at the ascension. In the case of believers, these two steps will be collapsed into one at the resurrection. Thus, the body of Jesus between his resurrection and ascension is not the model for what the believer's resurrection body will be. This view allows for both Luke 24:39 and 1 Cor 15:50 to be taken seriously and rather literally, and to be reconciled harmoniously. It also allows for more natural treatment of Matt 22:30 and its parallels, and possible implications thereof.[20]

While some may be inclined to think that all the issues of evangelical theology have been adequately resolved, I have suggested that there is much work yet to be done, not only on these issues, but on several others that could have been mentioned. We have also noted that beneath many of the topics yet unresolved lie more basic issues, which if given sufficient attention, may enable progress on the primary issues of discussion. The history of evangelical theological formulation has been a productive one. The future can be as well.

---

19. Ladd, *I Believe*, 96–99.
20. Orr, *Resurrection of Jesus*, 195–202.

Bibliography

Berkhof, Louis. *Systematic Theology*. Grand Rapids: Eerdmans, 1953.

Boyd, Gregory. *God of the Possible: A Biblical Introduction to the Open View of God*. Grand Rapids: Baker, 2000.

Beilby, James K., and Paul R. Eddy, editors. *Divine Foreknowledge: Four Views*. Downers Grove, IL: InterVarsity, 2001.

Geisler, Norman L. *The Battle for the Resurrection*. Nashville: Nelson, 1989.

Hodge, Charles. *Systematic Theology*. Vol. 2. Grand Rapids: Eerdmans, 1952.

Kaku, Michio. *Hyperspace: A Scientific Odyssey through Parallel Universes, Time Warps, and the 10th Dimension*. New York: Anchor, 1995.

Ladd, George E. *I Believe in the Resurrection of Jesus*. Grand Rapids: Eerdmans, 1975.

Moreland, J. P., and Scott B. Rae. *Body & Soul: Human Nature & the Crisis in Ethics*. Downers Grove, IL: InterVarsity, 2000.

Murphy, Nancey C. "Nonreductive Physicalism: Philosophical Challenges." In *Personal Identity in Theological Perspective*, edited by Richard Lints, Michael S. Horton, and Mark R. Talbot, 95–117. Grand Rapids: Eerdmans, 2006.

Nash, Ronald H. *When a Baby Dies: Answers to Comfort Grieving Parents*. Grand Rapids: Zondervan, 1999.

Orr, James. *The Resurrection of Jesus*. London: Hodder & Stoughton, 1908.

Packer, J. I. *God's Words: Studies of Key Biblical Themes*. Downers Grove, IL: InterVarsity, 1981.

Piper, John. *Let the Nations Be Glad! The Supremacy of God in Missions*. 2nd ed. Grand Rapids: Baker, 2005.

Robinson, John A. T. *The Body: A Study of Pauline Theology*. Studies in Biblical Theology 1/5. London: SCM, 1952.

Thorne, Kip S. *Black Holes and Time Warps: Einstein's Outrageous Legacy*. New York: Norton, 1995.

2

"Center," "Horizon," and Rhetorical Focus in Ignatius of Antioch

Robert B. Sloan

IN HIS *A BASIC CHRISTIAN THEOLOGY*, A. J. CONYERS DEMONSTRATES A wide-ranging knowledge of systematic theology, Scripture, and the great theologians of the church. He succeeds well in his goal of providing a "guide to Christian theology for those just entering their theological studies."[1] The value of the work lies precisely in its ability to introduce the basic categories of systematic theology while bringing to bear for the reader—whether to illustrate or substantiate arguments—the resources of Scripture and historical theology.

In honor of Conyers's broad grasp of biblical, historical, and ecclesiastical materials, I would like to look at Ignatius of Antioch, an apostolic father who is favorably cited by Conyers in support of the early Christian emphasis upon *mimesis* (imitation) as related to an appeal to unity.[2] In so doing, I hope to draw attention to a slight, but nonetheless perceptible shift in perspective between canonical first century Christian literature and its use of both biblical traditions and the history (theology and acts) of Jesus to reflect and/or *establish* apostolic traditions, on the one hand, and Ignatius's *reception* of those apostolic traditions as a new horizon of thought from which he made certain situationally important rhetorical and pastoral appeals. Thus, on his march to martyrdom, Ignatius pleads especially, against certain "unbelievers," for the *physicality* of the central apostolic traditions—particularly the suffering

---

1. Conyers, *Basic Christian Theology*, ix.
2. Ibid., 191–92.

of Jesus—as a basis for unity.³ With the prospect of his impending, violent death, and the urgency he feels to halt the theological inroads being made by these opponents, Ignatius shapes the received kerygma, especially traditional views of the cross, in ways that emphasize its physical starkness and highlight its power to unify.

It is no doubt always the interplay of sources, traditions, and contemporary circumstances that constitutes Christian theology, an interplay that Conyers well embodied in his life and writings. New Testament scholars are accustomed to speaking of the "horizon" and "center" of a given writer, as, for example, the "horizon" of Pauline theology is widely said to be Jewish apocalyptic and the Pauline "center" is the message of the crucified and risen Jesus. A given Pauline letter is then understood to be an occasional piece that, given the Pauline center, within its horizon of Jewish apocalyptic, will have different rhetorical foci. Romans, for example, argues for the faithfulness/righteousness of God in fulfilling his purposes for the world by saving Jews and Gentiles alike through the faithful obedience of Jesus Christ.

The purpose here is to look at the letters of Ignatius and offer in summary fashion a few remarks as to the larger social and literary provenance of his thought, while also looking at both the horizon and center of his thinking as revealed in his occasional pieces, followed by a description of his overriding rhetorical foci.

Introduction

When Serapion, Bishop of Antioch (in office ca. 198–211[4]) wrote to the Christian community of Rhosos (about thirty miles from Antioch) with regard to the *Gospel of Peter* and the question of its authenticity, he

3. My distinction between *canonical* first century literature and Ignatius neither prejudges the dating of the documents typically called the "Apostolic Fathers" nor presumes any theories of literary dependence on the part of Ignatius upon New Testament traditions. I do, in fact, think Ignatius is knowledgeable of Pauline and Johannine traditions, and I am inclined to believe he is familiar with Matthean and even Lukan (*pace* Brown, *Gospel and Ignatius of Antioch*, 1–3) traditions. The recent efforts of those in the Robinson, Borg, Koester, Crossan et al. schools of Gospel/sayings criticism are, in my opinion, far too willing to adopt the most complicated theories of the trajectories of the Jesus and Gospel traditions (oral and literary) over more satisfying and less speculative possibilities that work with the texts and traditions we actually have. See the magisterial discussion of these and related issues in Wright, *Jesus and the Victory of God*, 28–82.

4. Downey, *History of Antioch*, 303.

referred to a group of heretical teachers as "Docetae"[5] and became thereby the first in our extant literature to employ the noun *Docetists*.[6] The giving of a formal name to those who denied the real humanity (especially the passion) of the Savior reflects a stage in the historical trajectory of a sub-Christian theological impulse[7] that is well past its beginnings. In addition to the unwelcome reflections of the docetic tendency within New Testament communities (e.g., 1 John 4:2; 5:6, 8; 2 John 7; 1 Tim 3:16; Luke 24:39), there is, about a century earlier than Serapion, in the literary remains of Ignatius (one of Serapion's predecessors as bishop of Antioch), a decided, indeed virulent animosity toward those "unbelievers" who say "that he suffered in appearance only [τὸ δοκεῖν αὐτὸν πεπονθέναι] (it is they who exist in appearance only!). Indeed, their fate will be determined by what they think: they will become disembodied and demonic" (Ign. *Smyrn.* 2:1).[8]

Though it does not account for the basic structures of his theology, particularly the received traditions pertaining to the birth, death, and resurrection of Jesus, the vehement opposition of Ignatius to the docetic threat must have exerted some influence upon the shaping and application by him of those traditional materials in response to his opponents. From this point of departure, it is the threefold thesis of this paper that (1) the theology of Ignatius of Antioch, with regard to its "horizon," is the *apostolic tradition* of the early church, which has the emerging shape of what is, not very long after Ignatius, called the *regula fidei* (itself anticipating the Apostles' Creed); (2) within the framework of this received apostolic kerygma, the theology of Ignatius has for its "center" the *cross of Christ* as the unifying dynamic, the ongoing form, and the eschatological goal of Christian experience; and (3) unity, in various aspects, is the *rhetorical focus* of his seven pastoral letters. In this regard, the tension of his circumstances of arrest, no doubt magnified

---

5. Eusebius *Ecclesiastical History* 6.12.2–6 (2:40–43).

6. "Docetism" in *Oxford Dictionary of the Christian Church*, 413.

7. In light of its varied manifestations among quite diverse heretical (and orthodox?) movements, the term *docetism* may justly be used to refer broadly to those movements which, however different their Christologies may have been in other regards, held "that Christ was man only in appearance." Slusser, "Docetism," 172. In the case of Ignatius's docetic opponents, it was particularly their rejection of the genuineness of Christ's suffering that drew him to the attack.

8. Holmes, *Apostolic Fathers*, 250–51. Unless otherwise noted, all Greek texts and English translations used herein are from this source.

for Ignatius by the prospect of martyrdom in Rome on the one hand and the docetic threat encountered repeatedly on his trek across Asia on the other, has almost singularly fixed the Ignatian focus upon the necessity of a theological and ecclesiastical unity, the former around the received apostolic traditions and the latter around the bishop especially, but also around every major feature of the community's experience in worship, whether prayer, baptism, the Eucharist, or obedience.[9]

Social and Literary Provenance

Jean Daniélou points to "Jewish Christianity" as providing the larger context for understanding Ignatius's thought. By "Jewish Christian" is meant the kind of theology that, while not necessarily associated with Jerusalem Christianity or any of the traditionally labeled Jewish Christian communities, continues to use Jewish forms and thought structures in the expression of its faith.[10] Ignatius's thought seems clearly to fall within the scope of this broad definition. There have, of course, been attempts to interpret the thought of Ignatius from other historical points of reference, e.g., in terms of mystery cults,[11] the Gnostic redeemer myth,[12] and/or neo-Platonic conceptions.[13] It seems, however, that his basic theological perceptions are more heuristically explained in terms of biblical patterns, especially those of Paul and John.

---

9. In the early 1980s, I presented a paper on Ignatius of Antioch to the Second Century Seminar, also known as the Seminar on Early Catholic Christianity. Everett Ferguson, then of Abilene Christian University (now retired), graciously offered a very helpful response to the paper, from which I benefited greatly. His unpublished paper, "Response to Robert Sloan: The Unity of the Church in Ignatius," is the source for this and several other references.

10. "Jewish Christianity," thus broadly defined, is essentially the "third sense" described by Daniélou, *History of Early Christian Doctrine*, 9–10.

11. Bartsch, *Gnostisches Gut und Gemeindetradition bei Ignatius von Antiochien* as cited in Maurer, *Ignatius von Antiochien und das Johannesevangelium*, 7.

12. E.g., Schlier, *Religionsgeschichtliche Untersuchungen zu den Ignatiusbriefen*, 81: "Fassen wir zusammen, so ergibt sich ... für Ignatius, dass dem mit seiner Christologie verbundenen Heilsdrama ein Erlösermythos zugrunde liegt. Dieser hat zum wesentlichen Inhalt das verborgene Herabsteigen des Erlösers aus seiner himmlischen Heimat auf die Erde und sein offenbares Zurückkehren von hier nach dort. Mit diesem Mythos ist die christliche Gemeindetradition von dem gekreuzigten und auferstandenen Messias verbunden..."; cf. Maurer, *Ignatius von Antiochien*, 26–43.

13. Examples of this point of view with respect to the ἕνωσις θεοῦ in Ignatius are referred to in Snyder, *Continuity of Early Christianity*, 162–73.

Establishing the Jewish Christian provenance of Ignatius's theology requires, of course, more than mere assertion. The final proof for such a contention must emerge from the study of Ignatius's theology as a whole, if it is to be sustained. In anticipation of that point, however, it may be noted that more than one feature of Ignatian thought and language has been regarded as Syrian, and that, Jewish Christian in provenance. Though her conclusions with regard to the presence of Essenism in Antioch may be doubted,[14] Virginia Corwin has shown what seem to be clear resemblances between the Ignatian environment and the *Odes of Solomon*,[15] which many still argue to be an originally Syriac piece and also Jewish Christian, at least in its final form.[16] While also arguing for a Syrian/Jewish Christian background for the *Odes*, J. Daniélou has further maintained that theological developments in Ignatius clearly resemble other products of Syrian Christianity, particularly the *Ascension of Isaiah*.[17] Daniélou has in fact suggested extensive parallels between Ignatius and other Jewish Christian literature, conceptions, language, and liturgy.[18]

Others are less content to refer to "Jewish Christianity," especially when referring to language and literary style. More than one scholar

---

14. Corwin, *St. Ignatius and Christianity in Antioch*, 61.
15. Ibid., 71–79.
16. Cf. Hennecke, *New Testament Apocrypha*, 808–9.
17. Daniélou, *Theology of Jewish Christianity*, 40–42.
18. The following examples are taken from *The Theology of Jewish Christianity*. The connection of "the Name" with persecution (Ign. *Eph.* 1:2; 3:1; cf. 7:1), 156–57; the doctrine of an angel set over the earth (Ign. *Eph.* 17:1; 19:1), 188ff.; the hidden descent of the Son (Ign. *Eph.* 19:1), 207, 212; the Magi and the Star (Ign. *Eph.* 19:2–3), 217–24; the baptism of Jesus as a defeat of demonic powers (Ign. *Eph.* 18:2), 226–27; the descent into Hell (Ign. *Magn.* 9:2), 236–37; the cross as spiritual power (Ign. *Eph.* 9:1), 278, 288 (here it seems that Daniélou has missed other Ignatian passages characteristic of Jewish Christianity that establish a deeper and broader theological connection between the triumphant cross and the incorporating/unifying cosmic power of God: cf. Ign. *Smyrn.* 1:2; Ign. *Trall.* 11:1; Ign. *Phld.* 3:3; Ign. *Magn.* 5:2); the church as the goal of creation (Ign. *Eph.* inscr.), 294; the institution of Sunday worship (Ign. *Magn.* 9:1), 342–43. Daniélou (356) also argues that the organization of the Ignatian church in Antioch, with its strictly ordered hierarchy of bishop, presbyterate, and deacons, was Jewish Christian after the model of the Jerusalem organization, likely because of a great influx of Jewish Christians after the events of AD 70. This assertion is not, however, undisputed. See Brent, *Ignatius of Antioch*. Cf. Jay, "From Presbyter-Bishops to Bishops and Presbyters," 286–87. It is interesting to note that Daniélou mentions no parallels between Jewish Christian Eucharistic rites and the Eucharist as reflected in Ignatius.

has noted that Ignatius writes in a style common to the first and second centuries AD, known as Asianism.[19] Certainly there is not much in terms of Old Testament language or allusion in Ignatius, especially when compared to *I Clement* or *Barnabas*.[20]

Ignatius was likely no stranger to the religious and philosophical dualisms that threatened to undermine the reality of the primitive gospel traditions, as the repeated struggle of the early Christian community in Antioch against docetic, Gnostic, and/or mystery cults is well documented.[21] The association of the names of many second-century heresiarchs—Simon Magus,[22] Menander,[23] Saturninus,[24] Cerdo,[25] and (through Cerdo) even Marcion[26]—with Antioch and/or Syria illustrates at least a widely held perception—that of Justin, Irenaeus, Tertullian, and Eusebius, for example—of the susceptibility, if not fecundity, of the Antiochene environment with regard to all such, though varied, essentially dualistic movements.[27]

The description "Jewish Christian" is adequate if all one seeks is a general frame of reference to understand Ignatius, but it is really not helpful beyond implying that the more vertical and dualistic thought forms characteristic of Greek thought are not pervasively present. We must go beyond the generalization of Daniélou and try to be more specific.

What does seem clear is that the confessional traditions of early apostolic theology[28] form the clearest theological backdrop—as a kind of thought horizon—for Ignatius's pastoral exhortations.

The repeated references to such traditions—be they called apostolic kerygma or emerging forms of *regula fidei*—stand as the confessional

---

19. Cf. Ferguson, "Response to Robert Sloan"; and also Holmes, *Apostolic Fathers*, 174.

20. Ferguson, "Response to Robert Sloan."

21. See, for example, Wallace-Hadrill, *Christian Antioch*, esp. 1–26.

22. Irenaeus *Adv. Haer.* 1.23.2–4; Eusebius *Ecclesiastical History* 2.13-15.1 (1:136–43).

23. Justin *Apol.* 1.26.1, 4; Irenaeus *Adv. Haer.* 1.23.5.

24. Irenaeus *Adv. Haer.* 1.24.1–2.

25. Irenaeus *Adv. Haer.* 1.27.1; Tertullian *Adversus Marcionem* 1.2.3, 1.22.10, 4.17.11–12; Eusebius *Ecclesiastical History* 4.10 (1:326–27).

26. With the exceptions of the citations from Eusebius and Tertullian, the references in nn. 22–25 are from Foerster, *Gnosis*, 27–44, passim.

27. Cf. Downey, *History of Antioch*, 288–92.

28. Sloan, "Canonical Theology of the New Testament."

basis of his exhortations. The following citations illustrate the pervasive nature of these explicit apostolic tradition/*regula fidei* type passages in the Ignatian corpus.

Ign. *Ephesians*[29] 7:2

There is only one physician,	εἷς ἰατρός ἐστιν,
who is both flesh and spirit,	σαρκικὸς καὶ πνευματικός,
born and unborn,	γεννητὸς καὶ ἀγέννητος,
God in man,	ἐν ἀνθρώπῳ θεός,
true life in death,	ἐν θανάτῳ ζωὴ ἀληθινή,
both from Mary and from God,	καὶ ἐκ Μαρίας καὶ ἐκ θεοῦ,
first subject to suffering and then beyond it,	πρῶτον παθητὸς καὶ τότε ἀπαθής,
Jesus Christ our Lord.	Ἰησοῦς Χριστὸς ὁ κύριος ἡμῶν.

Ign. *Ephesians* 18:2

For our God, Jesus the Christ,	ὁ γὰρ θεὸς ἡμῶν Ἰησοῦς ὁ Χριστὸς
was conceived by Mary	ἐκυοφορήθη ὑπὸ Μαρίας
according to God's plan,	κατ' οἰκονομίαν θεοῦ,
both from the seed of David	ἐκ σπέρματος μὲν Δαυὶδ
and of the Holy Spirit.	πνεύματος δὲ ἁγίου·
He was born and was baptized	ὃς ἐγεννήθη καὶ ἐβαπτίσθη
in order that by his suffering he might cleanse the water.	ἵνα τῷ πάθει τὸ ὕδωρ καθαρίσῃ.

Ign. *Magnesians* 11:1

. . . but instead to be fully convinced	ἀλλὰ πεπληροφορῆσθαι
about the birth	ἐν τῇ γεννήσει
and the suffering	καὶ τῷ πάθει
and the resurrection	καὶ τῇ ἀναστάσει
that took place during the time	τῇ γενομένῃ ἐν καιρῷ
of the governorship of Pontius Pilate.	τῆς ἡγεμονίας Ποντίου Πιλάτου·
These things were truly and most assuredly done	πραχθέντα ἀληθῶς καὶ βεβαίως
by Jesus Christ, our hope . . .	ὑπὸ Ἰησοῦ Χριστοῦ, τῆς ἐλπίδος ἡμῶν

---

29. The Greek texts and English translations are from Holmes, *Apostolic Fathers*.

Ign. *Trallians* 9:1–2

... apart from Jesus Christ,	χωρὶς Ἰησοῦ Χριστοῦ ...
who was of the family of David,	τοῦ ἐκ γένους Δαυίδ,
who was the son of Mary;	τοῦ ἐκ Μαρίας,
who really was born,	ὃς ἀληθῶς ἐγεννήθη,
who both ate and drank;	ἔφαγέν τε καὶ ἔπιεν,
who really was persecuted under Pontius Pilate,	ἀληθῶς ἐδιώχθη ἐπὶ Ποντίου Πιλάτου,
who really was crucified and died while those in heaven and on earth and under the earth looked on;	ἀληθῶς ἐσταυρώθη καὶ ἀπέθανεν, βλεπόντων τῶν ἐπουρανίων καὶ ἐπιγείων καὶ ὑποχθονίων·
who, moreover, really was raised from the dead when his Father raised him up.	ὃς καὶ ἀληθῶς ἠγέρθη ἀπὸ νεκρῶν, ἐγείραντος αὐτὸν τοῦ πατρὸς αὐτοῦ,
In the same way his Father will likewise also raise up in Christ Jesus us who believe in him.	ὃς καὶ κατὰ τὸ ὁμοίωμα ἡμᾶς τοὺς πιστεύοντας αὐτῷ οὕτως ἐγερεῖ ὁ πατὴρ αὐτοῦ ἐν Χριστῷ Ἰησοῦ,
Apart from him we have no true life.	οὗ χωρὶς τὸ ἀληθινὸν ζῆν οὐκ ἔχομεν.

Ign. *Smyrnaeans* 1:1–2

[H]e is truly of the family of David with respect to human descent,	ἀληθῶς ὄντα ἐκ γένους Δαυὶδ κατὰ σάρκα,
Son of God with respect to the divine will and power, truly born of a virgin, baptized by John	υἱὸν θεοῦ κατὰ θέλημα καὶ δύναμιν, γεγεννημένον ἀληθῶς ἐκ παρθένου, βεβαπτισμένον ὑπὸ Ἰωάννου
in order that all righteousness might be fulfilled by him, truly nailed in the flesh for us under Pontius Pilate and Herod the tetrarch	ἵνα πληρωθῇ πᾶσα δικαιοσύνη ὑπ' αὐτοῦ, ἀληθῶς ἐπὶ Ποντίου Πιλάτου καὶ Ἡρῴδου τετράρχου καθηλωμένον ὑπὲρ ἡμῶν ἐν σαρκί,
(from its fruit we derive our existence, that is, from his divinely blessed suffering),	ἀφ' οὗ καρποῦ ἡμεῖς ἀπὸ τοῦ θεομακαρίστου αὐτοῦ πάθους,
in order that he might raise a banner for the ages through his resurrection for his saints and faithful people, whether among Jews or among Gentiles, in the one body of his church.	ἵνα ἄρῃ σύσσημον εἰς τοὺς αἰῶνας διὰ τῆς ἀναστάσεως εἰς τοὺς ἁγίους καὶ πιστοὺς αὐτοῦ, εἴτε ἐν Ἰουδαίοις εἴτε ἐν ἔθνεσιν, ἐν ἑνὶ σώματι τῆς ἐκκλησίας αὐτοῦ.

Ign. Polycarp 3:2

... the Eternal,
the Invisible, who for our sake became visible;
the Intangible,
the Unsuffering, who for our sake suffered,
who for our sake endured in every way.

τὸν ἄχρονον,
τὸν ἀόρατον, τὸν δι' ἡμᾶς ὁρατόν,
τὸν ἀψηλάφητον,
τὸν ἀπαθῆ, τὸν δι' ἡμᾶς παθητόν,
τὸν κατὰ πάντα τρόπον
δι' ἡμᾶς ὑπομείναντα.

The foundational character for Ignatius of the received apostolic traditions regarding the Davidic descent, birth, death, and resurrection of Jesus is thus hardly questionable; but the shaping of those traditions, especially in light of the docetic deniers of the truly (note the repeated use of ἀληθῶς)[30] physical quality of those events brings us to the heart—the center—of Ignatius's theology, i.e., the true "passion" of Christ.

The Letters of Ignatius:[31] A Theological Analysis

Much of the scholarly focus upon the center of Ignatian theology has orbited around the "imitatio" concept. G. F. Snyder, after an extensive study of the history of Ignatian studies, places himself in the tradition of von Campenhausen, Schlier, Bartsch, and Preiss (to which the names of Rathke and Brox could be added[32]) by maintaining that imitation is "the key to understanding the martyrdom of Ignatius."[33] Without entering into the discussion of "imitation" at this point, it is at least significant to note here that the one letter in which Ignatius predominantly devotes himself to the question of his impending martyrdom, that to

---

30. ἀληθῶς appears eleven times in the Ignatian corpus, primarily in the various confessional (i.e., kerygmatic or *regula fidei* type) passages.

31. Written as the Antiochene bishop was being taken, under arrest, to Rome. The first four letters (*Ephesians, Magnesians, Trallians,* and *Romans*) were apparently written from Smyrna; the last three (*Philadelphians, Smyrnaeans,* and *Polycarp*) from Troas. See Lightfoot, *Apostolic Fathers,* 1:35. According to the best sources, Ignatius met his death in Rome in AD 115. See Downey, *History of Antioch,* 292ff.

32. Rathke, *Ignatius von Antiochien und die Paulusbriefe*; and Norbert Brox, *Glaube als Zeugnis,* cited by Bommes, *Weizen Gotte,* 95. Bommes's discussion and criticism in this connection of Schlier (86–95) and von Rathke, Preiss, Brox, and von Campenhausen (95–197) is especially helpful.

33. Snyder, *Continuity of Early Christianity,* 231.

the Romans, contains only *one* reference to imitation (6:3).³⁴ Added to this point is the fact that the μιμητής, μιμέομαι word group occurs only seven times in the Ignatian correspondence, and no less than four of those occurrences refer not to Ignatius (or his martyrdom) but to his readers (Ign. *Eph.* 1:1; 10:3; Ign. *Trall.* 1:2; Ign. *Phld.* 7:2).

Others have attempted to find in the ideas of "atonement" and "vicarious sacrifice" the interpretive key to the thought of Ignatius. William C. Weinrich's excellent study of Ignatius, within the framework of his monograph *Spirit and Martyrdom*, contains a detailed analysis of ἀντίψυχον ("ransom" or "substitute," found four times: Ign. *Eph.* 21:1; Ign. *Smyrn.* 10:2; Ign. *Pol.* 2:3; 6:1) and περίψημα ("offscouring" or "sacrifice," used twice: Ign. *Eph.* 8:1; 18:1) and concludes that by the early second century, the latter term "had generally lost its strictly sacrificial meaning and had become more and more an expression of contempt or self-humiliation," and that the former term (which occurs only in connection with the Ephesian and Smyrnaean congregations) is more than likely related to the relationships of hospitality, friendship, and assistance that blossomed when Ignatius stopped in Smyrna on his way to Rome and received such extraordinary kindnesses from the congregation there and the beloved Ephesian emissaries (Ign. *Eph.* 21:1).³⁵

Let us now turn our attention to the present hypothesis, that the increasingly formal apostolic traditions constitute the horizon of Ignatian thought, the true (as opposed to apparent) passion of Christ its center, and "unity" its pervasive rhetorical focus. Attached to the present study [see Appendix I] is a listing, complete with texts, of the rather impressive constellation of Ignatian words and phrases that turn upon the idea of "unity."³⁶ There it may be observed that the notion of unity touches upon, in context, virtually every concern in the Ignatian

34. Cf. Goodspeed, *Index Patristicus*; and Heinrich Kraft, *Clavis Patrum Apostolicorum*.

35. Weinrich, *Spirit and Martyrdom*, 112–14. In this context, Weinrich has also examined Ign. *Rom.* 2:2 (πλέον δέ μοι μὴ παράσχησθε τοῦ σπονδισθῆναι θεῷ, ὡς ἔτι θυσιαστήριον ἕτοιμόν ἐστιν) and Ign. *Rom.* 4:2 (λιτανεύσατε τὸν κύριον ὑπὲρ ἐμοῦ, ἵνα διὰ τῶν ὀργάνων τούτων θεοῦ θυσία εὑρεθῶ), where obvious sacrificial terminology is employed. He concludes that these passages do not suggest that Ignatius dies *for others*, but rather that his martyrdom shows forth God, since martyrdom "is an expression of the passion of Christ" (114–15).

36. I am greatly indebted to Prof. Bruce Corley for his careful and detailed gathering of these words and phrases into such a useful format. Prof. Corley currently serves as president of the B. H. Carroll Theological Institute in Arlington, Texas.

corpus: church order, obedience to the bishop (and opposition to schismatics), the Eucharist, baptism, martyrdom, Christology (the birth, the cross, and the resurrection), God, Satan, prayer, song, and discipleship. If it be granted from the evidence of Appendix I that unity is the most comprehensive concept in Ignatius's thought (and the terms ἕνωσις and ἑνότης, among the apostolic fathers, are found only in Ignatius[37]), what must then be discovered is the generating center. Before attempting to demonstrate, by way of a more detailed look at three specific passages, that the cross of Christ is that center, we must first consider briefly the relationship of Ignatius's martyrdom to his thought.

There may be little doubt that his impending death, imagined by Ignatius in very gruesome images (see Ign. *Rom.* 4:1—5:3!), was quite naturally a significant force in at least the tone and application of his theology. It must not, however, be presumed from that fact that Ignatius was not also the receiver and bearer of apostolic tradition (see the *regula* type passages above). In at least two places (see below), the Antiochene bishop specifically relates, one to the other, his theology (traditionally expressed) and his martyrdom, indicating that the significance and validity of the latter depend wholly upon the truth of the former.

> Ign. *Trallians* 9:1—10:1
>
> 9:1 Be deaf, therefore, whenever anyone speaks to you apart from Jesus Christ, who was of the family of David, who was the son of Mary; who really was born, who both ate and drank; who really was persecuted under Pontius Pilate, who really was crucified and died while those in heaven and on earth and under the earth looked on; 2 who, moreover, really was raised from the dead when his Father raised him up. In the same way his Father will likewise also raise up in Christ Jesus us who believe in him. Apart from him we have no true life.
>
> 10:1 But if, as some atheists (that is, unbelievers) say, he suffered in appearance only (while they exist in appearance only!), why am I in chains? And why do I want to fight with wild beasts? If that is the case, I die for no reason; what is more, I am telling lies about the Lord.

Also, in Ign. *Smyrn.* 1:1—4:2, after beginning with a similar, creed-like statement of his theology,

---

37. Cf. Goodspeed, *Index Patristicus*; and Kraft, *Clavis Patrum Apostolicorum*.

> 1:1 [H]e is truly of the family of David with respect to human descent, Son of God with respect to the divine will and power, truly born of a virgin, baptized by John in order that all righteousness might be fulfilled by him, truly nailed in the flesh for us under Pontius Pilate and Herod the tetrarch.

Ignatius continues by arguing more expansively for the genuineness of Christ's suffering and resurrection before concluding, indignantly, with the assertion that,

> 4:2 [I]f these things were done by our Lord in appearance only, then I am in chains in appearance only. Why, moreover, have I surrendered myself to death, to fire, to sword, to beasts?

Occasioned and no doubt shaped (note the repeated use of ἀληθῶς and ἀληθινός in the creedal passages) by the docetists' assertions to the contrary with regard to the physicality of Christ, and more particularly that of his suffering, these confessional and embryonic *regulae fidei* materials point nevertheless to the centrality for Ignatius of the cross of Jesus.[38] For more explicit elaboration of this claim, we now turn to a few passages[39] where Ignatius gives more extensive expression to his theological impulses.

> Ign. *Trallians* 11:1-2
>
> 11:1 φεύγετε οὖν τὰς κακὰς παραφυάδας τὰς γεννώσας καρπὸν θανατηφόρον, οὗ ἐὰν γεύσηταί τις, παραυτὰ ἀποθνῄσκει· οὗτοι γὰρ οὔκ εἰσιν φυτεία πατρός. 2 εἰ γὰρ ἦσαν, ἐφαίνοντο ἂν κλάδοι τοῦ σταυροῦ, καὶ ἦν ἂν ὁ καρπὸς αὐτῶν ἄφθαρτος· δι' οὗ ἐν τῷ πάθει αὐτοῦ προσκαλεῖται ὑμᾶς ὄντας μέλη αὐτοῦ. οὐ δύναται οὖν κεφαλὴ χωρὶς γεννηθῆναι ἄνευ μελῶν, τοῦ θεοῦ ἕνωσιν ἐπαγγελλομένου, ὅς ἐστιν αὐτός.
>
> 11:1 Flee, therefore, from these wicked offshoots that bear deadly fruit; if anyone even tastes it, he dies on the spot. These people are not the Father's planting. 2 For if they were, they would appear as branches of the cross, and their fruit would

---

38. Note also in Ign. *Eph.* 18:1 the statement, "My spirit is a humble sacrifice for the cross, which is a stumbling block to unbelievers but salvation and eternal life to us," which is followed by the substantiating assertion that "our God, Jesus the Christ, was conceived by Mary according to God's plan, both from the seed of David and of the Holy Spirit. He was born and was baptized in order that by his suffering he might cleanse the water."

39. Indebtedness to Weinrich, *Spirit and Martyrdom*, 118–22, must be acknowledged for directing my attention, by his own excellent exposition of them, to the significance of the first two passages herein treated.

be imperishable—the same cross by which he, through his suffering, calls you who are his members. The head, therefore, cannot be born without members, since God promises unity, which he himself is.

Though the metaphors are abruptly introduced, and not completely consistent throughout, there is in the whole a tolerably clear depiction of Ignatius's intent. The unbelievers, those who say his suffering was only apparent (10:1), are to be zealously avoided. These unbelievers, because they are abnormal offshoots, who are in fact not the Father's planting,[40] bear only a poisonous fruit.[41] On the contrary, those who are a planting of the Father—and here the metaphor changes from the *persons* as the plant(ing) to the *cross* as the plant and the true believers as κλάδοι—are revealed as branches of the cross and bear an imperishable fruit, viz., eternal life by virtue of their union with the cross. This cross, which is the passion (of Jesus), is his *summons* to his members. The change of metaphor now to "head" and "members," though sudden, is nevertheless consonant with the theme of unity underlying the whole passage. Indeed, such union between the believer and Christ-in-passion and the Father must be so for Ignatius—and here metaphor and promise and theological "given" tumble in upon one another, respectively, in rapid disjuncture—since a head must have members, since God has in fact promised ἕνωσις, and since, moreover, God himself *is* union. At the center of this union, in fact the very means and *summoning power* of it, is Christ-in-(authentic)-passion, to which union the members themselves are testimony (ἐφαίνοντο), and in which union the promise of God finds its fulfillment (τοῦ θεοῦ ἕνωσιν ἐπαγγελλομένου).[42]

---

40. Whether Ignatius means here that the enemies as φυτεία are not the "planting" or "plant" of the Father (and thus are a separate, poisonous "plant") because they were not *planted by* the Father, or that they are abnormal "offshoots" *of* the Father is not perfectly clear: for metaphorical consistency with κακὰς παραφυάδας and κλάδοι τοῦ σταυροῦ the latter alternative is to be preferred, but in all likelihood Ignatius's intent is the former, which is conceptually more consistent with what follows and parallels the "weed" metaphors used elsewhere (Ign. *Phld.* 3:1), where clearly φυτεία refers to an alien plant itself. Cf. Grant, *Apostolic Fathers*, 79; and Lightfoot, 2:176–77.

41. Possibly there are Eucharistic overtones here, i.e., the "poison" is of a schismatic's Eucharist; cf. Grant, *Ignatius of Antioch*, 79; but the parallel, the "imperishable fruit" of true believers (the branches of the cross), is not easily correlated, as an image, to a Eucharist under the bishop's authority.

42. Here and elsewhere it may be seen that the contention of Bultmann, "Ignatius and Paul," 270, that Ignatius has no history-of-salvation perspective must be greatly qualified, if not in fact abandoned.

Ign. *Smyrnaeans* 1:2

ἀληθῶς ἐπὶ Ποντίου Πιλάτου καὶ Ἡρώδου τετράρχου καθηλωμένον ὑπὲρ ἡμῶν ἐν σαρκί, ἀφ' οὗ καρποῦ ἡμεῖς ἀπὸ τοῦ θεομακαρίστου αὐτοῦ πάθους, ἵνα ἄρῃ σύσσημον εἰς τοὺς αἰῶνας διὰ τῆς ἀναστάσεως εἰς τοὺς ἁγίους καὶ πιστοὺς αὐτοῦ, εἴτε ἐν Ἰουδαίοις εἴτε ἐν ἔθνεσιν, ἐν ἑνὶ σώματι τῆς ἐκκλησίας αὐτοῦ.

1:2 . . . truly nailed in the flesh for us under Pontius Pilate and Herod the tetrarch (from its fruit we derive our existence, that is, from his divinely blessed suffering), in order that he might raise a banner for the ages through his resurrection for his saints and faithful people, whether among Jews or among Gentiles, in the one body of his church.

This selection begins with the conclusion of one of Ignatius's creed-like passages, viz., a statement regarding the actual suffering on the cross of the Son of God. The use of ἀληθῶς and the double specification of dating—under Pontius Pilate and Herod the tetrarch—are obviously an anti-docetic polemic and introduce the point in the tradition of greatest contention, that he was "nailed" (to the tree) ἐν σαρκί. The following use of ὑπὲρ ἡμῶν could be an unreflective retention of the tradition (1 Cor 15:3) by Ignatius or, which is on balance more likely, an example of a shift in nuance given to the traditional elements, i.e., his being "nailed" is understood to be "for our sake" inasmuch as we are now his "fruit" (cf. Ign. *Trall.* 11:2, κλάδοι τοῦ σταυροῦ) and hence participate in his divinely blessed passion. Though awkwardly stated and as a metaphor once again abruptly introduced, it seems that the explanation of the ὑπὲρ ἡμῶν is the conviction that as a result of his passion we, as the "fruit" of the cross, are in union with the Father, who ordained his suffering (ἀπὸ τοῦ θεομακαρίστου αὐτοῦ πάθους).[43] Furthermore, the Father has through the Son's suffering on the tree raised a banner—here the use of Isa 5:26, 11:10, 12 (cf. also 49:22; 62:10) depicts the cross as an ensign to which the scattered people of God may now rally—so that his purpose (ἵνα) of unity—drawing together his holy and faithful ones, whether among Jews or Gentiles—might be fulfilled in the gathering together into one body (ἑνὶ σώματι) of his church.[44] The resurrection, moreover, far from

---

43. Cf. Weinrich, *Spirit and Martyrdom*, 121.

44. Note that the following context (2:1) again states the eschatological purposes for his suffering (ἵνα σωθῶμεν) and links as pointedly as ever the efficacy of his passion

being the final act that obliterates the memory of the previous scandal of suffering, is that which universalizes (εἰς τοὺς αἰῶνας) the cross and/or effects the raising of it as a banner/ensign. In Ignatius, it is not so much the cross that derives added meaning from the resurrection; rather, it is the resurrection that has significance only insofar as it is connected with (cf. Ign. *Smyrn.* 5:3), validates, and/or exalts the true passion of Christ.[45] Indeed, it is the resurrection that reveals, to his saints and faithful followers, the salvation historical meaning of the cross as the banner that draws them into unity and, ultimately, into the oneness of God.[46] It is out of this conviction that Ignatius may speak so glowingly of the Smyrnaeans, giving glory to "Jesus Christ, the God who made you so wise" with a wisdom that rejects all divisive, heretical insinuations and is characterized by their established, unshakeable faith, which keeps them "nailed . . . to the cross of the Lord Jesus Christ" (1:1).

Ign. *Magnesians* 5:1–2

5:1 Ἐπεὶ οὖν τέλος τὰ πράγματα ἔχει, καὶ πρόκειται τὰ δύο ὁμοῦ, ὅ τε θάνατος καὶ ἡ ζωή, καὶ ἕκαστος εἰς τὸν ἴδιον τόπον μέλλει χωρεῖν. 2 ὥσπερ γάρ ἐστιν νομίσματα δύο, ὃ μὲν θεοῦ, ὃ δὲ κόσμου, καὶ ἕκαστον αὐτῶν ἴδιον χαρακτῆρα ἐπικείμενον ἔχει, οἱ ἄπιστοι τοῦ κόσμου τούτου, οἱ δὲ πιστοὶ ἐν ἀγάπῃ χαρακτῆρα θεοῦ πατρὸς διὰ Ἰησοῦ Χριστοῦ, δι' οὗ ἐὰν μὴ αὐθαιρέτως ἔχωμεν τὸ ἀποθανεῖν εἰς τὸ αὐτοῦ πάθος, τὸ ζῆν αὐτοῦ οὐκ ἔστιν ἐν ἡμῖν.

5:1 Seeing then that all things have an end, two things together lie before us, death and life, and everyone will go to his own place. 2 For just as there are two coinages, the one of God and the other of the world, and each of them has its own stamp impressed upon it, so the unbelievers bear the stamp of this world, but the faithful in love bear the stamp of God the Father through Jesus Christ, whose life is not in us unless we voluntarily choose to die into his suffering.

"for us" (δι' ἡμᾶς, which, like the ὑπὲρ ἡμῶν above, refers not to sacrificial notions of substitution but to the union to which we are summoned and joined in the cross) with the physical reality of his suffering.

45. I am reminded here of Conyers's exposition of Moltmann's view of the relationship between the cross and the resurrection in *God, Hope, and History*, e.g., 103–7.

46. Cf. Ign. *Smyrn.* 3:1–3, where the physicality of even the resurrected Christ is adduced as an argument for the genuinely sarkic nature of his suffering against those who maintain "that he suffered in appearance only" (2:1).

In the midst of arguing for unity under the authority of the bishop (3–4), who is to preside over the church (6:1) and without whom there may be no undertakings of worship (7:1–2), Ignatius argues, with language reminiscent of Didache 1:1, etc., that there are two destinies, life and death, set before the human race. The τέλος of life belongs to those who bear the stamp (χαρακτῆρα) of God the Father, while unbelievers, bearing a worldly impress, are bound unto the τέλος of death. The stamp of the Father is effected "through Jesus Christ," an agency which is further qualified as consisting in the willing (αὐθαιρέτως, which recalls the dually proposed destinies of life and death) receipt of a "dying" that itself is shaped by and oriented toward his passion (τὸ ἀποθανεῖν εἰς τὸ αὐτοῦ πάθος). Paradoxically, it is the believer's willing union with Christ-in-passion that results in the presence of "his life in us." Though a word for "union" is not used, clearly there is here the expression, not of a simplistic "parallelism" between the death of Jesus and the "dying to self" of the believer, or even the death of Jesus and the literal death of the martyr, but rather of the believer's *present* (n.b., the present tenses: ἐστιν . . . ἔχει . . . ἐστιν) *connection with, and participation in*, the character of God (which is unity) expressed in and effected by Christ-in-passion. It may be noted here that the passage continues via a transition (actually, a return[47]) from this realized Ignatian "indicative" to the Ignatian "imperative" (6:1, οὖν): that therefore "all things" ought to be done commensurately with the "harmony of God" (παραινῶ, ἐν ὁμονοίᾳ θεοῦ σπουδάζετε πάντα πράσσειν), which things, moreover, imperatively involve unity with the bishop and those who preside (ἑνώθητε τῷ ἐπισκόπῳ καὶ τοῖς προκαθημένοις, 6:2). This latter, ecclesial unity serves as a "type and pattern"—here the notion of "parallelism" is appropriate—of the incorruptible life which is in his passion (εἰς τύπον καὶ διδαχὴν ἀφθαρσίας, 6:2).

. . .

Other passages could be treated to the same effect.[48] It is hoped, however, that in light of the above analyses, the threefold thesis of this paper

---

47. The "indicative" was itself a digression in the paranesis; cf. Grant, *Ignatius of Antioch*, 59).

48. E.g., the well-known Trinitarian passage in Ign. *Eph.* 9, where the cross is the "crane" (μηχανῆς) of Jesus Christ lifting believers into place to form as a unity the Father's temple, the edifice of God the Father; or Ign. *Rom.* 7:2, where the Living Water (the Holy Spirit, see the excellent discussion of Ign. *Rom.* 7:2 in Weinrich, *Spirit and*

has been well supported, if not established: that the Ignatian horizon—the commonly recognized apostolic traditions, i.e., the emerging creed-like kerygma which orbits around the Davidic descent, birth, suffering, and resurrection of Jesus—has found its center, its δύναμις—shaped no doubt by the impending crises for Ignatius of martyrdom and schism—in the passion of Christ, which is itself a branch-bearing tree, a summoning banner, and an elective impress of the Father's χαράκτηρ, with which the believer stands in vital union. This union, moreover, is manifested (though not consummated, cf. Ign. *Rom.* 5-7) in the eschatologically established one body of Christ and paralleled in the ecclesiastical order of the church (cf. Ign. *Eph.* 2:2; 3:2; 6:1; Ign. *Trall.* 3:1; 7:1-2; Ign. *Phld.* inscr.; 1:1; 5:1; Ign. *Smyrn.* 8:1-2) and as such represents in all its situational variety the repeated, rhetorical focus of the letters.

To repeat, the pressures of both an impending martyrdom and potentially serious fractures among the churches of Ignatius's purview have shaped the emotional content and rhetorical appeals of the letters. That fact notwithstanding, there is still in Ignatius a discernible appeal to the received apostolic traditions. On the other hand, he has surely shaped these materials by his necessary appeals to the genuineness of Christ's humanity, especially his suffering, and has also likely—by virtue of the imminent dissolution of his own flesh and the docetic denial of Christ's—drawn the cross of his Lord, hitherto a feature among others of his confessional *horizon*, into the generating *center* of his theology.

Appendix I: Expressions Relating to Union/Unity/Unison in Ignatius of Antioch

The Ignatian literature abounds in metaphors, synonyms, cognates, and stylistic phrases which cluster around the idea of union—union at every level of existence. Four such clusters—though other words and concepts are also indicated below—are: (1) general terms for union, unity, and

---

Martyrdom, 130–34) draws the martyr toward final union with the passion of Christ and the oneness of God; or the famous passage in Ign. *Eph.* 19 where the three mysteries of the virginity of Mary, her childbearing, and also the death of the Lord were hidden from the Prince of this world until revealed by the heavenly star, which precipitated the defeat of all the divisive powers of evil and the overthrow of the "ancient empire," which was at length consummated through the death and resurrection of Jesus. In all of these passages, the themes of unity, and/or the defeat of the Satanic forces of separation, are seen in inextricable relationship to the passion of Christ.

unison (ἕνωσις, ἑνότης, ὁμόνοια, σύμφωνος, συνήθεια) with corresponding antitheses (χωρίς, μερισμός, ἄνευ); (2) christological unity (πάθος, ἀληθής, σάρξ ... πνεῦμα); (3) ecclesiastical unity focused on the bishop and Eucharist (γνώμη, μιμητής, εἷς); and (4) union with Christ in martyrdom (τυγχάνω, ἄξιος, μαθητής). The central terms ἕνωσις and ἑνότης occur only in Ignatius among the Apostolic Fathers. The frequency distribution of significant terms can be set out in tabular form.[49]

	Eph	Mag	Trall	Rom	Phil	Smyr	Pol	Total
ἀληθής (–ῶς, –ινή, –εια, –ομαι)	6	1	5	5	1	7	1	26
ἄξιος (–όω, κατ–, αξιο +)	11	9	5	12	4	5	5	51
γνώμη	5	–	–	2	4	1	4	16
εἷς, μία, ἕν	9	5	1	–	4	1	–	20
ἕνωσις (–όω, –ότης)	5	5	1	1	8	2	3	25
εὑρίσκω	7	1	4	6	2	1	3	24
μαθητής (–εύω, μαθη +)	3	4	1	5	1	–	2	16
μιμητής (–ομαι)	2	1	1	1	1	1	–	7
ὁμόνοια	3	2	1	–	2	–	–	8
πάθος (–ημα, –ητος)	4	2	2	1	3	5	1	18
πάσχω	–	–	2	2	–	3	1	8
σάρξ ... πνεῦμα (–ικος, –ικῶς)	3	3	2	1	2	5	3	19
σύμφωνος	3	0	0	0	0	0	0	3
συνήθεια	1	0	0	0	0	0	0	1
τυγχάνω (ἐπι–)	4	2	3	9	1	3	3	25

The following compilation, arranged in the chronological order of the seven genuine letters, illustrates the wide range of unity terminology and expression.

---

49. Cf. the tables of Swartley, "*Imitatio Christi* in the Ignatian Letters," 92, 94, who detects a semantic shift in the last three letters owing to good news from Antioch. The frequency counts are derived from Kraft, *Clavis Patrum Apostolicorum*; and Goodspeed, *Index Patristicus*.

Ign. *Ephesians*

praes.   ... *united* and elect through genuine suffering....

ἡνωμένην

1:1   ... *imitators* of God....

μιμηταὶ ὄντες

1:2   ... and was hoping through your prayers to succeed in fighting with wild beasts in Rome—*in order that by so succeeding* I might be able to be a *disciple*....

ἵνα ... ἐπιτυχεῖν ... μαθητὴς εἶναι

3:1   ... I have *not yet been perfected in Jesus Christ*. For now I am only beginning *to be a disciple*, and I speak to you as my *fellow students*.

οὔπω ἀπήρτισμαι ἐν Ἰησοῦ Χριστῷ ... μαθητεύεσθαι ... συνδιδασκαλίταις μου

4:1   For your council of presbyters ... *is attuned to the bishop* as strings to a lyre.

συνήρμοσται τῷ ἐπισκόπῳ

4:1   [I]n your *unanimity* and *harmonious* love Jesus Christ is sung.

ὁμονοίᾳ ... συμφώνῳ

4:2   [J]oin this *chorus* ... so that by *being harmonious* in *unanimity* and taking your pitch from God you may *sing in unison with one voice* through Jesus Christ to the Father....

χορὸς γίνεσθε ... σύμφωνοι ὄντες ἐν ὁμονοίᾳ ... ἐν ἑνότητι, ᾄδητε ἐν φωνῇ μιᾷ

4:2   It is, therefore, advantageous for you to be in *perfect unity*, in order that you may always *have a share* in God.

ἀμώμῳ ἑνότητι ... μετέχητε

5:1 ...*fellowship with your bishop*...*united with* him [Ephesians with bishop], as the church is with Jesus Christ and as Jesus Christ is with the Father, so that all things may be *harmonious in unity*.

συνήθειαν ἔσχον πρὸς τὸν ἐπίσκοπον ὑμῶν ... ἐνκεκραμένους ... ἐν ἑνότητι σύμφωνα

8:1 [Y]ou *belong entirely* to God ... then you indeed *live God's way*.

ὅλοι ὄντες ... κατὰ θεὸν ζῆτε

8:2 [Y]ou *do everything in Jesus Christ*.

ἐν Ἰησοῦ ... Χριστῷ πάντα πράσσετε

9:1 [Y]ou are stones ... prepared beforehand for the building of God the Father, *hoisted up to the heights by the crane* of Jesus Christ, which is the cross, using as a rope the Holy Spirit ... and love is the *way that leads up* to God.

ἀναφερόμενοι ... διὰ τῆς μηχανῆς ... ὁδὸς ἡ ἀναφέρουσα

9:2 ...*participants together*... God-bearers... Christ-bearers....

σύνοδοι

10:1 ...that they *may find God*....

θεοῦ τύχωσιν

10:3 [L]et us be eager to *be imitators of the Lord*.... [W]ith complete purity and self-control you may *abide in Christ Jesus physically and spiritually*.

μιμηταί ... μένητε ... σαρκικῶς καὶ πνευματικῶς

11:1 [L]et us *be found in Christ Jesus, which leads to true life*.

ἐν Χριστῷ Ἰησοῦ εὑρεθῆναι εἰς τὸ ἀληθινὸν ζῆν

11:2 Let nothing *appeal* to you *apart from him* [Jesus Christ]....

χωρὶς τούτου μηδὲν ... πρεπέτω

11:2   [B]y which [chains] I hope, through your prayers, to rise again. May *I always share in them*....

ἀεὶ μέτοχον εἶναι

12:2   You are the highway of those who are being killed for God's sake; you are *fellow initiates of Paul* . . . may I be found in his footsteps *when I reach God*....

Παύλου συμμύσται . . . ὅταν θεοῦ ἐπιτύχω

13:1   [H]is [Satan's] destructiveness is nullified *by the unanimity* of your faith.

ἐν τῇ ὁμονοίᾳ

14:1   [A]nd the two [faith and love], *when they exist in unity, are God*.

ἐν ἑνότητι γενόμενα θεός ἐστιν

15:3   Therefore let us do everything with the knowledge that *he [the Lord] dwells in us*.

ἐν ἡμῖν κατοικοῦντος

18:1   *My spirit is a humble sacrifice* for the cross....

περίψημα τὸ ἐμὸν πνεῦμα

19:1, 3   ...three mysteries [Mary's virginity, birth and death of Jesus] to be loudly proclaimed, yet which were accomplished in the silence of God.... Consequently all magic and every kind of spell were *dissolved*, the ignorance so characteristic of wickedness *vanished*, and the ancient kingdom was *abolished* when God appeared in human form....

ἐλύετο . . . ἠφανίζετο . . . καθῃρεῖτο . . . διεφθείρετο

20:2   All of you, individually and *collectively, gather together* in grace, by name, in one faith and one Jesus Christ . . . in order that you may obey the bishop and the council of presbyters with *an undisturbed mind*, breaking *one bread*, which is the *medicine of immortality*....

κοινῇ πάντες . . . συνέρχεσθε . . . ἀπερισπάστῳ διανοίᾳ, ἕνα ἄρτον . . . φάρμακον ἀθανασίας

21:2   ... Jesus Christ, our *shared hope*.

κοινῇ ἐλπίδι

Ign. *Magnesians*

1:2   ... *I pray* that in them there may be a *union of flesh and spirit* that comes from Jesus Christ ... and of faith and love ... and—what is more important—of Jesus and the Father.

ἕνωσιν εὔχομαι σαρκὸς καὶ πνεύματος

1:3   In him *we will reach God*, if we patiently endure all the abuse of the ruler of this age and escape.

θεοῦ τευξόμεθα

3:1   [D]*efer to him* [bishop] as one who is wise in God; yet not really to him, but to the Father of Jesus Christ, the bishop of all.

συγχωροῦντας αὐτῷ

4:1   [S]ome ... call a man bishop but do everything *without regard for him*.

χωρὶς δὲ αὐτοῦ

5:2   [E]ach of them has its own stamp impressed upon it. ... [T]he faithful in love bear the stamp of God ... whose life is not in us unless we voluntarily choose *to die into his suffering*.

τὸ ἀποθανεῖν εἰς τὸ αὐτοῦ πάθος

6:1   [D]o everything in *godly harmony*, the bishop presiding in the place of God. ...

ἐν ὁμονοίᾳ θεοῦ

6:2   Let all, therefore, *accept the same attitude as God*. ...

ὁμοήθειαν θεοῦ

6:2   Let there be nothing among you that is capable *of dividing* you, *but be united with the bishop* and with those who lead....

μερίσαι, ἀλλ' ἑνώθητε τῷ ἐπισκόπῳ

7:1   Therefore as the Lord did nothing without the Father... (*for he was united with him*), so you must not do anything *without the bishop and the presbyters.*

ἡνωμένος ὤν ... ἄνευ τοῦ ἐπισκόπου καὶ τῶν πρεσβυτέρων

7:1   [G]athering together, let there be *one* prayer, *one* petition, *one* mind, *one* hope, with love....

ἐπὶ τὸ αὐτὸ μία προσευχή, μία δέησις, εἷς νοῦς, μία ἐλπίς, ἐν ἀγάπῃ

7:2   Let all of you *run together* as to *one* temple of God, as to *one* altar, to *one Jesus Christ,* who *came forth from one Father* and *remained with the One and returned to the One.*

εἰς ἕνα ναὸν συντρέχετε θεοῦ ... ἐπὶ ἕνα Ἰησοῦν Χριστόν, τὸν ἀφ' ἑνός ... εἰς ἕνα ὄντα

8:2   For the most godly prophets *lived in accordance with Christ Jesus.*

κατὰ Χριστὸν Ἰησοῦν ἔζησαν

8:2   [T]here is *one God who revealed himself* through Jesus Christ his Son, who is his Word that came forth from silence....

εἷς θεός ἐστιν ὁ φανερώσας ἑαυτὸν

9:2   [H]ow can we possibly live *without him,* whom even the prophets, *who were his disciples in the Spirit,* were expecting as their teacher?

χωρὶς αὐτοῦ ... μαθηταὶ ὄντες τῷ πνεύματι

10:1 [I]f he [Jesus Christ] *were to imitate the way we act,* we are lost.

μιμήσηται καθὰ πράσσομεν

12:1 [Y]ou have Jesus Christ *within you.*

ἐν ἑαυτοῖς

42　PART ONE: FAITH

13:2　*Be subject to the bishop* and to one another, as Jesus Christ . . . to the Father, and as the apostles were to Christ and to the Father, *that there may be unity, both physical and spiritual.*

ὑποτάγητε τῷ ἐπισκόπῳ . . . ἵνα ἕνωσις ᾖ σαρκική τε καὶ πνευματική

14:1　Remember me . . . *in order that I may reach God.* . . . For I need *your united prayer and love in God.* . . .

ἵνα θεοῦ ἐπιτύχω . . . τῆς ἡνωμένης ὑμῶν ἐν θεῷ προσευχῆς καὶ ἀγάπης

15:1　Farewell *in godly harmony* to you who possess an *undivided spirit*, which is Jesus Christ.

ἐν ὁμονοίᾳ θεοῦ . . . ἀδιάκριτον πνεῦμα

Ign. *Trallians*

praes.　. . . at peace *in flesh and spirit through the suffering* of Jesus Christ, who is our hope. . . .

ἐν σαρκὶ καὶ πνεύματι τῷ πάθει

1:1　[I]*n him* [*the bishop*] *I saw* your entire congregation.

ἐν αὐτῷ θεωρῆσαι

1:2　. . . I praised God when I found out that you were, as I had learned, *imitators of God.*

μιμητὰς ὄντας θεοῦ

2:2　[D]o nothing *without the bishop,* but be *subject also to the council of presbyters* as to the apostles of *Jesus Christ, our hope, in whom we shall be found, if we so live.*

ἄνευ τοῦ ἐπισκόπου . . . ὑποτάσσεσθε καὶ τῷ πρεσβυτερίῳ . . . ἐν ᾧ διάγοντες εὑρεθησόμεθα

3:1 *Without these* [deacons, bishop, presbyters] *no group can be called a church.*

χωρὶς τούτων

3:2 ... I received *a living example* of your love and still have it with me *in the person of your bishop.*...

ἐξεμπλάριον ... ἐν τῷ ἐπισκόπῳ ὑμῶν

5:2 [T]hough I am in chains and can comprehend heavenly things ... *despite all this I am not yet a disciple.*

ἤδη καὶ μαθητής εἰμι

6:2 *These people* [heretics], while pretending to be trustworthy, *mix Jesus Christ with themselves*—like those who administer a deadly drug mixed with honeyed wine....

ἑαυτοῖς παρεμπλέκουσιν Ἰησοῦν Χριστὸν

7:1 [C]ling *inseparably* to Jesus Christ and to the bishop and to the commandments of the apostles.

οὖσιν ἀχωρίστοις

7:2 *The one who is within the sanctuary* is clean, but the *one who is outside* ... is not clean. That is, whoever does anything *without the bishop and council of presbyters and deacons* does not have a clean conscience.

ὁ ἐντὸς θυσιαστηρίου ... ἐκτὸς ... χωρὶς ἐπισκόπου καὶ πρεσβυτερίου καὶ διακόνων ... οὐ καθαρός

8:1 [R]*egain your strength* in faith (which is the flesh of the Lord) and in love (which is the blood of Jesus Christ).

ἀνακτήσασθε ἑαυτοὺς

9:1 ... *apart from Jesus Christ*....

χωρὶς Ἰησοῦ Χριστοῦ

44 PART ONE: FAITH

9:2 ... will likewise also *raise up in Christ Jesus us* who believe in him.

ἡμᾶς ... ἐγερεῖ ... ἐν Χριστῷ Ἰησοῦ

11:2 ... the same cross *by which he, through his suffering,* calls you who are his *members*. The head, therefore, cannot be born without members, since *God promises unity, which he himself is.*

δι' οὗ ἐν τῷ πάθει ... μέλη ... τοῦ θεοῦ ἕνωσιν ἐπαγγελλομένου, ὅς ἐστιν αὐτός

12:2 ... I ... praying that *I may reach God,* exhort you: persevere in your *unanimity.* ...

θεοῦ ἐπιτυχεῖν ... ἐν τῇ ὁμονοίᾳ

12:3 ... I may be *reckoned worthy of the fate that I am eager to obtain,* lest I be found disqualified.

καταξιωθῆναί ... ἐπιτυχεῖν

13:2 [L]ove one another, each one of you, *with an undivided heart.*

ἐν ἀμερίστῳ καρδίᾳ

13:3 My spirit is dedicated to you, not only now but also when *I reach God.*

ὅταν θεοῦ ἐπιτύχω

Ign. *Romans*

praes. ... to those who are *united in flesh and spirit* to every commandment of his. ...

κατὰ σάρκα καὶ πνεῦμα ἡνωμένοις

1:2 [I]t is difficult *for me to reach God,* unless you spare me.

τοῦ θεοῦ ἐπιτυχεῖν

2:1 For I will never again have an opportunity such as this *to reach God.* ...

θεοῦ ἐπιτυχεῖν

2:2	Grant me nothing more than *to be poured out as an offering to God* while there is still an altar ready....
	τοῦ σπονδισθῆναι θεῷ
2:2	...*that I may rise to him.*
	ἵνα εἰς αὐτὸν ἀνατείλω
3:3	Nothing that is visible is good. For our God Jesus Christ is more visible now that he is *in the Father.*
	ἐν πατρὶ ὤν . . . φαίνεται
4:1	Let me be food for the wild beasts, through whom I can *reach God. I am God's wheat*, and I am being ground by the teeth of the wild beasts, so that I may prove to be pure bread.
	θεοῦ ἐπιτυχεῖν. σῖτός εἰμι θεοῦ
4:3	But *if I suffer, I will be a freedman of Jesus Christ* and will rise up free *in him.*
	ἐὰν πάθω, ἀπελεύθερος . . . ἐν αὐτῷ
5:1	Yet because of their mistreatment [by ten leopards, or soldiers] *I am becoming more of a disciple....*
	μᾶλλον μαθητεύομαι
5:3	Now at last *I am beginning* to be a disciple. May nothing . . . envy me, so that *I may reach* Jesus Christ.... [L]et these come upon me, only *let me reach* Jesus Christ!
	ἄρχομαι . . . ἐπιτύχω . . . ἐπιτύχω
6:1	*Him I seek....*
	ἐκεῖνον ζητῶ
6:3	Allow me to be an *imitator of the suffering of my God*. If anyone has him within, let that person understand what I long for and *sympathize* with me, knowing what constrains me.
	μιμητὴν εἶναι τοῦ πάθους . . . συμπαθείτω

7:2 *My passionate love has been crucified* and there is no fire of material longing within me, but only water living and speaking in me, saying within me, "Come to the Father."

ὁ ἐμὸς ἔρως ἐσταύρωται

7:3 I want the *bread of God*, which is the *flesh* of Christ ... and for *drink* I want his blood, which is incorruptible *love*.

ἄρτον θεοῦ θέλω ... σὰρξ ... πόμα ... ἀγάπη

8:3 Pray ... that *I may reach the goal*.

ἵνα ἐπιτύχω

9:2 But *I have been granted the mercy* to be someone, *if I reach God*.

ἠλέημαι ... ἐὰν θεοῦ ἐπιτύχω

Ign. *Philadelphians*

praes. ... the church ... that ... is firmly established *in godly harmony* and unwaveringly rejoices in the suffering of our Lord. ...

ἐν ὁμονοίᾳ

praes. ... if they [members of the Church] are *at one with the bishop*. ...

ἐν ἑνὶ ὦσιν σὺν τῷ ἐπισκόπῳ

1:2 [H]e [bishop] is *attuned to* the commandments as a harp to its strings.

συνευρύθμισται

2:1 *[F]lee from division* and false teaching.

φεύγετε τὸν μερισμὸν

2:2 [M]any seemingly trustworthy wolves attempt, by means of wicked pleasure, to take captive the runners in God's race; but *in your unity* they will find no opportunity.

ἐν τῇ ἑνότητι

3:2	For all those who *belong to* God and Jesus Christ are *with the bishop*....
	θεοῦ εἰσιν ... μετὰ τοῦ ἐπισκόπου εἰσίν
3:2	...all those who repent and *enter into the unity* of the church....
	ἔλθωσιν ἐπὶ τὴν ἑνότητα
3:3	[I]f any *follow a schismatic*... they *disassociate themselves* from the passion.
	σχίζοντι ἀκολουθεῖ ... τῷ πάθει οὐ συγκατατίθεται
4:1	[P]articipate in *one Eucharist* (for *there is one flesh* of our Lord Jesus Christ, and *one cup that leads to unity* through his blood....
	μιᾷ εὐχαριστίᾳ ... μία γὰρ σάρξ ... ἓν ποτήριον εἰς ἕνωσιν
4:1	(...*one* altar, just as there is *one* bishop, *together with* the council of presbyters and the deacons, my fellow servants), in order that whatever you do, *you do in accordance with God*.
	ἕν ... εἷς ... ἅμα ... κατὰ θεὸν πράσσητε
5:1	[Y]our prayer to God *will make me perfect*, so that *I may attain* the fate by which I have received mercy, since I have taken refuge in the gospel as the flesh of Jesus....
	με ἀπαρτίσει ... ἐπιτύχω
5:2	[B]ecause they [prophets] also believed in him, they were saved, since they *belong to the unity centered in Jesus Christ*... approved ... and *included* in the gospel....
	ἐν ἑνότητι Ἰησοῦ Χριστοῦ ὄντες ... συνηριθμημένοι
6:2	[G]ather together, all of you, with *an undivided heart*.
	ἀμερίστῳ καρδίᾳ

PART ONE: FAITH

7:2   [T]he Spirit itself was preaching, saying these words: "Do nothing *without the bishop*. Guard *your bodies as the temple* of God. Love *unity*. Flee from *divisions*. Become *imitators of Jesus Christ*, just as he is of his Father."

χωρὶς τοῦ ἐπισκόπου . . . σάρκα ὑμῶν ὡς ναὸν . . . ἕνωσιν . . . μερισμοὺς . . . μιμηταὶ

8:1   I was doing my part . . . as a man *set on unity*. But *God does not dwell where there is division and anger*.

εἰς ἕνωσιν κατηρτισμένος . . . μερισμός . . . ὀργή, θεὸς οὐ κατοικεῖ

8:1   . . . if in repenting they return to *the unity* of God and the *council* of the bishop.

ἑνότητα . . . συνέδριον

8:2   . . . I urge you to do nothing *in a spirit of contentiousness*, but *in accordance with the teaching of Christ*.

κατ' ἐρίθειαν . . . κατὰ χριστομαθίαν

9:1   All these [patriarchs, prophets, apostles, and Church] come together in the *unity of God*.

εἰς ἑνότητα θεοῦ

9:2   *All these things together* are good, if you believe with love.

πάντα ὁμοῦ

11:2   The Lord Jesus Christ will honor them; on him they set their hope *in body, soul, and spirit with faith, love, and harmony*.

σαρκί, ψυχῇ, πνεύματι, πίστει, ἀγάπῃ, ὁμονοίᾳ

Ign. *Smyrnaeans*

1:1   . . . having been *nailed*, as it were, to the cross of the Lord Jesus Christ *in both body and spirit*. . . .

καθηλωμένους . . . σαρκί τε καὶ πνεύματι

2:1	[H]e truly suffered... not, as certain unbelievers say, that *he suffered in appearance only*.... [T]*hey will become disembodied*....
	ἀληθῶς ἔπαθεν ... τὸ δοκεῖν αὐτὸν πεπονθέναι ... οὖσιν ἀσωμάτοις
3:2	And immediately they touched him and believed, *being closely united with his flesh and blood*.
	κραθέντες τῇ σαρκὶ αὐτοῦ καὶ τῷ αἵματι
3:3	[H]e ate and drank with them like *one who is composed of flesh, although spiritually he was united with the Father*.
	ὡς σαρκικός, καίπερ πνευματικῶς ἡνωμένος τῷ πατρί
4:1	...knowing that *you are of the same mind*.
	καὶ ὑμεῖς οὕτως ἔχετε
4:2	..."*near the sword*" means "*near to God*".... Only let it be in the name of Jesus Christ, so that *I may suffer together with him*! I endure everything....
	ἐγγὺς μαχαίρας, ἐγγὺς θεοῦ ... εἰς τὸ συμπαθεῖν αὐτῷ
5:3	...until such time as they change their mind regarding the *passion, which is our resurrection*.
	πάθος, ὅ ἐστιν ἡμῶν ἀνάστασις
6:2	They abstain from Eucharist and prayer because they refuse to acknowledge that the *Eucharist is the flesh* of our savior Jesus Christ, *which suffered* for our sins....
	εὐχαριστίαν σάρκα εἶναι ... τὴν ... παθοῦσαν
8:1	*Flee from divisions*.... Let no one do anything that has to do with the church *without the bishop*.
	μερισμοὺς φεύγετε ... χωρὶς ἐπισκόπου
8:2	...not permissible...to baptize...*without the bishop*.
	χωρὶς τοῦ ἐπισκόπου

PART ONE: FAITH

9:1   [T]he one who does anything *without the bishop's knowledge* serves the devil.

ὁ λάθρα ἐπισκόπου

9:2   *God is your reward*; if you endure everything for his sake, *you will reach him.*

ἀμοιβὴ ὑμῖν θεός . . . αὐτοῦ τεύξεσθε

11:1   [B]y your prayer *I may reach God.*

θεοῦ ἐπιτύχω

11:2   . . . to go to Syria to congratulate them, because . . . *their corporate life has been restored to its proper state.*

ἀπεκατεστάθη αὐτοῖς τὸ ἴδιον σωματεῖον

11:3   . . . that he might join in glorifying the *tranquility* that . . . has come to them, and because *they have now reached . . . a safe harbor.*

εὐδίαν . . . λιμένος ἤδη ἐτύγχανον

12:2   . . . individually and collectively, in the name of Jesus Christ and in his flesh and blood, his suffering and resurrection (*which was both physical and spiritual*), in *unity with God* and with you.

σαρκικῇ τε καὶ πνευματικῇ, ἐν ἑνότητι θεοῦ

13:2   . . . firmly grounded in faith and love *both physically and spiritually.*

ἑδράσθαι . . . σαρκικῇ τε καὶ πνευματικῇ

Ign. *Polycarp*

1:2   *Focus on unity*, for there is nothing better.

τῆς ἑνώσεως φρόντιζε

5:2   And it is proper for men and women who marry *to be united with the consent of the bishop.* . . .

μετὰ γνώμης τοῦ ἐπισκόπου τὴν ἕνωσιν ποιεῖσθαι

6:1	*Train together with one another*: compete together, run together, suffer together, rest together, *get up together*....
	συγκοπιᾶτε ἀλλήλοις ... συνεγείρεσθε
6:2	Be patient, therefore, *and gentle* with one another, as God is with you.
	ἐν πραΰτητι
7:1	...provided...that through suffering *I reach God*, so that I may prove to be a disciple....
	διὰ τοῦ παθεῖν θεοῦ ἐπιτύχω
8:3	...may you remain in him, *in the unity and care of God*.
	ἐν ἑνότητι θεοῦ καὶ ἐπισκοπῇ

Bibliography

Bartsch, Hans Werner. *Gnostisches Gut und Gemeindetradition bei Ignatius von Antiochien*. Gütersloh: Bertelsmann, 1940.
Bommes, Karin. *Weizen Gottes: Untersuchungen zur Theologie des Martyriums bei Ignatius von Antiochien*. Köln-Bonn: Hanstein, 1976.
Brent, Allen. *Ignatius of Antioch: A Martyr Bishop and the Origin of Episcopacy*. London: T. & T. Clark, 2009.
Brown, Charles Thomas. *The Gospel and Ignatius of Antioch*. New York: Lang, 2000.
Brox, Norbert. *Glaube als Zeugnis*. Munich: Kösel, 1966.
Bultmann, Rudolf. "Ignatius and Paul." In *Existence and Faith*. New York: Meridian, 1960.
Conyers, A. J. *A Basic Christian Theology*. Nashville: Broadman & Holman, 1995.
———. *God, Hope, and History*. Macon, GA: Mercer University Press, 1988.
Corwin, Virginia. *St. Ignatius and Christianity in Antioch*. New Haven: Yale University Press, 1960.
Daniélou, Jean. *A History of Early Christian Doctrine before the Council of Nicaea*. Vol. 1: *The Theology of Jewish Christianity*, translated and edited by John A. Baker. Philadelphia: Westminster, 1964.
Downey, Glanville. *A History of Antioch in Syria from Seleucus to the Arab Conquest*. Princeton: Princeton University Press, 1961.
Eusebius. *Ecclesiastical History*. Vol. 1: English translated by Kirsopp Lake. 1926. Loeb Classical Library. Reprint, Cambridge: Harvard University Press, 1949. Vol. 2: English translated by J. E. L. Oulton. 1932. Loeb Classical Library. Reprint, Cambridge: Harvard University Press, 1938.
Ferguson, Everett. "Response to Robert Sloan: The Unity of the Church in Ignatius." Unpublished paper.
Foerster, Werner. *Gnosis: A Selection of Gnostic Texts*. English translation edited by R. McL. Wilson. Vol. 1: *Patristic Evidence*. Oxford: Clarendon, 1972.
Goodspeed, Edgar J. *Index Patristicus*. Leipzig: Hinrichs, 1907.
Grant, Robert M. *The Apostolic Fathers: A New Translation and Commentary*. Vol. 4: *Ignatius of Antioch*. London: Nelson, 1966.
Hennecke, E. *New Testament Apocrypha*. Edited by W. Schneemelcher. English translation edited by R. McL. Wilson. Vol. 2. London: SCM, 1974.
Holmes, Michael W., editor and translator. *The Apostolic Fathers: Greek Texts and English Translations*. 3rd ed. Grand Rapids: Baker Academic, 2007.
Jay, Eric G. "From Presbyter-Bishops to Bishops and Presbyters." *Second Century* 1 (1981) 125–62.
Kraft, Heinrich. *Clavis Patrum Apostolicorum*. Munich: Kösel, 1963.
Lightfoot, J. B., editor and translator. *The Apostolic Fathers*. 2nd ed. Pt. 2: *Ignatius and Polycarp*. 2 vols. London: Macmillan, 1889–90. Reprint, Grand Rapids: Baker, 1981.
Maurer, Christian. *Ignatius von Antiochien und das Johannesevangelium*. Zurich: Zwingli, 1949.
The Oxford Dictionary of the Christian Church. Edited by F. L. Cross and Elizabeth A. Livingstone. 2nd ed. London: Oxford University Press, 1974.
Rathke, Heinrich. *Ignatius von Antiochien und die Paulusbriefe*. Berlin: Akademie, 1967.

Schlier, Heinrich. *Religionsgeschichtliche Untersuchungen zu den Ignatiusbriefen.* Giessen: Töpelmann, 1929.

Sloan, Robert B. "Canonical Theology of the New Testament." In *Foundations for Biblical Interpretation: A Complete Library of Tools and Resources,*" edited by David. S. Dockery, Kenneth A. Mathews, and Robert B. Sloan. Nashville: Broadman & Holman, 1974.

Slusser, Michael. "Docetism: A Historical Definition." *Second Century* 1 (1981) 163–72.

Snyder, Graydon F. *The Continuity of Early Christianity: A Study of Ignatius in Relation to Paul.* Ann Arbor, MI: University Microfilms, 1961.

Swartley, Willard M. "The *Imitatio Christi* in the Ignatian Letters." *Vigiliae Christianae* 27 (1973) 81–103.

Tertullian. *Adversus Marcionem.* Edited and translated by Ernest Evans. 2 vols. Oxford: Clarendon, 1972.

Wallace-Hadrill, D. S. *Christian Antioch: A Study of Early Christian Thought in the East.* Cambridge: Cambridge University Press, 1982.

Weinrich, William C. *Spirit and Martyrdom: A Study of the Work of the Holy Spirit in Contexts of Persecution and Martyrdom in the New Testament and Early Christian Literature.* Washington, DC: University Press of America, 1981.

Wright, N. T. *Jesus and the Victory of God.* Christian Origins and the Quest of God 2. Minneapolis: Fortress, 1996.

3

Reading Scripture as a Christian[1]

Randy Hatchett

> The problem is that we want to talk in universals and this book gives us particulars. When we ask for abstracts about an invisible God, it gives us concretes about visible people.... Our questions about abstract ideals are constantly answered with the concreteness of history.
>
> —A. J. Conyers, *How to Read the Bible*, 1986.[2]

A. J. CONYERS' WRITINGS WERE RICHLY PERSONAL, AS WERE MY OWN encounters with him. One of his gifts to the church is his persistent witness that theology is rooted in real life or that real life is necessarily theological. His wise embrace of the incarnation gave him discernment for sensing God's presence in the concrete circumstance. With this in mind I offer two personal parables in an effort to illustrate the necessity of recapturing the art of an explicitly theological reading from within the community of the church. I am unaware of Conyers taking up this precise topic. This endeavor seeks to extend his work that increasingly articulated the depth of meaning and beauty of belonging to a place and a people. We will rely upon several voices, from a growing chorus, who seek to ground the reading of Scripture in the church.

1. Several descriptions of a distinctively Christian manner of reading rightly find footing in Augustine's notion of charity. Alan Jacobs suggests this "hermeneutics of love" should characterize all reading and not only the reading of Scripture. While embracing this conviction, I address here only some necessarily Christian ways of reading of Scripture. See Jacobs, *Theology of Reading*, 9–32. For another exposition of Augustine's formative role in Christian reading, see Jeffrey, *People of the Book*, 79–89.

2. Conyers, *How to Read the Bible*, 26.

Grandfather and the Enlightenment

Firstly, my grandfather and grandmother, Earl and Irene, graduated from Southwestern Baptist Theological Seminary near the close of the great depression. My grandparents and I shared stories about seminary as I was later earning two degrees from the same institution. Granddad felt honored to have studied theology with W. T. Conner and I was honored to study with Conner's student James Leo Garrett. Remembering his orientation to the seminary, Granddad reported he was told he would learn to read Greek and use the best historical research tools—lexicons and texts. Thus equipped he would need to answer a crucial question before he served a Baptist church as pastor: "does the New Testament really say what the Baptists told me it said?" The spirit of modernity abided at the heart of this sales pitch (orientation speech); he was called to challenge his beliefs and hold them up to critical scrutiny armed with the newfound lenses of Greek grammar and a historically conscious methodology. The conversations taught me that modernity was not only for liberals. With Granddad's help I came to see that liberalism and fundamentalism were "peas in a pod"—they framed the questions the same characteristically modern way even if they rendered opposing answers. While Granddad was careful to distinguish himself from fundamentalism and liberalism, his training had a distinctively modern accent: as a learner, he was to set aside the convictions that are indebted to time, place, and the practices of a concrete community (all forms of corrupting tradition) in order to see for himself.[3] The careful articulation and adaptation of the modern thesis was tempered by precisely what modernity sought to overcome. Earl and Irene were well-formed believers who had left a community and place where they had learned who they were; they joined a closely-knit seminary family where professors led students along the same journey they themselves had previously traveled. With only a few casualties, Granddad and his classmates asked and answered the questions about Baptist identity and teaching in the affirmative. They left seminary with an enriched sense of what it meant to be a Baptist.

---

3. Granddad interpreted this in part as an exercise in the Baptist axiom of soul competency. Conyers never denied soul competency to my knowledge but was aware of the challenge that it be distinguished from the modern project.

Conyers was aware of the impoverishment that resulted in the wake of the modern quest to rise above the concreteness of lived experience. His later works, *The Long Truce* and *The Listening Heart*, hold many riches but include an essential motif: the modern project has failed to make good on its promise to enrich and liberate. Modern voices suggested that liberty would be found when we transcend the local and parochial features of life—our "rootedness" and "locatedness" in flesh and blood circumstance. He rightly argued that our place in a covenant community—our connection, loyalty, and appreciation for our place, people, and culture—are not destructive to the knowing process. Concrete circumstance is the venue where life is meaningfully lived. The voice of modernity has not brought the promised liberty but only other masters.[4]

Marriage and Theological Reading

A second parable reflects upon marriage. Grandfather performed the vows and my college philosophy professor, Larry Braidfoot, brought a charge crafted from Bonhoeffer's "Wedding Sermon from a Prison Cell." One phrase or theme stood out: Debbie and I were asking God to add his "yes" to our "yes." Conyers, by the way, cites this expression.[5] Bonhoeffer's expression instructed us that viewing our marriage as the sum of our initiative was not enough. We were challenged as a couple to see that our decision to marry was to be submitted to God and consequently to be seen as part of a much larger drama. If our prayer before the gathered community was answered, then our marriage was the product of more than hearts and hormones; God's "yes" meant that he was a party of interest and even a sponsor.

Our union knows many blessings: for example, we celebrate and admire four wonderful children. We have also journeyed together in hard seasons and places. Through everything we have come to walk together with the conviction that our walking together is a matter of decisions but also, dare I say, destiny. We believe, in keeping with the

---

4. Conyers, *Listening Heart*, 34–113; and *Long Truce*, 45–147. Consider another Baptist theologian, Barry Harvey, for modernity's influence upon theology and theological responses, in *Can These Bones Live?*, 39–47.

5. Conyers, *Listening Heart*, 171; see Bonhoeffer, *Letters and Papers*, 41–47.

sermon of Bonhoeffer, that God has invested in our marriage and our story is now found to be part of his story.

This conviction changes the way one thinks of marriage. We are still aware of how we came to marry. We can acknowledge with some emotional distance that we could have not married, could have not stayed married, or could have married others. But a persistent intuition presses upon us: our drama is not merely our own doing. A theological reading might say no more than God added his "yes" or that he gave permission. Our journey, however, brings me to a personal and intuitive exclamation of conviction that surpasses Bonhoeffer's notion.[6] Love gives boldness to declare mysteries when I say "you are a gift from God" or "God meant you for me." Again I acknowledge the capacity to step back and divorce myself from this explicitly theological reading. Our story is the story of two kids getting married; I poured great energy into the project; I asked the question and she said "yes;"[7] later we joined together to say "I do." Theologians of other varieties might readily have at hand an explanation for such mysteries or know some technique for harmonizing the decision dimension and destiny dimension of our union. Without embracing such strategies, I continue to believe that our humble journey, both remarkable and unremarkable, is sanctioned and crafted by God.

An independent investigator researching marriage may observe that we have a relationship that is successful and enduring by some point of comparative reference. But I am doubtful a researcher might ever sense what I have come to believe and hold as true through the years. These differing perspectives reside side by side; there is an objective, empirically driven posture of the imaginary researcher and there is my own profoundly personal and theological reading. Strangely theological readings do not come so easily to me; I hold few features of my story with such clarity and conviction. Saints, we are told, see the whole of creation in its theological frame of reference. Reading, and especially speaking with, Conyers almost always left me wanting to see more of what he could see through a sacred lens.

Conyers had learned to see the world theologically; his acquired theological vision provided discernment to assess the costliness of the

---

6. I humbly acknowledge that Bonhoeffer warns against pious presumption or "false piety" in *Letters and Papers from Prison*, 42.

7. Ironically, I proposed at Seminary Hill where my grandparents had attended.

modern point of view. Modernity is characterized by the rise of practices and convictions that weigh against sacred readings and findings. The Enlightenment disposition sought to attribute phenomena as belonging to either the natural or the supernatural arena. Such thinking distorts the Christian tradition, which sees God sustaining and orchestrating the creation instead of a self-standing, self-sustaining, mechanistic view of the world. The false bifurcation of natural and supernatural eventually leads to nature eclipsing God. It also ignores that creation is the chosen place for the divine drama; in a gospel-shaped world, God's incarnational presence stands as the centerpiece instead of viewing his work or presence as an alien intrusion.[8] The modern hostility towards a theological reading of events is stubborn. For the modern mind such sacred readings, like a divine sanction and underwriting of a marriage, are at best wishful habits of the immature mind or even worse an evil-spirited matrix designed to manipulate or appease others. What is left is the call to be brave and responsible to one's own sense of standards because there is no "bigger picture" but only man-made structures mistaken for God's work. Reflecting upon marriage again, partners may find a relationship mutually rewarding in a given season; but where enlightened thinking rules, there is little reason to be married in a church house before God and his gathered people. Conyers' critique of modernity makes the costly consequences clear: there are no marriages made in heaven. No doubt the incapacity to read, interpret, or see God's work in the concrete fabric of creation has consequences for how we read the Bible.

Another reflection upon marriage needs to be included. While recognizing the divine embrace, we must also depict the nature of the love required from the partners. Conyers compares "an abandonment of ourselves to the Word of God," to "the abandonment to the risk of marriage."[9] A faithful reading of the Bible "does not imply less than critical judgment, it does imply more." The "more" is one's emotion and will in addition to the intellect. The young man pondering marriage should not surrender critical acumen. Prudence requires him to anticipate or calculate the couple's future happiness, compatibility regarding religion and politics, and financial habits and disposition, to name only a few

---

8. Levering, *Participatory Biblical Exegesis*, 18–25, attributes this false dilemma as the consequence of nominalism's triumph.

9. Conyers, *How to Read the Bible*, 54.

issues. In time, however, his emotion and will take the lead, "though his intellect may give its consent." When the moment or season of commitment arrives his desire for an intellectual certainty is surrendered "for the sake of discovering more completely the mystery of the other person." A similar personal investment is necessary for a genuine reading of Scripture. Conyers argues that sympathy is necessary to understand Jeremiah and a willingness to believe is necessary to receive John's testimony.[10]

The method is sound, not foolhardy. Risk is essential and unavoidable for acquiring a certain dimension or kind of knowledge. The young man puts aside the practical questions not because he is willing to live with knowing less but because he passionately longs to know more. Practicing prudence, conducting feasibility studies, and collecting data finally reach a point of diminishing return. To really know her he must commit and surrender to love her and receive her love. The mystery of union with another person requires commitment and risk.

Reading the Bible requires a faithful risking; reading from detachment and distance is barren by comparison but still holds promise because the reader may be drawn into the experience of faith. Conyers writes, "with Sarah we laugh, with David we have remorse, with Peter our overconfidence evaporates at the crucial moment, with Paul we feel ourselves as the chief of sinners—we are led as full human beings into the presence of God."[11] The parable of marriage yields two lessons: one observes that theological readings—seeing human phenomena as possessing a divine sanction—have epistemic significance; the second observes that full participation in a Christian reading of Scripture, like participation in marriage, requires commitment and risk by virtue of their distinctive character.

Tradition: Reformation and Early Church

Advocates of a modern approach to reading propose that disinterested readers are the legitimate heirs to the Reformers in that they set aside tradition and relied instead upon Scripture. Popular retellings of the Reformation encourage this erroneous verdict when they picture the great Reformers, Luther and Calvin, as embracing a tradition-free

10. Ibid., 53.
11. Ibid., 53–54.

reading of Scripture. D. H. Williams' work offers an artful and constructive correction for such Protestant misimpressions.

Williams recounts that Luther desired a general council to address the needed reform of the church. In Luther's envisioning such a council should be grounded on the four great councils (Nicea, Constantinople, Ephesus and Chalcedon); it was these councils, he concluded, "which establish the norm of Christian doctrine." In a similar vein, Calvin could voice confidence in early church and even put forward that the Spirit had guided the council of Nicea in "expounding the real meaning of Scripture."[12] The contrast between Calvin and Wollebius, who occupies his chair one hundred years after Calvin, is also informative. Calvin, while cautious about the language of tradition, constantly reads from within the community in the light of church tradition; Wollebius by contrast depends upon rationalistic principles without any hint of the guidance Calvin had sought from the church in reading the text.[13]

Not only is the idea of reading Scripture in light of tradition and community the practice of the Reformers, it also touches the very identity of Christianity. Scripture can be read in a myriad of ways even once a canon has begun to function and take shape. Irenaeus addressed this issue with his image of an ancient mosaic. He tells the story of crude workers who disassemble a mosaic made of jewels that picture a king. The king's image is artful and involves a fitting and beautiful arrangement of the jewels which collectively represent the king in a noble manner. The reckless workers, however, poorly reassemble the pieces in a coarse and artless fashion to represent a dog or a fox instead of a king. Irenaeus confronted the gnostic readers on just this issue. The Gnostics read with the intent to reconfigure. The guiding image of the king functions like the rule of faith. Similarly, reading a text of Scripture in a Christianly fashion is to read it according to and in keeping with the rule of faith.[14] The rule of faith guides the reader in understanding the particular passages of the Bible, but also assists the reader to organize or construe the various passages into a larger narrative. Interestingly, some of the earliest uses of the word "canon" refer to a theological canon, the

---

12. Williams, *Evangelicals and Tradition*, 74.

13. Idem, "Scripture, Tradition, and the Church," 120–21; also compare his *Retrieving the Tradition*, 173–204.

14. Wilken, *Spirit of Early Christian Thought*, 67–68. He cites Irenaeus, *Against Heresies*, I.8.1.

rule of faith.[15] Reading in accord with the rule (canon) of faith is the discriminating trait between "Christianly" and "Non-Christianly" (e.g., Gnostic) reading.

Community

David Yeago joins a team of ecumenically oriented theologians who call the church to rediscover its trinitarian identity.[16] The rich sources of doctrine, liturgy, and practices serve as guides to this journey of reacquaintance. In light of these resources, Yeago identifies the church as the "privileged locus for scriptural interpretation." The church's worship and doctrine provide the reader with the requisite orientation to the very reality to which the Scripture itself bears witness. He recounts that the ancients, and indeed pre-moderns, held life in the church and faith as a necessity for the interpreter. Additionally, the Reformers shared the idea that knowledge of the tradition, wisdom, and Christlikeness gave a reader a distinctive advantage.[17]

Yet, the modern era reversed this longstanding conviction. As with my grandfather, a researcher is advised to neutralize, suspend, or transcend any loyalty to concrete experience. One's prejudgment or prejudice corrupted readers and lured them away from the bravery required to face the verdicts yielded by "critical" methods. A Cartesian-inspired method called for readers to never rely upon earlier verdicts influenced by the experience of living in the church.[18] The way forward depended upon brave readers who could rise above their life in the church to exercise a rational autonomy.[19]

The shift is dramatic. Belief and participation in the life of the church are recast as a corrupting influences rather than the necessary orientation for reading. This reevaluation is accompanied by numerous ironies. For one, as noted previously, the Reformers' articulation of *sola*

15. Williams, *Evangelicals and Tradition*, 58–65.
16. Buckley and Yeago, *Knowing the Triune God*.
17. Yeago, "Bible," 49.

18. Ibid., 56–57. Yeago engages the notion of Scripture's clarity arguing that Luther claimed the central gospel teaching was accessible, while acknowledging that Scripture is difficult.

19. Compare Candler's observation that St. Thomas held humility, as opposed to today's autonomy, as the first requirement for those training in *sacra doctrina*. *Theology, Rhetoric, Manuduction*, 109–11.

scriptura was depicted as a step toward reading independently of tradition and community. Another irony involves the Reformers' protest against the clerical privilege claimed by Catholicism which required the vexing task of interpretation to be left for the priests and bishop.[20] Modern-minded theorists ironically viewed the Reformation protest against clerical privilege as an incremental step toward embracing critical methods. Luther and Calvin were recast as proto-liberals,[21] despite the fact that their readings were thoroughly embedded in the church. Yeago highlights the incongruity when he observes that the "status elite" represented by the priest and bishop were not replaced by Luther's priesthood of believers but by a "meritocratic elite" of an academic guild. The guild's mythos seemed more plausible as secular moods and voices gained traction. The new mythos seemed commonsensical: freedom from tradition yielded accurate readings that rested on critical inspection and not pious preaching.

Today postmodern[22] eyes can see more clearly that the embrace of the "new liberty" was not achieved by abandoning the encumbrances of tradition and community, but was instead a phenomenon that even the ancients were familiar with: conversion. Modern folk were converting from one community to another.[23] The new guild also required certification of competence and compliance in academic life. Much theological training for ministry fell under similar sway. Some seminaries now sought to produce a new elite minister who could genuinely read the text depending upon criticism without creed.

Knowledge

Yeago anticipates several objections to his presentation for "ecclesial reading" and seeks to distinguish it from other viewpoints. The posture of reading from within the church does not lead him to a con-

20. The popular writer Benson Bobrick claims an interrogator's first question for suspected heretics was whether the subject knew any Scripture in the vernacular, in *Wide as the Waters*, 11.

21. Note the balance achieved by Linda Woodhead, *Introduction to Christianity*, 259.

22. In conversation, Conyers spoke of what I call "postmodern" as "John Locke on a skateboard." I took this to mean he viewed postmodernity as hyper-modernity.

23. It is fair to view some participants in the discussion as maintaining memberships in multiple communities.

structivist hermeneutic (whereby the reader is free to "construct" the meaning of the text). Also, it need not require a fundamentalist view of Scripture or inspiration: an omnipotent view of Scripture as comprised of miraculously given, though poorly organized, propositions that are capable of unambiguous reading. He argues that such an understanding of inspiration derives from an anti-Catholic agenda seeking to deny the teaching office of the church. Neither must an ecclesial reading ignore the Scriptures' "diversity."[24]

More importantly still, Yeago is eager to distinguish his view from the contemporary notion that one's circumstance determines one's reading. For example, a reader's circumstance or context of poverty may incline readers to attend to the issue of poverty; but poor people can offer incommensurate readings from their context in poverty. More important than one's circumstance is one's belief or conviction. He writes: "the Bible is not read as it is by the Christian poor simply because they are poor, but also because of what they believe to be true of God and the world, about poverty, and for that matter the biblical texts themselves."[25] Again the point is that readings are not the product of suspending one's convictions but of attending to them. Yeago claims that the church "knows something" of pressing relevance to the task of reading. He cites Athanasius' observation that knowing the resurrection had taken place provokes Peter in Acts 2 to apply Psalm 16 to a risen Jesus.[26] The central conviction that Jesus is raised still serves as the crucial factor for interpretation. At this point the notions of knowledge and community merge because the resurrection is intertwined in the liturgy, ritual, and practice of the church. Yeago claims "knowledge is embedded in the church's practice."[27] The central teachings and practices of the church are the very resource that provides a fruitful orientation for encountering the Bible's message.

In a recent interview, Kiku Adatto told a story about the theorist Roland Barthes that provokes consideration of the link between love,

24. Yeago, "Bible," 62, 75, 78. I have ventured to suggest that such over burdened descriptions of inspiration result in part from an unarticulated or weak view of God.

25. Ibid., 53.

26. Ibid., 54; citing Athanasius, *Against the Arians*, 2.16.

27. Yeago, "Bible," 56, argues that Irenaeus corrects a Gnostic depreciation of the flesh by recognizing its discontinuity with the Eucharist. Yeago shapes his article in part around the knowledge the church employs in reading Scripture; the knowledge includes that the Bible is inspired and it forms a unity (60–66, 70–85).

intimate knowledge, and interpretation; it is little wonder that readers who know the necessity of love develop a proprietary interest. Soon after the passing of his mother, Barthes discovered a photo of his mother that captured her soul; he offered explanations about how her expression, in this particular photo, revealed a little-known but vital dimension of her person. Some were surprised that he did not include this soul-revealing photo in the collection of photos intended for public viewing. He explained that onlookers might review the photo without understanding who she was. Intelligent but uninitiated viewers would gaze and fall upon many interesting observations about hair and fashion styles and technical insights. Barthes concluded, however, that without knowing her it seemed inappropriate to let them look upon what they could not "see," having no knowledge of her.[28]

Text and Teaching

Matthew Levering identifies the shift toward nominalism and away from a participatory metaphysic as the reason for the decline of theological reading. While he narrates modern complications that also stifle theological interpretation, the primary explanation is medieval and not modern. He holds that the roots of modernity are found in the medieval metaphysic of nominalism; nominalism fostered the triumph of "autonomous humanism" by displacing the reigning "participatory" approach. Nominalism tends to place the divine and human as rivals competing for turf. By contrast, a participatory metaphysic had made it possible to picture oneself, or one's place and moment in history "as marked by either divine presence," or as participating "in transcendental truth and goodness."[29] In the perspectives of Augustine and St. Thomas,[30] the world's relationship to God made it possible for a human undertaking to bring one to the intersection of the eternal and the temporal. For example, an artist's work of creative beauty may be thought to share in

---

28. Adatto, "Image of a Person's Face."

29. Levering, *Participatory Biblical Exegesis*, 20–21. Robert Barron, *Priority of Christ*, 15, joins Colin Gunton and John Milbank in a similar assessment of late scholasticism's influence. Cf. Harvey, *Can These Bones Live?*, 245–46.

30. Levering, *Participatory Biblical Exegesis*, 19, stipulates that Christians appropriated a participatory metaphysic from Plato and a teleological metaphysic from Aristotle with St. Thomas combining the two.

or participate in the work that God sanctions and exemplifies. Beauty's praises belong finally to God who structures the world so that beauty may be shared both by creating beauty and by acknowledging it with admiration. In such a participatory envisioning of the world, the artist and God are not competitive; instead, God becomes the ground, source, and inspiration for human achievement and excellence.

Within such a world, the Bible's production needs not be seen as a contest between divine and human authorship. For example, Levering notes that Augustine, in his chief work on interpreting the Bible, gathers all the variety and diversity of the Bible under the rubric of teaching; that is, God can be seen as offering instruction no matter what variety of human genres or circumstances may be encountered on the Bible's pages. The Bible is God's sacramental tool for divine instruction or teaching. Learning to read the Scriptures involves transforming participation in the triune God. Augustine would see no dissonance in his divine understanding of the Bible's nature and goal on the one hand, and the need to address the questions about understanding human communication on the other.[31]

Levering also explores reading the text in the community. Engaging with Jewish exegetes[32] he finds that avoiding communal exegesis is an impossibility. Following especially Michael Fishbane, Levering notes that the Bible itself is the product of communal exegesis wherein later biblical writings appropriate earlier biblical writings. He concludes well: "there is no biblical text, in other words, that comes to us unmediated by communal practices of interpretation; divine Revelation contains in itself, as a constitutive element, communal exegesis."[33] Nuanced critical study concludes that the object of its study is itself a product of communal reading.

A participatory metaphysic provides a suitable foundation for seeing the Scripture as a divine product without denying its human

---

[31]. Levering, *Participatory Biblical Exegesis*, 69–70. Levering cites Augustine; see Augustine, *Teaching Christianity: De Doctrina Christiana*. Augustine spends most of his energy, especially in books 2 and 3, treating technical challenges of understanding ambiguous human communication; in book 4 he advocates effective communication strategies. Compare Yeago, "Bible," 70, who views Scripture as a text with the Holy Spirit as its "one single speaker."

[32]. Barry Harvey, *Can These Bones Live?*, 60, traces a very constructive conversation in the face of the supersession question.

[33]. Levering, *Participatory Biblical Exegesis*, 103.

character.[34] These texts, humanly speaking, are in part the product of a communal process of interpreting and reinterpreting tradition. The ancient church clearly received or read them communally as well. Peter Candler Jr. argues that reading was not merely a tool for the Christian pilgrimage, but it was the very pedagogy of faith. Candler maintains that it is reading that allows pilgrims to know God "as the product not of immediate apprehension but of time-bound, transient learning, mediated to us by the community of God through the people gathered around his Word."[35]

Core Convictions for Christian Readings

Several core convictions sustain a Christian reading of the Scripture and find root in Conyers' wisdom. Owning one's tradition does not place one at an epistemological disadvantage but is an essential experience required for interpretation. An explicitly theological view of the Bible need not be surrendered; the Bible may be seen as a product of God's sponsorship and ownership. The dispositions of trust, risk, and commitment are necessary to know God and hear his voice.

Reading in the light of tradition is the distinguishing mark of Christian exegesis. Reading in light of the rule of faith, patristic exegetes suffered from no stifling uniformity but rather displayed a confounding variety; even still the rule of faith guided the church in identifying readings that deviated substantially from this theological canon; for example, the church could dismiss the alternative account offered by Marcion on the grounds of a functional orthodoxy long before the orthodox creeds were articulated. Similarly, the Reformers exercised independence from some traditions because they were loyal to other traditions.

Life in the church, with its practice, worship, and fellowship, provides the necessary orientation required for an authentic reading of Scripture. Also, Christian reading rests upon certain convictions or truth claims that influence the practice of interpretation. At the center of this network of convictions is the proclamation that God raised Jesus from the dead. Readings failing to appropriate these central convictions

---

34. I acknowledge there are other strategies for justifying a mediated view of God's working in the world.

35. Candler, *Theology, Rhetoric, Manuduction*, 35.

fall short of an explicitly Christian posture. Critical reading need not be the final enemy or master of theological reading.[36]

A metaphysical or theological model that embraces God's prerogative to act in and through his creation enhances an articulation of a Christian reading. By understanding that God's work may be mediated, we recapture the insight that God is not rightly understood as merely one actor among many others—one force among other competing forces. The text of Scripture is rightly seen as a human document rooted in context and culture but also as a divine book by which God teaches and edifies.

Conyers' wisdom is similarly fashioned. He discerned that modernity had impoverished the exercise of thinking by attempting to eclipse the resources of place and time. Yet at the same time he observed that God employs the concrete creation as rich tools in his larger purpose. He spoke and lived at the intersection of love and knowledge. His work serves as a commentary on both the love of wisdom and the wisdom of love.

We may be unable and find it undesirable to forbid outsiders to read Scripture as the early fathers had once scolded the Gnostics; we may also find it unwise to ignore or deny the critical study of the Bible; more negligent still, however, is our failure to acknowledge and take up the church's faith and practice as our hermeneutical habitat. Reclaiming this habitat will require the virtue of courage exhibited by A. J. Conyers. I trust that the entreaty to embrace the church as the locus of Scripture-reading will be a fitting tribute to his strong and contagious faith.

---

36. I recognize that Christian scholars seek to engage in critical exegesis with a mind to serving the church. For example, some scholars take up critical methods as a heuristic tool. More ambitiously, some believe that critical studies provide the raw materials for a subsequent theological reading. Such a simple division of labor may not be as commonsensical as it first seems. Levering compares the work of Stephen Fowl and Brevard Childs, both pioneers in the arena of theological interpretation. Among numerous points of interest, he explores the issue of the priority of critical studies as a prelude to theological readings embraced by Childs. Levering appeals to St. Thomas in supporting Fowl's challenge of critical scholarship's place of privilege and priority. Levering, *Participatory Biblical Exegesis*, 118–39. Cf. also the work of Daniel Treier, *Theological Interpretation of Scripture*, 85–92.

Bibliography

Adatto, KiKu. "How the Image of a Person's Face in a Photograph Has the Capacity for Intimate Representation of Inner Personhood." Mars Hill Audio Journal 96, disc1, tracks 3–4. Online: http://www.marshillaudio.org.

Augustine. *Teaching Christianity: De Doctrina Christiana*. Translated by Edmund Hill. Hyde Park, NY: New City, 1996.

Barron, Robert. *The Priority of Christ: Toward a Postliberal Catholicism*. Grand Rapids: Brazos, 2007.

Benson, Bobrick. *Wide as the Waters: The Story of the English Bible and the Revolution It Inspired*. New York: Penguin, 2001.

Bonhoeffer, Dietrich. *Letters and Papers from Prison*. New York: Macmillan, 1972.

Buckley, James J., and David Yeago, editors. *Knowing the Triune God: The Work of the Spirit in the Practices of the Church*. Grand Rapids: Eerdmans, 2001.

Candler, Peter M., Jr. *Theology, Rhetoric, Manuduction, or, Reading Scripture Together on the Path to God*. Grand Rapids: Eerdmans, 2006.

Conyers, A. J. *How to Read the Bible*. Downers Grove, IL: InterVarsity, 1986.

———. *The Listening Heart: Vocation and the Crisis of Modern Culture*. Waco: Baylor University Press, 2009.

———. *The Long Truce: How Toleration Made the World Safe for Power and Profit*. Dallas: Spence, 2001.

Harvey, Barry. *Can These Bones Live? A Catholic Engagement with Ecclesiology, Hermeneutics, and Social Theory*. Grand Rapids: Brazos, 2008.

Jacobs, Alan. *A Theology of Reading: The Hermeneutics of Love*. Boulder, CO: Westview, 2001.

Jeffrey, David Lyle. *People of the Book: Christian Identity and Literary Culture*. Grand Rapids: Eerdmans, 1996.

Levering, Matthew. *Participatory Biblical Exegesis: A Theology of Biblical Interpretation*. Notre Dame: University of Notre Dame Press, 2008.

Treier, Daniel J. *Introducing Theological Interpretation of Scripture: Recovering a Christian Practice*. Grand Rapids: Baker Academic, 2008.

Wilken, Robert. *The Spirit of Early Christian Thought*. New Haven: Yale University Press, 2003.

Williams, D. H. *Evangelicals and Tradition: The Formative Influence of the Early Church*. Grand Rapids: Baker Academic, 2005.

———. *Retrieving the Tradition and Renewing Evangelicalism: A Primer for Suspicious Protestants*. Grand Rapids: Eerdmans, 1999.

———. "Scripture, Tradition, and the Church: Reformation and Post-Reformation." In *The Free Church and the Early Church: Bridging the Historical and Theological Divide*, 101–26. Grand Rapids: Eerdmans, 2002.

Woodhead, Linda. *An Introduction to Christianity*. Cambridge: Cambridge University Press, 2004.

Yeago, David. "The Bible." In *Knowing the Triune God: The Work of the Spirit in the Practices of the Church*, 49–93. Grand Rapids: Eerdmans, 2001.

4

The Reformed Objection to Natural Theology
A Catholic Response to G. C. Berkouwer

Eduardo J. Echeverria

Introduction

GERRIT CORNELIUS BERKOUWER (1903–1996) WAS A RENOWNED Dutch Reformed theologian, holder of the Chair in Dogmatics (1945–1974) at the Free University, Amsterdam, a position previously held by his two illustrious neo-Calvinist predecessors, Abraham Kuyper (1837–1920) and Herman Bavinck (1854–1921).[1] He is the author of an eighteen-volume work, *Studies in Dogmatics*, as well as a highly regarded study and trenchant critique of Karl Barth, *The Triumph of Grace in the Theology of Karl Barth* (1954). Barth himself describes Berkouwer's study as "a great book on myself and the *Church Dogmatics*."[2] Throughout his dogmatic studies and elsewhere he engages the teachings of the Catholic Church as well as the works of both classical and contemporary Catholic theologians. Prior to the Second Vatican

---

1. By "Reformed" I mean that version of Protestant Christianity arising from the Calvinist Reformation in sixteenth-century Europe. The term "Neo-Calvinist" refers to a movement within Reformed Christianity that stems from the nineteenth-century Dutch educator, theologian, church leader, politician, and prolific writer Abraham Kuyper. Besides Kuyper, other genial spirits within this intellectual, cultural, and religious milieu include Bavinck, Berkouwer, and the philosopher Herman Dooyeweerd (1894–1977).

2. Karl Barth, *Church Dogmatics* IV/2:xii. Barth adds: "For all its reservations and criticisms this work is written with such care and goodwill and Christian *aequitas*." See also, *Church Dogmatics* IV/3:173–80.

Council he published two studies on Roman Catholicism.[3] He was officially appointed a "Delegated Observer" at that Council, which resulted in an important study of the Council and a more positive Reformed assessment of Roman Catholicism than in his earlier books.[4]

Of the many doctrinal themes that Berkouwer discusses in his *Studies in Dogmatics*, surely one of the most insightful overall is his treatment of the nature and reality of divine revelation, especially of the distinction between, and unity of, God's general and special revelation in his 1951 work *De Algemene Openbaring*.[5] By the middle of the twentieth century, according to Berkouwer, three problems had arisen, making it urgently necessary to devote a dogmatic study to this topic. The first two problems presuppose an antithesis between general and special revelation such that a theological position is developed that abandons either general revelation or special revelation. Either general revelation is abandoned on the basis of "the Christo-monistic conception of revelation [that] cannot recognize any *other* revelation than the one in the incarnated Word" (*AO*, 82 [102]), or special revelation is "gradually relativized by a *general* divine manifestation in the world" (*AO*, 8 [12]), and then eventually abandoned on the basis of a religious relativism that refuses to accept the uniqueness and exclusiveness of the revelation in Christ as a revealed truth. Men take offense at the claim "that God has revealed himself *in Christ* and that no one comes

---

3. *De Strijd Om Het Roomsch-Katholieke Dogma*; idem., *Conflict met Rome*; ET: *The Conflict with Rome*. See also, idem., *Nieuwe Perspectieven in de Controvers: Rome-Reformatie*.

4. Berkouwer, *Vatikaans Concilie en de nieuwe theologie*; (English ed., *The Second Vatican Council and the New Catholicism*). The words *nieuwe theologie* (literally "new theology") in the Dutch title of the book are a clear reference to the *nouvelle théologie* of Henri de Lubac et al. That reference is lost in the English translation, which speaks of "New Catholicism." Berkouwer continued his Reformed assessment of Vatican II and the *nouvelle théologie* in another book that remains untranslated, *Nabetrachting op het Concilie* ("Retrospect of the Council").

5. Berkouwer, *De Algemene Openbaring* (English ed., *General Revelation*). Further references to this work will be cited parenthetically in the text. Both sources will be cited, first the original as *AO*, followed by the pagination of the English translation in square brackets. See also Berkouwer, "General and Special Divine Revelation." Besides general and special revelation, Berkouwer's studies cover themes like faith and justification, sanctification, and perseverance, the providence of God, divine election, the sacraments, man and the image of God, the person and work of Christ, the return of Christ, sin, the church, and Holy Scripture (two volumes are devoted to each of the last four themes).

to the Father except *through Him* [John 14:6]" (*AO*, 9 [13]). The third problem—found chiefly in traditional Roman Catholic theology and, for example, in Vatican Council I of 1870—is the identification of general revelation with natural theology, with the implication that there is a natural knowledge of God *independent* of the special revelation in Jesus Christ. Let me briefly explain each of these problems in order to set the context for the topic of this essay.

First, the historic Christian teaching regarding the "*unique* and 'once-for-all' character of the redemptive revelation in Jesus Christ" (*AO*, 6 [9]) is "increasingly criticized from the viewpoint of 'general' revelation." "Christianity, it was argued," adds Berkouwer, "set too many boundaries to God's revelation by calling it 'special' and by localizing it. Did not all religions contain elements with hidden indications of a revelation of God? Was it still possible to accept the specific of God's revelation in Israel and in Jesus Christ? In this manner—as an attack on the Church—the plea was made for a general, universal revelation of God in the world."[6] Berkouwer wrote this statement half a century ago. Since then religious relativism has been championed by many theologians, making opposition to the distinction between general and special revelation even more stiff.

Of course, Berkouwer rejects any view of general revelation that undermines the sufficiency and absoluteness of special revelation in Jesus Christ. Yes, general revelation is necessary: it not only leaves men without excuse, establishing the impossibility of their guiltlessness, but also indicates that fallen man is not freed from the normative presence of God in and through the works of creation. In particular, general revelation, particularly through the reality of God's common grace—a non-saving grace that restrains the full consequences of sin from disclosing itself in reality—manifests "the power of God in revelation and in grace preserving life from total self-destruction."[7] Thus, general revelation is necessary.

Second, in reaction to those who argue that "general revelation" is sufficient and hence special revelation in Christ is unnecessary, a Christo-monistic idea of revelation is developed. "*The principal attack against the profession of general revelation came namely from the adher-*

---

6. Berkouwer, "General and Special Divine Revelation," 14.
7. Ibid., 21.

ents of Christo-monism" (*AO*, 90 [112]).[8] Some argue that it is religiously necessary "*to simply conclude from the exclusive salvation in Christ to the exclusive revelation in Christ*" (*AO*, 74 [93]). In other words, adds Berkouwer, "this monism denies all revelation in actual sense outside of the historic Christ and recognizes only 'witness' and 'indications' which as such indeed are connected with *the* revelation but still *are* not revelation" (*AO*, 90 [112]). There is also a version of Christo-monism that attempts to prove, says Berkouwer, "on the basis of fallen mankind's blinded eyes, that God has revealed himself *only* by his Word, and not already in the works of his hands" (*AO*, 233 [280]; italics added).

Now, as to its sufficiency and absoluteness, Berkouwer rejects any view of special revelation in Christ that opposes the biblical idea, as he rightly judges, that God reveals himself universally in and through the works of creation (see *AO*, 87 [108]). Yes, Jesus Christ is the fullness and mediator of all of God's revelation in word and deed, in Old Testament prophecy and promises, in his historical acts of revelation in times past, and in his creation as a source of revelation itself. These all truly point to Christ for their ultimate significance and meaning as the one historical revelation in whom the light of God's revelation arose in a full, unparalleled, and unsurpassable manner (see Col 1:15–20). But this "is something entirely different," says Berkouwer, "from revelation *commencing* with him. Asserting the latter is forcing the Scriptural data into an *aprioristic* scheme" (*AO*, 85 [106]).

But affirming the reality of general revelation, of the revelatory nature of creation, does not mean that it is concurrent with the supernatural special revelation in Christ. In other words, says Berkouwer, general revelation is *not* an independent source of natural knowledge of God in addition to special revelation, with the latter being the source of our supernatural knowledge of God, supplementing and completing the

---

8. Berkouwer charges Karl Barth with "Christomonism." He is not alone in making this charge. According to Henri Blocher, "Critics, not lightweights in the scholarly world, have complained [of Barth's] 'Christomonism': [for example] A. Moda lists Paul Althaus (first in print), Reinhold Niebuhr, Helmut Thielicke, K. Okayama, to whom we may add Richard Muller and even, though with a limiting 'perhaps', the faithful translator Geoffrey Bromiley.... Berkouwer [in *The Triumph of Grace in the Theology of Karl Barth*] introduced 'panchristism' and 'Jesucentric' to characterize Barth's thinking.... Webster notes that Barth, in his later writings, was alert to the danger of 'Christological totalitarianism'. The phrase, finally, that many Barthians prefer was coined by Barth to define his 1930 turn: 'christological concentration'. This comparatively neutral expression is unobjectionable" ("Karl Barth's Christocentric Method," 26–27).

former. "In general revelation we are not dealing with an independent source of knowledge; on the contrary, by faith we understand the act of divine revelation in created reality" (*AO*, 238 [289]). Berkouwer adds, "No true knowledge of the revelation of God in the works of his hands is obtainable without faith in Christ" (*AO*, 235 [285]).

This point brings us to the third problem, namely, the problem of natural theology and its identification with general revelation. Berkouwer strenuously insists that general revelation is not the same as natural theology, and he argues, on the one hand, that identifying the two has led some, such as the early Barth in the Barth-Brunner debate, to reject the former because they reject the latter.[9] On the other hand, some have argued, such as Etienne Gilson,[10] that accepting general revelation opens, in Berkouwer's words, "the door to natural theology" and guarantees it "a legitimate place in the theological system." Berkouwer adds, "General revelation and natural theology are thought to be on the *same plane* structurally." That is, a natural knowledge of God is mediated through created things by way of theistic proofs and logical inferences, rendering our knowledge of God the conclusion of an argument. Those who accept general revelation but reject natural theology are considered to be inconsistent. "Consistently—it is said—the idea of general revelation *must* lead to natural theology. Therefore, we must discuss the background of natural theology and ask whether general revelation and natural theology are indissolubly united" (*AO*, 11 [15]). Berkouwer argues that they are not the same: "only by separating between general revelation and natural theology can we do justice to the message of

---

9. See the debate in Brunner, *Natural Theology*. Oscar Cullmann is also unclear about the question of an original revelation in and through creation (natural revelation, as he calls it). He observes, on the one hand, "The concept of 'natural revelation', which emerges only later, is still foreign to the New Testament." On the other hand, he says, "Paul merely confirms the fact that the revelation through the works of Creation . . . does not effectually lead the Gentiles to Christ." In sum, "In the context of Rom 1:18, therefore, the mention of the divine revelation to the Gentiles among the works of Creation cannot have the aim of providing a basis for a natural revelation in addition to the Christian revelation given in redemptive history. It rather has only the meaning of showing that the Gentiles, like the Jews, are 'inexcusable'" (*Christ and Time*, 180–81). But as Berkouwer says regarding Cullmann's point that the effect of general revelation is to leave men without excuse: "Maar dit kan toch nooit de werkelijkheid dezer Openbaring te niet doen" [But this can nonetheless never eliminate the reality of [creation] Revelation] (*AO*, 23–24 n. 52).

10. Gilson, *Christianity and Philosophy*.

Scripture" (*AO*, 126 [153]). The message that Berkouwer has in mind is that the unbeliever "*does not know God at all*" (*AO*, 109 [139]). There is an epistemic gulf between general revelation and true knowledge of God. Berkouwer insists that the antithesis between knowing and not-knowing is deeply biblical. "There is no half-way stop between the idolatry, foolishness, and darkness of heathendom and the knowledge of God." "A man can leave the one for the other," he adds, "only by way of conversion as by the passage from life to death. This, too, is the only way of escape from the wrath of God" (*AO*, 119–20 [147]).

Yet, this antithesis does not eliminate general revelation. Berkouwer urges us to resist the identification of the noetic aspect of knowledge—how and what we can know—with its ontic aspect—the ontological foundation of what we can know—and hence always to distinguish sharply between knowing and being. In other words, man's lack of true knowledge of God apart from Christ in no way denies the objective reality of general revelation; the reality of the latter is not determined by man's lack of true knowledge. To draw that conclusion would be to confuse the noetic with the ontic, as Berkouwer repeatedly states. Rather, the effect of general revelation is to leave men without excuse, and thus "the not-knowing is unmasked in its guilty character precisely because there is and remains [general] revelation" (*AO*, 23 [31]). In sum, Berkouwer writes, "Precisely this distinction, yes, the *separation* [Dutch: *scheiding*] of general revelation and natural theology, is the most important question in the whole debate [between Barth and Brunner and hence on the relation of general revelation and natural theology]. It is impossible and unjustified to conclude that because man lacks the true knowledge of God, therefore *God's* [general] *revelation* is also absent" (*AO*, 35 [46]).

Since I personally agree with much of Berkouwer's theology of general revelation, in my Catholic response to his Reformed theological objections to natural theology I will only consider those aspects of his theology that bear upon those objections. For my purpose here, I am interested chiefly in three important questions: (1) what general revelation means and whether natural theology is implied in accepting it; (2) what human reason, if anything, can truly know of God; and, finally, (3) whether human reason has any power to know God after the fall into sin.[11] Before turning to these questions, I begin by summarizing Berkouwer's Reformed objections to natural theology.

Berkouwer's Reformed Objections to Natural Theology

Berkouwer's objections to natural theology might be summarized in four points. First, Berkouwer believes that natural theology in the Catholic tradition purports to be based upon God's general revelation in creation and hence it "does not pretend to be an *autonomous* theology" (*AO*, 47 [61]). This is an important and accurate observation to make about the basis of natural theology. A natural theology would be taken to be autonomous if it ascribes to reason's power self-sufficiency in acquiring knowledge of God. Autonomy here means that human reason purports to function in a world-immanent sense alone and hence without reference to God, grace, and revelation. But natural theology is based on the principle that any knowledge of God at all, including the knowledge acquired through the medium of creation, is solely due to God's self-revelation. In the case of natural theology, this is God's manifestation of himself in and through the works of creation. In other words, there is a certain action on the part of God making possible what can be known about him in and through creation. So Rome, says Berkouwer, "*really acknowledges a revelation of God in this created reality*" (*AO*, 60 [75]; see also, 66–67 [80–81]). "Nevertheless," adds Berkouwer, "one is *always amazed how little place this revelation idea gets in the exposition of natural theology*" (ibid.).[12] He explains why.

Vatican I mapped the fields of knowledge onto the realms of nature and grace and their corresponding epistemic principles of reason and faith.[13] There is a widely held view that regards the realm of nature to be self-contained and the practice of natural theology to be world-immanent, with the powers, and thus activities, of human reason in that practice taken to be essentially self-sufficient, religiously neutral, unaffected by sin, and reaching for knowledge of God *apart* from grace

---

11. In distinguishing these three questions, I am following von Balthasar, *Theology of Karl Barth*, esp. 302–25.

12. Karl Barth and Wolfhart Pannenberg make a similar charge, particularly against Vatican I. For the former, see *Church Dogmatics* II/1:79; for the latter, see *Systematic Theology* 1:75–76.

13. Deferrarr, *Sources of Catholic Dogma*, 446–47.

and revelation. Consequently, the practice of natural theology seems to function under presuppositions that are inconsistent with the idea of general revelation. It begins to take on the shape of an autonomous theology but also general revelation and natural theology are identified as one and the same.[14] Here we have the essence of Catholic rationalism. I agree with Gilson that there is some warrant for this interpretation, given the way that some Catholics have expressed themselves.[15]

Of course, Berkouwer acknowledges that this is not a rationalistic limitation of divine revelation: there exists a knowledge that is proper to faith. He also knows that Pius IX's *Syllabus of Errors* of 1846 clearly condemned rationalism: "All truths of religion flow from the natural power of human reason; hence, reason is the chief norm by which man can and should come to knowledge of all truths of whatever kind."[16] Nevertheless, the charge of rationalism is warranted because Rome defends the claim, according to Berkouwer, that reason left completely to itself has the power to attain knowledge of God mediated by creation.[17]

---

14. For an instructive account of how this historically came about, see Dupré, *Passage to Modernity*, 178–81.

15. Gilson, *Christianity and Philosophy*, 59.

16. Deferrari, *Sources of Catholic Dogma*, 435; *Syllabus*, no. 4.

17. Berkouwer writes: "Reformation thought . . . took a critical stance toward the proofs of the existence of God in Roman Catholic theology. These proofs prompted the impression that isolated human reason must lead to the conclusion of the existence of God. But such isolation is impractical and impossible because man's thinking exists and functions only in relationship to the whole man. In this totality the matter of human decision falls within the realm of the heart and of faith" ("General and Special Divine Revelation," 17). It isn't at all clear why theistic proofs are unavailable if knowing is an act of the whole man (which it surely is) and not only of the mind. Furthermore, Berkouwer dismisses theistic proofs because "in general [they] have wielded little influence. For they stand—especially in our times—in the shadow of a great many 'proofs' *against* the existence of God." What "proofs"? Unfortunately, he doesn't say. Moreover, "that God can be proved as the first causes or prime mover of all things finds less agreement these days among men. Even in Roman Catholic circles some voices say that the Roman Catholic proofs mean little or nothing *for those who do not already believe*. And in our times, in opposition to the proofs for the existence of God, a deep agnosticism elaborates the conviction of the absence of God; no longer recognizing the world as purposeful, this agnosticism abandons it to senselessness and absurdity and sees the existence of man in the world as a meaningless and purposeless jest" (ibid.). Berkouwer's insouciance regarding the availability of arguments for God's existence is troubling because it may lead some to conclude that the source of unbelief is not only our sinfulness but also our intellectual incapacity. On this point, see Terence Penelhum, "Revelation and Philosophy." Berkouwer's lack of epistemological self-confidence in theistic arguments half a century ago has been replaced with a modest confidence in

Still, Berkouwer suggests that Catholic rationalism is given a more extreme form with Vatican I's teaching that "God, the beginning and end of all things, can be known with certitude by the natural light of human reason from created things," which is interpreted to mean that theistic proofs or arguments are the source of that certainty. He notes, "It is true that the Vaticanum does not speak of the probability but of the certainty of knowing God. However, when the modernistic-oath of 1910 referred back to the Vatican Council's declaration of the natural light of reason, to this was added that God, who is knowable by the natural light of reason, 'can certainly be known as the cause of all things, and therefore can also be proved'" (AO, 53 [66–67]).[18]

Second, Berkouwer readily grants that Vatican I (1869–70) and, later, Pius XII's 1950 encyclical letter, *Humani Generis*,[19] distinguish the *de jure* possibility of acquiring knowledge of God by means of reason alone from the *de facto* actuality of doing so. One goes beyond the former condition to the latter condition, says Berkouwer, in that "most men do *not actually* come to knowledge of God by means of a rational world-and-life view but by another way" (AO, 50 [64]). That other way is the divine Word-revelation: our knowledge of God's general revelation is the fruit of knowing the gospel. In other words, there are obstacles hampering human reason's actual functioning, impeding its proper functioning so as to carry out its natural ability of grasping the truths about God mediated through creation. Therefore, the fathers of Vatican I write, "It is indeed thanks to this divine revelation, that those matters concerning God which are not of themselves beyond the scope of human reason, can, even in the present state of the human race, be known by everyone without difficulty, with firm certitude and with no intermingling of error."[20] But this only makes divine revelation relatively necessary respecting divine truths that, in principle, do not exceed reason's grasp. Such revelation makes it easier for human reason, in a

---

the availability of arguments for defending the rationality of theism. On this point, see Craig, "God Is Not Dead Yet."

18. Deferrarr, *Sources of Catholic Dogma*, "The Oath Against the Errors of Modernism," 549: "And first, I profess that God, the beginning and end of all things, can be certainly known and thus can also be demonstrated by the natural light of reason 'by the things that are made' [Rom 1:20], that is, by the visible works of creation, as the cause by the effects."

19. Pius XII, *Humani Generis*, no. 3.

20. Deferrarr, *Sources of Catholic Dogma*, 446.

concrete situation, as a *de facto actuality*, to acquire natural knowledge of God derived from the creation.

Yet, adds Berkouwer, "the restraining factors which make supernatural revelation relatively necessary are due to the *circumstances*, but *not* to the knowing agent, not to the power or ability of human reason itself" (*AO*, 52 [66]). According to Berkouwer, this means that Vatican I holds that the natural light of man's reason is sufficient for the *post lapsum* man to come to certain knowledge of God. He claims that this view is informed by an understanding of the relation between nature and grace in which the latter two are divided into two self-contained, externally juxtaposed levels—one natural, the other supernatural. Berkouwer explains: "It is true that Rome admits that sin has wounded human nature by the loss of special supernatural gifts, but the ... ability of human reason was neither destroyed nor disturbed, so that reason can still reach God. The nature of the intellect remained intact and so in a certain sense human nature is still *open* for the knowledge of God. Reason operates in the world of created reality and arrives thus, at *true*, though incomplete knowledge of God" (*AO*, 53 [67]). In addition to the fundamental misconception of how nature, sin, and grace are related, the other major problem with the Vatican's view of what the *post lapsum* man can know, according to Berkouwer, is that it is contrary to biblical teaching: the "real Pauline doctrine is that the [unregenerate] *do not know God at all*" (*AO*, 109 [139]).

But this claim surely begs the question: if unregenerate man is so fallen and estranged from God that he cannot have any true knowledge at all of God, then how can God's wrath be justified without this knowledge? Isn't this the knowledge that renders man without excuse? Doesn't he need to recognize sufficiently the truth about God in order to suppress it?[21] Isn't that what St. Paul implies in his statement, "For although they knew God, they neither glorified him as God nor gave thanks to him, but their thinking became futile and their foolish hearts were darkened" (Rom 1:21)? Isn't St. Paul speaking of those who "*having known* God, do not glorify him as God"? And without this knowledge, isn't his teaching regarding divine wrath nullified?[22]

21. Martin, "Revelation as Disclosure," 219.

22. On this connection, see Murray, *Romans*, 41: "The first part of verse 21 is causally related to the last clause in verse 20 and gives the reason why those concerned are without excuse—they are without excuse 'on this account that, knowing God, they

Berkouwer agrees that the clarity and irrefutability of general revelation leads St. Paul to speak of the "heathen as knowing God," and this is evidence of a fundamental relation between general revelation and knowledge that cannot be denied. "Man can never remove himself so far from divine revelation that the light of revelation no longer shines upon his life. But what does man do with this revelation, how does he react to his encounter with this revelation, to his 'knowing' of God in his revelation" (*AO*, 122 [150])? What kind of "knowing" is this if it is necessary to account for man's inexcusability yet fails, as St. Paul says, to lead man to give thanks or glorify God with his whole life? Why is Berkouwer skeptical that this act of "knowing" is an authentic act of knowing God?

In answering this question Berkouwer cites Dutch Reformed theologian Seakle Greijdanus (1871–1948), who writes that this "knowing" is "'not a right knowing which leads to recognition . . . but only a superficial notation. [God's Revelation] touches his consciousness and is active there, but issues in no true knowledge which reveals itself in true service of God'" (*AO*, 122–123 [150]).[23] Berkouwer adds emphatically, "There is a contact with revelation, but a contact which fails to lead to a true knowledge and acknowledgment" (*AO*, 123 [150]). What is, then, a true knowledge and acknowledgement? Berkouwer doesn't say, but I think we can surmise what he means. Francis Martin obliges us with a biblical understanding that Berkouwer would share: "The English word that captures most of the semantic field [of the notion of the knowledge of God] is 'recognize', which can mean both 'perceive' and 'acknowledge'. 'Perceive' extends to include not only 'discern' but also 'experience' and,

---

glorified him not as God, neither gave thanks'. The knowledge of God must in this context be the knowledge derived from the manifestation given in the visible creation. It is of this manifestation the apostle is speaking and it is this manifestation that is stated in verse 20 to leave men without excuse. Therefore the cognitive perception elicited from the manifestation of God's glory in the visible creation is spoken of as 'knowing God'. The inexcusableness resides in the fact that being in possession of this knowledge they did not render to God the glory and the thanks which the knowledge they possessed ought to have constrained." Murray's exegesis is shared by more recent commentaries, Catholic and Protestant alike. For the former, see Byrne, *Romans*, 66–67. For the latter, see Schreiner, *Romans*, 85–86. Moo, *Romans*, 98, writes: "*Every* person is 'without excuse' because every person—whether a first-century pagan or a twentieth-century materialist—has been given a knowledge of God and has spurned that knowledge in favor of idolatry, in all its varied manifestations."

23. Greijdanus, *De Brief van den Apostel Paulus*, 1:112.

in this sense, 'know intimately.' 'Acknowledge,' on the other hand, implies a movement of the will, a choice of someone or an acceptance of their authority. 'To know God,' therefore, means to discern his presence and action, to experience him and be in communion with him, but it also means to choose him and obey him."[24] Catholic thinkers such as Gilson do not suppose that the unregenerate person "knows" God's revelation in, by, and through his creation in this authentic sense. But Gilson does suppose that the unregenerate minds of the ancients and others affirmed "numberless errors mingled with . . . truth." But unlike Berkouwer, Gilson adds, "they were still truths."[25]

Berkouwer's chief concern is that a natural theology cannot be built upon this "knowing," upon so-called "elements of truth," because we will then diminish the extent of man's ignorance and estrangement from God, and hence misconceive the radical antithesis between knowing and not knowing God. Consequently, the attendant call to radical conversion that is clearly taught throughout the New Testament will be muffled. Therefore, concludes Berkouwer, "Romans 1 is good material for the confession of general revelation. But one must take care of how he uses it. This 'knowledge' can never be isolated from the prevailing theme of Romans 1—*the wrath of God*. The history of theology parades before us numerous attempts to isolate it from the context. It is only with such kidnapping of the phrase ["*having known God*"] from its context that it can be used to support a natural theology" (*AO*, 120–121[148]).

But why is the function of this knowledge completely exhausted by its religious relation to the wrath of God? For Berkouwer this is its only function because man's natural reason is completely closed to general revelation. Why can't we distinguish this knowledge, in whatever imperfect form it appears—mindful that it cannot be wholly correct, error free, and unaffected by its rejection of God's grace—from its function in the biblical context where it is necessary for establishing a connection between general revelation and guilt ("that they may be without excuse")? In short, why not use this knowledge—however incomplete and inaccurate—to legitimate the natural capacity of human reason to grasp the truths of God's general revelation? Otherwise, if human reason is completely closed to that revelation, as von Balthasar astutely points out, man "could by nature be an atheist and the act of

---

24. Martin, "Revelation as Disclosure," 229.

25. Gilson, *Christianity and Philosophy*, 35.

faith could in itself be neither reasonable nor shown to be reasonable."[26] Furthermore, he adds, "Paul is referring to, summoning and claiming man's natural faculty and in no way the purely supernatural faith.... Therefore, in this act of faith that is demanded here, it is *also* a question of the natural activity of human reason. *It is precisely human reason that is summoned not only to come to know God but to acknowledge him in its logical thinking.*"[27] This is the reason Vatican I cites the famous passage from Romans (1:19–20) as a warrant for natural theology.

Berkouwer would resist legitimizing natural theology. It is, he claims, biblically unacceptable because the true knowledge of God is far from being a mere *addition* of some knowledge acquired by faith to the knowledge that one already possesses by reason. This kind of *quantitative* view neglects the nature of the unregenerate mind's suppression of the truth and the call to radical conversion to the revelation of God in Christ through the internal testimony of the Holy Spirit (*AO*, 116, 123 [144, 147]. Furthermore, natural theology regards the knowledge of God as the conclusion of an argument: "*via causalitatis* to the *prima causa*" (*AO*, 123 [150]). And Berkouwer rejects the identification of general revelation with natural theology.

This brings us to a third point in Berkouwer's Reformed objection to natural theology. In an effort to show the limits of the knowledge of God that natural theology yields—"*how* and *how far* God is known in this way" (*AO*, 55 [69])—Berkouwer gives a brief account of the crucial question that a Kantian would raise about natural theology—indeed for the whole of Catholic theology and apologetics—which reflects the idea that none of our concepts, including the concept of causality, can apply to God but are limited in their applicability to the limits of our experience. Berkouwer informs us that "Rome adopts a completely different point of view. Kant's criticism is termed agnostic, and Rome maintains

---

26. Balthasar, *Theology of Karl Barth*, 320. Thus also Emil Brunner: "The denial of such a 'general revelation' preceding the historical revelation of grace in Jesus Christ can appeal neither to Paul nor to the Bible at large. It contradicts the fact of responsibility. If man did not know God, how could he be responsible? But he is responsible, for he knows about God on the strength of the divine self-revelation. The apostle does not speak of a past, now buried, possibility but of something actually present; for it is true of everyone that he is inexcusable in his godlessness. It is true of every godless man that he does not give the honor to the God who made himself known to him, but obscures the divine revelation by the productions of his own undisciplined imagination and arbitrariness" (*Letter to the Romans*, 17).

27. Balthasar, *Theology of Karl Barth*, 314–15; emphasis added.

that the argument from causality is not limited to the extent of our experience, but is also valid beyond that.... The transcendent value of causality makes *natural* knowledge of God possible" (*AO*, 54–55 [68–69]).

In particular, the idea that none of our concepts can apply to God rules out all analogy between Creator and creature, and hence without such analogy the whole of our speaking about God would "simply [be] a groping in the darkness of an unapproachable light" (*AO*, 57 [70]). Thus, without analogy, there is no possibility of natural theology. We can therefore easily understand the importance for Roman Catholic theologians, says Berkouwer, to readily affirm the *analogia entis*, i.e., the real analogies between the Creator and the creature, which is founded upon the doctrine of creation. Significantly, it has nothing to do with an essentialist analogy between Creator and creature. Berkouwer correctly states that Catholic theologians strongly oppose the idea of the analogy of being in which "there is one universal Being under which both God and man are subsumed." But Berkouwer adds, "it presupposes a *difference* between Creator and creature. There is a great difference, an 'infinite difference', between God, 'the source of being', and all created beings. But this infinite distance does not eliminate all analogy. There is also a 'line of similarity' which God has himself established. God is not a hidden God. The words with which we speak about God are not simply a groping in the darkness of an unapproachable light. There is analogy, in spite of the infinite diversity and analogy of *being*: 'Being and existence are in God, just as well as in the creatures'" (*AO*, 56–57 [70–71]). Thus, the analogy of being makes possible a natural knowledge of God. Does Berkouwer agree with this thesis?

Now, it isn't at all obvious why Berkouwer raises this Kantian point against the Catholic tradition of natural theology.[28] Perhaps Berkouwer's aim is not to endorse Kant's rejection of the transcendent value of causality, or of the application in general of concepts to God,

---

28. One might ask Berkouwer, why limit Kant's point to causality? Indeed, as Nicholas Wolterstorff asks rhetorically ("Herman Dooyeweerd: An Appreciation"), "What is it that the theologian is doing, if not applying concepts to God? And more basic, what is it that Christians around the world are doing when they confess their belief that God is the *maker of heaven and earth*? And more basic yet, what is it that St. Paul was doing when he said [2 Cor 5:19] that God was in Jesus Christ reconciling the world to himself [and not counting men's sins against them], if not applying the concept of *reconciling* to God?"

but rather simply to argue that natural theology doesn't yield *true* knowledge of God. Indeed, I think this is what he is getting at by raising questions from a Kantian perspective as well about the *analogia entis*. Natural theology, says Berkouwer, "results in knowledge of the formal *aspects* of God's *being*, in an *independent* natural theology of the first article (God the Creator) which has *nothing to do* [italics added] with the knowledge of God in the reality of his grace and mercy." Berkouwer continues: "When Christ says, 'And this is life eternal, that they should know thee the only true God, and him whom those didst send, even Jesus Christ' [John 17:3], then according to Rome this does not destroy the fact that there is also *real* and *true* knowledge of God wholly apart from Christ" (*AO*, 58 [72]). Berkouwer finds it "inconceivable that the Roman Catholic Church has not been repeatedly shocked" by the total difference between the God of the philosophers and the God of the Bible. In particular, natural theology leaves us with an "*empty, abstract*, and *formal* God-concept" (*AO*, 58 [72]), with a self-existent being, the prime mover, first cause, necessary being, the uncaused being, the true and the good, the rational designer, and so forth. "How is it possible that such considerations derived from the natural light of reason can be connected with the name, which God himself revealed to Moses when he said: 'I am that I am' [Exod 3:14]. Can one really be satisfied with this identification of the 'natural' conception of 'God as *being*' and this covenant name expressing his *faithfulness* to his people? When Moses meets God does that even for a moment concern only the isolated, abstract 'being' of God *in itself*, which a natural theology could also reach?" (*AO*, 59 [73]). Berkouwer answers these last two questions in the negative.

Of course, the knowledge attained of the God of the philosophers by natural reason is, according to Aidan Nichols, undoubtedly "finally poor stuff when compared with the full vision of the glory disclosed in the mercy and faithfulness of Jesus Christ, 'the love of God made visible in Christ Jesus our Lord' (Rom 8:39)."[29] Yet, Nichols rightly adds elsewhere, "The God of the philosophers is indeed the same God as the Father of Jesus Christ, but he is known in two different fashions."[30] Berkouwer begs the question by assuming that the God of the philosophers is totally different from the God of Abraham, Isaac, and Jacob, and the Father of our Lord Jesus.

29. Nichols, *Epiphany*, 17–18.
30. Nichols, *Grammar of Consent*, 16.

84 PART ONE: FAITH

Fourth, Berkouwer rejects the claim implied in the conception of natural theology—a true knowledge of God can be acquired through the natural light of reason—that general revelation is an independent source of knowledge of God in addition to special revelation of Holy Scripture. How then does Berkouwer understand the relation between general and special revelation, between the universality and particularity of all God's doings? Briefly, general revelation is God's self-revelation in and through the works of creation; it refers to the universality of God's actions in created reality (nature, history, and human existence) extending to the entire world and to all men. "He did not leave himself without witness" (Acts 14:17). "Therein lies the 'general' character of this revelation of God" (*AO*, 242 [294]). Special revelation refers to the particular, concrete and historically focused activity of God's revelation in the history of Israel, in the person and work of Jesus Christ, and in the witness of the Holy Scriptures to Jesus Christ. The particularity of God's redemptive deeds should not be severed from the universality of God's action in the totality of created reality. Regarding man's capacity to appropriate God's general revelation through the things that have been made, Berkouwer calls for the absolute necessity of special revelation because the noetic influences of sin block our ability to be able to know general revelation for what it is: "this revelation deals with the knowledge of God *himself*" (*AO*, 238 [289]). Berkouwer adds, "Calvin's reference to the glasses (of faith) as the only means whereby we can know God in this book of 'nature' is of decisive significance for all reflection on general revelation" (*AO*, 235 [285]; see also, 252–53 [306]).[31] Thus, in Jesus Christ there is the unity of God's general and special revelation, of his universal and particular activity.

Since without faith in Christ no *true* knowledge is available of God's self-revelation in general revelation, according to Berkouwer, is the unregenerate man so out of connection with the revelation of God,

---

31. Calvin, *Institutes*, bk. 1, ch. 6, no. 1: "Just as old or bleary-eyed men and those with weak vision, if you thrust before them a most beautiful volume, even if they recognize it to be some sort of writing, yet can scarcely construe two words, but with the aid of spectacles will begin to read distinctly; so Scripture, gathering up the otherwise confused knowledge of God in our minds, having dispersed our dullness, clearly shows us the true God" (70). Centuries earlier St. Bonaventure makes the same point: "The world was like a damaged [*deletes*] book which God brought to perspicacity [*illuminavit*] and rectified by the book of Scripture" (as cited in Martin, "Revelation as Disclosure," 206 n. 3).

so incapable of receiving revelation because of sin, that there are no "elements of truth" at all in non-Christian religions? Berkouwer himself asks, "Do the false religions present us with a complete darkness that has fallen upon human existence, with an ignorance of which nothing more can be said than that it is non-knowing? ... Is false religion wholly false, all lies, or has it, at least in its highest moments, a participation in elements of the truth of God?" (*AO*, 128 [154–55]).

Berkouwer answers the question whether all non-Christian religions are bereft of truth by arguing that man cannot escape the revelation of God in nature, in history, and in human existence; hence, by God's common grace, the natural knowledge of God survives in the unregenerate and is manifested in man's *sensus divinitatis* ("awareness of divinity"). True enough, "he can misconstrue, avoid, exchange and pervert" this revelation, Berkouwer says, and evidence of this twisting is, in sum, found in all religions. But "in all this, religion is not independent of revelation; it is rather, a reaction, an answer, a resistance to, and defense against revelation. All human life is estranged from the life and glory of God," adds Berkouwer, "but that does not mean that man has escaped the revelation of God" (*AO*, 136 [162]).

For Berkouwer, this raises the question of whether the working of common grace among unbelievers abolishes "the antithesis [between knowing and not-knowing the true God] at all" (*AO*, 139 [166]). The brief answer to this question here must be that the only way to make sense of this claim is, according to Berkouwer, to see the natural knowledge of God, or the seed of religion, surviving in fallen individuals as "sparks" (*scintillae*) or "remnants" and "vestiges" (*rudera*), as Abraham Kuyper indeed says.[32] These remnants, says Berkouwer, are not a point of contact that could form "a stairway to grace or a preparation for conversion" (*AO* 141; see also, 142 [167; see also, 169]). Speaking of religions as such, in contrast, Kuyper holds that "the Christian religion is the only absolutely true religion in the face of all other religions as untrue and unrighteous."[33] In these other religions *qua* religions, he sees, according to Berkouwer, "anomaly, degeneration of the truth, disturbance, apos-

---

32. Kuyper, *Encyclopaedie der Heilige Godgeleerdheid*, 2:254–55; see also 227, 231 (English ed., *Principles of Sacred Theology*, 301–2; see also 275, 279).

33. Berkouwer is citing Kuyper here from *Encyclopaedie der Heilige Godgeleerdheid*, 3:451. This volume remains untranslated into English. Kuyper further observes, "Christianity and paganism are related to each other as the *plus* and *minus* forms of the same series" (*Encyclopaedie*, 2:255; *Principles*, 302).

tasy" (*AO*, 141 [168]). These other religions are the "necessary products of the apostasy to which the natural knowledge of God in the sinner must come when left to itself." Ultimately, Kuyper believes, "the common point of departure for all false religions lies ... in man's corrupted natural knowledge of God."[34] In Berkouwer's eyes, Kuyper measures the reactions of these religions in light of the *normativity* of God's general revelation, and of man's fundamental relation to that revelation. Thus, these reactions are rightly described as a reflection of the primary act of man suppressing the truth in unrighteousness (Rom 1:18).

Response to Berkouwer's Objections

What does general revelation mean, and is natural theology implied in an acceptance of it? Berkouwer rightly affirms that any knowledge of God at all, including the natural knowledge of God acquired through the medium of creation, is solely due to God's self-revelation; it is his first gift, his personal self-disclosure in, by, and through the things he has made. This claim that God's revelation in creation is a free act of God is based on the basic principle expressed by St. Irenaeus, for one, at the end of the second century: "The Lord taught us that no one is able to know God unless taught by God. God cannot be known without the help of God."[35] Indeed, Irenaeus' principle—"the knowledge of God begins with God"—goes back to St. Paul's explanation of why he justifiably accuses men of suppressing the truth in unrighteousness: "Because what can be known about God is manifest among them: God has made it manifest to them" (Rom 1:19). The second half of this verse implies a certain action on the part of God: God himself has revealed what can be known about him.[36] Berkouwer, then, rightly observes that the Catholic Church does affirm God's creation revelation, but he is amazed that this revelation rarely functions, or at best, remains in the background, in the exposition of natural theology. Yes, on the one hand, all the great teachers of the Catholic tradition—for example, Irenaeus, Maximus the Confessor, William of St.-Thierry, Alexander of Hales, Thomas

---

34. Kuyper, *Encyclopaedie*, 3:451.

35. As cited by de Lubac, *Discovery of God*, 7. On the theological epistemology of Irenaeus, see Wilken, *Spirit of Early Christian Thought*, 1–24.

36. Martin, "Revelation as Disclosure," 219–20.

Aquinas—are a witness to Berkouwer's claim about the Church.[37] On the other hand, I think he is right about his statement that the idea of creation revelation rarely functions in the exposition of natural theology. I think we can surely understand why.

Speaking of general revelation—or alternatively, as Catholic theologians sometimes do,[38] of natural revelation—to some suggests an epistemic supernaturalism, or fideism, and hence a suppression of our natural activity of human reason in grasping this revelation. But this conclusion confuses the ontic aspect of the problem of knowledge with the noetic aspect. In other words, speaking of general revelation refers only to the ontic source of the knowledge that is naturally acquired through reason (noetic aspect). In the words of de Lubac, "[it] does not mean the suppression of our natural activity of mind; it indicates the prime condition and guarantee of its validity. It does not mean substituting another principle in the place of reason; rather it means digging down to its foundation. Going back, and up, to the source. It means saying, with St. Thomas, and according to the teaching of St. Paul, that God, the creative God, manifests himself to us through his works as in a book, and that he is, moreover, the principle of the knowledge which we have to acquire by the exercise of natural reason."[39] If I understand de Lubac correctly, he is alluding here to the classical distinction between the *causa essendi* (ontic) and the *causa cognoscendi* (noetic), that is, between the metaphysical and the epistemological order of things, between what there is and how we can know it.[40] To say that the knowledge of God is grounded in, rather than known by, human reason would subvert the metaphysical order of things. Rather, as de Lubac puts it, "God is the reality which envelops, dominates, and measures our thought, and not the reverse."[41] While many things about God are known from the bottom up, as it were—i.e., from the things that God has made that permit us to come to a knowledge of his eternal power and divinity (Rom 1:19–20)—they are not "grounded" in my knowledge, but in objective reality. A "ground of knowledge" and a "ground of existence" are

---

37. On this claim, see de Lubac, *Discovery of God*, 9–10 n. 15.

38. Ibid., 12, 89–90. See also von Balthasar, *Theology of Karl Barth*, 309–11.

39. Ibid., 7–8.

40. On the import of this distinction, see Bavinck, *Gereformeerde Dogmatiek*, 2:62 (English ed., *Reformed Dogmatics*, 2:89–90).

41. Lubac, *Discovery of God*, 38.

distinct; alternatively put, we must avoid confusing the ontic and noetic aspects of knowledge.

As Bavinck rightly explains, "Although in a syllogism the existence of God may be the *conclusion*—just as, generally speaking, one may infer the existence of a worker from the existence of a piece of work—that existence in reality is still in fact the *origin* and *ground* of the existence of all things; indeed, it is even posited as such in the conclusion."[42] Bavinck understands the philosophical difference between the *causa essendi* (ontic) and the *causa cognoscendi* (noetic) in the practice of natural theology, but Berkouwer does not (see *AO*, 60–68 [74–83]). Berkouwer rolls out the standard claim that the acceptance of natural theology implies that belief in God's existence is based on arguments and proofs and hence that God has no foundation apart from them. "The contrary," says Bavinck, "rather, is the case." "The so-called proofs may introduce greater distinctness and lucidity," he adds, "but they are by no means the final ground on which our certainty regarding God's existence is ultimately based."[43] Again, that is the importance of the philosophical distinction between the *causa essendi* (ontic) and the *causa cognoscendi* (noetic) in the practice of natural theology. Bavinck recognizes this difference and hence is still able to value theistic arguments unlike Berkouwer. And as long as we are clear on the difference, *pace* Berkouwer, we will avoid identifying general revelation with natural theology.

Yet, there is more to say about why the idea of creation revelation remains in the background of exposition of natural theology. General revelation and natural theology are often confused, but the scope of natural theology is also frequently narrowed to a philosophical knowledge of God that is acquired through arguments and proofs. This stems from our preoccupation with giving arguments and theistic proofs that rationally justify the Christian faith.

In this light, we can understand why Vatican I's main concern at the start of chapter 2 of the *Constitutio dogmatica de fide catholica* is, in opposition to fideism and rationalism, to affirm man's natural ability to grasp this revelation, that is, "the subjective, creaturely presupposition for perceiving it." Given this concern, it is understandable why, as von Balthasar also remarks, "this [creation] revelation is not at all named or described as such." Still, he adds, "The passage from Paul (Rom 1:20)

---

42. Bavinck, *Gereformeerde Dogmatiek*, 2:62 (*Reformed Dogmatics*, 2:89–90).

43. Ibid., 90.

cited by the Council frequently speaks in this context—from which it cannot be disengaged—of an act of revelation.... Certainly it was not part of the intention of the Council to thematize this side of the problem. But the *Acta [Apostolicae Sedis]* speak nonetheless of an act of revelation by God. Catholic dogmatics recognizes this.... Thus we may say that the 'inferential' ascent of thought to the Creator is always borne by the Creator's prior decision to reveal himself in this nature itself."[44]

We can also avoid equating general revelation and natural theology by distinguishing the pre-philosophical natural knowledge of God from the philosophical knowledge of God acquired through natural theological arguments. *Pace* Berkouwer, the inference of reason von Balthasar is referring to in the concluding sentence of this passage—and he is referring to St. Paul's famous dictum cited by Vatican I in support of the teaching that knowledge of God is attainable by natural reason through the things that God has made—does not necessarily mean the philosophical knowledge of God acquired through theistic proofs, reasoning, and argument. The affirmation of God's reality is not the conclusion of an argument—so says de Lubac,[45] who adds, "No proof gave me God."[46] In other words, affirming the truth of God's existence is not necessarily achieved by way of the deductive consequence of the premises of an argument.[47] Rather, von Balthasar is referring to the spontaneous

---

44. Balthasar, *Theology of Karl Barth*, 309–10. The *Acta Apostolicae Sedis* publishes the official acts of the Pope and of the Roman Congregations, such as the Congregation for the Doctrine of the Faith. Pannenberg agrees with the point made by von Balthasar. He writes: "Unlike Paul, the council did not in fact expressly present the knowledge of God from the works of creation as a result of divine self-declaration. On the other hand it was obviously not the intention of the council to rule out this basis of the knowledge.... Insofar as it is a matter of stating the fact of a knowledge of God from the works of creation by the light of human reason, we cannot contradict the council statement from the NT so long as it is presupposed that this fact has its basis in God himself, who made himself known to us in his deity from creation. When Vatican II adopted the statement of Vatican I ["God, the source and end of all things, can be known with certainty from the consideration of created things, by the natural power of human reason"] in its Constitution on Revelation (*Dei Verbum* 6), it set the natural knowledge of God in the framework of salvation history according to the divine decree of revelation" (*Systematic Theology*, 1:75–76).

45. Lubac, *Discovery of God*, 38: "The thought, which is our affirmation of God, is not the conclusion of an argument."

46. Ibid., 188. This claim doesn't render philosophical proofs for God's existence superfluous.

47. Ibid., 60.

inference of reason, without argumentation and proof, through which humans arrive at (in Bavinck's words) "some firm, certain, and unfailing knowledge of God"..."in the normal course of development and in the environment in which God gave them the gift of life."[48] This knowledge, too, is always mediated by the things that God has made. In sum, this distinction implies that Berkouwer is mistaken in stating that, as a matter of principle, the Catholic tradition identifies general revelation and natural theological arguments.

Yes, Vatican I affirms the natural knowability of God: "The same holy Mother Church holds and teaches that God, the origin and end of all things, can be known with certainty by the natural light of human reason from the things that he created," and Rom 1:20 is cited in support. But whether this knowledge is necessarily reducible to natural theology in the sense of theistic proofs and arguments is another question. Indeed, in this passage there is no mention, says von Balthasar, of "how one forms proofs for God's existence: it can be known, but it cannot be demonstrated—*cognosci posse*, but not *demonstrari posse*." He adds, "Nothing is said by this against the logical validity of conclusiveness of proofs for God's existence (of which, for example, the oath against Modernism will speak later)."[49] In my judgment, von Balthasar, de Lubac, and others like John Henry Newman,[50] Jacques Maritain,[51]

---

48. Bavinck distinguishes between an "implanted knowledge of God" (*cognitia insita*) and an "acquired knowledge of God" (*cognitia acquisita*). The former "is acquired naturally and spontaneously, without reasoning and argument," whereas the latter is "acquired by reasoning and argument, reflection and demonstration along the lines of causality, eminence, and negation" (*Gereformeerde Dogmatiek*, 2:42; *Reformed Dogmatics*, 2:71). Bavinck's distinction is at the root of the development of the epistemology known as "Reformed Epistemology" in the twentieth century, advanced by neo-Calvinist philosophers such as Alvin Plantinga and Nicholas Wolterstorff. For Plantinga's mature statement of this epistemology, see his *Warranted Christian Belief*.

49. Balthasar, *Theology of Karl Barth*, 322.

50. For Newman's mature statement of his religious epistemology, see *An Essay in Aid of a Grammar of Assent*.

51. Jacques Maritain writes regarding Rom 1:19–20 that St. Paul "was thinking not only of scientifically elaborated or specifically philosophical ways of establishing the existence of God. He had in mind also and above all the natural knowledge of the existence of God to which the vision of created things leads the reason of every man, philosopher or not. It is this doubly *natural* knowledge of God I wish to take up here. It is natural not only in the sense that it belongs to the rational order rather than to the supernatural order of faith, but also in the sense that it is *prephilosophic* and proceeds by the natural or, so to speak, instinctive manner proper to the first apperceptions

and Aidan Nichols are right in distinguishing these two kinds of natural knowledge of God. Nichols correctly observes: "It has sometimes been supposed that the council committed Catholics to seek a proof of God's existence in strict logical form, a demonstration in a quasi-mathematical sense. Yet the key words of the text are ample, broad, capable of multiple interpretation: a knowledge 'through the creation' (through some, or perhaps each and every, aspect of finite being), 'by the natural light of human reason' (human reason *tout court*, with no attempt to lay down in advance what mode or style of human rationality that might be)."[52]

But to answer the question whether the natural knowability of God (in either of the two ways[53]) is necessarily implied by general revelation, and whether the denial of the former is inconsistent with affirming the latter, we must, however briefly, say something about what human reason can know, if anything, truly about God.

What can human reason, if anything, truly know of God? In answering this question, we need to avoid equivocation and hence confusion about two things. First, Berkouwer at one and the same time says that the unregenerate do not know God at all and yet there are some who have, however imperfectly, yielded to God's manifestation of himself in and through creation and hence in some sense know God. Second, is Vatican I speaking only about a *quaestio iuris* rather than a *quaestio*

---

of the intellect prior to every philosophical or scientifically rationalized elaboration" (*Approaches to God*, 17–18).

52. Nichols, *Epiphany*, 16.

53. On interpreting Rom 1:19–20, Craig writes: "The passage itself permits either interpretation [pre-philosophical as well as natural theological arguments]. But the interesting phrase '*aórata . . . nooúmena kathorâtai*' (1:20) could very well indicate that inferential reasoning is involved in the perception of God's invisible nature in the creation, meaning something like 'God's invisible nature is perceived through reflecting on the things that have been made.' . . . This pattern of reasoning was characteristic of Greek and Hellenistic Jewish thought, and it is interesting that Paul's language bears the imprint of that influence: *aidios* is found in pagan Greek from early times and frequently in Philo, but only here and in Jude 6 in the New testament; on God's *dynamis kai theiotēs*, cf. *vis et natura deorum* (Cicero, *De natura deorum* 1.18,44). A very close parallel to the Romans passage—so close, in fact, that some commentators have suggested that Paul had it in mind—is the Hellenistic Jewish work Wisdom of Solomon 13:1–9, where inferential reasoning is clearly in view, especially, verses 4–5, where we *noēsatōsan ap'autōn . . . analogōs*. Moreover, Acts 14:17 states that although God let the Gentiles go their own way, still he did not leave them *amartyron*, that is, without evidence or witness, which is constituted by the created order. These passages, which doubtless reflect a common approach to Gentile audiences, may be plausibly interpreted as a legitimation of natural theology" ("Classical Apologetics," 39–40).

facti, about a possibility rather than a fact, when it teaches that from the things that God has made man can know with certainty the existence of God by human reason?

Regarding the first point, if man suppresses the truth about God, he needs to recognize sufficiently that truth, and hence *in some sense* know it, in order not only for him to suppress it but also for God's wrath to be justified against him ("man is without excuse"). Thus, I do think that Berkouwer is inconsistent when denying that man knows God truly in any sense while at the same time affirming the epistemic connection between general revelation and man's guilt. Still, we need to answer the question what it means to *know* God truly in its deepest sense: "'To know God' . . . means to discern his presence and action, to experience him and be in communion with him, but it also means to choose him and obey him."[54] This is obviously not the kind of knowledge that is naturally acquired by the unregenerate man; it fails to result in true service of God. In that sense Berkouwer is right that the unregenerate man does not know God at all. Yet, because of God's common grace, the natural knowledge of God, however imperfect, but in some sense still true, does survive in fallen man.[55] Berkouwer acknowledges this point but it remains in the background of his thinking. That is because he is chiefly concerned about avoiding interpreting the natural knowledge of God sustained by common grace as "a preparation for conversion" and hence as a preparation for

---

54. Martin, "Revelation as Disclosure," 229. See also Leon-Dufour, *Dictionary of Biblical Theology*, 298: "[W]hen it [knowledge of God] is understood in its full breadth, [this] knowledge . . . can rightly be called 'communion' (1 John 1:3), since it is a share in the same life (John 14:19f), a union perfect in the truth of love (John17:26; see also 1 John 2:3; 3:26)."

55. In support of this claim, I cited earlier in the text Berkouwer's predecessor Kuyper, who writes: "thanks to common grace . . . knowledge of God is still possible, either by way of tradition, or as the result of personal insight, such as has been found in generous measures in the midst of paganism, in its mysteries as well as with its poets and philosophers." Similarly, we find Berkouwer's other predecessor, Bavinck, writing: "However severely Scripture judges the character of paganism, it is precisely the general revelation it [Scripture] teaches that enables and authorizes us to recognize all the elements of truth that are present also in pagan religions. . . . The Reformed theologians . . . by their doctrine of common grace . . . recognize all the truth, beauty, and goodness that is present also in the pagan world. . . . An operation of God's Spirit and of his common grace is discernible not only in the science and art, morality and law, but also in the religions" (Bavinck, *Gereformeerde Dogmatiek*, 1:290–291; *Reformed Dogmatics*, 1:318–19).

the reception of the Gospel (see *AO*, 141–42 [167, 169]). But why can't knowing these truths be a divine preparation and education, helping the human heart to be open to the fullness of truth in Jesus Christ? Yes, Christianity is positioned antithetically to all that is false in non-Christian religions (the Church believes the truth of revelation to be exclusively true and incompatible with the claims of other religions), but whatever is true is fulfilled and perfected in Jesus Christ.[56]

Furthermore, the truths about God known by unbelievers—say, Aristotle or Plato or Plotinus—belong to their respective frameworks of thought and the latter contain many errors and confusions to a greater of lesser extent that require the purification, opposition, and elimination. Accordingly, the task facing the Christian thinker involves assimilating, integrating, and finally transfiguring these truths into a Catholic framework. For Catholic thought recognizes fully that although non-Christian thought can get at some truth, the truth it holds may be part of a false perspective. The assumption here is that whatever good is found sown in the minds and hearts of men like Plato, Aristotle, Plotinus, and others must be taken captive for the truth of Christ and for the glory of God (cf. 2 Cor 10:5). In short, in Etienne Gilson's wonderfully apt phrase, Christian thinkers must "put these fragments of truth in the service of revelation."[57] This service is, as von Balthasar rightly urges, "no mechanical adoption of alien chains of thought with which one can adorn and garland the Christian dimension externally."[58] No quantifica-

---

56. Why couldn't natural theological arguments increase a person's openness to divine revelation? I dare say that philosophical arguments for God's existence may be of significant service to persons in all sorts of particular frames of mind. In sum, as John Henry Newman puts it, "[1] They often serve as a test of honesty of mind; their rejection being the condemnation of unbelievers. [2] Again, religious persons sometimes get perplexed and lose their way; are harassed by objections; see difficulties that they cannot surmount; are a prey to subtlety of mind or over-anxiety. Under these circumstances the varied proofs of Christianity will be a stay, a refuge, an encouragement, a rallying point for Faith, a gracious economy; [3] and even in the case of the most established Christian they are a source of gratitude and reverent admiration, and a means of confirming faith and hope. Nothing need be detracted from the use of the Evidences [such as natural theology] on this score; much less can any sober mind run into the wild notion that actually no proof at all is implied in the maintenance, or may be exacted for the profession of Christianity" (*Fifteen Sermons Preached*, sermon 10, no. 44, 199).

57. Gilson, *Philosopher and Theology*, 188.

58. Balthasar, "Tasks of Catholic Philosophy," 155–56. This essay was originally published in 1946. That the point von Balthasar is making is in agreement with Aquinas

tion view of knowledge here! Rather, the task implied in Gilson's phrase could be described as the "art of *breaking open* all finite, philosophical truth in the direction of Christ, and the art of *clarifying transposition*."[59] Christians are deeply committed to the "all-embracing authority of Christ" (see Matt 28:18) over all forms of creaturely truth, because in Christ are hid all the treasures of wisdom and knowledge (Col 2:2–3). For this reason, Christians "cannot rest until they have brought all these forms of into the service of the one truth. 'Everything is yours; but you belong to Christ, and Christ to God' (1 Cor 3:23)."[60]

Regarding the second point, whether God can be known with certainty through creation by human reason, there seems to be a consensus that Vatican I meant to speak only of a *de jure possibility*, and hence it prescinds from the concrete and fallen order in which we live and from the question not only of what extent but under what conditions of actuality that possibility is *de facto* realizable.[61] Why is this point important? On the one hand, Vatican I only decided that human nature—and hence natural reason's capacity to know God—is not destroyed or turned into its opposite such that (to quote Berkouwer) "a complete darkness . . . has fallen upon human existence, with an ignorance of which nothing more can be said than that it is non-knowing" (*AO*, 128 [154]). Instead, natural reason's ability to know God continues to function. On the other hand, since Vatican I decided the *de jure* question but left open the *de facto* question, it did not address the actual difficulties of attaining certainty regarding the knowledge of God when reason is left completely to itself in man's fallen condition.[62] Berkouwer is simply mistaken when he charges Vatican I with diminishing the significance of this fallen condition for man's natural reason to arrive at knowledge of God without grace and being guided by revelation.[63] Recall his claim

---

may be seen from the following statement of Aquinas: "So those who use the works of the philosophers in sacred doctrine, by bringing them into the service of faith, do not mix water with wine, but rather change water into wine" (*Summa Theologiae*, Q.2, art. 3, reply 5).

59. Ibid., 156.

60. Ibid., 158.

61. On the issue that the Council decided the *de jure* question but left open the *de facto* question, see von Balthasar, *Theology of Karl Barth*, 302–9. See also Lonergan, "Natural Knowledge of God"; and Schmaus, *Katholische Dogmatik*, 164–69.

62. Gilson, *Christianity and Philosophy*, 60.

63. Hereon see Kuyper, *Encyclopaedie*, 53; *Principles*, 106–14, esp. 1067: "[I]n every

that, according to the Catholic tradition, neither the knowing agent nor the power or ability of human reason itself has been weakened and darkened by original and actual sins and thus stands in need of restoration by redeeming grace. Here, too, Berkouwer is mistaken. Indeed, St. Thomas Aquinas contradicts him on this very point. Aquinas holds that the ability of human reason suffers the wound of ignorance and is deprived of its direction toward truth.[64] Therefore: "The researches of natural reason do not suffice mankind for the knowledge of Divine matters, even of those that can be proved by reason."[65] This leaves the proper ordering of our intellectual powers to the truth in a precarious, confused, and disordered state. This deprivation may also affect "man's desire to know the truth about creatures," adds Aquinas in his critique of immanentism, for he may wrongly desire to know the truth by not "referring his knowledge to its due end, namely, the knowledge of God."[66]

Indeed, he is right. According to Vatican I (and again in Vatican II), "*Natural* reason has the ability to know God" even *within* the concrete context of man's fallen condition. Of themselves, truths about God are naturally knowable without the supernatural light of faith. Let us recall St. Paul's point, that it is precisely this knowledge that render man without excuse. Of course this naturally knowable certainty of God's existence may be weakened and darkened by original sin and hence not rise to the level of a demonstratively proven certitude. Thus, Berkouwer is wrong in stating that "the natural light of reason in the present situation has nevertheless not been affected" (*AO*, 52 [66]). It is precisely because of the noetic effects of sin that Vatican I insists on the "moral *necessity*"[67] of divine revelation so that man can attain knowledge of God in his present fallen condition "directly, with firm certainty and

---

theory of knowledge which is not to deceive itself, the fact of sin must henceforth claim a more serious consideration."

64. Aquinas, *Summa Theologiae*, I-II, q.85, a. 3, resp. See also Gilson, *Christianity and Philosophy*, 81.

65. Ibid., II-II, q. 2, a 4 ad 1.

66. Ibid., II-II, q. 167, a. 1.

67. This phrase "morally necessary" is used by Pius XII in making the same point: "Divine Revelation must be considered morally necessary so that those religious and moral truths which are not of their nature beyond the reach of reason in the present condition of the human race, may be known by all men readily with a firm certainty and with freedom from all error" (*Humani Generis*, no. 3).

without any admixture of error."[68] Elsewhere it makes this very point even clearer: "For the most merciful Lord stirs up and helps with his grace those who are wandering astray, so that they may be able to come to knowledge of the Truth."[69] Clearly, natural reason itself is wounded; it is fallen reason. Therefore, writes Newman, "Ye must be born again," is the simple, direct form of words which she [the Church] uses after her Divine Master; "your whole nature must be re-born, your passions, and your affections, and your aims, and your conscience, and your will, must all be bathed in a new element, and reconsecrated to your Maker, and, the last not the least, your intellect."[70]

Since the whole of human nature is wounded by original sin and needs to be redeemed, made holy, sanctified, this therefore also includes the knowing powers of human reason. The redeeming grace of Christ transforms the very roots of human reason. "Grace must first purify reason, dress its wounds and guide it towards an object of which it is no longer worthy; but as soon as grace does this, it is indeed the withered reason itself, which revives under grace, the same reason, but [now] healed, saved, therefore in another state, which sees and proves."[71] In short, grace transforms reason from *within*, calling on it, as von Balthasar astutely remarks, "to fulfill the most natural aspects of its identity."[72]

Does human reason have any power to know God after the fall in sin? The answer is quite clearly yes. Yet, in developing a Catholic natural theology, the Catholic thinker should reject all those presuppositions that sometimes have badly affected the practice of natural theology. That is, we should reject the view that regards the realm of nature to be self-contained and the practice of natural theology to be world-immanent and autonomous. Correlatively, we reject the notion that human reason, with its powers and its activities, is essentially self-sufficient, abstracted from the commitment of the will, religiously neutral, and unaffected by sin. Merely on a rational foundation it cannot attain knowledge of God *prior to* and *apart* from faith, grace, and divine revelation. For in the words of Vatican I: "Since man depends totally on God as his Creator and Lord, and created reason is wholly subject to uncreated Truth, we

68. Deferrarr, *Sources of Catholic Dogma*, no. 3, 444.
69. Ibid., ch. 3, no. 14, 446.
70. Newman, *Apologia Pro Vita Sua*, 246.
71. Gilson, *Christianity and Philosophy*, 22.
72. Balthasar, *Theology of Karl Barth*, 311.

are obliged to yield to God the revealer full submission of intellect and will by faith." In this light we can understand why the main reason a Catholic natural theology does not *begin* with theistic proofs and arguments is that they are by no means the final grounds on which our certainty regarding the existence of God is based. Rather, the starting point of a Catholic natural theology is the revealed Word of God.

I conclude now with the words of Etienne Gilson: "He who wishes to think truly as a Catholic will do well never to forget the great saying of Saint Paul to the Ephesians: 'that henceforward you walk not as also the Gentiles walk in the vanity of their mind: having their understanding darkened' [4:17–18]. Saint Thomas applies this text, which he himself quotes in his *Summa Contra Gentiles* [Bk. I, 4], precisely to the truths naturally knowable to man. A Catholic natural theology is therefore possible for the intellect assisted by the divine Word which dispels the darkness and shields it from vanity."[73]

---

73. Gilson, *Christianity and Philosophy*, 22.

Bibliography

Aquinas, St. Thomas. *Faith, Reason and Theology: Questions I–IV of his Commentary on the De Trinitate of Boethius*. Translated by A. Maurer. Medieval Sources in Translation 32. Toronto: Pontifical Institute of Medieval Studies, 1987.
———. *Summa Theologiae*. Vols. 2 and 3. Translated by Fathers of the English Dominican Province. New York: Benziger, 1948.
Balthasar, Hans Urs von. *The Theology of Karl Barth*. Translated by Edward T. Oakes. San Francisco: Ignatius, 1992 [1951].
———. "On the Tasks of Catholic Philosophy in Our Time." *Communio* 20 (Spring 1993) 147–87.
Barth, Karl. "Nein." In *Natural Theology*, translated by Peter Fraenkel, 67–128. London: Centenary, 1946.
———. *Church Dogmatics*. 5 vols. in 13 parts. Translated by G. W. Bromiley, and T. H. L. Parker et al., edited by G. W. Bromiley and T. F. Torrance. Edinburgh: T. & T. Clark, 1956–69.
Bavinck, Herman. *Greformeerde Dogmatiek*. 4 vols. Kampen: Kok, 1895. Translated by John Vriend, edited by John Bolt, as *Reformed Dogmatics*. 4 vols. Grand Rapids: Baker Academic, 2003–.
Berkouwer, G. C. *De Strijd Om Het Roomsch-Katholieke Dogma*. Kampen: Kok, 1940.
———. *Conflict met Rome*. Kampen: Kok, 1949. Translated by David H. Freeman as *The Conflict with Rome*. Grand Rapids: Baker, 1958.
———. *De Algemene Openbaring*. Kampen: Kok, 1951. Translated as *General Revelation*. Grand Rapids: Eerdmans, 1955.
———. *Nieuwe Perspectieven in de Controvers: Rome-Reformatie*. Mededelingen der Koninklijke Nederlandse Akademie van Wetenschappen. Amsterdam: Noord-Hollandsche, 1957.
———. "General and Special Divine Revelation." In *Revelation and the Bible: Contemporary Evangelical Thought*, edited Carl F. H. Henry, 13–24. Grand Rapids: Baker, 1958.
———. *Vatikaans Concilie en de nieuwe theologie*. Kampen: Kok, 1964. Translated by Lewis B. Smedes as *The Second Vatican Council and the New Catholicism*. Grand Rapids: Eerdmans, 1965.
———. *Nabetrachting op het Concilie*. Kampen: Kok, 1968.
Blocher, Henri. "Karl Barth's Christocentric Method." In *Engaging with Barth: Contemporary Evangelical Critiques*, edited by David Gidson and Daniel Strange, 21–54. London: T. & T. Clark, 2008.
Brunner, Emil. "Nature and Grace." In *Natural Theology*, translated by Peter Fraenkel, 15–64. London: Centenary, 1946.
———. *The Letter to the Romans, A Commentary*. London: Lutterworth, 1959 [1938].
Byrne, Brendan. *Romans*. Sacra pagina 6. Collegeville, MN: Liturgical, 1996.
Calvin, John. *Institutes of the Christian Religion*. Vol. 1. Translated by Ford Lewis Battles, edited by John T. McNeil. Philadelphia: Westminster, 1960.
Craig, William Lane. "God Is Not Dead Yet: How Current Philosophers Argue for His Existence." *Christianity Today*, July 3, 2008. Online: http://www.christianitytoday.com/ct/2008/july/13.22.html.

―――. "Classical Apologetics." In *Five Views on Apologetics*, edited by S. B. Cowan, 26–55. Grand Rapids: Zondervan, 2000.

Cullmann, Oscar. *Christ and Time: The Primitive Conception of Time and History*. Translated by Floyd V. Filson. London: SCM, 1951 [1946].

Deferrari, Roy. J., editor. *The Sources of Catholic Dogma*. 30th ed. of Henry Denzinger's *Enchiridion Symbolorum*. St. Louis: Herder, 1957.

Dupré, Louis. *Passage to Modernity: An Essay in the Hermeneutics of Nature and Culture*. New Haven: Yale University Press, 1993.

Gilson, Etienne. *Christianity and Philosophy*. Translated by Ralph MacDonald. London: Sheed & Ward, 1939.

―――. *The Philosopher and Theology*. Translated by Cecile Gilson. New York: Random House, 1962.

Greijdanus, S. *De Brief van den Apostel Paulus aan de Gemeente te Rome*, vol. 1: *Hoofdstukken 1–8*. Amsterdam: van Bottenburg, 1933. Online: http://www.reformationalpublishingproject.com/pdf_books/Scanned_Books_PDF/KommentaarophetNieuweTestamentI_VIII.pdf.

Gunton, Colin E. *A Brief Theology of Revelation*. 1993 Warfield Lectures. Edinburgh: T. & T. Clark, 1995.

Kuyper, Abraham. *Encyclopaedie der Heilige Godgeleerdheid*, vol. 3: *Tweede Herziende Druk*. Kampen: Kok, 1909. Translated by J. Hendrik de Vries as *Principles of Sacred Theology*. Grand Rapids: Baker, 1980 [1898].

Leon-Dufour, Xavier, editor. *Dictionary of Biblical Theology*. 2nd ed. Boston: St. Paul Books, 1995.

Lonergan, Bernard J. F. "Natural Knowledge of God." In *Lonergan: A Second Collection*, edited by William F. J. Ryan and Bernard J. Tyrrell, 117–33. Philadelphia: Westminster, 1974.

Lubac, Henri de. *The Discovery of God*. Translated by Alexander Dru et al. Grand Rapids: Eerdmans, 1996 [1956].

Maritain, Jacques. *Approaches to God*. Translated by Peter O'Reilly. New York: Macmillan, 1954.

Martin, Francis. "Revelation as Disclosure: Creation." In *Wisdom and Holiness, Science and Scholarship: Essays in Honor of Matthew L. Lamb*, edited by Michael Dauphinais and Matthew Levering, 205–47. Naples: Sapientia, 2007.

Moo, Douglas J. *The Epistle to the Romans*. NICNT. Grand Rapids: Eerdmans, 1996.

Murray, John. *The Epistle to the Romans*. NICNT. Grand Rapids: Eerdmans, 1959.

Newman, John Henry. *An Essay in Aid of a Grammar of Assent*. Notre Dame: University of Notre Dame Press, 1979 [1870].

―――. *Apologia Pro Vita Sua*. Introduction by Anton C. Pegis. New York: Random House, 1950 [1870].

―――. *Fifteen Sermons Preached before the University of Oxford between 1826 and 1843*. London: Longmans, Green, 1906.

Nichols, Aidan. *A Grammar of Consent: The Existence of God in the Christian Tradition*. Notre Dame: University of Notre Dame Press, 1991.

―――. *Epiphany: A Theological Introduction to Catholicism*. Collegeville, MN: Liturgical, 1996.

Pannenberg, Wolfhart. *Systematic Theology*. Vol. 1. Translated by Geoffrey W. Bromiley. Grand Rapids: Eerdmans, 1991.

Penelhum, Terence. "Revelation and Philosophy." In *Divine Revelation*, edited by Paul Avis, 67–86. Grand Rapids: Eerdmans, 1997.

Pius XII. *Humani Generis*. Encyclical letter, August 12, 1950. Online: http://www.vatican.va/holy_father/pius_xii/encyclicals/documents/hf_p-xii_enc_12081950_humani-generis_en.html.

Schmaus, Michael. *Katholische Dogmatik*. Vol. 1. 5th ed. Munich: Max Hueber, 1953.

Schreiner, Thomas R. *Romans*. BECNT. Grand Rapids: Baker, 1998.

Wilken, Robert Louis. *The Spirit of Early Christian Thought*. New Haven: Yale University Press, 2003.

Wolterstorff, Nicholas. "Herman Dooyeweerd: An Appreciation." Online: http://rowc.blogsome.com/on-dooyeweerd-in-english/.

5

On the Liturgical Consummation of a Christian Worldview

Worldview, Worship, and Way of Life

David K. Naugle

Introduction

> Glory be to the Father, and to the Son, and to the Holy Ghost.
> As it was in the beginning, is now and ever shall be.
> World without end. Alleluia, Amen.

THERE ARE THREE SETS OF QUESTIONS ADDRESSED IN THIS ESSAY, stated here as clearly as possible. First of all, what doctrinal guidance and influence should a Christian worldview have on the content and character of the corporate worship of the church? How can and should the church's biblically based, all-embracing vision of life inform the proclamation of the Word and the administration of the sacraments in the church's worship?

Second, in turn, how might the totality of the church's worship embody and convey a scripturally based, comprehensive account of the cosmos and human existence? How should the liturgy (of whatever kind) inform and shape the essential consciousness and worldview of a Christian community? How should worship help us better understand God, the universe, our world, and ourselves? How should it also articulate the unique identity of the church as well?

Finally, what is or should be the compelling influence of both worldview and worship on the spiritual and moral formation of believers and their way of life in the world? In what way might worldview-based worship form the heart of the church's essential *paideia* (education/training) in transforming the thought-styles, loves and desires, and habits of believers into a God-glorifying Christlikeness? What epistemic (knowledge) assumptions and kind of pedagogy (teaching methods) make such transformation possible, so that believers become "constituted differently."[1] These questions address matters of worldview, worship, and way of life. Or to put it in the terms of the title of this essay, they concern the "liturgical consummation"[2] of a biblical worldview in the wholly dedicated, transformed minds, and obedient lives of countercultural Christians, as St. Paul envisions in Rom 12:1–2:

> Therefore I urge you, brethren, by the mercies of God, to present your bodies a living and holy sacrifice, acceptable to God, which is your spiritual service of worship. And do not be conformed to this world, but be transformed by the renewing of your mind, so that you may prove what the will of God is, that which is good and acceptable and perfect.

A historic way of discussing the liturgical consummation of "the mercies of God" in this dynamic trilogy of worldview, worship, and way of life is found in the classic ecclesiastical terms *Lex Credendi* (the "rule/law of belief"), *Lex Orandi* (the "rule/law of prayer"), and *Lex Agendi* (the "rule/law of action or practice"). At the heart of this celebrated discussion has been the question of the priority of the first two of these elements, belief and prayer, and the relationship of both of these to the third, action and practice.

In the Roman Catholic and Eastern Orthodox traditions, priority has been given to prayer or worship, and the formula has read *Lex orandi est lex credendi et agendi*, that is, "the rule/law of prayer is the rule/law of belief and action."[3] Prayer or worship is the source of belief and right behavior. Liturgical experience is determinative for doctrine and its ethical adornment. For example, Orthodox theologian Alexander Schmemann explains that the formation of an Orthodox worldview is not derived intellectually, "but above all from that living and unbroken experience of the church which she reveals and communicates in her

---

1. Murphy, *Teaching That Transforms*, 102.
2. The title of this essay is adapted from Pickstock, *After Writing*.
3. Attributed to Pope Coelestinus or Celestine I (AD 422–32). See Muller, *Dictionary of Latin and Greek*, 175.

worship, in the *leitourgia* always making her what she is: the sacrament of the world, the sacrament of the kingdom—their gift to us in Christ."[4] Accordingly, if one desires a deeper theological understanding or a biblical outlook on life, one need not read a book or take a class, but instead should attend worship. The church's worship is the root of the worldview/theology tree, and "what is prayed indicates what may and must be believed."[5] In biblical language, the argument could be put like this: "O taste and see that the Lord is good" (Ps 34:8).

On the other hand, by attributing supreme authority to God's Word (*sola scriptura*), the Protestant tradition has sought to exercise biblical or doctrinal control over both worship and way of life, and has generated the essential Reformational conviction that *Lex credendi est lex orandi et agendi*, that is, "the rule/law of belief is the rule/law of prayer and action" (though this expression is used rarely in Protestant circles). The Reformers in particular sought to cleanse doctrine, liturgy, and Christian practice of its imperfections, based primarily on Scripture, recognizing that, because of her frequent lapses into error and sin, the church must be reformed and always reforming (*ecclesia reformata semper reformanda*).[6] John Calvin, for instance, taught in his *Institutes* that the church must be submissive to biblical authority since it is "built upon the foundation of the prophets and apostles"[7] (Eph 2:20). Accordingly, to foster theological understanding and worldview development, someone of this persuasion will not necessarily go to church or attend worship, but will probably read Scripture or a book, take a class, or go to a conference! Indeed, the Apostle Paul corrected the liturgical infidelities of the Corinthian church on doctrinal grounds by pointing out that "God is not a God of confusion, but of peace" (1 Cor 14:33).

All of these traditions—Catholic, Orthodox, Protestant—agree that there is, or at least should be, a harmony and interplay between the principles of belief (*Lex Credendi*) prayer (*Lex Orandi*), and way of life (*Lex Agendi*). But they disagree over which of these first two should "set the pace," and both emphases, it seems, contain dangers.[8] The Catholic and Orthodox stress on "prayer" has resulted in questionable "beliefs"

4. Schmemann, *Life of the World*, 8.
5. Wainwright, *Doxology*, 251.
6. Ibid., 218–19, 251–52.
7. Calvin, *Institutes*, 75 (1.7.2).
8. Wainwright, *Doxology*, 252.

(according to some). The Protestant concentration on "beliefs" has neglected "prayer" (according to others). In other words, the former liturgical tradition generates doctrinal anxieties, and the latter doctrinal tradition is liturgically deficient. Both, it seems, have something to learn from each other—respectively, the restoration of doctrinal direction to the liturgy, and the renewal of liturgical meaning to doctrine[9]—when it comes to this triad of worldview, worship, and way of life, or the liturgical consummation of a Christian *Weltanschauung* ecclesiastically and personally.

In making a choice between these alternatives, for me the primacy of Scripture and its authority in all matters of faith and practice takes precedence. Thus, I advocate that a Christian worldview, or what is believed biblically and theologically (*Lex Credendi*), ought to be foundational and determinative of the worship of the church (*Lex Orandi*) and of Christian practice (*Lex Agendi*).

At the same time, as a corollary, I affirm their integral, reciprocal relationship, and believe that the liturgy of the church (*Lex Orandi*) ought to manifest its biblical and theological beliefs and be expressive of a Christian vision of the world (*Lex Credendi*). Furthermore, I assert that a biblical worldview (*Lex Credendi*) and form of worship (*Lex Orandi*) are central to the formation of gospel Christians, and should have a transforming impact on their way of life in the church and world (*Lex Agendi*). Hence, my model is Trinitarian in a sense, involving the "perichoretic"[10] diversity and unity of these three fundamental elements, as the diagram below indicates:

---

9. Schmemann, *Church, World, Mission*, 145–46.

10. The theological concept of *perichoresis*, also known as "circumincession," denotes that the divine essence is shared by each person of the Trinity in a manner that avoids blurring the distinctions among them. By extension, this idea suggests that the others share any essential characteristic or action that belongs to one of the three. My use of this term here is meant to suggest the integrated and interactive nature of worldview, worship, and way of life. On the terms *perichoresis* and "circumincession," see Grenz, *Pocket Dictionary*, 90, 26.

Biblical Worldview
(*Lex Credendi*)

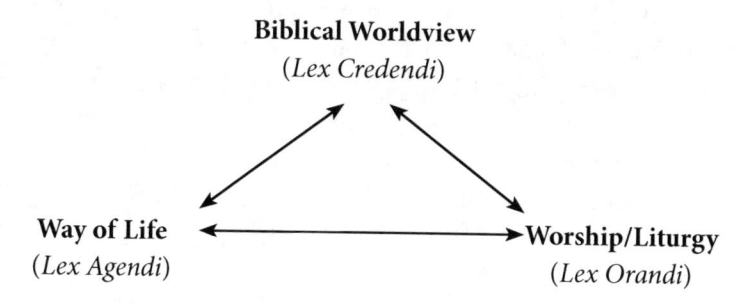

Way of Life ⟵⟶ **Worship/Liturgy**
(*Lex Agendi*)   (*Lex Orandi*)

But some problems remain. First of all, many churches understand and impart only a fragment of a Christian worldview—an "amputated" biblical vision, if you will. Second, as a result, a holistic, comprehensive Christian worldview is rarely on display in the worship of many churches. Third, this breakdown in worldview and worship has diminished the discipleship of believers, even dehumanized them, who are also encumbered, often un/subconsciously, by the idolatrous influences of contemporary culture that impact them and their congregations.

What we need, therefore, is fresh insight into the grandeur of the biblical picture of reality, its intended impact on the church and in her worship, and how this renewal of vision and worship can reconstruct the catechetical development of the saints and their walk in the world. We begin, then, with look at a biblical worldview and its theological implications that should inform and guide the church's rule or law of belief—her *Lex Credendi*.

Lex Credendi

> I believe in God the Father Almighty, Maker of heaven and earth.
>
> —Apostles' Creed

As an alternative to "worldview" definitions that are sometimes excessively cognitive in character (and perhaps bookish in tone), I propose what I believe is a biblical and more existential understanding of this notion. Since in Scripture the "heart"—in its deep connection with the human body—is the seat and source of thought, affection, volition, and worship, it seems to me that life proceeds "kardioptically," out of a vision of the embodied heart. That's what I think a worldview is: a vision or perception of God, the universe, our world, and ourselves corporally grounded in the human heart. So conceived, worldview is not just an intellectual construct, but involves the world engaging powers of the whole, embodied person as *imago Dei* in the mysterious interplay of spirituality, thought, emotion, will, and body, focused and unified in the heart. While the process of worldview formation itself is something of an enigma,[11] such a holistic outlook is pragmatically determinative for persons individually, for communities of various kinds, and for even larger groupings, all of which affect the course of human history in micro-political or macro-political ways. It is imperative, therefore, for followers of Jesus and for the church to find its cosmic bearings through an immersion and fluency in the master narrative of the canon of Holy Scripture and its graciously revealed account of truth and reality. "For too long," writes Robert Wilken in an article on "The Church's Way of Speaking," "Christianity has relinquished its role as teacher to society. Instead of inspiring the culture, it capitulates to the ethos of the world. The Church must rediscover herself, learn to savor her speech, delight in telling her stories, and confidently pass on what she has received."[12]

Similarly, from my own experience and observation, I detect that many churches and many believers lack a cohesive, comprehensive, and holistic worldview orientation. A *bits and pieces syndrome* where biblical faith is known and experienced in a fragmented, piecemeal fashion, shatters the needed cohesiveness—lots of stars but no constellation. A fundamental *disconnection between the Old and New Testaments* and its unified theological message from creation to new creation damages a needed canonical comprehensiveness—like going to a movie an hour late. An egregious *dualism and religious compartmentalization* fractures the sacred wholeness of human existence in which, as Dietrich Bonhoeffer explains, "the cause of Christ becomes a partial and provincial matter within the limits of reality," thus forming the most "colossal obstacle" to genuine faith.[13]

These three problems—one incoherent (bits/pieces), another uncanonical (OT/NT disconnect), and the other heretical (dualism)—

---

11. "As an individual passes through the various stages of human development, the heart obtains a vision of reality, even though it cannot explain exactly how." Based on William James, *Pluralistic Universe*, 13; quoted in Naugle, *Worldview*, 271.

12. Wilken, "Church's Way of Speaking."

13. Bonhoeffer, *Ethics*, 196–97.

are responsible for a severe diminishment of biblical faith, and may account, in part, for what J. I. Packer has called the "stunted ecclesiology" of evangelical Christianity, and its loss of a genuine "churchliness."[14] However, if with G. K. Chesterton we affirm that "Christianity even when watered down is hot enough to boil all modern society to rags," just think about what it would be and do if it were mixed to full strength and filled to the brim![15]

Is there, then, an alternative that is more maximalist than minimalist when it comes to substance of a Christian *Weltanschauung* and its ecclesiastical and spiritual implications? To be sure, there is, and for better or worse, I call it the worldview-driven church.[16] Churches, I propose, ought to be "driven," that is, informed and guided by the Christ-centered metanarrative of Scripture with its fulsome themes of creation, fall, redemption, and consummation, and their radical consequences in every department of life. In this I am encouraging us to recover what has been known traditionally as the "catholicity" or comprehensive wholeness of genuine biblical religion under the sovereignty and blessing of the Triune God.

Now since people rarely seem changed by routine preaching or moral exhortation, but might, indeed, be altered significantly by a "transformed imagination,"[17] at the heart of my proposal is the need for a radical enhancement and grasp of God's greatness and his larger creative and redemptive purposes for the world stirring us up at the center of our souls. Such an expanded perspective can purge our spiritual sight of the "film of familiarity,"[18] renew our "heartset" (a fusion of intellect, emotion, will, spirituality), and enable us to picture things

---

14. Packer, "Stunted Ecclesiology?" 120–27.

15. Chesterton, *Orthodoxy*, 323. He continues this thought by stating immediately afterward: "The mere minimum of the Church would be a deadly ultimatum to the world."

16. The "worldview-driven church" may be an infelicitous expression, but for the time being, I will employ this nomenclature since it suggests a unified, coherent, "big picture" conception of biblical faith that is all-embracing, universal, and cosmic in scope.

17. Brueggemann, *Hopeful Imagination*, 25.

18. Shelley, "Defense of Poetry," 497. In context, Shelley is speaking about the effects of poetry itself, and by proxy, the imagination. Thus he adds that poetry (the imagination) can create "anew the universe, after it has been annihilated in our minds by the recurrence of impressions blunted by reiteration."

anew. "Glory be!" said C. S. Lewis's old London cabby, who was turned inside out when he witnessed the founding of Narnia unexpectedly. Its unspeakably beautiful music and thousand glorious stars in the night sky shook him to the core. "I'd ha' been a better man all my life," he said, "if I'd known there were things like this."[19] The cabby's imagination was affected profoundly by this new revelation, and his life would have changed drastically had the disclosure not come too late. A similar kind of revolution in consciousness and conscience can occur in Christian people (and in the churches that comprise them) if and when they encounter a coherent, canonical, and holistic presentation of God and the total cosmos that transfigures the imagination and causes it "to fly beyond the stars!"[20] Such an expanded vision, a new "kardioptic," this vigorous perspective fixed in the embodied heart, consists of these basic theological and ministerial components.

At the theological level, a transformed Christian imagination begins with the incomparable majesty of God the Trinity, and the intention to recover the church's central purpose of worship—to glorify, love, and fear God in order to insure that the means of the church's ministry (e.g., evangelism and discipleship) are not substituted for her final end. *Biblically*, as has already been suggested, it entails the recovery of the *whole* canonical story of Scripture as creation, fall, redemption, and consummation, and understands her theological identity and purpose in the world in the context of the whole counsel of God. *Christologically*, it is committed to a view of the person and work of Jesus as the Cosmic Christ—the Creator and Redeemer of all things, the One in whom are hidden all the treasures of wisdom and knowledge (Colossians 1:15–23; 2:3)—in an effort to counteract the unfortunate effects of a limited, pietistic, and sentimental conception of the Savior. *Soteriologically*, it emphasizes the centrality of the redemptive focus of the kingdom of God, or God's redeeming reign or rule in Christ in its confrontation with evil, both as a present mystery and future hope, with converting significance for the whole of life to offset the confusion and neglect surrounding this crucial theme. *Anthropologically*, it consists of an embrace of the dignity and wholeness of the human person in body and soul as God's image and likeness and the essential offices of prophet, priest, and king, in order to overturn diminished perspectives on personhood and activ-

---

19. Lewis, *Magician's Nephew*, 100.
20. Schaeffer, *Art and the Bible*, 61.

ity, and what it means to be either male or female. *Ecclesiologically*, it maintains that Christ's church is the new, spiritual Israel in substantial continuity with the people of God in the Old Testament from Adam to Abraham to David to Jesus, showing the unity of God's purposes in redemptive history from creation to new creation, thus thwarting unwarranted discontinuities. *Eschatologically*, it understands the church as the community of saints upon whom the last days and the ends of the ages have already come (1 Cor 10:11; Heb 1:2). It recognizes that the church presently lives and ministers "at the hyphen"[21] between present kingdom redemption ("already") and the Second Advent ("not yet"). When Christ returns, he will terminate history in judgment and resurrection when all things are fully restored in the new heavens and earth where God will abide with his saints forever.

At a ministerial level, this proposal for a renovated Christian imagination through a biblical worldview-driven church begins with a *liturgical reinvigoration* of the ministry of Word and sacraments, and a call to consider the historic worship practices of the church (e.g., Christian calendar) as an ancient and yet fresh way of remembering God's mighty deeds and edifying believers. *Homiletically*, it encourages the church's preachers and teachers to rediscover the Christ-centered focus of Scripture (Luke 24:27, 44), and to adopt the canonical context of creation, fall, and redemption as the guiding hermeneutical principles for interpreting and proclaiming God's Word. *Socially*, it emphasizes the importance of cultivating Christian community as a redeemed form of human relations and alternative to contemporary uncharitable selfishness and radical individualism. *Catechetically*, it recommends the classical vision of Christian humanism as the goal of sanctification and Christian discipleship, undercutting gnostic and legalistic interpretations of spirituality and the Christian life that tend toward dehumanization. *Vocationally*, it urges congregations to promote the biblical doctrines of giftedness and calling as the basis for service, valuing the roles and contributions of *all* believers who are making a difference in the church and the world with a resolute sense of purpose. *Evangelistically*, and as the culmination of the preceding theological and ministerial components, a renewal of Christian vision entails the proclamation of the whole gospel for the whole person for the whole

---

21 Gonzalez, *¡Alabadle!*, 16; quoted in Plantinga and Rozeboom, *Discerning the Spirits*, 164.

world in the whole of life as the basis of evangelism, mission, and cultural transformation.

How utterly idiosyncratic is the church's divinely revealed account of reality! Its ontology of the Trinity, its "engraced"[22] cosmology of creation, its epistemology of revelation, and so on provide believers with an exceptional way of understanding and living in the world. In this perspective, divinely revealed theology is, indeed, restored to her proper role as the queen of the sciences, both inside and outside the precincts of the temple, so to speak. For these and other reasons, then, the church and her worldview must *not* be regarded simply as another world religion or spiritual option among a smorgasbord of possibilities. Rather, the church is absolutely unique among institutions, the product of God's creative and redemptive deeds with an identity and purpose from above for below.

At this point, my worldview church proposal intersects significantly with a variety of contemporary biblical scholars, ethicists, and theologians and the escalating movement known as radical orthodoxy. As leaders in these disciplines and this group point out, the church offers an alternative *mythos* or story (canonical gospel), a new set of rituals (Word and sacraments), and a distinctive manner of life (cruciform discipleship). This vision also entails an alternative language, history, politics, literature, psychology, economics, aesthetics, and semiotics, etc. that are central to her constitution as the *villanova* (new city), and its countercultural vision of the world.[23] In our day, this distinguishing ecclesiology stands in sharp contrast to "modern cities of eternal aspiration" rooted in human pride, and to "postmodern cities of endless desire," grounded in unbridled avarice, gluttony, and lust (especially the latter). In general, how different the biblical church, with its theology and creeds, is to "Babylon" or any ruling "culture of seduction" at any

---

22. Milbank, *Being Reconciled*, 115, quoted in Smith, *Introducing Radical Orthodoxy*, 122.

23. Leithart, *Against Christianity*, 7–8, 36. Leithart explains that this understanding of the church as a new culture, city, nation, etc. is a common theme in recent theology as seen in "New Testament scholars (N. T. Wright, Richard Horsley, James D. G. Dunn, Krister Stendahl), systematicians (John Milbank, George Lindbeck, Oliver O'Donovan), ethicists (John Howard Yoder, Stanley Hauerwas), sociologists of religion (Rodney Stark), historians of early Christianity (Wayne Meeks), and more popular writers (Rodney Clapp, Wes Howard-Brook, Barry Harvey)" (8).

time.[24] In our context, how different the church is (or should be) to the prevailing assumptions of liberal, democratic capitalism, and its humanistic, consumerist, therapeutic, and nationalistic ethos. But her immersion in this environment makes perception of her own heavenly citizenship and divine calling difficult.

The question, then, is this: how can the church as a "third race" display in worship her revealed explanation of the world and her matchless ecclesial identity through the chief liturgies of Word and sacrament? How can the church also shape believers as citizens of the divine commonwealth or kingdom who bow the knee, not to any "Caesar," but to Christ as Lord (cf. Phil 1:27; 2: 9–11; 3:20)? In other words, in light of the worldview of divine revelation, of what should the rule or law of the church's worship consist—her *Lex Orandi*?

Lex Orandi

> Almighty God, whose Son our Savior Jesus Christ is the light of the world, grant that your people, illumined by your Word and Sacrament, may shine with the radiance of Christ's glory, that He may be known, worshipped and obeyed to the ends of the earth. Through Jesus Christ our Lord, who lives and reign with You and the Holy Spirit, one God, now and forever, Amen.
>
> —Collect for the second Sunday after Epiphany,
> *Book of Common Prayer*

Many worship styles abound today, even generating what some have referred to as the "worship wars." In the midst of this rather heated exchange, I would like to suggest that, regardless of approach, the content of the church's governing narrative and her countercultural, kingdom identity ought to be clearly embodied and conveyed in the two non-negotiable ecclesiastical liturgies of Word and sacrament.[25] Whatever

---

24. Ward, *Cities of God*; quoted in Smith, *Introducing Radical Orthodoxy*, 136, 245.

25. Word and sacrament were joined together in Sunday worship by the middle of the second century as this statement from Justin Martyr, quoted in Wainwright, "Preaching and Eucharist," 444, indicates: "And on the day called Sun-day an assembly is held in one place of all who live in town or country, and the records of the apostles or writings of the prophets are read for as long as time allows. Then, when the reader has finished, the president in a discourse admonishes and exhorts us to imitate these good things. Then we all stand up together and offer prayers; and as we said before, when we have finished praying, bread and wine and water are brought up, and the president

else churches may do, these two functions are central and should reflect the church's deepest convictions and basic character. The proclamation of the Word and the rituals of baptism and Communion depict an alternative world—indeed, the true one—and participation in them constitutes the church's powerful method of education and training (i.e., *paideia*) that resocializes believers in every significant relationship and opens up astonishing new possibilities for Christian human existence.[26] We must sketch how Word and sacrament, properly construed, might accomplish this.

The Proclamation of the Word. The proclamation of Scripture, especially through reading and preaching, is an essential component of the church's liturgy. These activities are designed to exalt God, as he is made known through the declaration of his mighty deeds as Creator, Judge, and Redeemer of the world, and to build up believers in faith, hope, and love.

Bonhoeffer speaks of "the right way of reading the Scriptures together," which has application to the church at worship. He is convinced that brief verses cannot and should not take the place of reading the Scriptures as a whole. A verse or two for the day is insufficient since Holy Scripture, as he says, "is a unit and is intended to be used as such." Hence, he recommends the reading of Scripture as a narrative so that its inner theological coherence and Christ-centeredness is clear.

> As a whole the Scriptures are God's revealing Word. Only in the infiniteness of its inner relationships, in the connection of the Old and New Testaments, of promise and fulfillment, sacrifice and law, law and gospel, cross and resurrection, faith and obedience, having and hoping, will the full witness to Jesus Christ the Lord be perceived.[27]

In the matter of preaching, we must first critique the notion, quite common in evangelical churches, that the sermon should be the focal

---

likewise offers prayers and thanksgivings to the best of his ability, and the people assent, saying the Amen; and there is a distribution, and everyone participates in the elements over which thanks have been given; and they are sent through the deacons to those who are not present (*Apology* 1, 67)." John Calvin, *Institutes*, 1023 (4.1.9), also identifies a true church by these two distinguishing marks: "Wherever we see the Word of God purely preached and heard, and the sacraments administered according to Christ's institution, there, it is not to be doubted, a church of God exists."

26. Leithart, *Against Christianity*, 16; Murphy, *Teaching That Transforms*, 151.

27. Bonhoeffer, *Life Together*, 50–51.

point of the service. Should everything else either lead up to or follow from the pastor's preaching as mere preliminaries or appendices? For many, worship services are really preaching services, and little more.

Instead, I suggest that, without diminishing its importance, the sermon needs to be decentered and rightly relocated in the larger context of the total liturgy where it finds its proper place among other necessary components. It is even better not just to resituate the sermon in the context of the liturgy as a whole, but also even to say that preaching itself is a doxological act before God. Indeed, it is comparable to the Eucharist or Communion as an endeavor that recalls God's mighty deeds, whose efficacy requires the work of the Holy Spirit, and whose larger context is the eschatological purposes of God in history.[28] Doxological preaching has the potential to reconceptualize Christian consciousness and renovate Christian conduct. In Murphy's words, "As it maintains its rootedness in liturgy, . . . preaching is the Scripture-driven, worship centered act (art) that makes meaning for a community's life together as it strives to bear witness to the truth of the gospel in the world."[29]

To ascertain the true meaning of things through the preached Word, a biblical passage must be interpreted in the total context of Scripture and in light of its christocentric focus. There is no way to understand the multiplicity of Bible *stories* apart from a clear grasp of the whole biblical *story*, and it is impossible to understand Scripture correctly apart from the person of Jesus who fulfills it all. As Bonhoeffer indicated, the Bible is not a cookbook of recipes for successful living, nor is it "a box or casket of gems and jewels to be mined."[30] Rather it is a comprehensive, unified narrative that tells the true story about how God in Christ created a very good world, judged its egregious sin, and redeemed it wholly out of his mercy and grace.

These themes form the broad paradigm or pattern of thought within which the discrete texts and tales of Scripture must be interpreted, with Jesus at the center of them all. Any passage read outside this governing framework will be a misunderstood passage. A Christ-centered theology of creation, fall, and redemption, therefore, forms the proper hermeneutics for homiletics. If it fails to do so, then presuppositions and worldviews alien to the faith will undermine the interpretive

---

28. Murphy, *Teaching That Transforms*, 144.
29. Ibid., 145.
30. Sanders, "Contextual Hermeneutics," 228.

process, resulting in Scripture twisting, false consciousness, Christian malformation, and the diminishment of the divine glory.

On the other hand, when hermeneutics and homiletics are in alignment with the truth of God's Word, then the results are significant. First, the preached language of the Bible, coupled with the church's historic linguistic traditions in theology, worship, and witness, provide a new *vocabulary* by which to name and explain reality Christianly. Second, liturgically centered preaching over time also transforms the Christian *imagination* and cultivates new images of the world and the church, and the place of a reimagined self within both. Third, the homiletic dimension of biblical worship is central to *catechesis* by changing a believer's essential desires, and cultivating a variety of virtues, skills, and habits commensurate with the character of Christ.

Reading and preaching God's Word, therefore, always envisions a world that is fundamentally different from and in conflict with the fallacious ways the fallen world views the world. This new preached biblical vision is always directed toward life change and God's glory. It should engender multiple responses, not the least of which is participation in the sacraments of baptism and Holy Communion, which are also revelatory of the God's grandeur and the nature of the church's true theological identity. All who proclaim God's Word, pray, then, in this way:

> Lord, teach me that I may teach Your people; sanctify and enable all my powers, that in their full strength I may deliver Your message reverently, readily, faithfully, and fruitfully. Make Your Word a swift Word, passing from the ear to the heart, and from the heart to life and conversation, that as the rain returns not empty, so neither may Your Word, but accomplish that for which it is given, through the Word incarnate, who lives and reigns with You and the Holy Spirit, one God, forever and ever, Amen.[31]

The sacrament of baptism. Over against modernity's anti-ritualism and postmodernity's empty ritualism, and in light of the contemporary loss of significant cultural symbols and festivities (not to mention evangelicalism's suspicion of all things ritualistic, symbolic and festive), the biblical church recognizes the immense importance of her rituals—powerful expressions of a reverse conception of the world. As Stanley Hauerwas notes, "These rites, baptism and eucharist, are not just 'reli-

---

31. Adapted from a prayer by George Herbert.

gious things' that Christian people do. They are the essential rituals of our politics. Through them we learn who we are."[32]

Commissioned by the resurrected Christ (Matt 28:19–20), baptism itself is a *sacrament of initiation* into the kingdom of God and fellowship of the church. It is a royal act and a communal celebration. Through it, the person baptized is given a new identity and launched upon a lifelong vocation to manifest faithfully the commitments and character that are native to the rite itself. Despite the unfortunate superficiality and sentimentality that characterizes baptismal services in many congregations today, the act is truly a matter of death and life. It immerses baptismal candidates into Christ's death to sin and simultaneously identifies them with the triumph of his resurrection, making believers dead to sin and alive to God. It is both an exit and an entrance, a funeral and a birthday. As Paul states in Romans 6:4, "Therefore we have been buried with Him through baptism into death, in order that as Christ was raised from the dead through the glory of the Father, so we too might walk in newness of life."

By the fourth century, the church had established a relatively uniform baptismal procedure and its rather dramatic or even theatrical nature demonstrated the revolutionary significance that was attached to it. Baptisms, which were typically held during Eastertide, culminated a three-year educational or catechumenal process in which candidates received instruction in the Christian faith. During this time, they participated in worship up to the Eucharist, whereupon they were dismissed from the service in order to receive further teaching. When the day of baptism finally arrived, the candidates participated in a six-step process. First, in a rite of renunciation, the candidates stripped off their clothing as a sign of the leaving their old lives behind. They faced west, denounced Satan and all his works, and even spat upon him as a symbol of rejection. Then they turned eastward, facing the baptistery to receive the oil of exorcism. Second, the candidates were then immersed in the baptismal waters three times in the name of the Father, Son, and Holy Spirit, as a sign of dying and rising with Christ. Third, the candidates were then clothed in a white baptismal robe, symbolic of putting on Christ. Fourth, the new believers received the sign of the cross, indicating divine possession or ownership, and assuming the responsibility of

---

32. Hauerwas, *Peaceable Kingdom*, 108; quoted in Smith, *Introducing Radical Orthodoxy*, 239.

a cruciform life. Fifth, the candidates were *Christ-ened*, that is, they were anointed with oil and then called Christians. Sixth and finally, these new Christians were given candles as symbols of the light of Christ's resurrection. Once these steps were complete, the newly baptized participated in the Communion meal for the first time, sealing the meaning of their initiation into the faith.[33]

From this elaborate process, we can see how this profound action signifies an altered perception of life and the world, confers a new identity in Jesus Christ, and imparts a vocation of holiness upon those who submit to it. In essence someone baptized says:

> I used to see and live in the world this way; then I met Jesus, and now I understand everything differently. This watermark is my testimony to a radical change in my perspectives and allegiances, and with God's help, I intend to keep what my baptism signifies in a godly character and way of life.

The baptismal rite, then, testifies to the utterly new way of interpreting the meaning of life based on the story of the gospel to which baptismal candidates have committed their lives. It calls those who submit to this sacrament to embody its meaning in behavior that does justice to this new vision, and manifests grateful submission to their new Lord. This is why a failure to live accordingly constitutes a renunciation of one's essential baptismal calling. Acts of unfaithfulness are fundamentally acts of spiritual idolatry and treason, for it amounts to a repudiation of all that being a baptized Christian is meant to convey. To thwart unfaithfulness, the collect from the *Book of Common Prayer* for the first Sunday after Epiphany, commemorating Christ's baptism, seems more than appropriate:

> Father in heaven, who at the baptism of Jesus in the River Jordon proclaimed him Your beloved Son and anointed him with the Holy Spirit: Grant that all who are baptized into his Name may keep the covenant they have made, and boldly confess him as Lord and Savior; who lives and reigns with You and the Holy Spirit, one God, in glory everlasting. *Amen.*

The sacrament of Communion. The kingdom community of the church created through baptism is nurtured not only by the proclamation of God's Word, but also by frequent participation in Communion,

---

33. Murphy, *Teaching That Transforms*, 167–68.

or Holy Eucharist. For one thing, the Eucharist, or "Great Thanksgiving" as it is called, is a miniature expression of the larger cosmic sacrament. Just as we offer bread and wine in Christ to God in thanksgiving for Jesus and his sacrifice, so we are to offer gratitude to God for all we receive from him through the gifts of his creation, seeing his presence and glory in them all. James 1:17 is clear on this: "Every good thing given and every perfect gift is from above, coming down from the Father of lights, with whom there is no variation or shifting shadow." Or as Alexander Schmemann has explained it, "All that exists is God's gift to man, and it all exists to make God known to man, to make man's life communion with God."[34]

Thus, to live in this world, to receive and enjoy its gifts, and to offer them back to God in thanksgiving and praise is our fundamental function as human beings. Christ is the model as the perfect Eucharistic God/man who gave thanks to God for everything, offering his all to God. In following Christ in this, we find our true fulfillment as human beings made as the image and likeness of God. The church's regular Eucharistic celebration certainly *remembers* Christ and his self-giving act through bread and wine, but it does even more: it discloses to us the sacred character of the world as God's creation, our offering it and ourselves to God as Christ did, revealing our own identity and purpose in it as its grateful prophets, priests, and kings.

By participating in this sacrament, the church also recognizes her countervailing character as the body of Christ. Texts depicting the institution of the Supper in the Gospels, Acts, and the Epistles (Matt 26:26–29; Mark 14:22–25; Luke 22:17–20; John 6:52–59; Acts 2:42–47; 1 Cor 10:14–22; 11:23–25) disclose the particulars of the church's distinctive theological, moral, and spiritual identity, which including the following features.

- A community of food and festivity
- A community of gratitude
- A community of sharing
- A community of the blood and covenant
- A community of sacrifice and service
- A community of forgiveness and reconciliation

34. Schmemann, *Life of the World*, 14.

- A community of the eschatological kingdom
- A community of hope and expectation
- A community of symbol and memory or remembrance
- A community of prayer, worship and praise
- A community of life eternal
- A community of resurrection
- A community of divine and human fellowship and friendship
- A community of knowledge and teaching
- A community of awe, signs and wonders
- A community of gladness and joy
- A community of proclamation, evangelism, mission, salvation
- A community of oneness and unity
- A community of exclusive worship
- A community of examination and judgment

Indeed, the church consists of and should foster these features of her identity in God. In seeking to reach out to her contemporaries, therefore, the Christian community should not sell out to the values of the surrounding culture, for non-Christians neither need nor want more of what they already have. Rather she should strive to be and present what she actually is, namely, a divinely ordained "new way to be human" that eschews idolatry and dehumanizing ideologies of the age. "In the celebration of the Eucharist," Murphy states, "the church embodies a visible politics as an imaginative, utterly real alternative to the false and destructive powers and principalities. The Eucharist is the politics of the church, a Christian economy (*oikonomia*) in a world of . . . folly and injustice."[35] Pray, then, in this way:

> Lord, grant that all who share this bread and cup may become one body and one spirit, a living and holy sacrifice to Christ, to the praise of your Name. . . . Through Christ, and with Christ, and in Christ, all honor and glory are yours, Almighty God

---

35. Murphy, *Teaching That Transforms*, 194.

and Father, in the unity of the Holy Spirit, for ever and ever. AMEN.[36]

Word and sacrament, then, are the two crucial, non-negotiable elements of Christian worship that reflect the content of the biblical vision from which they come. They inform and shape the consciousness of the Christian community and help it to understand itself and the world, and to live in it aright.

Now if it is true that we learn what we do, and are shaped by the worship we offer, then the ministry of Word and sacrament ought to form the church into the wise, committed, and thankful people of God. When a Christian worldview is consummated liturgically in worship, it should also generate the peculiar way of life of biblical Christians. In fact, the church's chief apologetic resides not so much (or only) in arguments as it is in life—in Christ's first, then in the life and ministry of the church.[37] The belief and prayer of the church, then, must translate naturally into its rule or law of action and practice—its *Lex Agendi*.

Lex Agendi

> But prove yourselves doers of the word, and not merely hearers who delude themselves.
>
> —James 1: 22

Just as there should be no disconnection between worldview and worship, there should be no disjunction between worship and way of life—the liturgy of life after the liturgy of worship, establishing a fully consummated Christian worldview. Belief and mission, preaching and justice, baptism and service, Eucharist and hospitality, among other "mutually authenticating"[38] conjuncts, ought to constitute a unified whole. Word, worship, and work, in other words, should fit beautifully together. For Martin Luther, the church's theology in the Eucharist carried profound moral responsibilities to minister to those in need. He writes:

---

36. From the Holy Eucharist II in *The Book of Common Prayer*.
37. Leithart, *Against Christianity*, 100.
38. Wolterstorff, *Until Justice and Peace Embrace*, 215.

> Here your heart must go out in love and learn that this is a [Eucharistic] sacrament of love. As love and support are given to you, you must in turn render love and support to Christ in His needy ones. You must feel with sorrow all the dishonor done to Christ in His Holy Word, all the misery of Christendom, all the unjust suffering of the innocent, with which the world is everywhere filled to overflowing. You must fight, work, pray, and—if you cannot do more—have heartfelt sympathy.[39]

This suggests that Word and worship segues appropriately into the church's ethic, that is, "it is the enactment, the ritual performance, of a moral vision out of which the people of God are called to live justly and ethically.... It is to be formed by the truthful habits of speech and gesture, learned in worship, that shape the character of persons and communities for faithful witness in the world."[40] Undoubtedly, in the church's past and present, there have been and now are countless numbers of churches and Christians who have wed belief, prayer, and action together and walked in a manner worthy of the calling with which they have been called (Eph 4:1). From Paul's collection for the saints at Jerusalem to present-day multifaceted social action on the part of dedicated believers, Christians of all kinds have demonstrated their faith by their works, and have even sealed the offering of their lives to their Master in their own blood. There should be no shortage of recognition or appreciation for the expressions of Christian faithfulness throughout the history of the church.[41]

However, today we are experiencing a crisis in Christian behavior, especially in the evangelical church in North America, whose moral vision and virtue appear to be rather weak. There is a remarkable separation of *Lex Credendi* and *Lex Orandi* from *Lex Agendi*, for many, it seems, believe and pray, but fail to ground their moral lives in their prayers and beliefs.

The evidence for this concern is more than anecdotal or intuitive, as Ronald J. Sider's book *The Scandal of the Evangelical Conscience* suggests. "How bad are things?" Sider asks. "What is the depth of the

---

39. Martin Luther, "Blessed Sacrament of the Holy and True Body of Christ," quoted in Lathrop, *Holy Things*, 159.

40. Murphy, *Teaching That Transforms*, 211.

41. For example, see Schmidt, *Under the Influence*. In this work, Schmidt documents the faithfulness of the Christian community and the transformative influence of believers in fourteen key cultural domains.

scandal?" His statistics on divorce, giving, sexuality, racism, and other moral matters paint a depressing picture of undistinguished Christian ways of life.[42]

Assuming Sider's analysis is accurate, we must ask the reasons for this hypocrisy, for this nauseating lukewarmness, for this overall spiritual self-deception and slothfulness. What are the causes for this behavioral meltdown in the evangelical church today?

Far be it from me to say for sure, but I will hazard a guess that the church has succumbed to the triple jeopardy that I mentioned before. First of all, churches understand and impart only a fragment of a biblical worldview. Second, as a result, a biblical worldview is rarely on display in the churches' worship. Third, this breakdown of worldview and worship has diminished the discipleship of believers who are also encumbered, often un/subconsciously, by the deadly, idolatrous influences of contemporary culture. In short, any vestige of a biblical worldview in the church remains liturgically unconsummated, and fails to be embodied in a Christian way of life.

In terms of this third point just mentioned, *what Christians bring with them to church culturally* is as much of a problem, if not a greater one, than the church's own sins of omission or commission. As Murphy explains, "It is not always easy to recognize what we bring with us to worship—much of it is subtle and unspoken, rooted in the broader cultural socialization each of us undergoes as a citizen of the wider world, a socialization that often goes unreflected and uncommented upon. But what we bring with us to worship has everything to do with how we worship and how we are shaped [or not shaped] by the worship we offer."[43]

Murphy herself is not reticent to name and critique what she thinks are the two most powerful, modern/postmodern cultural forces that shape most people in North America today and make serious Christian discipleship so difficult. The first of these "powers" is *consumerism* and its accompanying hedonism, narcissism, and therapeutic sensibilities. The second is a *nationalism*, which confuses the flag and cross, and tends to exclude those beyond one's own borders from the hospitality of the gospel. All these sources of infidelity, however, can be reduced to one, and that is that well-intended churches and believers, even with-

---

42. Sider, *Scandal of the Evangelical Conscience*, passim.
43. Murphy, *Teaching That Transforms*, 119.

out knowing it, have simply been caught in the jaws and masticated by the teeth of the behemoth of modern and postmodern culture. Rather than being *in* the fallen world, but not *of* it, as Jesus commanded (John 17:14–18), many Christians and churches, ironically, are *of* the fallen world, but not really *in* it.[44]

What then does the breakdown in the behavior of believers suggest if not the intensity of the cultural competition, not only in terms of its moral allurements, but also in terms of its metaphysics and epistemology, that is, in its perceptions of reality and in its way of knowing and doing the truth? Not only this, but the issue of the disordered loves of believers must be addressed. Since we mostly do what we love, if our loves are disordered, so are our lives.[45] When these alien perspectives and passions invade a church already weakened by a breakdown of its own worldview and worship, the consequences can be deadly. What is to be done?

Conclusion

What we should do is what I have suggested throughout the course of this paper. First, it seems to me that piecemeal, reductionistic interpretations of the Christian faith need to be replaced with a robust biblical worldview with all of its attendant metaphysical, epistemic, and ethical implications—its countercultural *Lex Credendi*. Second, this generous vision of Christian faith and the cosmos as a whole must be embodied and communicated appropriately in the worship of the church through Word and sacrament—its countercultural *Lex Orandi*. Finally, as believers engage regularly in the liturgy and are shaped by the church's dramatic story and moral vision, Lord willing, they will be transformed at the root of their being and in the fruit of their lives, especially in the reordering of their loves and lives in all things—its countercultural *Lex Agendi*. A biblical worldview manifested in the wholly dedicated, transformed minds, and obedient lives of countercultural Christians in the church will demonstrate that her view of the world revealed in Holy Scripture is being, at least in part, liturgically consummated. To such an end, let us pray:

---

44. I owe this expression to Ken Myers.
45. See Naugle, *Reordered Love, Reordered Lives*, passim.

O Lord, my God, Ruler of heaven and earth, please direct and sanctify, set right and govern my heart, my body, my sentiments, my words, and my actions in conformity with Your law and Your commandments, that I might adorn the gospel with works of righteousness, and be found faithful to the end, by Your help and grace, O Lord Jesus Christ, who lives and reigns with You and with the Holy Spirit, one God forever and ever. *Amen.*[46]

---

46. Adapted from the *Divine Office* II. See also Trickle, *Divine Hours*, 6, 75.

Bibliography

Bonhoeffer, Dietrich. *Life Together*. Translated by John W. Doberstein. San Francisco: Harper & Row, 1954.

———. *Ethics*. Translated by Eberhard Bethge. New York: Macmillan, 1955.

Brueggemann, Walter. *Hopeful Imagination: Prophetic Voices in Exile*. Minneapolis: Fortress, 1987.

Calvin, John. *The Institutes of the Christian Religion*. Edited by John T. McNeil. Translated by Ford Lewis Battles. Library of Christian Classics 22. Philadelphia: Westminster, 1960.

Chesterton, G. K. *Orthodoxy*. In *Collected Works*, vol. 1, edited by David Dooley. San Francisco: Ignatius, 1986.

Gonzalez, Justo L. *¡Alabadle! Hispanic Christian Worship*. Nashville: Abingdon, 1996.

Grenz, Stanley, et al. *Pocket Dictionary of Theological Terms*. Downers Grove, IL: InterVarsity, 1999.

Hauerwas, Stanley. *The Peaceable Kingdom: A Primer in Christian Ethics*. Notre Dame, IN: University of Notre Dame Press, 1983.

James, William. *A Pluralistic Universe*. New York: Longmans, Green, 1925.

Lathrop, Gordon W. *Holy Things: A Liturgical Theology*. Minneapolis: Fortress, 1998.

Leithart, Peter J. *Against Christianity*. Moscow, ID: Canon, 2003.

Lewis, C. S. *The Magician's Nephew*. New York: Collier, Macmillan, 1955, 1970.

Milbank, John. *Being Reconciled: Ontology and Pardon*. Radical Orthodoxy Series. London: Routledge, 2003.

Muller, Richard A. *Dictionary of Latin and Greek Theological Terms: Drawn Principally from Protestant Scholastic Theology*. Grand Rapids: Baker, 1985.

Murphy, Debra Dean. *Teaching That Transforms: Worship at the Heart of Christian Education*. Grand Rapids: Brazos, 2004.

Naugle, David K. *Worldview: The History of a Concept*. Grand Rapids: Eerdmans, 2002.

———. *Reordered Love, Reordered Lives: Learning the Deep Meaning of Happiness*. Grand Rapids: Eerdmans, 2008.

Packer, J. I. "A Stunted Ecclesiology?" In *Ancient and Postmodern Christianity: Paleo-Orthodoxy in the 21st Century. Essays in Honor of Thomas C. Oden*, edited by Kenneth Tanner and Christopher A. Hall, 120–27. Downers Grove, IL: InterVarsity, 2002.

Pickstock, Catherine. *After Writing: On the Liturgical Consummation of Philosophy*. Challenges in Contemporary Theology Series. Malden, MA: Blackwell, 1998.

Plantinga, Cornelius, Jr., and Sue A. Rozeboom. *Discerning the Spirits: A Guide to Thinking about Christian Worship Today*. Grand Rapids: Eerdmans, 2003.

Sanders, James A. "Contextual Hermeneutics." In *The Company of Preachers: Wisdom on Preaching, Augustine to the Present*, edited by Richard Lischer, 218–29. Grand Rapids: Eerdmans, 2002.

Schaeffer, Francis A. *Art and the Bible*. Downers Grove, IL: InterVarsity, L'Abri Pamphlets, 1973.

Schmemann, Alexander. *For the Life of the World: Sacraments and Orthodoxy*. Crestwood, NY: St. Vladimir's Seminary Press, 1973.

———. *Church, World, Mission*. Crestwood, NY: St. Vladimir's Seminary Press, 1979.

Schmidt, Alvin J. *Under the Influence: How Christianity Transformed Civilization.* Grand Rapids: Zondervan, 2001.

Shelley, Percy B. "A Defense of Poetry." In *The Norton Anthology of English Literature,* edited by M. H. Abrams, vol. 2. Rev. ed. New York: Norton 1962, 1968.

Sider, Ronald J. *The Scandal of the Evangelical Conscience.* Grand Rapids: Baker, 2004.

Smith, James K. A. *Introducing Radical Orthodoxy: Mapping a Post-Secular Theology.* Grand Rapids: Baker Academic, 2004.

Tickle, Phyllis. *The Divine Hours: Prayers for Autumn and Wintertime.* New York: Doubleday, 2000.

Wainwright, Geoffrey. "Preaching and Eucharist." In *The Company of Preachers: Wisdom on Preaching, Augustine to the Present,* edited by Richard Lischer, 443–52. Grand Rapids: Eerdmans, 2002.

———. *Doxology: The Praise of God in Worship, Doctrine, and Life.* New York: Oxford, 1980.

Ward, Graham. *Cities of God.* Radical Orthodoxy Series. London: Routledge, 2001.

Wilken, Robert L. "The Church's Way of Speaking." *First Things* 155 (Aug–Sept 2005) 27–31.

Wolterstorff, Nicholas. *Until Justice and Peace Embrace.* Grand Rapids: Eerdmans, 1983.

6

Share in the Joy

The Eschatology of A. J. Conyers

William D. Shiell

WHEN INTERVARSITY PRESS RELEASED A. J. CONYERS' *THE END: WHAT Jesus Really Said about the Last Things* in 1995, they chose an erupting "fire and brimstone" volcano for the front cover. The sales division apparently never read the book, and the marketing department was not on the same track as the theological section. I remember the incredulous look on Conyers' face as he explained how the cover illustrated why he wrote this exposition of Mark 13. He wanted to avoid the tendency of modern approaches that either sensationalizes the end (the problem with the cover) or trivializes eschatology. Both views "eclipsed" a proper perspective on heaven.[1] He rejected the fear and speculation of pre-millennial dispensationalism.[2] Whether from Hal Lindsey or Tim LaHaye, these views represent ancient Gnosticism in modern attire and distract the believer from paying attention to "the times." Such sensationalism has a tendency to scapegoat people and movements deemed offensive while masking their own proclivities toward evildoing.[3] They exhaust the church, keep believers from showing love in the world, and function as a means to an end of greater domination.[4] He equally rejected the other "enlightened" view of twentieth-century modernity that trivialized the end. From this perspective, the means of progress, technology,

---

1. Conyers, *Eclipse of Heaven*, 49.
2. Idem, *Basic Christian Theology*, 225–26.
3. Idem, *The End*, 96; and later in *The Listening Heart*, 173–78. Here he was notably influenced by Stanford professor René Girard's *The Scapegoat*. This was a theme throughout his career.
4. Idem, *The End*, 19, said that speculation distracted people and caused fatigue.

and science simply would overcome the end of an apocalypse through greater knowledge, power, resources, scientific achievement, and technological advances.[5]

Three experiences shaped his thinking. The first two were deeply personal: (1) his encounter with the devastation of hurricane Hugo in 1989; and (2) his battle against cancer, living in light of the end while he courageously taught, studied, worked, and worshiped in his last season of life. Professionally, his eschatology grew from his study of Joachim de Fiore, Dale Moody, Erich Voegelin,[6] and Jürgen Moltmann.[7] With Moltmann, Conyers viewed the end not as a cause for chronological speculation but qualitative anticipation.[8] Eschatological time was marked by a series of epochs that reflected the Trinity. This view of the end left the possibility open for a new kind of future based on trinitarian hope, love, and freedom. The future defined the present by casting a bright shadow from the resurrection onto the present circumstances.[9]

A believer responds to this new kind of future with humility and service to Jesus as Lord. Hope, love, and freedom do not destroy the hierarchical systems of history or theology. Conyers viewed hierarchy as one of the gifts to the created order. Historians and theologians, however, both use hierarchy and eschatology as a means to perpetuate power and domination. Conyers suggested that humility through service and hope in God's promised future counters the power of domination. Humility, hope, hierarchy, and eschatology conquer the enemy of power.[10]

---

5. Idem, *Eclipse of Heaven*, 109–13.

6. Voegelin, *Politischen Religionen*, 40–42, discusses Joachim de Fiore, the epochs, and apocalyptic time.

7. Moltmann, *Trinity and the Kingdom*, 203–4.

8. Conyers, *God, Hope, and History*, 170, on the Joachites and Moltmann.

9. Idem, *Eclipse of Heaven*, 37–38.

10. Conyers parts with Moltmann at this point. According to Moltmann, Trinitarian love liberated people from a monotheistic hierarchical domination system and offered the hope of a future to people open to a new project. According to Moltmann, the hierarchy within the modern church and state perpetuated this domination system. Conyers, however, resisted Moltmann's tendency to abandon hierarchy. In Conyers' view, a hierarchy existed in the natural order that reflected the proper relationship between the servants of God and the Lordship of Christ. To move toward a new project would lead away from the people, nature, and life that to which the Trinity related. Compare Conyers, *God, Hope, and History*, 199–201, to Moltmann, *Trinity and the Kingdom*, 216.

This way of eschatological living as a humble servant fits Jesus' parable of the talents. The passage occurs near the end of Jesus' eschatological discourse in Matthew 25:14–30. The parable is most notably associated with the commendation delivered at many funerals: "Well done, good and faithful servant." A cursory reading of the parable, however, indicates that the themes allude to a hierarchy of master and servant. The servants are not rewarded with an eternal dwelling but are given the opportunity to have a larger responsibility and increase their share of the master's estate. As a reward, the master tells them to "Share in the joy of the master."

Most commentators view this phrase as an invitation to a banquet[11] or a characteristic of God's future eternal kingdom.[12] First-century listeners, however, likely understood the phrase in light of the "faithful household servant" tradition in the Mediterranean world. Households used servants to manage finances, oversee farms, supervise people, and educate their children.[13] Long before they were manumitted, or even

---

11. Scott, *Hear Then the Parable*, 225. For the banquet: Jeremias, *Parables of Jesus*, 60, 67; Davies and Allison, *Matthew*, 3:408; Derrett, *Law in the New Testament*, 27, 29; Snodgrass, *Stories with Intent*, 532, 535; Wohlgemut, "Entrusted Money," 108; Witherington, *Matthew*, 463. For an alternative view entirely on semiotics see Martin, "Parabole des Talents," 17.

Jeremias has controlled the discipline on this word with his "Aramaism." In the received tradition of interpretations, most of the arguments about "share in the joy" stem from the questions raised by Jeremias: "Was this phrase (and others) the *ipsissima vox* of Jesus?" The logic then follows: (1) the early church hoped for an eternity in heaven; (2) this phrase was not something Jesus said because the phrase was not part of the original form of the parable; (3) this had to be an addition by the writer or the early church; (4) this addition must then refer to the messianic banquet or wedding feast because this was one of the common hopes of the early church. For example, see Wohlgemut "Entrusted Money," 8, citing Jeremias and Scott. Wohlgemut, however, arrives at different conclusions. I am raising a different question: how the first-century audience understood the phrase in light of their culture as it was performed as a part of the Gospel of Matthew in its final form. The only notable exceptions to this interpretation are Garland, *Reading Matthew*, 464; and Hauerwas, *Matthew*, 210.

12. Brisson, "Matthew 25:14–30," 308; Ackerson et al., *Storyteller's Companion*, 93; Hultgren, *Parables of Jesus*, 278. Hagner, *Matthew 14–28*, 736, states, "The invitation may refer to the happiness of a like prosperity. For Christian readers (both in the first century and in the present), however, the language cannot fail to connote the joy of eschatological blessing, just as the judgment of the wicked servant points to eschatological judgment." This might be true, but the parable indicates that the faithful servants received the wicked servant's talent. Apparently, there were still things that could be accomplished with that talent in the present.

13. Shiell, *Reading Acts*, 15.

if slaves were never freed, masters offered incentives that benefited the slave and brought rewards and pleasure to the master. By the first century, this long-standing tradition had become a part of the culture of master-slave relationships in such a way that the average person recognized the relationship in the parable. The "joy of the master" was not an invitation to an event at the end of time but a mutually beneficial command to be experienced as part of the household.

The Faithful Household Servant in Antiquity

In order to explain how an audience understood a turn of phrase such as the one found in Matthew, we will set the phrase in the context of three ancient literary traditions in the culture through the early second century AD.[14] These Greco-Roman, Jewish, and early Christian texts offer a sense of the audience's expectation as they heard the parable in the first century.[15]

Faithful household servants can be found in each tradition. Many of these slaves were eventually freed. Some faithful servants, however, remained in the house and were rewarded by masters. In the ancient world, masters of households can treat slaves with a variety of punishments and rewards.[16] They use fear and punishment as frequent motivators. In some cases, however, they commend these faithful servants and slaves for carrying out their duties or increasing the master's wealth. They give the slaves greater responsibility and the privilege of bearing

---

14. For the purposes of this essay, I have avoided later rabbinic and Greco-Roman texts that indicate how later audiences might have viewed this work. For a helpful list of rabbinic texts related to this parable that fall outside this period, see Snodgrass, *Stories with Intent*, 522.

15. This is just one view of the ancient audience. For instance, Richard Rohrbaugh focuses on the matter of the third servant in the parable. He discusses the parable through a social-scientific lens from the perspective of a peasant in a "limited good" agrarian society. He suggests that peasants would have taken the side of the third servant and have been offended by the rewards of the first two. I am suggesting here that peasants were not the only ones in the audience and proposing that some slave peasants would have responded positively to this parable in light of this household servant tradition. Peasants' views would have been just as varied as those of others in the first century ("Peasant Reading," 33). Scott reads the parable in light of patron-client relationships in Palestine. For a critique of these views see Wohlgemut, "Entrusted Money," 119.

16. Bradley, *Slaves and Masters*, 40.

children. When the master commends the slaves, they share in the joy of the master's satisfaction, happiness, and pleasure.

Greco-Roman Examples

The Greek household codes of Xenophon and Pseudo-Aristotle provide a model for rewarding faithful servitude,[17] and Xenophon's influence extended into the first century AD.[18] In both cases the slaves carry out the work of the household as well as the unseemly work of sexual favors for the master.

Xenophon uses a dialogue to teach conduct in a household. In this case, Socrates and Isocrates discuss the expectations and rewards of a housekeeper. Socrates states:

> Now, when we appointed our housekeeper, we looked for the one who seemed to have the greatest degree of self-control in eating, drinking wine, sleeping, and intercourse with me, and who, furthermore, seemed to have memory and the foresight both to avoid being punished by us for negligence and to consider how, by pleasing us in any way, she might be rewarded by us in return. We taught her to be loyal to us by giving her a share of our joy when we were happy, and if we had any trouble, we called on her to share it too. We trained her to be eager to improve the estate by taking her into our confidence and by giving her a share in our success. We instilled a sense of justice in her by giving more honour to the just than to the unjust, and showing her that the just live lives that are richer and better suited to a free citizen than the unjust. And so we appointed her to this post. (Xenophon *Oeconomicus* 9.11–13)

A writer using the pseudonym of Aristotle shared similar views:

> Every slave should have before his eyes a definite goal or term of his labour. To set the prize of freedom before him is both just and expedient since having a prize to work for, and a time defined for its attainment, he will put his heart into his labours.

17. Harrill, *Slaves in the New Testament*, 101–3.

18. Columella *De re rustica* 1.1.12; 11.1.5 (65–70 AD) knows Varro (first century BC), Cato (third century BC), and Xenophon. Bradley, *Masters and Slaves*, 23. Cato the Elder and Cicero (*De officiis* 2.87) cite Xenophon, "making Xenophon's handbook accessible to Varro, Columella, Pliny the Younger, and Quintilian, who quote or paraphrase Cicero's translation rather than the Greek original." Harrill, *Slaves in the New Testament*, 100–101.

> ... We should also keep festivals and give treats, more on the slaves' account than on that of the freemen; since the free have a fuller share in those enjoyments for the sake of which these institutions exist." (Aristotle *Oeconomicus* 1.5.6)

In Xenophon, the slave shares in the pleasure and satisfaction of the master as well as the trouble. They receive a share of the profits and the pleasure of the master.[19] In Aristotle, the "festivals and treats" are the means by which the master gives joy even though the prize of freedom is the ultimate goal.

Roman writers described household slaves who demonstrated fidelity above and beyond the call of duty. In some cases they gave their lives for their masters.[20] In a working relationship, however, where the slave is neither freed nor facing impending death, masters rewarded slaves similarly to their Greek predecessors in a household.[21] In the Roman period, however, masters went further, following Stoic advice that mutually benefited master and servant and rewarding servants with holidays.

Varro's and Columella's household codes discuss how slaves in the Roman period share in their master's joy. Varro from the first century BC discusses the role the foremen:

> The foremen are to be made more zealous by rewards, and care must be taken that they have a bit of property of their own, and mates from among their fellow-slaves to bear them children; for by this means they are made more steady and more attached to the place.... The good will of the foremen should be won by treating them with some degree of consideration; and those of the hands who excel the others should also be consulted as to the work to be done. When this is done they are less inclined to think they are looked down upon, and rather think that they

---

19. Pomeroy, *Xenophon Oeconomicus*, 65.

20. Valerius Maximus discussed several examples "Of the Fidelity of Slaves" in his book of sayings (6.8.1–7). Six are examples of slaves who gave their lives for their masters. One master, C. Plotius Plancus, offered his life in exchange for his slaves when they were trying to protect him (6.8.5). Antius Restio experienced fidelity and infidelity. His slaves looted his house when trying to escape. A slave whom he had bound in chains allowed Antius to escape with some crafty ingenuity and gave his life for him (6.8.7). Seneca mentions an incident between Caesar Augustus, a Senator named Rufus, and his slave (*De Beneficiis* 3.27).

21. Bradley, *Slaves and Masters*, 40, indicates that the rewards served as a means of "social control."

are held in some esteem by the master. (Varro *De re rustica* 1.17.5–7)

In his household manual for operating a farm, Columella offers advice on rewarding female slaves for good work and behavior. Helping slaves was good for business.

> I now and then avenge those who have just cause for grievance, as well as punish those who incite the slaves to revolt, or who slander their taskmasters; and on the other hand, I reward those who conduct themselves with energy and diligence. To women, too, who are unusually prolific, and who ought to be rewarded for the bearing of a certain number of offspring, I have granted exemption from work and sometimes even freedom after they had reared many children. For to a mother of three sons exemption from work was granted; to a mother of more her freedom as well. Such justice and consideration on the part of the master contributes greatly to the increase of his estate... If he has made it a practice to do all this for many years, he will maintain a well-ordered discipline when old age comes; and whatever his age, he will never be so wasted with years as to be despised by his slaves. (Columella *Rust.* 1.8.18–20)

The Stoic philosopher Seneca carries this theme further. The rewards for slaves extended beyond incentives for good work or the chance to bear children. In some cases, masters bestowed gifts to slaves, and the slaves reciprocated. Seneca discusses the joy that comes to a grateful giver and recipient of a gift. The giver and recipient share mutually in joy:

> But he who is happy in having received a benefit tastes a constant and unfailing pleasure, and rejoices in viewing, not the gift, but the intention of him from whom he received it. The grateful man delights in a benefit over and over, the ungrateful man but once. But is it possible to compare the lives of these two? For the one, as a disclaimer of debts and a cheat are apt to be, is downcast and worried, he denies to his parents, to his protector, to his teachers, the consideration that is their due, while the other is joyous, cheerful, and, watching for an opportunity to repay his gratitude, derives great joy from this very sentiment, and seeks, not how he may default in his obligations, but how he may make very full and rich return, not only to his parents and friends, but also to persons of lower station. For, even if he has received a benefit from his slave, he considers, not from whom it came, but what he received. (Seneca *De beneficiis* 3.17.4)

> Consider, rather, whether in the case of slaves, a manifestation of virtue is not the more praiseworthy the rarer it is, and too, whether it is not all the more gratifying that, despite their general aversion to domination and the irksomeness of constraint, some slave by his affection for his master has overcome the common hatred of being a slave. So therefore, a benefit does not cease to be a benefit because it proceeded from a slave, but is all the greater on that account because he could not be deterred from it even by being a slave. (Seneca *Ben.* 3.19.4)

Seneca observes that these rewards benefit the entire household when the slave "supplies more than he contracted to do":

> When he exceeds the bounds of his station and goodwill toward his master, and surpasses the expectation of his master by daring some lofty deed that would be an honour even to those more happily born, a benefit is found to exist inside the household. (Seneca *Ben.* 3.22.2)

This kind of joy applies to slaves who bestow gifts on their masters. His work on the estate is viewed as a benefit.

Masters used holidays to reward some slaves and abuse others.[22] Dionysius of Halicarnassus mentions how the Roman holidays of Saturnalia and Compilatia made the slaves "more agreeable to their masters and be less sensible of the severity of their condition" (*Antiquitates romanes* 4.14.4). For five days during Saturnalia some slaves appeared to have the same freedom as their masters. Many of Martial's epigrams were written about these holidays. During Saturnalia, Martial writes, "Play, frisky slaves, do nought by play. These [whips] I shall keep under seal for five days" (Martial *Epigrams* 14.79).[23]

---

22. Ibid., cites a number of potential holidays depending on the master's relationship with the slave including Matonialia in March, Fors Fortuna on June 24, Saturnalia in December 17–23, and Compatilia in January 3–5. August 13 was a holiday for slaves alone.

23. Rimell, *Martial's Rome*, 141, 175. A slave like Flaccus, however, was sexually abused during the festivals (Epig. 11.98). Ironically, Martial describes banquets and festivals full of hedonistic pleasures that some slaves would have wanted to take refuge from.

Jewish Tradition

Jewish literature records a faithful servant tradition[24] most notably in the events surrounding Joseph, Potiphar, and Pharaoh.[25] The stories contain similar characteristics as those from the Greco-Roman traditions. Joseph serves as a household servant. His masters praise him, rejoice in his presence, promote him within the household, and reward him with greater responsibility.

The tradition begins in the Hebrew Bible with Genesis and is echoed later in the Psalms. Joseph serves in the house of Potiphar and eventually Pharaoh and is promoted from interpreter of dreams to a household servant supervisor (Gen 39:4–8; 41:39–43). The tradition is echoed in Psalm 105:21. Josephus varies the tradition a bit and notes how Joseph enjoyed the rewards and happiness that the Pharaoh bestowed on him (*Antiquities* 5.7, 6.1). Philo combines the thread of the faithful servant from ancient Judaism with the pleasure of the master in the present life (*De Abrahamo* 22.108). Household servants can be trusted not only to do their jobs but also to fight in battle and receive the rewards and spoils of the battle. They rejoice in the presence of their master (*Abr.* 40.235). In his case, those who are slaves to God are already free even if they are enslaved to an earthly master. For example, Joseph is a model of the faithful servant in a household (*De Iosepho* 8.37–40), and he notes that Joseph received the praise and acclaim of the Pharaoh and his advisers in addition to his promotion (*Ios.* 21.1–4). At one point, the Pharaoh has such a relationship with Joseph that he considers himself to be a father figure (*Ios.* 242).[26] Joseph, however, fits Philo's broader

---

24. Daniel in the house of Nebuchadnezzar also seems to fit this tradition. He rewards his servant Daniel with gifts and authority in Babylon (Dan 2:46–49). Jewish tradition was very familiar with slavery but rarely followed, if at all, the instructions regarding Jubilee. Other than the exodus events, the only two instances of manumission recorded in the Hebrew Bible are Jer 34:8–11 and Neh 5:13. Hezser, *Jewish Slavery in Antiquity*, 307.

25. Hellenistic Jewish literature contains other references to the Joseph story, e.g., *Jub.* 34.10–11; 34.18–19; 39.5–8; 40.6–9; *T. Jos.* in the Testament of the 12 Patriarchs; Wis 10.13–14; *4 Macc.* 2.1–6; and 1 Macc 2.53. The texts mentioned here feature the themes of the faithful household servant similar to other Greco-Roman and early Christian literature. For a helpful survey of the Hellenistic images of Joseph, see Gruen, *Heritage and Hellenism*, 73–109.

26. Compare his comment to *Jub.* 43.19, which also refers to Joseph as a father to Pharaoh. This picture of Joseph is not consistent in Philo's writings. Compare the contrasting retelling of the story in *De Somniis* where Joseph appears to be pursuing

argument in *Every Good Person Is Free* that those who are slaves to God have already been freed. One of the characteristics of that freedom is happiness while they are working (*Prob.* 18.121).[27]

The Hellenistic Jewish novel *Joseph and Aseneth* employs this theme in the marriage of Joseph to Aseneth, the daughter of Pentephres the priest. The story is set during the seven years of plenty when Joseph served in Pharaoh's household. Aseneth is the ultimate reward for this faithful servant because she would have been pledged to one of Pharaoh's sons. Instead Joseph insists that Pharaoh should preside over the wedding. Pharaoh blesses the union publicly (a commendation), throws a feast, rejoices in the presence of the bride and groom, and rewards both with crowns on their heads (*Jos. As.* 21.1–7). The mutually beneficial relationship is reiterated at the conclusion of the story. After one of Pharaoh's jealous sons fails in an attempt to take Aseneth, the writer refers to Joseph as one "like a father" to Pharaoh's younger son (*Jos. As.* 29.9).[28]

Early Christian References

Jesus' parables reflect elements of the faithful servant tradition in antiquity where a servant or slave is responsible for a master's or king's possessions or supervises other slaves.[29] Four parables fit the picture of a master who commends and rewards faithful service with greater responsibility without granting manumission.[30] In Matthew 25:14–30, the master not only rewards the servants with more responsibility but also invites them to "share in the joy of the master."

The Shepherd of Hermas echoes this tradition in a parable reminiscent of *Joseph and Aseneth*. In this case, the son approves of the master's joy. In the parable, a faithful servant oversees a vineyard. While the master is away, he generously helps the servants he oversees. The servant first turns a vineyard full of weeds into a flourishing crop. With

---

personal glory. Gruen, *Heritage and Hellenism*, 89. His promotion, however, in Potiphar's and Pharaoh's households are consistent in these writings.

27. Garnsey, *Ideas of Slavery*, 162–63.

28. Gruen, *Heritage and Hellenism*, 99.

29. Matt 13:24–30; 18:23–25; 20:1–15; 21:33–46; 24:45–51; 25:14–30; Mark 12:1–12; 13:34–36; Luke 12:36–38; 12:42–46; 16:1–8; 17:7–9; 19:11–27; and 20:9–19.

30. Matt 24:45–51; 25:14–30; Luke 12:42–46; 19:11–27.

his son's approval, the master rewards the servant by making him a joint heir with the master's son "because, when he had a good thought he did not put it on one side, but carried it out" (Herm. *Sim.* 5.2.7). During the celebration feast, the servant shared the food the master gave him and gave the food to his fellow servants. According to the parable, "His master heard all these events, and again rejoiced greatly at his conduct. The master again assembled his friends and his son and reported to them what he had done with the food which he had received, and they were still more pleased that the servant should be made joint heir with his son" (Herm. *Sim.* 5.2.10–11). In this context the servant, master, son, and fellow servants rejoice together that the servant is a joint heir.

Philippians employs the rhetoric of a joyful servant. Paul refers to himself as a servant (1:1) who prays with joy (1:4) and whose joy grows (1:18). He urges the audience to grow in their joy (1:26) and to identify with Christ by imitating his humble service (2:6).[31]

Summary

Greco-Roman, early Jewish, and early Christian works reflect a common tradition in the ancient world. Masters rewarded household servants or slaves for faithful service even if they were not in the process of manumission. The beneficent masters gave servants not only tangible gifts and greater responsibility but also the pleasure, joy, and commendation of the master. This joy could be characterized by a variety of rewards: words of commendation, a holiday, a promotion with greater responsibility, or a share of the inheritance. The examples from the ancient world indicate that the servant received the benefit associated with joy immediately. He did not wait, delay gratification, or hope for a reward in the afterlife. The servant experienced the joy as part of his occupation.

In some cases, the master receives a mutually beneficial joy that comes with the faithful servant. Not only does the master profit from the servant's work, but in each tradition the master is pleased because the servant does so well. The master is happy because the servant is happy, and vice versa.

---

31. Service is not the only motif at work here. Suffering plays a critical role in the argument in Philippians. Service, however, informs the content of this joy that accompanies suffering. Bloomquist, "Subverted by Joy," 270–77. Polycarp, *To the Philippians* 1.3, uses a similar phrase in his writings.

The Faithful Servants in the Parable of the Talents

The Matthean parable of the talents fits the faithful household servant theme from antiquity. The faithful servants receive tangible benefits of greater responsibility and the intangibles of commendation and joy. The master also benefits from the servants' faithfulness.

The Context of the Parable in Matthew

The parable of the talents is one of four parables featuring a managerial slave in Matthew (18:23–35; 21:33–41; 24:45–51; and 25:14–30). The third and fourth of these are the only two in which managers are commended for faithful service.[32] In addition, the parable of the talents is the third of four eschatological parables that conclude this section of the Gospel (24:45—25:46).[33] These four are interwoven conceptually and lexically. They emphasize preparation, obedience, and faithful living in light of the end.[34] Each parable shows how faithfulness can be demonstrated in different ways: the wise servant is faithful because he works when the master comes (24:45–51); the bridesmaids prepare for the wedding wisely (25:1–13); the faithful servants invest the master's resources (25:14–30); and the sheep, unlike the goats, care for the less fortunate (25:31–46).

All these parables describe blessings for the faithful and tragic consequences for the unfaithful or unprepared (24:51; 25:12; 25:30; 25:46). Two of them share the judgment of "weeping and gnashing of teeth" (24:51; 25:30). Three involve absent characters (24:46; 25:5; 25:19), two of whom are delayed (24:48; 25:5). Three involve faithful servants who are commended (24:45–46; 25:21, 23; 25:34). Two discuss possessions (24:47; 25:14).[35] All of them share varying degrees of judgment or punishment for the unprepared or unfaithful. The rewards, however, alternate between a present reality and eternal benefits.

---

32. Glancy, *Slavery in Early Christianity*, 113, notes that Matthew's particular interest in managerial slaves is not found in the other Gospels.

33. Snodgrass, *Stories with Intent*, 494.

34. Hultgren, *Parables of Jesus*, 274, notes that the first two focus on the responsibilities of all. The parable of the talents discusses the responsibilities of those given gifts.

35. Snodgrass, *Stories with Intent*, 494.

In the parable of the ten bridesmaids the maidens prepare for a banquet and await the arrival of the groom. But it is only when the groom appears that the wise, the truly prepared, are invited to the wedding feast. In the parable of the sheep and goats, the glorious king divides the people as a shepherd would the sheep from the goats. He commends those on his right for acts of service to the prisoners, naked, and poor and invites them to enter eternal life. But he turns to those on his left—those who ignored the plight of the poor and imprisoned— and condemns them to eternal punishment.

The other two parables in this series share similar themes. The parable of the wise and foolish servants opens the section (24:45–50), placing faithful service in the context of a surprise visit from the master. The audience hears and understands that faithful work is part of the responsibility even while waiting for the master to return. And when he does return, the faithful servant is rewarded with more work and responsibility.[36] The issue confronting us here, however, is how the "joy of the master" functions in this context.

The Master's Rewards

The master entrusts talents to three servants while he is away on a journey. Two of them are found faithful; one is not and is thrown into the outer darkness. His talent is taken from him and given to the others to invest. Like the wise servants in Matthew 24, these servants are responsible for the master's possessions. In this case, a talent represents a share of the master's money. The faithful servants respond to what their master has entrusted them to do.[37] These servants do not have the prospect of liberation in their immediate future much like other household servants in the ancient world. They do, however, have responsibility for a portion of the master's estate much like the stewards in the manuals of Xenophon (*Oeconomicus* 9.11–13) and Varro (*Rust.* 1.17.5–7). In the parable, two servants invest the master's talents and multiply his fortune. When the master returns, he offers three benefits: (1) a commendation, "well done, good and faithful servant"; (2) a promotion, "you have been

---

36. Such parables of surprise are part of the theme of Matthew in this section of the Gospel.

37. Witherington, *Matthew*, 464.

faithful in a few things; I will put you in charge of many things"; and (3) a command, "Share in the joy of your master."

The first two benefits echo similar benefits in other parables of rewarded household servants (Matt 24:45–51; Luke 12:42–46; 19:11–27). These no doubt fit the listeners' expectations. As we have shown, the commendation and promotion resemble similar treatment for Greco-Roman servants in the household codes (Xenophon, Varro, and Columella 1.8.18–20) and Joseph as a servant in Pharaoh's house (Philo *De Iosepho* 21.1–4). The third benefit, sharing in the master's joy, combines elements of the other two. In other words it benefits both servant and master.

The Mutual Benefits

Unlike the other parables that feature the rewarded household servant (Matt 24:45–51; Luke 12:42–46; 19:11–27), the master commands an additional benefit not found in the other parables: "Share in the joy of the master." This command combines the servant's promotion, greater responsibility, delight in his achievement, the master's delight in greater earnings, and his pleasure toward his servant.

From the context of Mediterranean culture, the five function together as mutually beneficial rewards for master and servant. Based on the literary evidence, the first-century listener was familiar with the joy that a servant shares because of good work. Seneca indicates how these benefits brought joy to the recipient (*Ben.* 3.17). Masters rewarded slaves with holidays for times of celebration (Dionysius of Halicarnassus *Ant. rom.* 4.14.4). Jewish tradition indicates rewards for slaves' good work (Philo *De Abr.* 40.235). Josephus attests to Joseph's happiness and joy because of Pharaoh's pleasure (*Antiquities* 5.7, 6.1).

Masters experienced joy because of the profits they shared and the pleasure they found in their servants. Seneca indicates that servants could bestow gifts on their masters overcoming the "hatred" for being a slave (*Ben.* 3.19.4). A master rewards a servant because of the pleasure of increased profits (Columella *Rust.* 1.8.18–20). A master's pride grows because the servant surpasses expectations, and the master enjoys extending the benefits (*Ben.* 3.22.2).

The Function of the Benefits

We can imagine how this was understood by the auditors of Matthew. The audience identified with the faithful household servants who experienced the benefits of the kingdom of heaven before they reached the end.[38] As servants, they received their responsibilities as trustees of the kingdom.[39] Much like the wise servants and the bridesmaids, they are given more time than they expected; now they must choose how to respond.[40] Knowing the greater responsibility of the task ahead as disciples on the journey, the community heard the parable as commendations to them. They could view the responsibilities, issues, and concerns of the community as signs of greater trust by the master and opportunity for them to extend the mission in the world.[41] They could experience the joy of the master by taking the words of commendation to heart, accepting the responsibility of their service and resources,[42] and sharing in the pleasurable joy of the master.

Therefore, the phrase "the joy of the master" in this parable refers to the work, responsibility, and resources that Jesus (as master) continues to bestow on the community of faithful disciples.[43] In earlier sections

---

38. Glancy, *Slaves in Early Christianity,* 129. Ackerson, *Storyteller's Companion,* 93, suggests that this is the third in a series of parables "that help the church know how to prepare for Jesus' return." Also "The parable urges the Christian community to respond to God's rule in the pattern of the first two servants. God wants the church to increase the radius of the shining of its light of good works and testimony" (110).

39. Wohlgemut, "Entrusted Money," 119, argues against the traditional allegorical rendering and views this as a call to "take steps which would lead them to share in the kingdom's wealth."

40. Boring, *Matthew,* 453.

41. Garland, *Matthew,* 242. Witherington, *Matthew,* 464. For the traditional allegorical reading of the parable where the faithful servants=faithful listeners, wicked servant=unfaithful people, master=God, see Blomberg, *Interpreting the Parables,* 216. Hultgren, *Parables,* 278, extends the allegory. Talents=gifts entrusted to disciples, including money. He also links the parable to the spiritual gifts mentioned in Rom 12:6 and 1 Cor 12:4.

42. Garland, *Matthew,* 242: "In the situation of the Christian community, the resources that have been given it apply to its task of mission in the world (10:1; 24:14; 28:19)."

43. Hauerwas, *Matthew,* 210. This joy comes as the community receives these gifts "without regret." Hauerwas says that the responsibilities are learning to tell the truth and love our enemies. I think the parable suggests that the audience would have seen any resource God has given as something worth doing. See also Snodgrass, *Stories with Intent,* 535.

of the Gospel, the audience has heard instructions about "entering" the kingdom of heaven (5:20; 7:13, 23, 19:23). This parable shows that the listeners participate in the kingdom of heaven in this life through faithful service. They do not wait until after death for a delayed reward.[44] Joy is experienced by master and servants mutually now. They share the benefits of faithful service: words of commendation, greater responsibility, and the joy that is the master's to give.

It should be noted that the number or size of responsibilities matter little. The master offers the same commendation to both servants even though the quantity of their talents differs.[45] They are not only honored by being asked to take on this responsibility, but they take great joy in the opportunity to please the master. The master experiences mutual satisfaction and shares the joy of the servant because the servant has been faithful.

The faithful servants manage the talents well because they are motivated by the master's joy rather than fear of the master's punishments.[46] They recognize that with responsibility comes accountability. The difference between fidelity and indolence resides squarely in the servants' view of the master. The third servant assumes that the master is harsh; thus acting out of fear, he buries the talent.[47] Matthew's parable highlights how accountability in the kingdom of heaven does not require fear as a motivator. In this community, the mutual joy shared by master and slave drives obedience.

The community faithfully uses the resources and experiences the joy of service because Jesus continues to enjoy seeing his servants do well, grow, and benefit. He is joyful because the servants do well. He benefits from the risky investment. His joy grows and offers something to share because material and emotional benefits extend faithful stewardship.

---

44. Brisson, "Matthew 25:14–30," 308; Ackerson et al., *Storyteller's Companion*, 109; Hultgren, *Parables*, 278; Hagner, *Matthew 14–28*, 736.

45. Snodgrass, *Stories with Intent*, 542.

46. In this way, the theme of joy subverts a cultural fear of servants to masters as well as the misunderstanding of the statement of the third servant: "I knew you were a hard man . . . so I was afraid."

47. Snodgrass, *Stories with Intent*, 535–36.

Share in the Joy

In A. J. Conyers' eschatology, "the joy of the master" fits the blessings of this life in anticipation of the life to come.[48] The end was always "at hand," but the responsible believer faced several choices. In light of the end, he could live sensationally or obediently. He could relegate the end to an appendix to the Christian life[49] or choose to live expecting God's promises to be fulfilled "on earth as it is in heaven."

Conyers chose the expectant life of a servant. From his study of theology he knew well that a Christ follower may suffer as a "station on the way"[50] and that even those further responsibilities are gifts for the journey.[51] For him to serve God meant to live life with eyes wide open to the kingdom of God breaking into the present. And despite his great sufferings, Conyers labored hopefully on the edge of eternity because hope comes to the world from God.

As he reflected on the hierarchy in Philippians 2, Conyers echoed the same language found in my reading of the parable of the faithful household servants in Matthew 25:

> The eschatological Lordship of God is received by those who, like Christ, "empty" themselves and become servants (Phil 2:7), who count others as better than themselves (Phil 2:3). ... Historically speaking, the mode of Christian faith is hope; hierarchically speaking, the mode of Christian faith is humility. Both constitute an openness to the unresolved promise of God. Humility resolves the apparent contradiction between the open promise of God in history and the order of hierarchy.[52]

Humble service positions a person to be attentive to Jesus' coming. Because the Parousia is "at hand," a believer can be alert to the kingdom breaking in through the circumstances of life. Suffering can—and perhaps should—be received as a gift. In community with others obedience gives the freedom to live within a trinitarian concept of love. And so while anticipating the end, a true believer speaks truth to society, sees

---

48. So too Moltmann, *Spirit of Life*, 299. God's joy is a part of the beginning of an experience of homecoming in the Eucharist of the Spirit.

49. Conyers, *Basic Theology*, 203.

50. Idem, *Listening Heart*, 170.

51. Idem, *The End*, 146–47.

52. Idem, *God, Hope and History*, 199.

through the mirage of dependence on technology, and embraces the world with love by imitating Christ. Based on this reading of Matthew 25, the joy of the master brings these qualities together.[53] For servants who share the same fidelity to Chip Conyers' master, we continue to share this joy.

---

53. Conyers, *The End*, 141–45.

Bibliography

Ackerson, Bruce J., Ronald J. Allen, Randall Graves, Corinne Stavish, and Michael E. Williams. *The Storyteller's Companion to the Bible. The Parables of Jesus 11.* Edited by Dennis E. Smith and Michael E. Williams. Nashville: Abingdon, 2006.

Aristotle. *Oeconomica.* Translated by G. Cyril Armstrong. 2 vols. LCL. Harvard: Cambridge University Press, 1958.

Blomberg, Craig L. *Interpreting the Parables.* Downers Grove, IL: InterVarsity, 1990.

Bloomquist, L. Gregory. "Subverted by Joy: Suffering and Joy in Paul's Letter to the Philippians." *Interpretation* 61 (2007) 270–82.

Boring, M. Eugene. *Matthew.* NIB. Nashville: Abingdon, 1987.

Bradley, K. R. *Slaves and Masters in the Roman Empire: A Study in Social Control.* Collection Latomus 185. Bruxelles: Latomus, 1984.

Bradley, Keith. *Slavery and Society at Rome.* Cambridge: Cambridge University Press, 1994.

Brisson, E. Carson. "Matthew 25:14-30." *Interpretation* 56 (2002) 207–10.

Carter, Warren, and John Paul Heil. *Matthew's Parables: Audience-Oriented Perspectives.* Catholic Biblical Quarterly Monograph Series 30. Washington, DC: Catholic Biblical Assciation of America, 1998.

Cato, Marcus Porcius. *On Agriculture.* Translated by William Davis Hooper. LCL. Cambridge: Harvard University Press, 1954.

Charlesworth, James H. *The Old Testament Pseudepigrapha.* 2 vols. New York: Doubleday, 1983–1985.

Columella, Lucius Junius Moderatus. *De re rustica.* Translated by Harrison Boyd Ash. 3 vols. LCL. Cambridge: Harvard University Press, 1941.

Conyers, A. J. *A Basic Christian Theology.* Nashville: Broadman & Holman, 1995.

———. *God, Hope, and History: Jurgen Moltmann and the Christian Concept of History.* Macon, GA: Mercer University Press, 1988.

———. *The Eclipse of Heaven: Rediscovering the Hope of a World Beyond.* Downers Grove, IL: InterVarsity, 1992.

———. *The End: What Jesus Really Said about the Last Things.* Downers Grove, IL: InterVarsity, 1995.

———. *The Listening Heart: Vocation and the Crisis of Modern Culture.* Dallas: Spence, 2006.

———. *The Long Truce: How Toleration Made the World Safe for Power and Profit.* Dallas: Spence, 2001.

Davies, William David, and Dale C. Allison. *A Critical and Exegetical Commentary on the Gospel According to Matthew.* 3 vols. ICC. Edinburgh: T. & T. Clark, 1997.

Derrett, J. Duncan M. *Law in the New Testament.* London: Darton, Longman, and Todd, 1970.

Dionysius of Halicarnassus. *The Roman Antiquities.* Translated by Earnest Cary. 7 vols. LCL. Cambridge: Harvard University Press, 1937.

Garland, David E. *Reading Matthew: A Literary and Theological Commentary on the First Gospel.* New York: Crossroad, 1995.

Garnsey, Peter. *Ideas of Slavery from Aristotle to Augustine.* W. B. Stanford Memorial Lectures. Cambridge: Cambridge University Press, 1996.

Girard, René. *The Scapegoat.* Translated by Yvonne Freccero. Baltimore: Johns Hopkins University Press, 1986.

Glancy, Jennifer A. *Slavery in Early Christianity*. Oxford: Oxford University Press, 2002.

Gruen, Erich S. *Heritage and Hellenism: The Reinvention of Jewish Tradition*. Hellenistic Culture and Society 30. Berkeley: University of California Press, 1998.

Hagner, Donald A. *Matthew 14–28*. WBC 33b. Dallas: Word, 1995.

Harrill, James Albert. *Slaves in the New Testament: Literary, Social, and Moral Dimensions*. Minneapolis: Fortress, 2006.

Hauerwas, Stanley. *Matthew*. Brazos Theological Commentary on the Bible. Grand Rapids: Brazos, 2006.

Hezser, Catherine. *Jewish Slavery in Antiquity*. Oxford: Oxford University Press, 2005.

Hultgren, Arland J. *The Parables of Jesus: A Commentary*. Grand Rapids: Eerdmans, 2000.

Jeremias, Joachim. *The Parables of Jesus*. Translated by S. H. Hooke. 2nd ed. New York: Scribners, 1972.

Martial. *Epigrams*. Translated by David Roy Shackleton Bailey. 3 vols. LCL. Cambridge: Harvard University Press, 1993.

Martin, F. "Parabole des Talents." *Semiotique et Bible Bulletin d'etudes et d'eschanges* 84 (1996) 14–24.

Moltmann, Jürgen. *The Spirit of Life: A Universal Affirmation*. Translated by Margaret Kohl. Minneapolis: Fortress, 1993.

———. *The Trinity and the Kingdom: The Doctrine of God*. Translated by Margaret Kohl. Minneapolis: Fortress, 1980.

Nolland, John. *The Gospel of Matthew: A Commentary on the Greek Text*. New International Greek Testament Commentary. Grand Rapids: Eerdmans, 2005.

Philo. *De Somniis*. Translated by F. H. Colson and G. H. Whitaker. LCL. Cambridge: Harvard University Press, 1958.

Polycarp. *To the Philippians*. Translated by Kirsopp Lake. 2 vols. LCL. Cambridge: Harvard University Press, 1985.

Pomeroy, Sarah B. *Xenophon Oeconomicus: A Social and Historical Commentary*. Translated by Sarah B. Pomeroy. Oxford: Clarendon, 1994.

Rimell, Victoria. *Martial's Rome: Empire and the Ideology of Epigram*. Cambridge: Cambridge University Press, 2008.

Rohrbaugh, Richard L. "A Peasant Reading of the Parable of the Talents/Pounds: a Text of Terror." *Biblical Theology Bulletin* 23 (1993) 32–39.

Scott, Bernard Brandon. *Hear Then the Parable: A Commentary on the Parables of Jesus*. Minneapolis: Fortress, 1989.

Seneca. *De Beneficiis*. Translated by John W. Basore. 3 vols. LCL. Cambridge: Harvard University Press, 1958.

Shepherd of Hermas. *Similitudes*. Translated by Kirsopp Lake. 2 vols. LCL. Cambridge: Harvard University Press, 1985.

Shiell, William D. *Reading Acts: the Lector and the Early Christian Audience*. Biblical Interpretation Series 70. Boston: Brill, 2004.

Shillington, V. George, editor. *Jesus and His Parables: Interpreting the Parables of Jesus Today*. Edinburgh: T. & T. Clark, 1997.

Snodgrass, Klyne. *Stories with Intent: A Comprehensive Guide to the Parables of Jesus*. Grand Rapids: Eerdmans, 2008.

Turner, David L. *Matthew*. BECNT. Grand Rapids: Baker Academic, 2008.

Udoh, Fabian E. "The Tale of an Unrighteous Slave (Luke 16:1–8 [13])." *Journal of Biblical Literature* 128 (2009) 311–35.

Valerius Maximus. *Memorable Doings and Sayings*. Translated by David Roy Bailey. 2 vols. LCL. Cambridge: Harvard University Press, 2000.

Varro, Marcus Terrentius. *On Agriculture*. Translated by William Davis Hooper. LCL. Cambridge: Harvard University Press, 1954.

Voegelin, Erich. *Die Politischen Religionen*. Stockholm: Bermann-Fischer, 1939.

Witherington, Ben. *Matthew*. Smyth and Helwys Bible Commentary. Macon, GA: Smyth & Helwys, 2006.

Wohlgemut, Joel R. "Entrusted Money (Matt. 25:14–28)." In *Jesus and His Parables: Interpreting the Parables of Jesus Today*, edited by V. George Shillington, 103–20. Edinburgh: T. & T. Clark, 1997.

7

Speaking about Transcendence
Three Medieval Theologians

Phuc Luu

> There is one body and one Spirit, just as you were called to the one hope of your calling, one Lord, one faith, one baptism, one God and Father of all, who is above all and through all and in all.
>
> —Paul of Tarsus, Ephesians 4:4–6

A. J. CONYERS WAS FASCINATED WITH THE WORD "TRANSCENDENCE" both in its sound and its meaning. The word "transcendence" has a phonetic ring, which makes it something of a joy to say. In addition to its internal alliteration, the idea of transcendence was one of paramount importance to Conyers, as he tried to articulate the state and implication of theology in our modern/postmodern world. Conyers expressed the idea of transcendence in terms of the biblical notion of "heaven," urging, "Only heaven can prevent theology from becoming psychology."[1] For Conyers, transcendence is spoken as the world "over us," as something greater than us. As modernity attempted to replace a theological narrative with the story of the autonomous human person, the light of transcendence has been eclipsed by the dark shadow of the "Enlightenment." The demise of a transcendent perspective in the modern world has led to slavery, violence, and religious intolerance.[2] The removal of the transcendent created a void that was filled with all the

---

1. Conyers, *Eclipse of Heaven*, 193.

2. Ibid., regarding toleration, 151–53; regarding power and violence, 92–103. See also idem, *Long Truce*, 169–95; *Listening Heart*, 68–95.

horrors that the moderns were trying to prevent. Heaven's eclipse was also the eclipse of the earth and all that was good, noble, and beautiful.

To highlight the premium that Conyers placed on the idea of transcendence would be to recall the long history of speaking about God's relationship to God's creation. For centuries theologians of the church and philosophers of the academy have wrestled to express the appropriate relationship between God and the world. Medieval thinkers sought to articulate the idea of God's transcendence in order to give due respect to the biblical witnesses, church doctrine, and their philosophical milieu. This article focuses on the expression of divine transcendence by Augustine of Hippo, Anselm of Canterbury, and Thomas Aquinas, and their dialogue across centuries of Christian thought.[3] Many others have added to the discussion of transcendence, but modern reflection on transcendence has centered largely on these three figures. Therefore, I have chosen these three theologians as exemplars. Here, I seek to show that, taken together, these theologians show a stream of theological development that is a synthesis of philosophy and revealed truth. I suggest ways to understand their accounts as continuous with each other and therefore an important starting point on how theology should be done in the present. How did Augustine's retreat into his soul provide him with a theology of God's greatness? Building on Augustine's notion of the supremacy of God, how did Anselm's proofs for God's existence seek to remain faithful to Augustine and yet do what Augustine had not done? How did Aquinas' "five ways" and his use of analogical predication respond to the Anselmian tradition and expand it? As a Baptist, Conyers' theological sentiment was to be Protestant in principle and [C]atholic in substance.[4] Christian theology must not reject a long tradition of thinking about God, yet it must also undergo continuous reforms. By providing a narrative of how these medieval theologians addressed transcendence, the Protestant principle of *ecclesia reformata, semper reformanda* (the church reformed, always reforming) is kept alive.

---

3. I am indebted to the faculty and students at the Center for Thomistic Studies, University of St. Thomas, Houston, for their important work in the field of medieval philosophy.

4. Conyers, "Protestant Principle, Catholic Substance," speaks about catholic with as small "c" as universal, but I use the word in a proper sense in order to tie it to the tradition of the Catholic Church, lest Protestants forget whence they came.

Confessing Transcendence in the Soul

Aurelius Augustine (354–430 AD) wrote against his intellectual opponents, the Manicheans, the Donatists, and Pelagius, and in the context of political unrest. Christianity was still in the midst of formulating a tradition of thought that was christologically unique to its Judaic roots and yet drew from the biblical tradition of Israel. Forming a conception of God that was based in the sacred texts and that spoke the language of the Greco-Roman philosophical tradition was a new endeavor, but only through Augustine's intellectual and spiritual journey could he take up this task.[5]

The often quoted prayer of Augustine in the *Confessions*, "Our hearts [*cor*][6] are restless oh God until they find rest in thee," is not only a statement about a spiritual journey but an epistemological approach. Later in the *Confessions*, the bishop pleas: "Who will enable me to find rest in you? Who will grant me that you come to my heart and intoxicate it, so that I forget my evils and embrace my one and only good, yourself?" For Augustine, knowledge of God starts with a retreat into the soul, the place of the tri-partite powers: memory, understanding, and the will.[7] The "rest" that Augustine achieved came by way of a Neo-Platonic perspective passed on by his mentor, Ambrose, and the writings of Plotinus.

In book 7, Augustine narrates his journey from the dualism of the Manicheans to the Neo-Platonism that would allow Augustine to have the conceptual apparatus in order to understand God's nature. This starts with an understanding of the relationship between the incorruptible and what Augustine had perceived in his mind:

> With all my heart I believed you to be incorruptible, immune from injury, and unchangeable. Although I did not know why and how, it was clear to me and certain that what is corruptible

---

5. What Wilken, *Spirit of Early Christian Thought*, 3, says about early Christian thinking could easily be applied to Augustine's approach: "Christian thinkers were not in the business of establishing something; their task was to understand and explain something."

6. Augustine, *Confessions*, 2. English translations are from Chadwick, except where noted. Latin insertions mine. Here, it is important to get the sense of *cor* as heart, emphasizing emotional focus, but also the sense of mind (*mens*) and soul (*anima*), which are synonymous in Augustine's epistemology.

7. Augustine, *De Trinitate* 10.11.

> is inferior to that which cannot be corrupted; what is immune from injury, and unchangeable. Although I did not know why and how, it was clear to me and certain that what is corruptible is inferior to that which cannot be corrupted; what is immune from injury I unhesitatingly put above that which is not immune; what suffers no change is better than that which can change. (7.1)[8]

Augustine points out that although uncertain, he has an intuitive sense of the relationship between those things which are incorruptible, do not suffer change, and are immune to injury with the things that are corruptible, do suffer change, and are prone to injury. These properties, incorruptibility and corruptibility, express a hierarchy of goods. However, Augustine sees the order in the "physical images," literally, the "phantasms" (*phantasmata*) of his mind. Since they are sensory impressions that come from seeing the world they do not provide a clear way to see God's true nature.

Sense perception failed Augustine because it forced him to "imagine something physical occupying space diffused either in the world or even through infinite space outside the world," even though he knew that God was not composed "in the shape of a human body." But if God was not a form of something and neither the absence of the form, then what was God? Augustine, in frustration says, "So, my heart had become gross and I had no clear vision of my own self."[9] His conception of God as both permeating everything, since God is the greatest of all things, yet separate from all things was not compatible.

The Manicheans maintained the untenable position of both God's corruptibility and incorruptibility in their presentation of their problem of evil. For them, and for Augustine at this point, the immediate observation of the evil in the world must produce the conclusion that both evil and God exist diametrically. However, Augustine saw problems in their account:

- Darkness is in opposition to God.
- If God does not oppose this evil, then God would be opened to evil's corruption.
- God then is corruptible.

---

8. Augustine, *Confessions*, 111.
9. Ibid., 7.1 (112).

Augustine makes the last conclusion by asking, "What could [evil] have done to you, if you had refused to fight against it? If they were to reply that you would have suffered injury, that would make you open to violation and destruction."[10] The following Manichean descriptions of the soul follow loosely from the previous arguments:

- The soul, which is a part of God, is mingled with what is not God and is therefore corrupt.[11]

- The only way in which to save the soul from corruption is to free it through God's word, which is described as "free, pure, and untouched from corruption."

- Because the word emanates from the same source of the soul, then it is also corrupt and cannot save the soul.[12]

The final conclusion that Augustine makes is that (1) either God is corruptible and cannot save the soul or (2) God is incorruptible and the logic of the Manicheans does not follow. The problem of the soul's ability to understand God is not far removed from the problem of evil. Evil's corruption is on the created order and the soul that does not know God. But how can one know God, by seeing the fallen world in a state of disorder? And how can one know God if one's soul is not directed toward God? The only way out of this conundrum is what Augustine says in the beginning of book 1: "You have been preached to us. My faith, Lord calls upon you. It is your gift to me. You breathed it into me by the humility of your Son, by the ministry of your preacher."[13]

Augustine moves from his dissatisfaction of the Manichean account back to the relationship of evil to the immunity of God to solve the problems they could not resolve for him:

---

10. Ibid., 7.2 (112–13).

11. The soul is described as a "member" (*membrum*) or an "offspring" (*proles*), signifying something as a part of God or generated by God. This recalls the words of Paul of Tarsus at the Areopagus in Athens (Acts 17:28); he makes his defense of the Christian faith based on the words of the Greek poet Aratus (c. late fourth century BC). Aratus was influenced by Stoic philosophy, which believed Zeus to be not a god in the form of a person, but an entity that permeated all things, including mortal beings. See Aratus, *Phaenomena*, esp. 73.

12. Augustine, *Confessions*, 7.2 (113).

13. Ibid., 1.1 (3).

> But a problem remained to trouble me. Although I affirmed and firmly held divine immunity from pollution and change and the complete immutability of our God, the true God who made not only our souls but also our bodies, and not only our souls and bodies, but all rational beings and everything, yet I had no clear and explicit grasp of the cause of evil. (7.3)[14]

Here the question of supremacy is related to the question of evil. If God is the supreme creator of all things then did God create evil? If God is then the creator of evil then does this come back to another type of dualism, a dualism within God, a god who is both good and evil? If this is not the solution then, as Augustine will later ask, *Unde est malum*? (Whence is evil?).[15]

Augustine had a sense that free will figured into the answer but could not discern how. So he moves on to address "other principles," namely, insights brought on by deduction. The following shows Augustine's attempt to form an *a priori* and deductive view of supremacy and creation revealing God's nature:

> In this way I made effort to discover other principles. I had already established that the incorruptible is better than the corruptible, and so I confessed that whatever you are, you are incorruptible. Nor could there have been or be any soul capable of conceiving that which is better than you, who are the supreme and highest good. Since it is most true and certain that the incorruptible is superior to the corruptible, as I had already concluded, had it been the case that you are not incorruptible I could obtain something better than my God. (7.4)[16]

The *resolutio* of Augustine's struggle came in the form of the Neo-Platonic philosophy that replaced Manichean dualism. The Manicheans held that good and evil were polar opposites and therefore a valuation could not exist in order for Augustine to see God's supremacy over evil.

In establishing the "principles" for his arguments, Augustine first deduced the following:

---

14. Ibid., 113.
15. Ibid., 7.5 (115).
16. Ibid., 114.

1. The incorruptible is better than the corruptible.
2. God is incorruptible.
3. God is the supreme and highest good.[17]

From this first conclusion, that God is the "supreme and highest good," further conclusions are made by Augustine, in the mode of a *reductio ad absurdum*:

1. If God is corruptible, then God would not be the highest being.
2. Then there is something better than God.
3. However, one cannot conceive of anything better than God.
4. Therefore, God is the highest being.[18]

Since (2) and (3) form a contradiction, then (4) must be true. Augustine repeats this conclusion again: "Indeed, why need we say repeatedly 'Why is the being of God not a corruptible substance?' If it were so, that would not be God."[19]

The idea that the incorruptible is greater than the corruptible can be traced back even before Plato to Parmenides. In his poem, Parmenides argues that those things that are incorruptible hold being (they are considered "what is"). The common opinion was that those things that are corruptible are in process of becoming (both "what is" and "what is not").[20] For Parmenides, change, the movement from "what is" to "what is not," between being and not being, is illusory. Can one say the cup of hot coffee sitting on the table is something that is "what is not"?

Plato's "divided line" solves the question of how to account for that which is corruptible.[21] The incorruptible (what is) is compared to the corruptible—to things that are in the process of becoming (what is and is not) and to things that do not have being (what is not). Plato's contribution is in giving an account of visible objects as participating in the realm of the forms (therefore having being), but also as corruptible (as non-beings in some respects). In this way, the soul is able to *perceive* of the objects in the world and *know* what is true in form. The "divided

17. Ibid.
18. Ibid., 7.4 (114).
19. Ibid., 115.
20. Parmenides' *Poem*.
21. Plato, *Republic*, in *Plato*, 509d6–511e3.

line" (*Republic*, bk7, 509d6–511e3) sets the stage for the doctrine of the participation of forms, which Augustine will use to show that all beings participate in God.

Evidently, part of Augustine's problem in articulating a theology of transcendence was the problem of evil:

> I search for the origin of evil, but I searched in a flawed way and did not see the flaw in my very search. I placed before my spirit a conspectus of the entire creation–all that we can perceive in it, earth, sea, air, stars, trees and mortal animals, and all that we cannot perceive, the firmament of heaven above, all the angels, and all the spiritual beings. (*Confessions* 7.5) [22]

In placing all things, both perceptible and imperceptible, before him Augustine understood the infinitude of God. If all things participated in God, and if there was a vast amount but finite number of things, then only an infinite God could cover this vast expanse of things. The "sea/sponge" (*mare/spongia*) image provides a visually compelling picture but is incomplete. If God was like "a single sea" and all of creation was like a sponge, then the sponge would be filled in every part by the "immense sea." [23] In this way, Augustine imagined creation to be full of God, but also giving God eminence over creation because God is infinite. From this Augustine concluded:

- God has created all things.
- God is good and superior to all things in all ways.
- God created good creatures.
- God, being good, "surrounds and fills" these good creatures.[24]

But then the question, "Therefore, where is evil and whence did it come, and how did it creep in?" comes back into the equation.[25] This is an essential question of *quiddity*. If evil is not (*non est*) and without being, why then must we fear what is not?[26] Augustine is not engaging in ques-

---

22. Augustine, *Confessions*, 115.
23. Ibid.
24. Ibid.
25. *Ubi ergo malum et unde et qua huc inrepsit*? Translation mine.
26. Aquinas will build on Augustine's concept of evil in *De Ente et Essentia* and the *De Malo*. Evil can be predicated as both "is" and "is not." Evil "is" when we can speak about it as "blindness is in the eye." Evil is a privation that is the lack that something

tions of theodicy, but questions of ontology, the substance of things, which is at root of his questions about God's relationship to creation. If God is the creator of all, then what, in the world, is evil?

Questions of ontology must lead to questions of substances: What is matter? Plato and Platonism provide an explicit formal cause of created substances, but the view of visual objects as a shadow of the real forms provides a weak account of the material cause of things. The form of a triangle provides the quiddity or being for all triangles that exist in the world. Also "triangularity" participates, in essence, in the Form of the Good. But the material question, the relationship between form and matter is not answered. Therefore, Augustine asks a series of questions, which I will summarize, as result of the question, *unde est malum*?:

1. If God made all things good, is the matter from which God made things somehow evil?
2. If so, then God gave form and order to things, but are things that are given to matter not able to be transformed into good?
3. If so, why did God not transform matter into good if God was all-powerful?
4. If so, why then did God not eliminate matter and, thus, evil altogether?[27]

In another series of questions, Augustine speculates on the implications of matter's existence if matter is indeed evil:

1. Could matter exist contrary to God's will?
2. If matter does exist to give substance to forms, then it is eternal. Why then was matter able to exist prior to the forms in an unordered state, i.e., before matter is given a form?
3. If all things made by God are necessarily good, then why did God not make matter good?
4. If God did not create matter and if God needed matter to create good things, then is God less than all-powerful?[28]

---

potentially has. It would not make sense to say, "the rock is blind." In another way, evil is spoken of as "is not," because it does not have any real existence.

27. Augustine, *Confessions* 7.5 (115–16).
28. Ibid.

These questions weighed heavily on Augustine's "unhappy breast," for his heart had not resolved them. But Augustine paused in the midst of questioning to declare, "There is a firm place in my heart for the faith, within the Catholic Church, in our Christ, 'our Lord and Saviour.'"[29] It is noteworthy to state that in Plato's "divided line," belief or faith (πίστις translated as *fides*) is a lower form of cognitive awareness than "understanding" or *intellectus*. However, the bishop does not discount faith as a way to understanding and he goes on to say, "In many respects this faith was still unformed and hesitant about the norm of doctrine. Yet my mind did not abandon it, but daily drank from it more and more."[30]

What the Neo-Platonic books provided was a tool for him to interpret the Scriptures. Augustine shows where he read about the *logos* in the prologue of John's Gospel (1:1–18), in "the same sense and supported by numerous and varied reasons" as the Plotinus's texts (*Confessions* 9.13).[31] He also read the Epistle of Paul to the Philippians (2:6–11) in the same way, but clarifies that the Neo-Platonic texts did not have the same content. These Christian texts point to the intimacy between the Son—preexisting as the *logos* and being himself God—and God. However, the preexistence of the *logos* is not only a mediating principle, as the Neo-Platonists taught, but also, as Vaught describes, "a dynamic source from which finite beings unfold continuously."[32] All things created came through the *logos* as attested by the Scriptures, but this also points to the doctrine of participated beings.

This insight would cumulate in Augustine's vision named the "first vision passage" by Scott MacDonald:[33]

> By the Platonic books I was admonished to return into myself. With you as my guide I entered into my innermost citadel, and was given power to do so because you had become my helper (Ps. 29:11). I entered and with my soul's eye, such as it was, saw above that same eye of my soul the immutable light higher than

---

29. Ibid.

30. Since faith (πίστις) is a low level of cognitive awareness in Plato's divided line, perhaps further inquiry can be made as the value of faith and therefore, what *kind* of faith is actually expressed in Christian devotion.

31. Augustine, *Confessions*, 121.

32. Vaught, *Encounters with God*, 42.

33. MacDonald, "Divine Nature," 71–72, n. 4, argues that there are three vision passages all of which describe the same event and not different visions and all of which "report a successful vision of God."

my mind—not the light of every day, obvious to anyone, nor a larger version of the same kind which would, as it were, have given out a much brighter light and filled everything with its magnitude. It was not that light, but a different thing, utterly different from all our kinds of light. It transcended my mind, not in the way that oil floats on water, nor heaven is above earth. It was superior because it made me, and I was inferior because I was made by it. (10.16)[34]

Augustine's retreat into his soul led him a vision of a transcendent light. In order for Augustine to understand the *objects* of this world—both intelligible and visual—he must have a source of illumination greater than that of natural light. This light transcended his mind not with a spatial magnitude, but a metaphysical magnitude; the light was greater than him because it gave him existence, not as only the proximate source of his being, but the ultimate source of his being. Augustine could not fall back on the Manichean mistake in seeing "infinite" as being a factor of space.[35] God, as ultimate being who provides being to God's creatures, is seen in God's identity expressed when Moses encountered God: "Indeed truly, I am who I am" (Exod 3:14).[36] And in encountering the God who spoke as the "I AM," Augustine's doubt left him and he heard "in the way one hears within the heart."[37] Only after experiencing this vision of God's "invisible nature" did Augustine turn to the truth that is "understood from the things that are made" (Rom 1:20).[38]

In regard to the created universe there was still the persistent problem of evil. However, Augustine's vision of God's transcendence brought him the solution. In relation to God, at least two things can be said about the existence of things:

---

34. Augustine, *Confessions*, 123.

35. See the parallel passage in ibid., 7.20 (130): "But from the disappointment I suffered I perceived that darknesses of my soul would not allow me to complete these sublimities. Yet I was certain that you are infinite without being infinitely diffused through finite space. I was sure that you truly are, and are always the same; that you never become other or different in any part or by any movement of position, whereas all other things derive from you, as is proved by the fact that they exist."

36. Translation mine. Cf. Augustine's *Immo uero ego sum qui sum* to the Vulgate's *ego sum qui sum* of the same passage in Exodus.

37. Augustine, *Confessions*, 124.

38. Ibid. This passage from Romans is repeated in the other vision passages, twice in xvii (23) and once at the beginning of 7.20.

1. Things cannot be said absolutely to be.
2. Things cannot be said absolutely not to be.[39]

Again this is a problem solved by Plato, drawn out in Parmenides. What Augustine adds is the following:

1. Things cannot be said absolutely to be because they are not God.
2. Things cannot be said absolutely not because they are made by God.[40]

Because all things exist in an intermediate state (between "what is" and "what is not") they are contingent. And then there is an extrapolation: [NL 1-2]

1. All things are good because they are made by God.
2. All things are corrupted because they are not completely good, i.e., they suffer privation.

He concludes:

1. God makes incorruptible substances, e.g., the heavens, and they are a greater good.
2. God makes corruptible substances and only those things that are good can be subjected to corruption.[41]

Evil therefore is the lack of the good, not a substance, but lacking in substance. Augustine concludes: "For you evil does not exist at all [*non est*], and not only for you but for your created universe, because there is nothing outside it which could break in and destroy the order which you have impose upon it" (13.19).[42] Evil is then a privation that affects the created order and corruptible substances. Finally, Augustine could have a view of God's supremacy that worked out the problem of the effects of evil, particularly its non-existence.

A final key in Augustine's understanding of the greatness of God is a unified view of creation. Things taken individually are themselves good (*bona*), but things taken collectively are very good (*valde bona*; 12.18).

39. Ibid., 7.11 (124).
40. Ibid.
41. Ibid., 7.12 (124–25).
42. Ibid., 7.13 (125).

Seeing the goodness in things in themselves and reasoning about their existence and privation were not enough. The unification of all things displayed the highest good, and this superlative was in a quality of being not in a quantitative sense. Under the Manichean understanding of infinite Augustine saw God's infinite and eternal nature as a factor of space and time. Under a Neo-Platonic view he envisaged God's infinity and eternality as a factor of quality in that God provided being (15.21).[43] Evil was not substantive, but a lack of substance that "twisted away from the highest substance, you O God" (16.22).[44]

Neo-Platonism, which could easily be accused of a mind/body dualism, provided Augustine a way to know the highest good through the powers of his soul. It is not that Augustine's spiritual journey ended in this discovery. Neo-Platonism provided the conceptual basis to know God as incorruptible, supreme, and true, providing a basis for a vision of God that was consistent with the biblical witness and the teachings of the Christian faith. This insight did not only provide a philosophical basis for understanding God's transcendence, but created the foundation of his conversion and worship of God: "The person who knows the truth knows it, and he who knows it knows eternity. Love knows it. Eternal truth and true love and beloved eternity: you are my God. To you I sigh 'day and night'" (Ps 42:2).[45] The words of Augustine are the mingling of passion and mind, all which make up the soul.

Speaking about Transcendence through Being

Perhaps the most important and most discussed contribution of Anselm of Canterbury (1033–1109) is the so-called ontological argument for the existence of God.[46] What Anselm sought to do was to build

---

43. Cf. Porphyry's tree (in *Isagoge* or *Introduction*), which reveals a hierarchy of forms in the relation of *genus*, and *differentiae* that applies to the sensible world. However, Porphyry, unlike Plotinus, saw Aristotle's *Categories* not as a treatise about ontology.

44. Augustine, *Confessions*, 126. Again note *substantia* is the highest *genus* on the Porphyrian tree (from *genus* to *specie*: substance, body, animated body, rational animal, and human).

45. Ibid., x (16), 123.

46. The "ontological" argument was criticized by Kant in *Critique of Pure Reason*, "On the Impossibility of an Ontological Proof of the Existence of God," and therefore the name was then on associated with Anselm's proof. Anselm's argument is "ontologi-

on Augustine's statement that one cannot conceive of anything greater (*melius*) than God.[47] Philosophers have interpreted the arguments in *Proslogion* 2 and 3 as *a priori* arguments, stating that the very concept of God is necessarily instantiated in the definition of God. The merits and demerits, as well as proponents (Barth, Hartshorne, Plantinga, Malcolm) and critics (Kant, Russell) of the argument, are too numerous to account for in this essay, so my attempt is to sketch briefly the argument and show what the archbishop hoped to do in relation to what Augustine had done centuries before.

There are two versions of the proof; in both the impetus of the arguments is based in the Psalmist's assertion that "the foolish person says in their heart that there is no God" (14:1). In the *Proslogion* (1077–1078) the first is in chapter 2:

1. God is defined as "a being than which nothing greater can be conceived."[48]

2. God, as something that is understood, cannot exist in the understanding alone.

3. Existence in reality (*in re*) is greater than existence in the intellect (*in intellectu*).

4. Since that which exists in reality is greater than that which exists in the understanding, and this being, "is one than which no greater can be conceived," it follows that this being cannot exist in the understanding alone.

5. Since this is a contradiction, then "there is no doubt there exists a being, than which nothing greater can be conceived, and it exists both in the understanding and in reality."[49]

cal" insofar as it predicates necessary existence to God, therefore making claims of "being." In order not to prejudice this argument, I will not use this label. See also, Marion, "Is the Ontological Argument Ontological?"

47. "Nor could there be any soul capable of conceiving that which is better than you, you who are the supreme and highest good" (*neque enim ulla anima umquam potuit poteritve cogitare aliquid quod sit te melius, qui summum et optimum bonum es*). Augustine, *Confessions*, 114.

48. Anselm, *Basic Writings*, 53. All translations from this collection, translated by Deane, except otherwise noted. "And indeed, we believe that you are a being than which nothing greater can be conceived" (*Et quidem credimus te esse aliquid quo nihil maius cogitari posit*). For Latin text see Schmitt, *Anselmi Opera Omnia*, vol. 1.

49. Ibid., 53–54.

In this first case Anselm sets out to prove the existence of something in reality (*in re*) as being greater the conception of something in the intellect (*in intellectu*). In the definition of God one must include the existence of God as something that exists in both the understanding and reality. Two mistakes are often made by readers (and hearers) of this argument. The first is that this proof bases the existence of God on one's ability to conceive of God. This could not be further from Anselm's intent, and his illustration of the painter in chapter 2 illustrates this point:

> For, it is one thing for an object to be in the understanding, and another to understand that the object exists. When a painter first conceives of what he will afterwards perform, he has it in his understanding, but be does not yet understand it to be, because he has not yet performed it. But after he has made the painting, he both has it in his understanding, and he understands that it exists, because he has made it.[50]

Having an understanding of something and understanding it to exist are different things. A lack of distinction lies in a Cartesian reading of Anselm's argument. Whereas Anselm sought to clarify the difference between something that exists in the understanding and something that exists in reality, Descartes sought to base his own "ontological" proof on an *idea* or *concept* of a supreme being through extra-sensory perception.[51] Anselm clarifies this point in the brief but important chapter 15:

> [God] is greater than can be conceived.
>
> Therefore, O Lord, you are not only that than which a greater cannot be conceived, but you are a being greater than can be conceived. For, since it can be conceived that there is such a being, if you are not this very being, a greater than you can be conceived. But this is impossible.[52]

The second mistake is a derivative of the first, that somehow Anselm's proof is a movement from conception to reality.[53] This is not Anselm's proof, but Gaunilo of Marmoutier's objection, often called *Gaunilo's*

---

50. Ibid., 53.
51. Descartes, "Fifth Meditation," in *Meditations on First Philosophy*, 45–51.
52. Anselm, *Proslogium*, 68.
53. Schufreider, "Classical Misunderstanding," 499, says he agrees with Losoncy on this point.

Reply on Behalf of the Fool.[54] This Benedictine monk attempted to reframe Anselm's argument and then debunk the proof based on an incorrect reading:

> And the proof of this is as follows.—It is a greater thing to exist both in the understanding and in reality than to be in the understanding alone. And if this being is in the understanding alone, whatever has even in the past existed in reality will be greater than this being. And so that which was greater than all beings will be less than some being, and will not be greater than all: which is a manifest contradiction.
>
> And hence, that which is greater than all, already proved to be in the understanding, must exist not only in the understanding, but also in reality: for otherwise it will not be greater than all other beings.[55]

If we compare Anselm's original formulation, "that than which no greater than can be conceived," with "that which is greater than everything [*maius omnibus*]," then evidently Gaunilo's conclusion is not Anselm's. What is claimed in Anselm's definition is if one can conceive of a being greater than God, then this being is not God. What Gaunilo thinks as Anselm's argument is that God is "proved to be in the understanding" and if reality is greater than understanding then God is proved to exist in reality. This existence in understanding leads to the conclusion that God is greater than everything because of God's existence in reality is something great. We can think of God as we can think of the greatest of islands. Only taking Anselm in this way can Gaunilo's famous "lost island" proof can be used to invalidate what he takes as Anselm's proof because the greatest things do not have to exist just because we have conceived of them. In other words, it is true that the greatest possible island exists, whatever that means, but it is not true that the greatest possible island exist because a person thought of that greatest possible island or that it could exist.

The second proof can be seen in chapter 3 of the *Proslogion*:

---

54. Losoncy, "Saint Anselm's Rejection," argues that what has passed as Anselm's account has actually been Gaunilo's *Reply*. In addition, even though Gregory Schufreider ("Classical Misunderstanding," 489–99, 493) disagrees with Losoncy as to "why we should reject Gaunilo's version of the argument of *Proslogion* II"; Schufreider sees that Aquinas' use of Anselm is closer to the Gaunilo argument than Anselm's own.

55. Gaunilo's *In Behalf of the Fool*, in Anselm, *Proslogium*, 303. Latin text in Schmitt, *S. Anselmi Opera Omnia*, 125.

1. God cannot be conceived not to exist.
2. If God can be conceived not to exist, then that is not God.
3. A being that cannot be conceived not to exist is greater than a being that can be conceived not to exist.
4. If that which no greater can be conceived can be conceived not to exist, then it is not that which no greater can be conceived to exist.
5. Since this generates a contradiction, then a being than which nothing greater can be conceived *cannot* be conceived not to exist.[56]

Its basic premises are the same; yet the conclusion is not only of existence but also of *necessary* existence.[57] The import here is that God holds a type of existence different from all other things that exist. Hartshorne states: "The Proof claims to show that one and only one property, divinity, is related by necessity to the existence of a unique individual having the property, so that to conceive the property is to conceive the necessary existence of that individual."[58] Things do not require that we conceive of their actual existence. I can conceive of a tree in my head and there does not necessarily need to be the existence of the tree. This tree could have any property that I want it to have—a million feet high, purple leaves, hamburgers as fruit. In the same way, I can conceive of a hippogrith,[59] a phoenix, or tooth fairy and these things do not exist or necessarily exist. However to state that God is "that than which nothing greater can be conceived" is not only to necessarily conceive of God's existence, but to also posit that God necessarily exists and this claim of necessary existence shows that God is something that is greater than anything else. The proof, therefore, is not merely an *existentialist* proof, but one that shows the unique property of necessary existence, that only God possesses. In this way, Anselm, like Augustine, seeks to establish

56. Anselm, *Proslogium*, 54–55.

57. Before Anselm, the Arabic philosopher Avicenna (c. 980–1037 AD) sought to prove God's necessary existence through a different method based on God's essence. See Kenny, *New History of Western Philosophy*, 292–93.

58. Hartshorne, introduction to Anselm, *Basic Writings*, 5.

59. A hippogriff has the head and wings of an eagle and the body of a horse, not to be confused with a griffin, which has the head and wings of an eagle and the body of a lion.

a hierarchy of being with God surpassing all other beings because of God's necessity of being. Therefore, the proof in *Proslogion* 2 ties inextricably into 3,[60] God not only exists, but God's existence is greatest because of its necessity.

A year before Anselm put the pen to the *Proslogion*, he wrote the *Monologion* and opened the first chapter by discussing "a being which is best, and greatest, and highest of all existing beings." Here Anselm uses a teleological proof to show that there is a basis and goal of all of our desires. Humans are drawn to what they consider as good; and since "good" is said of different ways of different things, then there must be an ultimate source of the good that is the goal of all human desire.[61] In Anselm's example, if we say that a horse is swift and strong, then we can say that this horse is good. But if we say that a thief is swift and strong, then we cannot call the thief himself good, but only in that he is a good thief. So that a thing is good is not said to be good through itself (*per se*) but through another (*per aliud*). Only one being can be said to be *per se* good, being the source of goodness to all things; this one being is therefore supremely good. Anselm concludes by saying that "that which is supremely good is also supremely great." The combination of that which is "supremely good" and that which is "supremely great" makes this being the "highest of all existing beings."[62]

Albeit argued in a different manner, what is present in the *Proslogion* arguments that is not present in the *Monologion* argument is the simple elegance of the proofs. But one can quickly tell that the goal of both is the same: to set God apart from other things. It appears that Anselm is trying to do two things in *Proslogion* 2: (1) express what must be thought of as God when we say "God" and (2) to show God in relationship to other things in this world, that he holds the unique property of necessary existence. These arguments are framed in the cognitive abilities of the person to think about God, but it is not the cognitive ability to think about God that makes God real. Instead, the arguments set the boundaries of what is required in talking about the existence

---

60. Schufreider, *Confessions of a Rational Mystic*, 156–68, considers the relationship between II and III.

61. Cf. Aristotle's *Nicomachean Ethics* (Bk I, 7) concerning the "good."

62. Schufreider, *Rational Mystic*, 29, sees "a tight-knit connection between ontology and axiology—between being and value—which is not uncharacteristic of medieval thought as a whole."

or non-existence of God. They are the rules that guide the intellect in thinking about God and God's relationship to the world.

If there are any misconceptions about Anselm's view of human cognitive abilities, then in the first chapter of the *Proslogion* he makes this clear:

> Our labors and attempts are in vain without God. Man cannot seek God, unless God himself teaches him; nor find him, unless he reveals himself. God created man in his image, that he might be mindful of him, think of him, and love him. The believer does not seek to understand, that he may believe, but he believes that he may understand: for unless he believed he would not understand.[63]

Anselm, who is often credited as the father of scholasticism, labored under the banner of *fides quaerens intellectum* ("faith seeking understanding," which was said to be the original title of the *Proslogion*) and not "understanding seeking faith."[64] He believed that he was faithful to Augustine and continued in the Neo-Platonic tradition,[65] even though some, like Hartshorne, think that his classical argument went beyond what he was trying to prove. Nevertheless, Anselm is far from being a "rationalist" in the modern sense.[66] He is faithful as a Christian and this faith seeks to understand what it is he believes, even if the subject of the faith is beyond the grasp of total comprehension.

Did this philosophical view of theology produce a view of God that is consistent with the biblical witnesses, or in other words, did Anselm show that "that than which nothing greater can be conceived" is the same as the God of the Bible? Perhaps he did and perhaps he did not. What is important to recognize is that Anselm was faithful to a formulation of God that respects the relationship between Creator and creature; that they are both ontologically different and that the former provides being to the latter. Only in this respect can the arguments be deemed as ontological. This difference is consistent with the biblical witnesses and allows one not only to think of the existence of not only God, but also God's creatures.

63. Anselm, *Proslogium*, 49.
64. Ibid., preface, 47.
65. See Charlesworth's introduction in Anselm, *St. Anselm's Proslogion*, 26–30.
66. Schufreider, *Rational Mystic*, 13, uses the phrase "rational mystic" to deter emphasis on one aspect of Anselm's thought or another.

Predicating Transcendence through Existence and Analogy

Thomas Aquinas (c. 1224/5–1274) wrote the *Summa contra Gentiles* (*SCG*) between the years 1256 and 1264 to be used as a manual for Dominican missionaries to the Arabic-speaking, Spanish world. Over a century and a half had passed since the writing of the *Proslogion*. In book 1, chapter 10 of *SCG*, Thomas addresses the question of whether one can "assert that the existence of God is self-evident" (*per se notum*). Aquinas summarizes these "self-evident" arguments in §2:

> Those propositions are said to be self-evident that are known immediately upon the knowledge of their terms. Thus, as soon as you know the nature of a whole and the nature of a part, you know immediately that every whole is greater than its part. The proposition God exists is of this sort. For by the name God we understand something than which a greater cannot be thought. This notion is formed in the intellect by one who hears and understands the name God. As a result, God must exist already at least in the intellect. But He cannot exist solely in the intellect, since that which exists both in the intellect and in reality is greater than that which exists in the intellect alone. Now, as the very definition of the name points out, nothing can be greater than God. Consequently, the proposition that God exists is self-evident, as being evident from the very meaning of the name God.[67]

Thomas says, "as the very definition of the name points out, nothing can be greater than God," but does not say here that "God is that which nothing greater can be conceived." This is closer to Gaunilo's use of the term *maius omnibus* rather than what is used in Anselm's argument.[68] Is there a difference in saying that there is nothing greater than God and saying God is "that which nothing greater can be conceived?" The former assumes the existence of God as *per se nota* and the inferiority of things as existing in relationship to God. The latter shows the limit as to what can be thought of as God, "that than which nothing greater can be conceived." In other words, the second statement asks, "Can you think of something greater than God?" and then replies, "If you can, then that

---

67. Aquinas, *Summa Contra Gentiles*, 79. All translations from this edition, translated by Anton C. Pegis, unless otherwise noted.

68. Schulfreider, "Classical Misunderstanding," 490.

which you call God is not God." In the first statement, a person assumes that God's existence is self-evident; but in the second, to conclude God's existence based on what can be understood as God is not the same as saying that one assumes God's existence is self-evident. In other words, to say "God exists" is not the same as saying "It is self-evident that God exists."

Later, Aquinas goes on to treat the two senses of "self-evident":

> In part, however, the above opinion comes about because of a failure to distinguish between that which is self-evident in an absolute sense and that which is self-evident in relation to us. For assuredly that God exists is, absolutely speaking, self-evident, since what God is is His own being. Yet, because we are not able to conceive in our minds that which God is, that God exists remains unknown in relation to us. So, too, that every whole is greater than its part is, absolutely speaking, self-evident; but it would perforce be unknown to one who could not conceive the nature of a whole. Hence it comes about, as it is said in *Metaphysics* II [Ia, 1], that "our intellect is related to the most knowable things in reality as the eye of an owl is related to the sun." (SCG 1.11. 2)[69]

Thomas understands that being self-evident can be said in more than one way, absolutely (*simpliciter*) and in relationship to us (*quoad nos*). God exists as God's own being; that in itself is true, since God is God's existence (*sit suum esse*). However, we cannot know of that existence, since, according to Thomas, we do not directly know the nature of things. Proponents of Aquinas's argument admit that Aquinas's attacks are levied against his Franciscan contemporary, Bonaventure. Fellow theologian Bonaventure argued that the existence of God was so self-evident that it could not be thought not to exist (following on the heals of *Proslogion* 2).[70]

Aquinas then proceeds to say that we cannot presume to know the existence of something just because we understand what it means to say "God." Here is where Aquinas uses something closer to Anselm's phrase: "God is that than which nothing greater can be conceived" (*quod Deus sit id quo maius cogitari non posit*). Now Aquinas uses this definition of God in order to take up the point of existence *per se nota* that was

---

69. Aquinas, *Summa Contra Gentiles*, 81.
70. Schufreider, "Classical Misunderstanding," 489–99.

argued in the previous chapter. Aquinas now is not only concerned with the claim of the existence of God, but also the claim of the necessary existence of God, especially for those who do not believe in God. Thomas uses the definition of God, set out in *Proslogion* II, and argues against it and its implications in *Proslogion* III. His points are as follows:

1. The signification of the name of God does not necessitate knowing of the existence of God.
2. The meaning of the signification is not known to all, even to those who say that God exists.
3. People could define God in whatever way they chose, e.g., as the world.
4. Even when people do understand the name of God, it is not necessary that God exist in reality.
5. A thing and its definition are "posited in the same way," i.e., in the mind.
6. Since the thing is conceived in the intellect, it does not follow that it needs to exist outside of the intellect.
7. There is no difficulty for someone who posits that God does not exist.
8. The only one who has to resolve the difficulty of something existing in the mind and reality is the person who believes that "God is nothing greater than which can be conceived."[71]

For Aquinas, there is nothing in the definition of a name that requires it to have existence. Existence (*esse*) is a factor not of the definition but of the essence of a thing; its existence is not dependent on our cognitive abilities to think about it. Aquinas counters the second argument even more succinctly:

> Nor, again, is it necessary, as the second argument advanced, that something greater than God can be thought if God can be thought not to be. For that He can be thought not to be does not arise either from the imperfection or the uncertainty of His own being, since this is in itself most manifest. It arises, rather, from the weakness of our intellect, which cannot behold God

---

71. Aquinas, *Summa Contra Gentiles*, 81–82.

Himself except through His effects and which is thus led to know His existence through reasoning.[72]

A person does not have to necessarily think about God's existence. This inability does not have to do with God's own nature, since the proof of God's existence can be demonstrated in another way. And how is God's existence clearly known since Aquinas has said previously that we cannot know of God's nature? What is clear in Aquinas's arguments against the Anselmian tradition is that Thomas, like Anselm, (1) seeks to show the limits of the human mind in its understanding of God (God cannot be known *per se notum*) and (2) to show the relatedness between God and God's creation. Wippel clarifies: "Thomas's primary concern is not so much to refute Anselm as to reject the more general position which regards God's existence as self-evident."[73] Nevertheless, Aquinas argues that the only way speak of God's existence is through revelation or a demonstration from the effects to causes.[74]

In Aquinas's unfinished *Summa theologiae* (*ST*), he takes up the task of arguing from effects to cause in his famous *quinque viae*, or "five ways." C. F. J. Martin asks and answers, "Does God exist? Apparently Not."[75] So, Aquinas needs to first establish *that* God is before *what* God is, since God's existence is not self-evident:

> Now because we do not know the essence of God, the proposition is not self-evident to us; but needs to be demonstrated by things that are more known to us, though less known in their nature—namely, by effects.[76]

Aquinas posits this in the context of his statement that we can know *that* God is, but not *what* God is. This first needs to be demonstrated through what is first self-evident. In Aquinas's own terms, these demonstrations are said to be *quai* ("that") demonstrations, namely, starting with effect and determining cause, opposed to *propter quid* ("on account of what") arguments, from cause to effect.[77] In doing so, we can determine that

---

72. Ibid., 82.

73. Wippel, *Metaphysical Thought*, 397, outlines these texts of Aquinas in reference to Anselm (391–99).

74. Aquinas discusses the nature of sacred doctrine and scripture in Q. 1 of the *ST*.

75. Martin, *Thomas Aquinas*, 110, translates the objection, *Videtur quod Deus non sit*.

76. *Summa Theologiae* Ia, Q. 1, A. 1, *respondeo*.

77. *Summa Theologiae* Ia, Q. 2, A. 2, *respondeo*. Also, Aquinas uses these terms in the *SCG* and spends time refuting the viability of Anselm's arguments.

God exists but cannot determine the essence of God. The only method by which we can talk of God's essence is through speaking about what God is not and by analogy.[78]

To summarize the five ways as presented in the *Prima Pars* (first part) of the *ST* (Ia, Q2, A3, co.): the first is demonstrated by way of motion, the second by causality, the third by possibility and necessity, the fourth by gradation, the fifth by order. Aristotle's *Physics* is used to take up the first two arguments, but Aquinas moves beyond natural proofs. Menn describes the third and forth way as "ontological" not in the Anselmian sense, "but simply because they start from the fact of being (in the sense of existence) and not from contingent facts about the physical world."[79] Indeed, the fourth way shows the relationship in which a thing said to be "more X or less X," in comparison to its being. The value in this type of discussion is that it shows the connectedness between God and other beings that goes beyond physical proofs, as Menn affirms: "The advantage of a "metaphysical" proof of God's existence, if it could be made to work, is that it would lead us, by thinking through the questions about God and being that it raises, to a deeper conception of God, and of God's causal connection to other things, than simply conceiving him (say) as the first cause of motion."[80] But what deeper connection can a metaphysical proof or metaphysical understanding provide? Here is where we turn to Aquinas's use of analogy to understand God's essence. Since we cannot know God's essence except by what God is not, the only way to understand what God is not is through the comparison to the things that are. To say that things exist in the world have being and to say that God has being, asks the question of the relation of being between the two. These analogical relationships are also metaphysical relationships. Analogy helps us by using what is immediately intelligible to grasp that which is only intelligible in itself (*per se notum*).[81]

---

78. "Apophatic" or negative theology is influenced by the theology of the Neo-Platonist, who went by the moniker of Dionysius, but whom we call Pseudo-Dionysius.

79. Menn, "Metaphysics: God and Being," 147–48.

80. Ibid., 148.

81. Aristotle, *Physics*, Bk I, 7, 191a8; and Wallace, *Modeling of Nature*, xi, 73, in a treatment of nature and analogy (κατ' ἀναλογίαν).

Aquinas speaks about univocal, equivocal, and analogical predication in the *SCG* in the following ways:[82]

1. Nothing is univocally of God and other things (*SCG* 1.32)—"the heat generated by the sun and the sun are not called univocally hot" [2].

2. Not all the names are said of God and creatures in a purely equivocal way (*SCG* 1.33)—"For in equivocals by chance there is no order or reference of one to another, but it purely accidental that one name is applied to diverse things" [2].

3. Names are said of God and creatures analogically "according to an order or reference to something one" (*SCG* 1.34).[83] This is done in two ways: (1) "extrinsic attribution" when there is a relation to some third, and (2) "intrinsic attribution" or proportion, as related to each other.[84]

When we say things are "good" and that God is "good" we are referring to some one thing ("something one," *aliquid unum*) that is common in the two, i.e., "good." This can be something outside the nature of the two things or an intrinsic part of the nature of the two. In the *SCG*, Aquinas rejects "extrinsic" attribution for the "intrinsic" kind.[85] In scholastic terminology, the thing that is common is called the "analogon," and the instances of the differences that convey their commonality are called "analogates." For example, a "great painter" is the analogon when we are talking about Degas and Rembrandt, who are the analogates. In extrinsic attribution, the analogon is not only in the nature of one analogate, but in accidental relationship to other things.

Aquinas's example is that "health" is in the description of the subject of that which is healthy; let's say an animal or person. But we can

---

82. Aquinas also speaks about these forms of analogical predication in the earlier *Scriptum super libros Sententerium* (a commentary on the *Sentences* of Peter Lombard) I Sent. d. 19, q. 5 and in the later *Summa Theologiae* Ia, Q. 13.

83. *Secundum ordinem vel respectum ad aliquid unum.*

84. I am indebted to the work and help of Knasas at the University of St. Thomas, Center of Thomistic Studies, Houston, and his *Being and Some Twentieth-Century Thomists*.

85. Even though Aquinas does not use the terms "extrinsic" and "intrinsic," these Thomistic terms can be helpful descriptions. For a detailed discussion of analogy of attribution or proportion see Owens, *Elementary Christian Metaphysics*, 91, and n. 16.

call other things healthy in relationship to "one health." Medicine can be called healthy because it is the cause of health. Food can be called healthy because it is the preserver of health. Urine is called healthy because it is a sign of health, but these things are called healthy not because they exist in the subject of the healthy person; these are referred to a third thing, i.e., health. In other words, the medicine is called healthy not because of the healthy body (since it is the cause of health), but because by being absorbed by the body it then produces health. The relationship between health and medicine is causal and not inherent in the medicine itself; it is not in itself healthy. This causal relationship is the "third thing" of which Aquinas is speaking.

Because there is another way that substance and accident can be related, Aquinas rejects the above use of analogy for the "intrinsic" type of attribution, saying, "Thus, *being* [*ens*] is said of substance and accident according as an accident has reference to a substance, not according as substance and accident are referred to a third thing."[86] If we apply this image to God and God's creatures, then there is a relationship between God and creatures that one thing is internally related to another in the same way that substance is related to accidents. Again, the language of Aristotelian metaphysics is invoked. Being is divided into substance and accident, an accident being non-essential and non-necessary to a substance. For example, I am human being who is sitting down and typing on my computer at this moment. "Sitting" and "typing" are accidents of the substance of "human," but they also come out of my nature as rational creature that can sit and type. Accidents are carried along with substances and this relationship is "intrinsic" to the substances. In the same way, being is related to substance and accident. When applied to God, this analogy is theologically consistent because we can predicate "good" to God because "good" is what God gives to God's creatures.

Knasas provides a "non-metaphysical example" in that when we talk about the holiness of a person, this term is "ideally realized in Chirst and subsequently realized in some follower."[87] There is not one "analogate" that totally embodies what is meant by holy. Christ is the ideal realization of what is meant by holy and others are holy by virtue

---

86. Aquinas, *Summa Contra Gentiles*, Bk. I, c. 34, 3, distinguishes betweens being in terms of a "being" (*ens*) and being in terms of an act of being (*esse*), but here *ens* is used in a generic sense as the existence of something. See Aquinas' *De Ente et Essentia*.

87. Knasas, *Being and Some Twentieth-Century Thomists*, 145–46.

of their imitation of Christ. This is how the accident is related to the substance. It is in this way that God is related to God's creatures; there is being in the creatures of God that God bestows and this is seen in the existence of the creature.

What Anselm is working out in a direct way in the *Proslogion* and especially in the *Monologion* is put forth by Aquinas in an indirect way. It is indirect because the predication of "good" is seen in an analogical relation, through understanding what further in relation to us by that which is most immediate to us. If we go back to Anselm's image of a good horse, we can say that "good" is predicated of "horse" because of the goodness of God. The relationship is causal, but in a way that is intrinsic to God and God's creatures. Therefore, Aquinas helps us to understand the unity in the difference between the two.

Continuing to Speak about Transcendence

These three examplars have provided—through a philosophically motivated and divinely revealed theology—ways to understand the relationship between God and God's creation. A superficial reading of these arguments would show a history of contradictory thought in the theological tradition. Instead, I have noted the differences and tried to show a development in medieval thinking. Modern philosophical and theological views have misread and reacted to the work of these theologians in absence of their contexts. If modern philosophies have sought to reject God and transcendent premises, then modern theologies have sought to replace the transcendent God articulated by the medievals with something like the panentheism of the Process theologians.[88] Instead, the conclusions reached by the medievals were first principles in Conyers's theology.

The notion of an ordered universe is intimately tied to the notion of transcendence, and Conyers's reliance on the medieval view of hierarchy is evident in his earliest works. In both praising Jürgen Moltmann's

---

88. Panentheism is a theology that speaks of God as greater than the universe, but also permeating the entire universe with God's being, so that the universe is infused in God. This is different than pantheism, which claims that the universe is God and both are the same. Panentheism asserts that the two are ontologically different. In asserting this however, Process theologians make the same Manichean mistake that Augustine once made in his sea/sponge analogy.

eschatology of hope and critiquing his rejection of hierarchy, Conyers argues:

> A task for any Christian theology that is thoroughly aware of its grounding in eschatological promise may be less the leveling of the hierarchies and the casting aside of domination than heightening of the dialectical tension between domination and freedom. These two ideals, like faith and works, or law and grace, stand side by side in biblical thought. The kingdom of God is both an image of power, even of dominating hierarchical rule, and an image that calls into question every other ruling authority. It is the end of all rule (and thus liberation), and it is the epitome of rule (thus lordship).[89]

Conyers asks us to imagine a world where earthly authoritarian rule gives way to another kind of reign, a reign ordered and rooted in transcendence.

Conyers' *The Eclipse of Heaven* is not an apology about a celestial afterlife filled with angels and harps, but a defense of life lived with boundaries, between heaven and earth, between the other and us. Understanding a world "over us," and therefore its limits, implies the possibility of relationships: "[The idea of heaven] answers the question whether this great, incomprehensible reality is one that I *can* relate to; or whether it is, in the final analysis, chaotic, purposeless, and impersonal, or else indifferent with regard to my life."[90] Transcendent values have immediate ramifications; it gives humans a way to relate to the world.

Conversely, closing ourselves off to the transcendent brings about catastrophic effects. Conyers refers to the political philosopher Eric Voegelin, saying "that once society becomes closed to those experiences by which it is shaped, namely its reach for transcendent meaning, and the human quest focuses instead on worldly goods, the competing demands are satisfied by nothing short of bloodshed and revolution."[91] Conyers rightly observes that the modern elevation of choice replaced transcendent calling and community and has resulted in catastrophic consequences: "human beings naturally reach for meaningful action, and not finding it, resort to irrational and destructive action."[92]

---

89. Conyers, *God, Hope, and History*, 13; revisited in *Long Truce*, 213.
90. Conyers, *Eclipse of Heaven*, 19.
91. Conyers, *Listening Heart*, 5.
92. Ibid., 6.

A society brought up on transcendent values—when void of these values—will seek its replacement in any way possible, even in destruction.

Conyers sensitively notices that our world is "a world hungering for the rumor of heaven."[93] It is a "rumor" because modernity (for Conyers, postmodernity is only an extension of modernity) rejected heaven, thinking it a product of the Dark Ages and associating it with inquisitions, marauding Germanic tribes, and declining cultural and intellectual achievement. Rather, the medieval theologians illustrated an intimacy between an all-giving Creator and creation. What we inherited from Augustine, Anselm, and Aquinas is a heartfelt confession drawn with theological and philosophical rigor, a striving to understand Christian faith through the limits of the intellect and a seeking to peer into God's unfathomable nature through the existence of God's creation. To deny God's greatness is, in the same sense, to remove the closeness that God has to God's creatures. "Chip" Conyers was a devoted defender of a life lived in a world of surpassing beauty because its source was divinely revealed and intellectually perceptible, not artificially generated by our modern schemas. He spoke of this kind of life in formal lectures and informal conversations around meals. He addressed these sublime realities from his hospital bed as he fought the good fight against cancer. I can still hear him softly and carefully whispering the word "transcendence" over us.

---

93. Conyers, *Eclipse of Heaven*, acknowledgments.

Bibliography

Anselm. *St. Anselm's Proslogion, with A Reply on Behalf of the Fool by Gaunilo and the Author's Reply to Gaunilo.* Translated by M. J. Charlesworth. Oxford: Claredon, 1965.

———. *Basic Writings: Proslogium, Monologium, Cur Deus Homo, Gaunilo's In Behalf of the Fool.* Translated by S. N. Deane. 2nd ed. La Salle, IL: Open Court Classics, 1962.

Aquinas, Thomas. *Summa Contra Gentiles.* Edited by P. Marc et al. Textus Leoninus diligenter recognitus. Italy, 1961.

———. *Summa Contra Gentiles. Book One: God.* Translated by Anton C. Pegis. Notre Dame, IN: Notre Dame University Press, 1955.

———. *Summa Theologiae.* Italy: Marietti, 1962.

———. *The Summa Theologica of St. Thomas Aquinas.* Translated by Fathers of the English Dominican Province. 3 vols. New York: Benziger, 1947.

Aratus. *Phaenomena.* Translated by Douglas Kidd. Cambridge Classical Texts and Commentaries 34. Cambridge: Cambridge University Press, 2004.

Augustine. *Confessions.* Translated by Henry Chadwick. Oxford: Oxford University Press, 1991.

———. *Confessions.* Translated by William Watts. 2 vols. LCL. New York: Macmillan, 1931.

———. *Confessions.* Translated by F. J. Sheed. 2nd ed. Indianapolis: Hackett, 2006.

Conyers, A. J. "Protestant Principle, Catholic Substance." *First Things* 67 (1996) 15–17.

———. *The Eclipse of Heaven: Rediscovering the Hope of a World Beyond.* Downers Grove, IL: InterVarsity, 1992.

———. *The Listening Heart: Vocation and the Crisis of Modern Culture.* Dallas: Spence, 2006.

———. *The Long Truce: How Toleration Made the World Safe for Power and Profit.* 2nd ed. Dallas: Spence, 2008.

———. *God, Hope, and History: Jürgen Moltmann and the Christian Concept of History.* Macon, GA: Mercer University Press, 1988.

Descartes, René. *Meditations on First Philosophy with Selections from the Objections and Replies.* Translated by Michael Moriarty. Oxford: Oxford University Press, 2008.

Gersh, Stephen. "Anselm of Canterbury." In *Routledge History of Philosophy,* edited by C. C. W. Taylor, 132–49. London: Routledge, 1997.

Kant. *A Critique of Pure Reason.* Edited and translated by Paul Guyer and Allen W. Wood. Cambridge: Cambridge University Press, 1998.

Kenny, Anthony. *A New History of Western Philosophy,* vol. 2: *Medieval Philosophy.* Oxford: Clarendon, 2005.

Knasas, John F. X. *Being and Some Twentieth-Century Thomists.* New York: Fordham University Press, 2003.

Losoncy, Thomas A. "Saint Anselm's Rejection of the 'Ontological Argument'—A Review of the Occasion and Circumstances." *American Catholic Philosophical Quarterly* 64 (Summer 1990) 373–85.

MacDonald, Scott. "The Divine Nature." In *The Cambridge Companion to Augustine*, edited by Eleonore Stump and Norman Kretzmann, 71–90. Cambridge: Cambridge University Press, 2006.

Marion, Jean-Luc. "Is the Ontological Argument Ontological? The Argument According to Anselm and Its Metaphysical Interpretation According to Kant." *Journal of the History of Philosophy* 30.2 (1992) 201–18.

———. "L'argument relève-t-il de l'ontologie?" *Archivio di Filosofia* 58 (1990) 43–69.

Martin, C. F. J. *Thomas Aquinas: God and Explanations*. Edinburgh: Edinburgh University Press, 1997.

Menn, Stephen P. "Metaphysics: God and Being." In *The Cambridge Companion to Medieval Philosophy*, edited by A. S. McGrade, 147–70. Cambridge: Cambridge University Press, 2006.

Owens, Joseph. *An Elementary Christian Metaphysics*. Toronto: Bruce Pub., 1963.

Plato. *The Republic*. Translated by G. M. A. Grube, rev. by C. D. Reeve. In *Plato: Complete Works*, edited by John M. Cooper. Indianapolis: Hackett, 1997.

Schmitt, F. S., editor. *S. Anselmi Opera Omnia*. Vol. 1. Edinburgh: T. Nelson, 1946.

Schufreider, Gregory. "A Classical Misunderstanding of Anselm's Argument." *American Catholic Philosophical Quarterly* 66 (Autumn 1992) 489–99.

———. *Confessions of a Rational Mystic*. West Lafayette: Purdue Universtity Press, 1994.

Vaught, Carl G. *Encounters with God in Augustine's Confessions: Books VII–IX*. Albany, NY: SUNY Press, 2004.

Wallace, William A. *The Modeling of Nature: Philosophy of Science and Philosophy of Nature in Synthesis*. Washington, DC: Catholic University of America Press, 1996.

Wilken, Robert Louis. *The Spirit of Early Christian Thought: Seeking the Face of God*. New Haven, CT: Yale University Press, 2003.

Wippel, John F. *The Metaphysical Thought of Thomas Aquinas: From Finite Being to Uncreated Being*. Monographs of the Society for Medieval and Renaissance Philosophy 1. Washington, DC: Catholic University of America Press, 2000.

8

"These Are the Masks of God"
Martin Luther and the Protestant Life of Vocation

Brian C. Brewer

> I sing a song of the saints of God,
> patient and brave and true,
> who toiled and fought and lived and died
> for the Lord they loved and knew.
> And one was a doctor, and one was a queen,
> and one was a shepherdess on the green;
> they were all of them saints of God, and I mean,
> God helping, to be one too.[1]

IN 2008, RANDY PAUSCH, A COMPUTER SCIENCE PROFESSOR AT Carnegie Mellon University, wrote the well-acclaimed national bestseller, *The Last Lecture*, expressing his philosophy of life, happiness, and fulfillment as sage words for his surviving family, students, and readership to remember for themselves even as Pausch died of cancer. Two years prior, Spence Publishing published posthumously what amounted to A. J. Conyers' last lecture, *The Listening Heart: Vocation and the Crisis of Modern Culture*. Conyers completed the final draft just days before his death from the same disease in 2004. For Conyers, the postmodern notion that life comprised a series of individual choices merely wrought a culture of individual isolation. Instead, he urged this generation and the Church to return to the ancient, Christian idea of vocation, seeing life as more than self-fulfillment but living instead in response to a transcendent calling. Congruent with much of Conyers' thought was

---

1. Scott, "I Sing a Song of the Saints of God." Traditionally sung to the John H. Hopkins tune "Grand Isle."

the Protestant notion of a universal priesthood and the divine calling of service for all Christians through a life of vocation. The fount of this thought among Protestants was the former Augustinian monk, Wittenberg professor, and "Father of the Reformation," Martin Luther.

Foundational Doctrines to the Protestant Understanding of Vocation

One need not read Luther's writings more than cursorily to see his repeated theme of justification by grace through faith as foundational to his theology. Rejecting the Catholic understanding of meritorious works, Luther grounded his soteriology in the promise of Romans 10:9–10 ("If you confess with your lips that Jesus is Lord . . ."), Rom 10:4 ("Christ is the end of the law . . .") and 1:17 ("He who through faith is righteous shall live."), among other such passages. Thus, Luther concluded:

> It is clear that the inner man cannot be justified, freed, or saved by any outer work or action at all, and that these works, whatever their character, have nothing to do with the inner man. On the other hand, only ungodliness and unbelief of heart, and no outer work, make him guilty and a damnable servant of sin. Wherefore it ought to be the first concern of every Christian to lay aside all confidence in works and increasingly to strengthen faith alone and through faith to grow in knowledge, not of works, but of Christ Jesus, who suffered and rose for him. . . . No other work makes a Christian.[2]

Indeed, Luther went further by maintaining that the very purpose of the Decalogue was to underscore human ineptitude to accomplish the Law and attain righteousness. In his despair, the human instead seeks assistance from beyond himself, finding the Law satisfied only by the One who initially commanded it.[3] Luther then astonishingly concluded:

> It is clear, then, that a Christian has all that he needs in faith and needs no works to justify him; and if he has no need of works, he has no need of the law; and if he has no need of the law, surely he is free from the law. . . . This is that Christian liberty,

---

2. Luther, "Freedom of a Christian," in *Luther's Works* [hereafter *LW*] 31:347.
3. "He alone commands, he alone fulfils." *LW* 31:349.

our faith, which does not induce us to live in idleness or wickedness but makes the law and works unnecessary for any man's righteousness and salvation.[4]

To his critics, Luther's notion of Christian liberty more resembled Christian libertinism. Yet the reformer's view of justification by faith alone was not so inflated as to be subject to antinomianism, regardless if his enemies charged him with the same.[5] Instead, paradoxically, the Christian is released from the burdens of the Law which had condemned in order unrestrainedly to serve God by serving her neighbor. Humans then come to self-understanding only by grasping Christ's salvific work on their behalf. By obviating the requirement for human works to attain or even cooperate with divine grace, God liberates grateful Christians to serve, motivated solely by the latter's thankfulness to their Liberator. Thus, out of Luther's formation of the Protestant view of justification, work ceases to be the human contribution to one's salvation and instead is interpreted as an anthropomorphic expression of love for God and neighbor.

Luther notoriously articulated this thought through two dialectical propositions: "A Christian is a perfectly free lord of all, subject to none. A Christian is a perfectly dutiful servant of all, subject to all."[6] Several Lutheran scholars have noted of these two paradoxical statements: "The whole course of the Lutheran Reformation and the subsequent history of Lutheranism might be described as an extended commentary on these contradictory theses."[7] While this sentiment may be hyperbolic, it nevertheless underscores how essential both freedom and work are to Luther and the Protestant Reformation he inaugurated. However, the juxtaposition of being a "free lord" yet also a "servant" or even "slave" produces an enigmatic understanding of the human condition of the believer. In the midst of this theological quagmire, Martin Marty rhetorically questions:

> Does not the introduction of Luther's second phrase about being a slave . . . take away the effect of the Gospel? At first reading it would seem that the second phrase throws man back under the powers of sin, death, devil—the very powers from which he

4. *LW* 31:349–50.
5. See Luther, "Against the Antinomians," *LW* 47:104–5.
6. *LW* 31: 344.
7. Maxfield et al., *Pieper Lectures*, 2:vii.

has been freed and rescued by faith, by the activity of God in Christ, by Baptism. In that case, what good is "freedom" if it is to be soon balanced or even cancelled by its opposite?[8]

However, one must understand this dialectic being solved through the believer's response to God's gracious action through love, her love of God and her corresponding love for neighbor. As Marc Kolden observes, "Faith spontaneously springs into acts of love, according to Luther. It does not let us remain 'in heaven' but returns us to earth. This is another way of saying that the gospel frees us from the law for the law. The gospel returns us to the law; it frees us to use the [l]aw for the good of our neighbor."[9]

Luther explained further:

> Here we see that all works and all things are free to a Christian through his faith. And yet, because the others do not yet believe, the Christian bears and holds with them what he is not obliged to do. But this he does freely, for he is certain that this is pleasing to God also, and he does it gladly, accepts it as any other free work which presents itself without his selecting it, because he desires and seeks no more than to do in faith the works which are pleasing to God.[10]

Christian freedom then originates in God's justification of believers through faith, which is God's action alone; and faith itself comes as a divine gift and not by human effort. "Faith," Luther noted, "works truth and righteousness by giving God what belongs to him. Therefore God in turn glorifies our righteousness."[11] Thus, humans play no role in the accomplishment of their salvation and, consequently, find their freedom therein. Such a divine act enables believers to love God. At the same time, however, Christians, now united with Christ, share also in his benefits and responsibilities. These responsibilities encompass their love for one another. Robert Kolb equates these two relationships to a child's relationship to her parents and to her siblings and playmates. God, like a parent, gives life, establishes the child's genetic qualities, and forms the essential identity for his child. God alone is responsible for human identity. Yet, Kolb maintains, "from that identity as his creatures

---

8. Marty, "Luther on Ethics," 202–3.
9. Kolden, "Luther on Vocation," 385.
10. Luther, "Treatise on Good Works," *LW* 44:36.
11. Luther, "The Freedom of a Christian," *LW* 31:351.

and children proceeds the performance of activities which reflect that identity. Human creatures identify themselves as God's creatures when they live according to that identity which God has given them."[12] The human relationship to God is one established through God's grace and lovingkindness alone. But the believer's relationship to other people is subsequently determined by this newly discovered divine relationship, binding the Christian "to the rest of creation as people who are held accountable for exercising God-given responsibilities" to the others.[13] Thus Luther wrote:

> A man does not live for himself alone in this mortal body to work for it alone, but he lives also for men on earth; rather, he lives only for others and not for himself. . . . Although the Christian is thus free from all works, he ought in his liberty to empty himself, take upon himself the form of a servant, be made in the likeness of men, be found in human form, and serve, help, and in every way deal with his neighbor as he sees that God through Christ has dealt and still deals with him. This he should do freely, having regard for nothing but divine approval. . . . Hence, as our heavenly Father has in Christ freely come to our aid, we also ought freely to help our neighbor through our body and its works, and each one should become as it were a Christ to the other that we may be Christs to one another and Christ may be the same in all, that is, that we may be truly Christians.[14]

From this notion that the Christian life is one of both freedom and selfless, loving service, Luther famously wrote, "Hence, all of us who believe in Christ are priests and kings in Christ."[15] Scripturally grounding the claim of a universal Christian priesthood in 1 Peter 2, as well as Exodus 19 and Revelation 5, Luther's adaptation of the word "priest," a term that had heretofore been reserved for the Western church's clergy, for parishioner and cleric alike produced both a theologically significant insight but also a politically strategic maneuver in subverting much of the theology, power, and polity structure of the church. The power and responsibility of the priest to consecrate the sacraments, Luther argued, come not from the pope but from the congregation the priest

---

12. Kolb, "Two Kinds of Righteousness," 42.

13. Ibid., 43.

14. Originally cited in Luther, "Freedom of a Christian," *LW* 31:364, 366, 367–68; here cited in Hoyer, "Christianhood, Priesthood, and Brotherhood," 179.

15. Luther, *LW* 31:354.

represents. Likewise, it is not the papal hierarchy alone which holds the responsibility to set the church's doctrine. Questioned Luther, "If we are all priests, as was said above, and all have one faith, one gospel, one sacrament, why should we not also have the power to test and judge what is right or wrong in matters of faith? . . . Therefore it is the duty of every Christian to espouse the cause of faith, to understand and defend it, and to denounce every error."[16] On this same basis, Luther denounced sacerdotalism while arguing for the layperson's ability to partake of both elements in the Supper. Additionally, he posited one's right for private confession, acknowledging Christ's promise of binding and loosing as the prerogative of all Christians, saying: "Christ has given to every one of his believers the power to absolve even open sins."[17]

The powers to absolve sin, to read and interpret the Scriptures, and to proclaim and defend the faith, among other rights and responsibilities of the collective universal priesthood of Christians, are bestowed upon each believer in his baptism. In *The Babylonian Captivity of the Church*, Luther argued that ordination to the priesthood was not a legitimate, biblical sacrament but was, at best, an ecclesiastical ceremony. From this point, Luther argued against the present separation between clergy and laity in the Roman Church:

> They have sought by this means to set up a seed bed of implacable discord, by which clergy and laymen should be separated from each other farther than heaven from earth, to the incredible injury of the grace of baptism and to the confusion of our fellowship in the gospel. Here, indeed, are the roots of that detestable tyranny of the clergy over the laity. . . . Here Christian brotherhood has perished, here shepherds have been turned into wolves, servants into tyrants, churchmen into worse than worldlings. If they were forced to grant that all of us that have been baptized are equally priests, as indeed we are, and that only the ministry was committed to them, yet with our common consent, they would then know that they have no right to rule over us except so far as we freely concede it. . . . Therefore we are all priests, as many of us are Christians.[18]

---

16. Luther, "To the Christian Nobility," *LW* 44:135–36.
17. Luther, "Babylonian Captivity," *LW* 36:88.
18. *LW* 36:112–13.

For Luther, baptism, when accompanied by faith, does not so much clean a sinner as allow her to die (as by drowning).[19] In so doing, through the sacramental faith accompanied by water baptism, the believer also puts to death her obligations to the works of the Law in order to find the promise of salvation in Christ's work on the cross.[20] Baptism then initiates the believer into a life of Christian freedom and service to neighbor in God's name, hence, inducting her into the spiritual priesthood to the other. Therefore, instead of the medieval sacrament of ordination to signify a holy calling for a certain few, the new Protestant view of baptism grants it to all who believe. Luther concluded: "See to it first of all that you believe in Christ and are baptized. Afterward, see to your vocation."[21]

In sum, when seen through the lens of Luther's notion of spiritual freedom, the doctrine of the priesthood of all believers is not simply to be perceived as entrusting the believer with great heavenly privilege but especially with great earthly responsibility. Writes Gustaf Wingren: "Freedom in externals is freedom to the law, to the full hands of the work of one's vocation, unto bondage before one's neighbor."[22] The layperson is freed not only for appropriate ecclesial service but is especially called to love his neighbor through his particular divinely given gifts in his regular setting of work, family, and daily activity. No longer is one's occupation separated from another's as sacred and secular, spiritual and temporal. Instead, Luther sanctified the profane:

> It is pure invention that pope, bishop, priests, and monks are called the spiritual estate while princes, lords, artisans, and farmers are called the temporal estate. This is indeed a piece of deceit and hypocrisy. Yet no one need be intimidated by it, and for this reason: all Christians are truly of the spiritual estate, and there is no difference among them except that of office. Paul says in I Corinthians 12 [:12–13] that we are all one body, yet every member has its own work by which it serves the others. This is because we all have one baptism, one gospel, one faith, and are all Christians alike; for baptism, gospel and faith alone make us spiritual and a Christian people.[23]

19. *LW* 36:68.
20. Kolden, "Luther on Vocation," 388.
21. Luther, *Luthers Werke* [hereafter *WA*], 37:480.
22. Wingren, *Luther on Vocation*, 94.
23. Luther, "To the Christian Nobility," *LW* 44:127.

Thus, as Baptist historian Robert G. Torbet once remarked, the Protestant Reformation sought less to "unfrock the clergy as it ordained the laity."[24] The cleric does not receive a higher calling than the layperson. Instead, each person receives the call of God, from the humblest peasant to an archbishop. By virtue of one's baptism, the Christian is called of God to a life of service in faith. Regardless how basic, tedious, or ordinary one's task, a person may serve God and express her faith through it. Thus, based upon his notions of justification by faith, Christian freedom, and universal priesthood, Luther developed his important doctrine of Christian vocation: that all who believe in the divine Word are called to God's service through their everyday labors.[25]

The Language of Vocation

The Latin word *vocatio*, meaning "vocation," is derived from the Latin verb *vocare*, which is rendered "to call." Over the centuries, "vocation" pertained to one's religious calling. The Latin terminology ostensibly paralleled the Greek word *klēsis*, a noun used nearly a dozen times in the biblical epistles. For example, Paul admonished the early Christians, saying, "Consider your calling [*klēsis*], brothers and sisters, not many of you were wise by human standards" (1 Cor 1:26). Therefore, according to Scripture, one's calling pertained to the divine call of God to be and to live as Christians. However, by the fourth and fifth centuries, as Christianity became the state religion and was thereby diluted of much of its countercultural and religious substance, the use of the word "vocation" underwent reinterpretation to the effect that only those in the culture who felt "called" to the newly developed monastic orders held a "vocation." Thus, a separation gradually began to develop between lay Christians who were perceived as carrying out secular work and ordained clergy who were especially "called" to their religious professions. The latter usurped such terms as "convert," "profession," and "vocation" as pertaining exclusively to those in the religious orders, an act that stripped the lay Christian of much theological vocabulary and self-understanding.[26] By the twelfth century, clergy were viewed as having a closer relationship with God than laypersons through a perceived

---

24. Torbet, *Baptist Ministry*, 9.
25. Bennethum, *Listen!*, 45.
26. Karlfried, "Luther on Vocation," 122–24.

elevated calling, rank, and work, a notion that granted to them a greater sense of nobility, at least as it pertained to spiritual status.[27]

The usurpation of such occupational terminology, especially of the word "vocation," became the focus of much of Luther's polemics. One of his most popular treatises, *The Babylonian Captivity of the Church*, accused the clergy of enslaving the laity through a highly developed, exclusive, and tyrannical hierarchy.[28] Instead, through the doctrines of justification by faith and the priesthood of all believers, as previously outlined, Luther redefined vocation, or *Beruf* in German, once again as spiritually fulfilling work enjoyed by all baptized Christians. Rather than being called out from the world's concerns like the monastic orders had prescribed, Christians possess the highest position and perform the highest service for God through their ordinary work in the world. Luther even warned lay Christians to not enter religious orders or the priesthood for the purpose of pleasing God. Such works, he maintained, differed in no way from the farmer's or the housewife's. The worthiness of one's vocation came only when performed before God by faith alone.[29] Luther then wrote:

> Therefore there is nothing to the monks and their dung who say and assert, "It's nothing to live in the common stations and offices and to pursue their calling; but to enter a cloister and become a monk, now that's something." They think this way: Common works even the heathen do. Therefore they are nothing special before God. So they think, those who judge offices and works apart and without God's Word. Whoever has God's Word, however, speaks this way: It is true, if one wants to figure according to the work itself, it is a very small thing that a lad goes to school and studies, a lass spins and sews; and a housemaid cooks, washes, sweeps, totes children around, wipes, and bathes them. For such things the heathen and non-Christians also do. But they do it without God's Word, that is, they do not do it in faith, neither believing that service and obedience is done to God with such works nor knowing His command. A son, daughter, and maid who are Christians, however, know from the Fourth Commandment that God commands and wants to have such a work.[30]

27. Bennethum, *Listen*, 44.
28. Ibid., 41.
29. See *LW* 36:78.
30. Cited in Ahl, "Called and Freed," 82.

God, then, blesses all offices and worldly duties. In fact, if one is to detect a hierarchy of offices in Luther's writings, it is one which favors the peasant, for the earthly work which produces goods and services for the betterment of the world surpasses the "holy" offices which may not address a wider human need than one's own. "Hence," Luther asserted, "when a maid milks the cows or a hired man hoes the field—provided that they are believers, namely that they conclude that this kind of life is pleasing to God and was instituted by God—they serve God more than all the monks and nuns."[31] While the ordinary work done by a Christian may look no different from that done by a nonbeliever, the distinction lies in the Christian's attitude of love for God and God's Word, and a life led in obedience to God. The Lord, in turn, blesses the works of the Christian who approaches her vocation with faith. All Christians, then, are divinely called to use their gifts in service to and out of love for the world and one another in it. Consequently, "vocation" once again became a term applicable to the work of all Christians. God has called Christians be and to do for him. Thus, this world is the arena of one's vocation.[32]

Vocation and Creation

Because of this earthly focus, Luther's notion of *Beruf* is inextricably tied to the doctrine of creation. Luther emphasized that God created the world and declared it to be "good." However, God's creative work is no one-time event but is unceasing (*creare est simper novum facare*). First, a Christian comes to know that God works passively in the world. By bestowing on the earth such gifts as gold and silver beneath its surface, great trees, plants and fertile soil, God supplies humanity with the resources for its ongoing work in this world. Luther asked rhetorically, "Does the labor of man do this? To be sure, labor no doubt finds it, but God has first to bestow it and put it there if labor is to find it. Who puts into the flesh the power to bring forth young and fill the earth with birds, beasts, fish, etc.? Is this accomplished by our labor and care? By no means."[33] God then works in secret; humanity's blessings come from God's hidden hand.

31. *LW* 3:321.
32. See Wingren, *Luther on Vocation*, 1–10.
33. Luther, "Exposition of Psalm 127," *LW* 45:327.

God now chooses lovingly to work inexorably by sustaining and renewing creation through the cooperation of humanity. This ongoing creative work is to maintain God's goodness in the world. That Christ became incarnate in order to redeem humanity is a powerful affirmation of this idea. If God the Father sends his own Son to earth to redeem it, then the Christian life should likewise not be one of worldly escape but a calling into the areas of humanity's greatest needs in order to imitate and even continue God's good creation and redemption of it.[34] Since the biblical creation narrative includes both God declaring the world as "good" and commissioning humanity to its work (Gen 1:28), it follows that work itself is good and is associated with God's intention for all humans in God's creation.[35]

Through Luther's view of a highly developed theism, God is seen as intensely active in the world. This, for the Wittenberg reformer, is evidence of God's ongoing creative work. However, God's work typically occurs in palpable ways through human hands by those who labor in faith. As humanity requires continual sustenance, God uses the work of other people to be his co-laborers in serving such human needs. Consequently, Luther wrote:

> God's people please God even in the least and most trifling matters. For He will be working all things through you; He will milk the cow through you and perform the most servile duties through you, and all the greatest and least duties alike will be pleasing to Him.[36]

It is especially through faithful humanity that God is making all things new.

Varieties of Christian Vocation

Occupation as Vocation

Naturally, when we consider the notion of vocation, what initially comes to mind is one's occupation, and Luther devoted a great deal of ink to this aspect of the Christian's calling. Each person has been given unique

---

34. Kolden, "Luther on Vocation," 386.
35. Bennethum, *Listen!*, 50.
36. Originally cited in *LW* 6:10; here cited in Beenethum, *Listen!*, 51.

gifts to use in service to the world around him. Provided one understands this selfless purpose to his work, he begins to perceive God's intention for vocation. Whether one is a baker, blacksmith, butcher, or brewer, she can find through her occupation an avenue of service to love her neighbor. Through her everyday work, she finds her divine calling. In the regular vocations in which they find themselves, Christians learn to be priests to one another. Through ordinary work, when expressed in selfless love, God commissions the believer to proclaim the gospel of grace; it is a tangible means of preaching the Word of God.[37] Luther powerfully expressed this sentiment this way:

> If you are a manual laborer, you find that the Bible has been put into your workshop, into your hand, into your heart. It teaches and preaches how you should treat your neighbor. Just look at your tools—at your needle or thimble, your beer barrel, your goods, your scales or yardsticks or measure—and you will read this statement inscribed on them. Everywhere you look, it stares at you. Nothing that you handle everyday is so tiny that it does not continually tell you this, if you will only listen. Indeed, there is no shortage of preaching. You have as many preachers as you have transactions, goods, tools, and other equipment in your house and home. All this is continually crying out to you: "Friend, use me in your relations with your neighbor just as you would want your neighbor to use his property in his relations with you."[38]

Luther's theology of universal priesthood and vocation for every Christian naturally developed from his anti-monasticism. He came to understand that God's particular call of the individual was not necessarily one to a new ministry: "Every occupation has its own honor before God, as well as its own requirements or duties.... God is a great lord and has many kinds of servants."[39] For instance, when preaching from John 21, where Christ commanded Peter to feed Christ's sheep, Luther subverted the medieval interpretation that God then calls a chosen few to such a spiritual task, accomplished through rigorous personal sacrifice, holy vows, and ordination to public ministry. Such a person absconded himself from secular life to one which ostensibly focused entirely on the transcendent. However, Luther maintained that the Christian faith

37. Bennethum, *Listen!*, 48.
38. *LW* 21:237.
39. Luther, "Sermon on Keeping Children in School," *LW* 46:226.

was centered on a God who came in the "hidden" and humble form of a man, Jesus of Nazareth. Correspondingly, Christians hear the call of God through the concealed forms of their ordinary, unassuming occupations. Therefore, as Lutheran scholar William Lazareth wrote, "In short, when we love to do what we ought to do and have to do, then we have answered Christ's call: 'Take up your cross and follow me.'"[40]

The work of one's occupation becomes transformed through faith into one's calling. The work, then, is not a means of attaining God's grace but the outflow of one's love for the One who grants his grace unconditionally. Thus, Luther wrote:

> God gives us grace not so that we can walk all over it as the world does, but because God takes an interest in all that we do to our neighbors, good and bad, as though we were doing it to God. If only everyone would regard [his] service to [his] neighbors as service to God, the whole world would be filled with *Gottesdienst* ["God-service," the German word for worship]. A servant in the stable, a maid in the kitchen, a child in school—these are merely God's workers and God's servants, if they with diligence do what their father and mother, or lord and lady of the household gives them to do. Thus would every house be filled with *Gottesdienst*, indeed every house would be a true church in which nothing other than pure *Gottesdienst* was practiced.[41]

Much of Luther's writing on vocation is flavored with instruction for laypersons to remain in the occupations in which they found themselves. Finding a Scriptural warrant in 1 Corinthians 7:20f ("Let each of you remain in the condition in which you were called . . ."), Luther continually repeated this theme, ostensibly out of his anti-monasticism and in order to promote societal stability. The reformer sanctified the secular position by arguing creatively even from the Lukan Christmas pericope:

> Christian freedom is not bound to any particular work [i.e., to ordained ministry], for all works which come along are of equal worth to a Christian. The shepherds did not run off to the desert, don cowls, shave their heads, or change any of their external practices in clothing, time, food or drink. They returned instead to serve God by caring for their flocks. For Christian faith does not consist in external activities which man has to change, but

---

40. Lazareth, *Luther on the Christian Home*, 135.
41. Originally cited in *WA* 36:339–40; here cited in Bennethum, *Listen!*, 50.

in an inward transformation by which he receives a new heart, spirit, will and disposition.[42]

However, while Luther urged fellow Christians to find God through obedient and faithful service in their present positions—both for theological reasons and for the purpose of providing a stable society—he did not discourage social mobility. Through education, children became acquainted with their God-given gifts, which, in turn, provided them greater volition and competency for the particular service through which they might best serve God.[43] Luther could not deny the social mobility to others that he, the son of a miner, experienced by advancing through law school and theological training. At the same time, Luther urged Christians to understand that God did not favor one occupation over another but merely the attitude of one's love expressed through it. Thus, the work of one's occupation is not an end in itself but a means for serving the God who has already worked in and who now works through it.[44]

Marriage and Family as Vocation

While occupations are typically seen as coterminous with vocations today, the former do not fully comprise Luther's broad acceptation of *vocatio*. In his lectures on Genesis, the reformer actually observed three "orders of creation" in which one's vocation might be carried out:

> This life is profitably divided into three orders: (1) life in the home; (2) life in the state; (3) life in the church. To whatever order you belong—whether you are a husband, an officer of the state, or a teacher of the church—look about you, and see whether you have done full justice to your calling.[45]

Therefore, a Christian would likely find herself within more than one order and carry out God's calling through multiple obligations or stations (*Stände*). This is because vocation, while including one's occupation, more generally pertains to God's call to live life in the world and not to be hermetically sealed away from it in order to pursue "spiritual"

---

42. *WA* 10.II:137.
43. See Luther, "Sermon on Keeping Children in School," *LW* 46: 213–58.
44. Bennethum, *Listen!*, 52.
45. *LW* 3:217.

ends. Therefore the responsibilities to family represent a significant station in which Christians live out their vocations.

Among the Ten Commandments, Luther placed primacy in the injunction to honor one's parents. It becomes the backbone not only to the family but to societal structure and order.[46] Like the other two orders, the life in the home requires each person to be subject to the others. It was God's design for humanity to depend upon and serve one another rather than for each person to act independently. In fact, Luther maintained, humanity's sin was an attempt to be like God and reject the responsibilities one has for the others. But proper interdependence becomes a source of self-discipline and mortification. The Christian, then, operates willingly and lovingly through joyful obedience to the appropriate authorities in work, in the state and in the family. Correspondingly, the responsibility of parents, spouses, and house workers are essential callings for the Christian home.[47] Wrote Luther:

> How is it possible that you are not called? Are you not either a husband or a wife, a son or a daughter, a servant or a maid? Take for example the most humble of estates. As a married man, do you not have enough to do in governing your wife, child, household, and property so that everything is done justly and in obedience to God's will? . . . Instead we spend our time counting rosary beads and doing other such things which do not serve our callings in the least.[48]

Thus, the responsibilities of fatherhood and motherhood far outweigh the medieval "holy" works of "foundations, fastings, dress, celebrations, priestcraft, monkery, and nunnery." The latter, when compared to the former, is "nothing but human vanity."[49] Instead, the Christian's first responsibility is to what he or she has already been given in life—from one's occupation to one's spouse, from one's duty as a church member to one's responsibility to care for aged parents or dependent children. Christians are called to minister in love in the stations in which God has already placed them before they consider extraordinary works outside such responsibilities.

46. Lazareth, *Luther on the Christian Home*, 138.
47. Ibid., 142.
48. WA 10.I.2:308.
49. WA 10.I.2:307.

Undoubtedly, the Christian calling lived out in marriage became foundational to Luther's order of home and family. Luther refused to label marriage as a sacrament because he understood it to be grounded not in God's redemptive work but as ordained instead as part of God's creation and as a remedy for humanity against sins of the flesh (1 Cor 7:2, 9b). However, as his Protestant theology matured, Luther began to maintain that marriage was also a significant part of a Christian's vocation, as a spouse is one's "nearest neighbor."[50] In his treatise *On Married Life*, Luther argued against the Greco-Roman view that a wife is a "necessary evil," arguing instead that marriage is part of God's design for humanity to produce children and an estate pleasing to God.[51] When engrafted with faith, a Christian enjoys marriage, assured by the confidence that one is not only participating in an important social institution but now also a divine calling. Consequently, each person is strengthened in her daily tasks, be they domestic or occupational, mundane or extraordinary, exhilarated by the thought that she is carrying out God's intended vocation[52]:

> See here, when natural reason, the clever whore, looks at married life, she lifts her nose into the air and says, Oh, am I supposed to put the baby to sleep, wash the swaddling-clothes, make the beds, and put up with those awful smells, stay awake nights, get up when the baby cries, and take care of the eczema and sickness? ... Am I supposed to be a prisoner in marriage? ... For when a man washes the swaddling-clothes or does some other menial task for the benefit of a baby, someone will undoubtedly make fun of him and take him for a fool or at least henpecked. But if he does these tasks out of faith, who really has the last laugh? Certainly God also laughs with all the angels and creatures, not because of the swaddling-clothes but because of the faith.[53]

Both husband and wife, then, may wash dirty diapers to the glory of God!

One may readily observe in his writings that, while not anticipating the advancement of women in the workplace in the subsequent centu-

---

50. Lazareth, *Luther on the Christian Home*, 217.
51. WA 10.II:294.
52. Lazareth, *Luther on the Christian Home*, 219.
53. WA 10.II:295–96.

ries, Luther does provide an understanding of vocation that spiritually matches the work of women to that of men—a progressive notion for the sixteenth century! The daily work of motherhood is understood as a God-ordained estate and is granted vocational status equal in spiritual value to that of her husband's work. The care of the home and children becomes a selfless, divinely inspired calling for wives. One might also observe from the citation above that Luther, again progressively, intended husbands to participate with their wives in such domestic tasks, since God's callings are not limited to one's occupation as to remove the male from menial, domestic chores.

While the husband and wife live in faithful service to one another,[54] a marriage that begets children also becomes theologically pregnant with divine purpose. The raising of children carries with it not only noble social implications in providing a proper home, a well-grounded society and a respect for civil authority; more importantly Christian parents are charged with the task of training their children in the faith:

> You see how rich the estate of marriage is in good works. For into the bosom of the family God places children who are conceived from the parents' own bodies and in need of their Christian works. For example, in making known the gospel message to them, parents act as the children's apostles, bishops, and pastors. In short, there is no greater, more noble power on earth than the religious and civil authority exercised by parents over their children.[55]

Children, in turn, who honor and obey their parents and are responsive to their spiritual and civil leadership, also live out the early divine callings of their young lives. Thus, when instilled with faith and acted out in love, the estate of the family becomes an integral part of the vocations of all Christians.

---

54. Some scholars have criticized Luther for not fully developing the vocational purpose of marriage within the couple and not merely for its procreational purposes. For instance, Lazareth noted: "When it comes to spelling out how this faith is active in loving service and devotion in a Christian's marriage, . . . Luther still disappoints us" (*Luther on the Christian Home*, 221).

55. Originally cited from *WA* 10.II:301; here cited in Lazareth, *Luther on the Christian Home*, 220.

Public Service as Vocation

Luther saw the office of the state as a worthy office and calling through which a Christian may and even ought to serve God. In fact, the Christian who maintained high moral character is an ideal person to serve in such a capacity. Though they approach the problem differently, both the church and the state concerned themselves with confronting sin. The Christian magistrate, whom Luther often refers to more generally as the "public individual," is divinely charged to "punish and judge evil men, to vindicate and defend the oppressed, because it is not they but God who does this. They are his servants in this very matter.... [As a public official] no man acts in God's place for the sake of himself and his own things, but for the sake of others."[56]

Luther proposed two kingdoms in which each Christian was a member: the church and the state. While the devil often commandeers the latter, God remains the head of both. Christians, then, who live out their callings through service in and through the state, must be vigilant that they do not allow their borrowed powers to overcome their Christian impulse to act altruistically and lovingly to their law-abiding citizenry by succumbing to corruption and egotistical fulfillment:

> For it does not follow that because the kingdoms of the world fight against the kingdom of Christ, they are bad in themselves; even as it does not follow that the spear, with which the side of the Lord was laid open on the cross, was not a good creation. We ought to differentiate between a creature or thing and the abuse of it. The creature is good, even if it be abused. The abuse does not spring from the thing, but from a depraved mind. Even so civil righteousness, laws, trades, and human efforts are things which are by nature good; but it is abuse that is bad, because the world misuses these gifts against God.... Abuse does not inhere in the substance. That thing is good in which the devil activates abuse.[57]

However, the righteous Christian can and does withstand such corruption and rightly protects the civil order of the community. In so doing, he represents God's justice in the temporal order.

---

56. Luther, "Two Kinds of Righteousness," *LW* 31: 04–5.
57. Luther, "Exposition of Psalm 2," *WA* 40.II:203.

The Ministry as Vocation

Karlfried Froehlich once wrote that "Luther did not eliminate priests or do away with the priesthood. Instead he eliminated the laity!"[58] But as entirely positive as this might at first appear to Protestant sentiments, the notion of an egalitarian priesthood elicits a considerable ecclesial problem: If all Christians are priests, what then is the particular role of the actual priest or ordained minister? When taken to its logical conclusion, one might initially believe Luther to be moving in a Quaker-like trajectory, dissolving the ordained office of pastor through his universal priesthood of all believers. However, just as God calls "the butcher, the baker, and the candlestick maker" each to his respective vocation, God also calls certain individuals to carry out the vocation of minister in the church.

While each Christian's baptism ordained her to the priesthood, it is, ironically, regarding the priest's most prominent act, proclamation (i.e., preaching), that Luther finally separates clergy from laity. Though every Christian shares the same authority pertaining to the Word and sacraments, for the sake of good order only a person who has received the consent of the congregation or been called by the majority thereof should actually administer them.[59] In addition to carrying out the public duties of preaching, baptism, and Communion, the pastor is tasked with educating "the various estates on how they are to conduct themselves outwardly in their several offices and estates so that they may do what is right in the sight of God."[60] Even though the priesthood of all believers qualifies all Christians to participate in the mission and ministry of the Church with the gifts each is given, for the purpose of good order the priestly acts of preaching and administering the sacraments are reserved for the chosen and ordained few to represent the whole of all Christians. While he encouraged each person to remain within the calling with which she found herself, Luther was particularly protective of the clergy from imposters and those who misconstrued the universal priesthood to convey a universal theological authority. To those who attempted to influence the direction of their pastor's homilies, Luther

---

58. Froehlich, "Luther on Vocation," 127.
59. See Brewer, "Baptist View," 156–58.
60. Originally cited in *LW* 46:226; here cited in Bennethum, *Listen!*, 52.

scolded, "You fool, you simpleton, look to your own vocation; don't you take to preaching, but let your pastor do that."[61]

As a common right of all Christians collectively, no one Christian can arise by his own authority and assume alone that which belongs to the entire church. Instead, Luther argued, each congregation should choose "faithful men" who are "able to teach," and to entrust to them the responsibility of carrying out these priestly functions on behalf of all.[62] Those chosen are to be viewed by others as worthy and able to fulfill this representative calling. While any Christian, Luther argued, can preach, baptize, and pray, and all should at times, especially in emergencies, the selected minister(s) should normally carry out these rites and perform these functions publicly so that everything might be done in order (1 Cor 14:40). Those chosen for this specific function should be called "ministers, deacons, stewards, [or] presbyters," and not "priests," for, again, all Christians are priests.[63]

The Hidden Work of God through Christian Vocation

To understand fully Martin Luther's mature Protestant theology of vocation, one must not overlook an essential underlying theme: God chooses to use faithful humanity to carry out God's own work in the world. God works through all Christian vocations, no matter how simple, menial, and worldly they might at first appear. God intends each Christian to be useful in service to the world. God doesn't need nor does he depend upon human work. The Lord has the capacity to heal without a physician, but most often chooses medicine to accomplish this divine healing. God does not need farmers, ranchers, butchers, and bakers to feed humans, for God has allowed manna to fall from heaven in the past. Nor does God even need adults to procreate children; he is fully capable of forming them out of dust. Nevertheless, the Lord chooses to work obliquely through humans. By permitting human cooperation in such work, God allows the faithful to be his hands and feet in the world.

Through dozens of writings, Luther consistently provided examples of God's hidden work through the vocations of the faithful in each

61. Originally cited in Luther, "Exposition of John 1 and 2," WA 46:735; here cited in Wingren, *Luther on Vocation*, 114.
62. Luther, "Concerning the Ministry," *LW* 40:36.
63. *LW* 40:34–5.

of the reformer's three estates. Regarding the family, for instance, while he could have populated the world with humans directly, like the other divine estates God chooses instead to work passively or circuitously through the faithful work of husbands and wives. Creation is thereby perpetuated as spouses work through God and on God's behalf. Luther colorfully argued:

> From where do we all have our origin if it is not from marriage and domestic arrangements? It is as though the papists were born from tree trunks and stones! If mothers did not bear, suckle, clean infants and keep them warm, the whole human race would have to perish. But since God Himself is the Author of these offices, there are no grounds at all for thinking that the worship of God is hindered by these matters, but they were most excellent and most pleasing exercises of godliness toward God and men. For God wants the fetus to be borne in the womb and to be suckled and kept warm by the earnest care of mothers that it may be nourished and grow, and so He has placed milk in the breasts. . . . Careful attention must be paid to the Author, because it is God who sets up, praises, remunerates, and adorns domestic work.[64]

Likewise, the Christian ruler must be reminded of Paul's declaration: "All power is from God, and he who resists the power resists God" (Rom 13:1–2). Therefore, a righteous ruler must act with justice, knowing that he is somehow representing God himself by rightly punishing a murderer or an adulterer and not succumbing to bribery or corruption. "But," Luther encouraged, "if hatred or enmity results, he should commend himself and his welfare to the Lord in faith; then he will feel that he is being defended by God."[65] Moreover, when the magistrate encounters resistance and hardship as a result of his vocation, it is a sign that he is actually working in accordance with God's will and rightly working in God's stead, for the sinful world will undoubtedly rebel from such judiciousness.

Finally, the cleric finds himself acting in God's stead both in the pulpit, where he faithfully speaks on behalf of God the words his congregants must hear, and when he administers the sacraments. In contradistinction to the Roman Church which had generally accepted sacerdotalism, which granted a priest, by virtue of his ordination, the

---

64. Luther, "Lectures on Genesis," *LW* 6:347–48.

65. Ibid., 3:328.

ability not only to administer the sacraments but also to dispense grace through them, Luther argued that the power of the sacrament emanated from an even higher source. In the new Protestant view, the rite of ordination does not provide sacramental potency to the ordinances. For instance, regarding baptism Luther noted that

> we can clearly see the difference in baptism between man who administers the sacrament and God who is its author. For man baptizes, and yet does not baptize. He baptizes in that he performs the work of immersing the person to be baptized; he does not baptize, because in so doing he acts not on his own authority but in God's stead.... Ascribe both to God alone, and look upon the person administering it as simply the vicarious instrument of God, by which the Lord sitting in heaven thrusts you under the water with his own hands, and promises you forgiveness of your sins, speaking to you upon earth with a human voice by the mouth of his minister.[66]

Therefore, in addition to one's occupation, Luther identified God working in and through the Christian in each of Luther's three estates. Thus the notion that God works through the deeds, chores, parenting, governing, and occupations of humanity is indispensable to the reformer. Through the human efforts of God's faithful people, God himself is the one who is truly at work. This is not merely intended by Luther to be an empty expression but a profound theological statement. God hides himself in the common work of ordinary Christians. Thus Luther wrote: "What else is all our work to God—whether in the fields, in the garden, in the city, in the house, in war, or in government—but just such a child's performance, by which He wants to give His gifts in the fields, at home and everywhere else? These are the masks of God, behind which He wants to remain concealed and do all things."[67]

Luther argued that while God could do and, in essence, actually does everything, God still wants us to participate with him and "do what belongs to our calling."[68] Subsequently, Luther outlined how God's work precedes and accompanies our own:

> He gives bread to nourish and preserve the body; but He gives it to him who labors, sows, reaps, etc. And when you sow the land,

---

66. *LW* 36:62–63. Cf. Kelling, "Martin Luther."
67. Luther, "Exposition of Psalm 147," *LW* 14:114.
68. Ibid.

you must not think that nothing will result from your labor. For it is God's command that you should do your duty, and He wants to work through you. Therefore you must devote yourself to your work and duty with all your strength and attention, and leave the rest to God.[69]

A Christian's work, then, begins and ends in faith. One's vocation arises in earnest when her work commences out of love for neighbor and as an expression of love for God. It ends each day trusting God that such work will provide for one's basic needs and fulfill the intention of one's divine calling. Throughout, however, Protestant Christians come to learn that it is God himself who works through them: "For He will be working all things through you; He will milk the cow through you and perform the most servile duties through you, and all the greatest and least duties alike will be pleasing to Him."[70]

Conclusion

Martin Luther developed his view of Christian vocation over against the reigning medieval view. Five centuries later, his understanding of vocation poses significant problems for the modern context. Miroslav Volf, for instance, has argued that Luther's notion of Christian vocation is inadequate for our contemporary setting because it is unresponsive to those individuals alienated through work that they either dislike or are forced to do. Luther does not speak to those occupations that are dehumanizing, which Christians should rightly denounce rather than accept as one's lot in life. Such indifference, when compounded by a theology of divine calling for every occupation, fails to elicit a Christian critique of unfair trade, dangerous work environments, and the tragic continuation of human slavery. Instead, Volf contends, Luther simply but dangerously admonished his followers: "Let each one remain in his vocation, and live content with his gift."[71] While Luther's words in this context should always be associated with his critique of the medieval thought which regarded monasticism as the singular vocation, a mod-

---

69. Luther, *Lectures on Genesis*, LW 3:290.

70. Ibid., 6:10. Wingren, *Luther on Vocation*, 9, paraphrases this passage: "God himself will milk the cows through him whose vocation that is. He who engages in the lowliness of his work performs God's work, be he lad or king."

71. Volf, *Work in the Spirit*, 107–9.

ern reader might indeed construe Luther's writings as discouraging social advancement.

A. J. Conyers too found the Lutheran vocational trajectory problematic. Drawing upon the writings of Origen, Conyers preferred to root vocation not in justification by faith but rather in the ongoing work of being created in God's image. Thus, people must see their vocations as a continual, eschatological process whereby they inexorably seek to conform to God's likeness. Likewise, Conyers pointed out, via Bonhoeffer, that Luther's view of vocation, which in effect sanctified the secular, fails to strike a balance between the Christian's embrace of society and her rejection of the world. There seems only room for the former, to the effect that most people identify the word "vocation" today with secular works that retain no theological underpinnings.[72]

Such critiques notwithstanding, a return to Luther's notion of vocation would serve as a necessary corrective to the modern secular hegemony of vocation as serving merely pecuniary functions or as a means for self-fulfillment. Luther's call to see one's life as an avenue of service to neighbor and an expression of one's love for God is significantly constructive. Under such a perspective, universities would return to a liberal arts education as the proper foundation for their professional schools, and all Christians would be led to find how best to use God-given gifts to fulfill human needs. Luther eschewed the medieval dichotomy between spiritual and temporal estates. While many interpreters perceive the Wittenberg reformer as promoting the secular in society, more rightly we might understand Luther as elevating all tasks heretofore relegated to the profane, when done in faith, as sacred. The Protestant view of life as a means for serving God, or even more profoundly, as God serving humans through other humans, is a needed corrective to self-serving postmodern perspectives. A Christian's vocation serves as God's incarnational work, the "masks of God" in love of and service to one's neighbor. Thus, Luther concluded: "We have the saying, 'God gives every good thing, but not just by waving a wand.' God gives all good gifts; but you must lend a hand and take the bull by the horns; that is, you must work and thus give God good cause and a mask."[73]

---

72. Conyers, "Vocation and the Liberal Arts," 125–27.
73. Luther, "Exposition of Psalm 147," *LW* 14:115.

Bibliography

Ahl, Dennis C. "Called and Freed for Obedience and Service." In *Martin Luther: Companion to the Contemporary Christian*, edited by Robert Kolb and D. Lumpp, 82–92. St. Louis: Concordia, 1982.

Bennethum, D. Michael. *Listen! God Is Calling!: Luther Speaks on Vocation, Faith and Work*. Minneapolis: Augsburg Fortress, 2003.

Brewer, Brian C. "A Baptist View of Ordained Ministry: A Function or a Way of Being?" *Baptist Quarterly* 43.3 (2009) 154–69.

Conyers, A. J. "Vocation and the Liberal Arts." *Modern Age* (Spring 2003) 123–31.

Froehlich, Karlfried. "Luther on Vocation." In *Harvesting Luther's Reflections on Theology, Ethics and the Church*, edited by Timothy J. Wengert, 121–33. Grand Rapids: Eerdmans, 2004.

Hoyer, George W. "Christianhood, Priesthood, and Brotherhood." In *Accents in Luther's Theology*, edited by Heino O. Kadia, 148–98. St. Louis: Concordia, 1967.

Kelling, Hans-Wilhelm. "Martin Luther: The First Forty Years in Remembrance of the 500th Anniversary of His Birth." *Brigham Young University Studies* 23 (Spring 1983) 131–46.

Kolb, Robert. "Luther on Two Kinds of Righteousness." In *Harvesting Luther's Reflections on Theology, Ethics and the Church*, edited by Timothy J. Wengert, 38–55. Grand Rapids: Eerdmans, 2004.

Kolden, Marc. "Luther on Vocation." *Word and World* 3 (1983) 382–90.

Lazareth, William H., *Luther on the Christian Home*. Philadelphia: Muhlenberg, 1960.

Luther, Martin. "Against the Antinomians." In *LW 47: The Christian Society IV*.

———. "The Babylonian Captivity of the Church." In *LW 36: Word and Sacrament II*.

———. "Concerning the Ministry." In *LW 40: Church and Ministry II*.

———. *D. Martin Luthers Werke: Ritische Gesammtausgabe*. Weimar: H. Böhlau, 1883–.

———. "Exposition of John 1 and 2." In *WA 46*.

———. "Exposition of Psalm 2." In *WA 40.II*.

———. "Exposition of Psalm 127." In *LW 45: The Christian in Society II*.

———. "Exposition of Psalm 147." In *LW 14: Selected Psalms III*.

———. "The Freedom of a Christian." In *LW 31: Career of the Reformer I*.

———. *Lectures on Genesis*. In *LW 1–8*.

———. *Luther's Works*. Edited by H. T. Lehmann. 55 vols. St. Louis: Concordia; Philadelphia: Fortress (Muhlenberg), 1955–.

———. "A Sermon on Keeping Children in School." In *LW 36: Word and Sacrament II*.

———. "To the Christian Nobility of the German Nation Concerning the Reform of the Christian Estate." In *LW 44: The Christian Society I*.

———. "Treatise on Good Works." In *LW 44: The Christian Society I*.

———. "Two Kinds of Righteousness." In *LW 31: Career of the Reformer I*.

Marty, Martin E. "Luther on Ethics: Man Free and Slave." In *Accents in Luther's Theology*, edited by Heino O. Kadia, 199–229. St. Louis: Concordia, 1967.

Maxfield, John A., Daniel Preus, and Martin Noland. *The Pieper Lectures: The Lutheran Doctrine of Vocation*. 2 vols. St. Louis: Concordia Historical Institute and Luther Academy, 2008.

Scott, Lesbia. "I Sing a Song of the Saints of God." Hymn no. 243 in *The Hymnal of the Protestant Episcopal Church in the USA*. New York: Church Pension Fund, 1940.

Torbet, Robert G. *The Baptist Ministry Then and Now*. Philadelphia: Judson, 1953.

Volf, Maroslav. *Work in the Spirit: Toward a Theology of Work*. New York: Oxford University Press, 1991.

Wingren, Gustaf. *Luther on Vocation*. Philadelphia: Muhlenberg, 1957.

PART TWO

Culture

9

Here I Stand ... or Do I?

Jean Bethke Elshtain

WHEN I WAS IN LUTHERAN CONFIRMATION SCHOOL, COMMITTING Luther's "Small Catechism" to memory—for we confirmands were grilled before the congregation on Confirmation Sunday on our knowledge of this pedagogical text—I loved to come to the conclusion of an article, the place where Luther puts his foot down and declares: THIS IS MOST CERTAINLY TRUE.

Not: this is likely true, or there's a high degree of probability that this is the case, or, this is "true" in scare quotes, given my construction of "truth" in the context of the representations of my time. You no doubt see the product of contemporary academic querulousness and muddiness in this last one.

Nowadays we may feel the need to apologize for Luther's alleged Eurocentrism and his masculinism and even intolerance in claiming "this is most certainly true"—on and on in this vein. By the time we're finished, Luther is reduced to a wraith whispering, "I think maybe this is true depending on what you mean by 'true'."

And as to Luther's thundering "HIER STEHE ICH. ICH KAN[N][1] NICHT ANDERS"—here we have another likely embarrassment. When we stir in the element of context, no doubt, a contemporary critic might claim that we all know that the ground on which Luther stood and felt so secure is shifting sand, not a foundation; clearly, Luther deluded himself in this regard. Sound and fury signifying much less than he claimed for, as Marx so correctly put it, "all that is solid melts into air." What we

---

1. From the editors: Modern German differs from that of Luther's day, spelling "can" (as in, "I can") with a double "n" rather than a single.

once thought solid vaporizes the moment that we turn our withering critical gaze in that direction.

I am exaggerating contemporary academic concepts and manias, no doubt. There is, after all, much that is salutary that emerges from paying critical attention to the words of titanic figures. This helps us to more reasonably sort out historic "truths" that may not be as unassailable as we once thought. Reason reminds us that we should not sacralize historic persons—they are flesh-and-blood mortal figures, not gods. That said, surely we have gone too far. In constantly pulling the rug out from under people's sources of meaning, solace, and purpose and leaving naught save a giant hole where once a powerful, historic tableau existed, what really, have we accomplished?

In one of his many powerful songs, Bob Dylan sings, "Ya gotta serve somebody." Wittingly or not, he underscored an abiding truth, and we should not pretend that we don't serve something (or somebody) outside ourselves. Alas, our critical powers may well become a fetish, the very altar at which we worship. One can discern, at times, an undercurrent of gleeful aggression in showing people their allegedly simplistic credulities. A will to power—to triumph over the simple folks—is at work here.

I am reminded of this when I see bewildered senior citizens listening stoically and submitting quietly as their traditional hymns are junked, their liturgy is rearranged, Scripture is made politically correct, old norms are abandoned as unenlightened and even "unChristian." They are no longer at home in their church home.

Some of this, to be sure, is inevitable; things do change and some things should, for example, any historic uses to which Scripture was put to justify egregious prejudices and mean-spiritedness. But that worry—far too bloated in Protestant mainline circles—is not what I'm talking about here. Rather, my sights are set on the fact that we have destroyed our capacity and authority to state boldly, *Hier stehe ich. Ich kan nicht anders* ("Here I stand. I cannot do otherwise"), and in the spirit of Luther, "This is most certainly true."

Must we jettison all we have been deeded as ineluctably tainted by its emergence within eras that were in so many ways "benighted" by our own standards? Correlatively, it is certainly the case that my claim—"This is most certainly true"—may be used by the ideologue in such a manner that aims to *silence other voices*, so that it becomes a monologue rather than a dialogue that is not only rightly intolerant of egregious errors but also dismissive of alternative, reasonable claims.

So: "Here I stand ... or do I?" Must Luther, a battered diminished Luther, be banished to the outer annex of the history museum where the has-beens are sent, or can Luther stand in his historic strength and determination as we appreciate the many features of this titanic personality's life and work? Mustn't we rather insist that he not only should be but *is* an immoveable, inflexible rock, if he is to be the vital Luther of historic memory? Can we, in the end, rehabilitate Luther and other historic figures and open the windows to new breezes that, while perhaps ruffling Luther's hair and sending his ecclesiastical robes flapping in the wind, nonetheless refuse to lay him low altogether?

Again: What remains of Luther's "Here I stand" and "This is most certainly true"? Who is Luther for us today? Unquestionably, Luther's is a complex and mixed legacy. For example, one essential dimension to Luther is Christian freedom. Here, alas, Luther is both liberator and jailor. He is bold in insisting that the Christian is free to serve, free to love God, free to worship, free to enact his or her vocation in the world. At the same time, the Christian is bound: bound in service to others, bound in obedience to God, bound to Scripture. This all sounds good; however, history tends to muddy things up—to put it mildly. The waters got muddied here because, over time, freedom became de-tethered from "bound," from service to and for others. We were free insofar as we were free from constraint, including the constraining ties that bound us in family, friendship, and community.

Nearly five centuries removed, Luther's legacy tilts in the direction of the jailor. What do I mean? What I have in mind is Luther's "imprisoned self"—i.e., the self that needs saving and justifying—all alone, naked before God. This is the self that is now free to serve, yet which in our own era has been transmuted into the autonomous self, i.e., the self which stands as the sole judge of the self. It goes without saying that Luther would be appalled at many of the dimensions of modern freedom in what I have called "the sovereign self," the master of all he or she surveys.

It would be grotesquely unfair, in my view, to saddle Luther with the lion's share of the responsibility for contemporary narcissism and self-servingness. At the same time, in assessing Luther's complex legacy, we do have to ask ourselves whether he guarded against the unleashing of the sovereign self. Perhaps, in his eagerness to break from the medieval church, he broke us too free from the ties that bind in institutions. Or perhaps it was not he, but we. He was not an altar-smasher. He criticized those who, in his name, in the name of the priesthood of all believers, entered churches only to destroy them and who hounded monks and nuns and even killed them. That he could be thus misunderstood, however, suggests that perhaps, in his brilliant and thundering rhetoric, he did too little to offer intrinsic constraints. This is a question around which many battles, past and present, are waged; but it is one which those concerned with Luther and his legacy cannot avoid.

Finally, there is the matter of Luther and the claims of truth, the issue with which I began. Here I want to defend Luther against his detractors. On this score, I must be firm: Christians have been altogether too timid. One need not be a rigid fundamentalist to insist that "This is most certainly true." In Robert Bolt's *A Man for All Seasons*, the words placed in Thomas More's mouth tell us that God created human beings to "serve him wittily" in the tangle of their minds. There are truths to be discovered and rediscovered. There are lessons to be learned and relearned. We serve neither ourselves nor others well if we temper our fundamental convictions. Luther, in line with the "Great Tradition," teaches us: "I believe in God the Father Almighty, I believe in Jesus Christ His only begotten Son . . ." Without these fundamental convictions, one endorses a sentimental orientation to "do good in the world, but one loses faith.

Permit me to share a personal illustration of what I have in mind. Not too long ago I accompanied a young woman, at her request, on a visit to a pastor. She was carrying a heavy burden. She had left her church and had decided to return. But, first, she had to unburden herself. She told the pastor of what she had done and the number of people she cared about who had been harmed. Simply and with decisive force, she stated, "I have sinned." Said the pastor: "You made a mistake." This, to me, was an extraordinary move. "Mistake" has none of the force that "sin" does. The conceit at present that we can substitute psychobabble for serious theological terms is damaging; it undermines theological seriousness and it undercuts our ability to come to grips with the realities of sin and what it does to individual persons and to entire cultures.

Here Luther would come to our aid. Luther's "bondage of the will" is nothing if not a corrective to human hubris. Does this language go too far in its reach, seeming to eradicate nearly all space or human agency? Perhaps, but the corrective is one that we need. Yet, we do not seek this corrective out, for the most part. This means that Luther is an outlier in most discussions. He looms, but only as a rather absent figure, even to communicants of the church that bears his name.

Let me offer one further illustration drawn from my experience. Some years ago I was invited as an "outside expert" to sit down with a group that was working on a statement from a Lutheran perspective on issues of war and peace. I entered the room, took my seat at the head of the table, made a few preliminary remarks and then indicated that it was probably best to proceed through questions. The first question went like this: "We have a problem. We have this albatross around our necks named 'Martin Luther.' What can we do about that?" I suppose I should not have been surprised—there is very little that should surprise us any longer. But it did shock me somewhat. Seated before me were those who claimed a long historic lineage and a complex, powerful heritage yet who were running as fast as they could in the opposite direction from their founder. Because Luther located himself in the just-war tradition and was no quasi-pacifist, he would no longer do.

Let us turn to another question that should be salient for all parents in contemporary American society, namely, education. In order to better assay the pedagogical dimensions of Luther's work, we need to remember that Luther embraced a notion of education as formation, the formation of a self to prepare the self for Christian vocations. These vocations included the plowman in the fields, the housewife in the kitchen, and the husband teaching his child carpentry. Luther criticized the notion that there were specifically Christian vocations of a highly spiritual nature to which but a few were called and, further, that these were superior to the lives and work of ordinary people. In asking whether Luther any longer makes sense to us we are, in effect, launching an inquiry into what we transmit to future generations and whether anything of the Christian heritage is passed on as being of essential if not inestimable worth.

Consider Luther at the Diet of Worms in 1521. We are familiar with the famous confession, "Here I stand. I cannot do otherwise. God help me. Amen." But ponder the words preceding this powerful proclamation: "I am only a man, not God. If I have spoken evil, bear witness against me. Unless you can convince me by Scripture, I am bound by the text. My conscience is captive to the word of God." We do well to consider the terms "conscience" and "captive." Nowadays we would likely say of conscience, "Of course, it is vital that consciences be formed. But we don't want consciences that are too strict because we don't want to be judgmental about others." For Luther the very substance of conscience, the heart of the matter, is "the word of God"—to which he is captive. He is not a free agent in this regard. But here, alas, we would cavil mightily. Conscience, to be conscience, must, in our view, be utterly "free." But what precisely do we mean by freedom? Luther's view of freedom and the modern notion, which has sometimes been called "subjective" or "expressive" individualism, do not comport; in fact, they clash at every point.

The self we extol today is a masterless self, captive to no one and nothing. It is a sovereign self, as I characterize it elsewhere in my work. Characteristic of this sovereign self is the assumption that I am a law unto myself, that my obligations to others are of a freely contracted nature, that rights trump obligations, and that nobody and nothing might have any prior claims on me. Now, we most assuredly would not convey such notions directly and baldly to students; nevertheless, they are in the air that we breathe in twenty-first-century America, and we imbibe these. Education from a Lutheran perspective can and should challenge such notions, but I suspect this is not done in any systematic way—in part, because we do not really accept the "bondage of the will." In fact, we have become exceedingly uncomfortable speaking of original sin or, as I indicated earlier, sin at all.

Here we do well to recall Luther's famous treatise on Christian freedom. The self is twinned, as it were, tethered to an interiorized self and the external world. It is in the inner man that righteousness dwells, if it has a home anywhere; external things do not produce Christian righteousness. Luther's thinking proceeds from two famous propositions: a Christian is *a perfectly free* lord of all, subject to none; and a Christian is *a perfectly dutiful servant* of all, subject to all. What have we, Luther's interpreters, done? Culturally, we have split the bound self from the free self. The free self triumphs; the bound self falls through the memory hole in which unpleasant historic truths disappear. The Lutheran distinctive that faith alone justifies necessarily begins with a recognition of our helpless sinfulness. Only grace and faith heal. We are free from the fear that law and works merit our justification—this is the benefit of Christian liberty. *Sola fides*: faith alone. In being saved we can, in fact, recapture something of our prelapsarian condition. Unfortunately, however, we cannot remain in the moment of incandescent grace—we are, after all, sinners. Without ongoing reminders of how we are bound, we convince ourselves that our being "saved" unbinds us altogether.

To say that Luther would find this contemporary misconstrual of ours disturbing is to understate the matter. For it is in and through our bondage to the word of God that we are called to service in behalf of our neighbor. By their fruits, after all, we shall know those who are properly "bound." We cannot live just for ourselves—precisely what the free, unbound self does. We are under the command of love as articulated by St. Augustine: to harm none and to serve all as best we can. Luther works to guarantee that we internalize awareness that we are bound. This is reflected in his insistence that children are bound in obedience to their elders, as they are to their parents, teachers, and, yes, secular rulers. All these expect to receive obedience and well they should. Obedience begins in the family and then extends more generally. Is obedience any longer crucial to our vocabulary, our understanding, our pedagogy?

Clearly not. We expect reasonably decent behavior but *we do not like* the sound of "obedience." It seems fundamentally not to comport with our understanding of freedom, nor with our view of what the young should be in relation to their elders. Without legitimate authority we cannot sustain either relationships or institutions. A signal error of modern liberal society is to conflate authority with something suspect, even with tyranny. This egregious error is stated explicitly in the work of the classic nineteenth-century liberal thinker John Stuart Mill, in his essential text *On Liberty*. Mill sets up an explicit antinomy between "liberty," on the one hand, and "authority," on the other. In consequence, this misguided error helped to fuel distrust of even legitimate authority. It muddied the waters where our ability to distinguish legitimate from illegitimate exercise of authority is concerned, and it pounded the final nail into the coffin of the "medieval right of resistance," which turned precisely on our capacity to separate authority from tyranny. To be sure, such notions lingered on in rather anemic form. But the die was cast.

Is Luther in any way culpable on this score? Many would argue "yes" because of his enormous distrust that government performed a positive ethical function. That view he associated with Aristotle, whom he despised, and Thomism, which he opposed strenuously. Ironically, because the only barrier that stands between an overweening and tyrannous state is the individual conscience rather than strong institutions—including church in the medieval sense—it became easier for those barriers to fall. Please do not think I am conflating Luther with such classical liberal thinkers as Mill—I am not. But Luther's mixed legacy includes his complex understanding of Christian freedom and his correlative views on secular authority and the extent to which it must be obeyed. He analogizes: even as Christ's commands are precisely that—commands—even so those entrusted by God with authority make commands that, for the most part, should be obeyed. This does not mean rulers can do whatever they want. But the secular or temporal sword is given extraordinary free reign in Luther's work. Even those who belong to the kingdom of God—a small, select minority—should obey so as not to give scandal to the vast majority who are citizens of the earthly kingdom. We need the sword because the great majority of citizens do not belong to the kingdom of God.

We are subject to the powers that be, and this need for obedience must be taught, all other things being equal. The temporal sword is frequently bloody, Luther tells us, because there is so much mischief afoot and the reign of the wicked cannot be permitted to triumph. Even the hangman is not to be despised. This role, too, is a service. Christians are enjoined to suffer evil without avenging themselves on behalf of others. The only ground for disobedience is if you are required to renounce your faith; otherwise, governing authority is a divine service.

Is this a view that we teach? Certainly not. It does not comport with the principles articulated as the grounds for colonial disobedience to the British King. That was derived in part from the work of John Locke, who himself had been educated in a curriculum that made contact with the medieval scholastic tradition, one in which authority was clearly distinguished from tyranny. So the issue of how far temporal authority extends remains a highly controversial question. It is surely this debate, this controversy, that should be conveyed rather than to ignore the difficulties and even the troubling features of what Luther had to say on such matters. While I have not examined the curriculum of Lutheran K-12 schools, I suspect this is not routinely studied. I would be happy to learn that I am wrong in this respect.

So, here too, as in Luther on the bondage of the will, I suspect Luther no longer makes sense to us, at least not Luther in the main rather than a Luther shorn of all his bite and even his bluster. I have suggested that Luther, bowdlerized (if you will), severs earthly governance from normative imperatives to a great extent, and that this confounds the question of obedience to authority. In thinking along these lines I have the experience of Nazi Germany in mind and an issue that has long vexed me: why did Lutherans obey? The Deutsche Christen allied with the state, Lutheran bishops offering the Hitler salute and positioning the swastika on Christian altars. What in the Lutheran tradition permitted this in such a wholesale way? The historic record, still being revealed, demonstrates that Catholic Bavaria actually did considerably better in this regard, although this is not our topic and not a matter to debate here. But why such obedience, particularly when Luther is consistently credited with helping to presage the age of democratic revolutions in the sixteenth and seventeenth centuries—revolutions that involved rebellions again monarchical overreach and, in America, the drive towards constitutionalism?

Can both elements—Luther's understanding of human freedom and his view of secular authority—be true? Yes, I believe they can, unfortunately. It depends to a great extent on what portion of Luther's legacy one embraces, endorses, and conveys. No wonder Luther has been called Janus-faced by many cultural critics and political historians. His revolt led directly both to *cuius regio, euius religio* (Augsburg, 1555) and to the territorial state (Westphalia, 1648). This was a fateful development indeed, for an official state religion—part of the official governing apparatus, so to speak—is much less likely to undertake the kind of critical scrutiny that can lead directly to disobedience should that apparatus violate its mandate. If we turn to Dietrich Bonhoeffer's indictment of Nazi German rule, one might be required, in a sense, to abandon one's citizenship. Clearly, I am not suggesting this was an explicit aim of Luther—not at all—but this is one of the fraught unintended consequences of his revolt and the language in which it was cast.

Let us turn once more to a critical interpretation of Luther by contemporary analysts in order to take a direct look at his complex legacy. Again, we are justified in asking, is his position intelligible and accessible to us, whether we agree or disagree? Can it be conveyed clearly to young Americans, or children of the West more generally? Consider the words of the distinguished historian Constantin Fasolt: "The promise of freedom and self-determination, that revelation of his self to the world, that ruthless honesty that gave Luther credibility. Theology mattered to those who wanted reasons. Without theology, Luther himself could scarcely have acted as he did. In that sense theology is crucial to understanding the history of the Reformation.... Henceforth conscience was never again to disappear from the stage of politics. Conscience was there for good."[2]

We see here the putting together of what contemporary society—certainly contemporary liberalism in its dominant form—pries apart. There are two strands: monist and pluralist. Monism insists that there must be one dominant site of legitimate authority in society. Liberalism is of two minds on this. One strand tends toward plural sites of authority, purpose, meaning, legitimacy. Another—and one that prevails in many academic arguments—privatizes all institutions that are not the state, so that the state takes on a monist drive. It is this monism of authority that I here lament and that is the trajectory of Luther's thought, given the way in which he stresses individual conscience and deemphasizes the legitimate public authority of church. In this sense, he prepares the way for the political theology that underlies the emergence of what I have called the Protestant nation-state. In this light, Fasolt is correct that "modern politics is unimaginable without the redefinition of the relation between politics and religion that Martin Luther... demanded and obtained. It was the Reformation that made the separation of religion, law, and politics inevitable."[3] The problem is not per se this separation—the drive towards a secular state as he knows it lies therein—but rather the privatization of religion. We rightly applaud the disestablishment of religion—not official state religion—but we should be very concerned about religion's subsequent privatization.

The most serious issue is the way in which Luther's political theology unleashes the prince by diminishing the authority of any other entity. For Luther, there is nothing human beings can do to bind God. That is, whatever God wills is right because God wills it. If God wills it, it is right. "What God wills is not therefore right because he ought or ever was bound so to will; but on the contrary, what takes place is therefore right because he so wills."[4] Even though God is a God of the

2. Fasolt, *Limits of History*, 17.

3. Ibid., 49.

4. Luther, *Bondage of the Will*, section 88.

will, he remains trustworthy. If we conjure a model of earthly rule that exists as a kind of mimesis of Luther's understanding of God, it suggests that there is nothing we can do to bind the prince. If he wills it, it must belong within the sphere of his legitimate exercise of authority. Of course, Luther knows this cannot be entirely right. But, as I already indicated, the difficulty is that institutional barriers to an unbound prince decline. We do not get a sense in Luther's thought that the prince is hemmed in by a dense thicket of law.

But the problem remains: how to bind the prince? Our consciences do not bind the prince. We enter the world of Luther's "two kingdoms" doctrine. What is done in temporal rule cannot possibly touch on our internal state, what Luther calls our "innermost being." For the most part, the temporal ruler should be obstructed in his often grim work neither by the pope above nor the people below. Thereby do we teach that Luther set the conditions for free exercise of religion, even when the Reformation seemingly yielded not so much free exercise as official state religion? Notwithstanding this impression, he did disentangle the state from an explicit normative and theologically justified purpose. Given Luther's bias against institutions and his greatest fear—disorder and chaos—he is compelled to rely on secular authority. Alas, the prince's conscience is the weak reed that checks his exercise of power. This is, of course, problematic because by no stretch of the imagination does Luther believe most temporal authorities will be authentic Christians and therefore self-binding, that is, servants to all as well as lords of all.

Mind you, Luther's is not a view of the divine right of kings; rather, it is a doctrine that temporal authority is divinely instituted. The state's tasks are both punitive and positive in that the prince must protect the exercise of faith. Luther articulates his thesis concerning temporal authority forthrightly, as I have already indicated. He acknowledges that most temporal rulers are usually a bunch of fools or knaves, so one must expect the worst and hope for a bit better until that rare bird, the Christian prince, comes along. For guidance on the law of the temporal swords, Luther turns to the story of the Israelites and their kingdom, an account that includes the scriptural warrant for the temporal sword and the law. On this account, the sword must not be shy. The prince should exercise his authority boldly, lest chaos and criminality thrive. The world cannot be ruled without blood. It follows that the temporal ruler's sword is often bloody; he is God's rod and vengeance. There are some—likely the vast majority—who need this coercive and positive sword more than do true Christians. Even as human beings are twinned, so classes of human beings are divided into those who belong to the kingdom of God and those who belong to the kingdom of the sword.

Alas, it will never be the case in this vale of tears that all the world is truly faithful; thus, the sword is required in perpetuity. Some humans—those who are citizens of God's kingdom—go much beyond what the law requires to help their neighbors and give of themselves. But they cannot do this work of *caritas* if disorder is threatening and chaos persists. Given Luther's assumptions, it is more rather than less likely that force is needed to bind human beings to one another and to the law. Were we "naturally" more good and less wicked, the hand of temporal authority could rest more lightly on our heads. But we are not. For this reason, worldly authority has the power to punish and punish severely. This is its legitimate task.

There exist both mild and strong interpretations of Luther on the will and the state. The strong interpretation, for Luther, holds that human reason is the devil's plaything. It follows that our self-willing is invariably inflicted by the sin of pride Adam's ur-sin of disobedience. According to weaker interpretations, Luther hopes to tame strong notions of the efficacy of the will in order to keep believers both humble and prayerfully aware that their salvation lies not in self-worth and deeds but in grace, prayer, and God's forgiveness. Most assuredly, Luther's self cannot be said to be sovereign, even in its innermost part. The weakness of the human will is such that to pretend we can consistently will the good is folly. We are consistently reminded by Luther of our creaturely status.

But what about the nagging conundrum of temporal authority? Human beings—all human beings—are subjected to a form thereof. That this is so is unrelated to one's interest in a common good or one's hope that the least harm might be done. Only if *all persons* belonged to the kingdom of God would the need for temporal law vanish. Temporal rule restrains the unchristian and the wicked. Those believers who, naively, hold that one can rule by the gospel alone would, were they in ascendance, unleash the beasts on the world to devour, slash, and slay as they would will. On this earth, by Luther's reasoning, if the lion lies down with the lamb, the lamb must be replaced frequently.

Although they are under temporal authority, Christians are not of its totality; however, they should, if called upon, fulfill temporal offices, including even that of the hangman. Government, ordained of God, is not to be despised. Soldiers, too, can be Christians insofar as they serve others even unto sacrifice of self. Christ, it is true, did not bear the sword, but neither did he abolish it. In a sort of pre-Machiavellian move, Luther urges temporal authority not to punish too much or too little. The prince acts under a norm of ordinary requirements and under the claim of necessity. Necessity may call for the temporary use of unusual authority by the sword with a particular problem at a particular moment—a formulation that carries through to the present. Luther believed the so-called Peasant Revolt, for which he was an inadvertent catalyst with his "priesthood of all believers," should be put down bloodily as it threatened temporal peace. Luther's reaction to the revolting peasants is a rather ugly one, but nevertheless intelligible given his fear of anarchy and chaos and his insistence that one should not literalize Scripture politically speaking. Theology alas is not a one-way ticket to public policy, as we might put it nowadays. Luther finds the peasants—and by extension any person or group—who identify their cause with Jesus Christ to be an "outrageous folly and perversion of the gospel." Those who do should be smitten, slain, and stabbed. Finally, and most fatefully, the tumult Luther reflected and contributed to stirred things so much that Europe was soon riven by upheavals, wars, and confessional controversies, even unto use of the sword. There was no higher unity—no higher sovereign (save God)—to appeal to any longer, the papacy and empire having been denuded of much of their previous authority both in theory and in practice.

But how shall we convey any and all of this in a highly voluntaristic, individualistic society? Carefully streamlined, with troubling bits hived off, Luther can be properly placed in the category of champion of freedom, and this unambiguously. In this way, we can make a "thinned out" Luther both accessible and more or less acceptable. The moral and political reality is far more interesting, far more complex, far more disconcerting, because Luther challenges us on so many fronts, beginning with his view of the self. That self is forged in the interstices of the spiritual dimension of the self, while the locus for formation, including education, is the family. Any discussion of Luther on education, then, must acknowledge the importance of the family. Disintegration and weakening of the family is, therefore, a matter of signal import to spiritual as well as temporal existence. Certainly all the empirical evidence available to us shows the terrible costs to individuals and society as a whole when families break apart. There is really no contest on this score, although idealogues remain who deny the evidence as if any constructed set of intimate arrangements will do. They will not. And they do not. Because we have been so immersed for so long in the view that to advance a normative view of family life is perforce to be intolerant, judgmental, bigoted, and all the rest, we remain silent on such issues lest we appear to be out of step.

To conclude, permit me to further comment on the family as the heart of the educative and pedagogical matter. We can then assess whether even this part of Luther's legacy is any longer fully accessible to us. If not, what is our alternative? The Christian family is the epicenter of human social existence. The family is an arena of compassion, concern, kindness, and emotion; but Luther also locates learning obedience to authority within the family, since the Bible commands children to honor and to obey their fathers and their mothers. But Luther not only finds the source of parental authority in that commandment, he goes further:

> For all authority has its root and source in parental authority. For where a father is unable to bring up his child alone, he takes a teacher to teach him; if he is too weak, he takes his friend or neighbor to help him; when he departs this life, he gives authority to others who are chosen for the purpose. So he must have servants, men and maids, under him for the household, so that all who are called master stand in the place of parents, and must obtain from them authority and power to command. Wherefore in the Bible they are called fathers.[5]

So important is our understanding of authority and obedience that Luther prophesied "the end of the whole world" should the "rule of the parents" be lost.

If the child does not learn obedience in the home, the temporal order is threatened insofar as the child will be a willful and rebellious subject. Luther tied the nature, structure, and purpose of the secular order to that of the family. He saw the family not simply as an analogue or microcosm of the state, but found the origin of all authority in the scriptural injunction to parents. Luther, however, did not follow classical patriarchal theories in collapsing parental and political rule, nor is there a grant here of unlimited absolute dominion. Rather, he adopts a perspective that seeks the origin and prototype of secular rule in the

5. Luther, *Large Catechism*, iv.

rule of fathers, declaring that an important relation between political and parental rule exists even when parental rule is natural and political rule is not. Parental rule is antecedent to all political forms; it is given in the order of creation itself.

Representing the future of society, the child is to be dearly beloved as well as disciplined to obey. While it is true that we in the present do dearly love our children, we are doing a very poor job, it seems to me, of instilling in them a sense of legitimate authority and the extent to which it should be obeyed. We may think (or wish) that democracy has overtaken any such need. But, if anything, democracy requires self-discipline and authority more than authoritarian societies. We rely on the individual who is bound by inner conscience rather than external threat. The formation of inner conscience is a project that cannot be successfully carried out unless the child is reared in a situation of freedom *and* bondage, love *and* discipline. To the extent that one exists to the exclusion of the other, the inner voice of conscience is either not formed fully or is malformed. The results we see around us in society every day. The essential question, however, is whether this argument of Luther is within our repertoire of ethical, moral, theological, and political understandings any longer. If it is, it is in weakened form. And that should be a cause for some concern. The more one ponders these and related matters, the more Luther's status as one of Western history's most titanic figures is confirmed, even as his status as a cardboard cutout saint of freedom evaporates. And that is as it should be.

Bibliography

Fasolt, Constantin. *The Limits of History*. Chicago: University of Chicago Press, 2004.
Luther, Martin. *The Bondage of the Will*. Translated by H. Cole. Peabody, MA: Hendrickson, rep. 2007.
———. *The Large Catechism*. Translated by F. Bente and W. H. T. Dau, 565–77. In *Triglot Concordia: The Symbolical Books of the Evangelical Lutheran Church*. St. Louis: Concordia, 1921.

10

Reclaiming Tolerance
A. J. Conyers and Fethullah Gülen

David B. Capes

In his book *The Long Truce* (2001) A. J. Conyers argues that tolerance, a principle doctrine in Western democracies, is not a public virtue; rather he contends that it is a political strategy employed to centralize power and guarantee profits. Tolerance, of course, seemed to be a reasonable response to the religious wars of the sixteenth and seventeenth centuries, but tolerance based upon indifference to all values except political power and materialism has relegated ultimate questions of meaning to private life. Conyers offers another model for tolerance based upon values and resources already resident in pre-Reformation Christianity.

In this essay, we consider aspects of Conyers' case against the modern, secular doctrine of tolerance. We examine his attempt to reclaim the practice of Christian tolerance based upon humility, hospitality, and the "powerful fact" of the incarnation. Furthermore, we bring the late Conyers into dialogue with Fethullah Gülen, a Muslim scholar, prolific writer, and source of inspiration for millions of moderately inclined Muslims. We explore how both Conyers and Gülen interpret their scriptures and traditions in order to fashion a theology and political ideology conducive to peaceful coexistence.

Fethullah Gülen was born in 1941 near Erzurum, Turkey. He grew up in a religiously observant home, the son of an imam. He became a state preacher in 1959 and took his first post in Izmir. Inspired by the teachings of Said Nursi and Mevlana Jalal ad-Din Rumi, Gülen advocates a spiritual form of Islam that is open to science, promotes education, and is deeply committed to interfaith dialogue. One of his principle ideas is *hizmet* (Turkish), the notion that all true believers have a duty to serve the "common good" of the community, nation, and world. As a result he has inspired a transnational civic movement often referred to as the Gülen movement.[1] His followers have founded schools (more than 500) and hospitals and organized various charitable and educational institutions in many countries around the world. In his many books, publications, and audio recordings Gülen condemns terrorism as un-Islamic and appeals instead for understanding, dialogue, and tolerance based on religious principles. In the late 1990s Gülen immigrated to the United States for health reasons, although many suspect that it had more to do with tensions between him and the secular Turkish authorities. Gülen had been accused—but was later acquitted—of advocating the establishment of an Islamic state in the Ataturk's Turkey.

In many ways Conyers is a suitable dialogue partner with Gülen on the question of tolerance.[2] Until his untimely death, Conyers had distinguished himself as a gifted Baptist theologian with an ever-increasing audience. He was a consummate "Southern gentleman," kind, welcoming, sincere. As a scholar, he had benefited from a positive relationship with Jürgen Moltmann, whose influence appears consistently, though not uncritically, in his work.[3] As a Baptist, Conyers was a member of a denomination in the U.S. that is not typically associated with tolerance but is with strong convictions, passion, and fervency in faith. Still, despite popular perceptions, there is a significant tradition of tolerance and freedom of conscience within many Baptist thinkers in Europe, beginning with Thomas Helwys. Baptists, of course, were a religious minority at the turn of the seventeenth century, and so they faced hostility from both established churches and government officials. As a result, they advocated for religious liberty initially for themselves but by extension for all. They formulated the doctrine directly from Christian Scripture, reason, and human experience. Essentially, they argued that government should not meddle in matters of religion and conscience. Had they known it, they would have agreed wholeheartedly with the Qur'anic injunction that there is no compulsion in religion (2:256). Baptist leaders scandalized some by advocating religious liberty for

1. For a useful description of the Gülen movement written by an insider who is also a social scientist, see Muhammed Çetin, *Gulen Movement*.

2. For an overview of Gülen's life see Ünal and Williams, *Advocate of Dialogue*, 1–42.

3. E.g., Conyers, *God, Hope, and History*.

Roman Catholics, Turks, Jews, and heretics alike.[4] Religious uniformity, they believed, was not necessary to ensure the domestic tranquility.[5] In the last century this Baptist distinctive is articulated carefully in the work of E. Y. Mullins,[6] and Conyers builds and expands on that tradition in his own way. Conyers then represents one of the most recent and articulate advocates for tolerance in American Baptist life. But Conyers also recognizes that the practice of toleration is "not an exclusively Christian predisposition, for the practice of toleration is often touchingly and effectively expressed in such religious philosophies as one finds associated with Hinduism, Taoism, Confucianism, and among the Sufi mystics of Islam."[7] This is all the more reason to bring Conyers and Gülen into conversation.

Conyer's Critique

Since the seventeenth century tolerance has often been considered a public virtue. In the last decades of the twentieth century tolerance/toleration became one of the principle virtues, institutionalized in Western democracies in a variety of ways.[8] Conyers, however, questions whether tolerance should be considered a virtue at all. Compared with other, classical virtues such as love, courage, and moderation, Conyers argues that tolerance is different because everyone acknowledges that there must be limits regarding toleration. When John Locke wrote famously regarding tolerance,[9] he argued that tolerance is not limitless. Some are not to be tolerated, including atheists and Roman Catholics according to Locke. While we might disagree with where the line of toleration is drawn, everyone acknowledges that the line has to be drawn some-

---

4. Helwys, *Mistery of Iniquity*, 69.
5. McBeth, *Baptist Heritage*, 85–86.
6. See, e.g., Mullins, *Axioms of Religion*.
7. Conyers, *Long Truce*, 228.
8. Marcuse, "Repressive Tolerance," 1, argues that tolerance is an end in itself. Marcuse, who is a Hegelian, sees history as eventually telling the "truth." So the end of this virtue itself is played out in "extralegal means," i.e., violence and revolution. The irony is in how the original purpose of tolerance, namely, to assuage the problems of religious wars in earlier centuries, will climax in violence. This is one of the reasons why Conyers sees the twentieth century as being the most violent. See Conyer's, *Listening Heart*.
9. Locke, *Letter Concerning Toleration*.

where. When the Boniuk Institute for the Study and Advancement of Religious Toleration at Rice University held its inaugural conference in September 2005, the theme of that conference was "Tolerance and Its Limits." In Conyers' view, true virtue has no limits. He writes:

> A virtue strengthens our relationships. From a Christian perspective, all virtues serve the interests of love, love being the chief virtue and goal of life. Humility, patience, and prudence make it possible to love God, the world, and human beings, all in their proper order and proportion. Virtues are interconnected and, in a sense, are all one. They are themselves the goal of human life. We are created for this: to be capable of loving.[10]

For Conyers, all lesser virtues serve the chief virtue, love. There is never a time when love is out of place or courage is inappropriate or moderation is unwise. But everyone agrees that tolerance cannot be without limits.

So then, what is tolerance if it is not a virtue? Conyers proffers that tolerance is a modern strategy to establish centralized power and to protect economic prosperity. While it may depend on virtues such as humility, moderation, patience, etc., tolerance is in fact a policy to achieve a particular end. That particular end itself is a good. Tolerance aims to ease the tensions rooted in the significant differences facing a shrinking, global world; as such it is not an end but a means to an end, a strategy that seeks harmony and peace within our common life.[11] Now, Conyers advocates for peaceful coexistence as a good worthy of all our efforts. But he questions whether the modern strategy of tolerance advocated in secular democracies has a sufficient basis. He bases his argument upon an analysis of key writers on tolerance, including Thomas Hobbes, Pierre Bayle, John Locke and others.[12]

Conyers begins his critique of the modern doctrine of tolerance by noting that its genesis in the thought of John Locke and John Stuart Mill arose along with the establishment of the modern nation-states.[13] Prior to that time, human societies had been composed of a variety of "natural" associations based on ethnic, religious, familial, and economic ties.

10. Conyers, *Long Truce*, 7–8.
11 Ibid.
12. Ibid., 66–168.
13. Ibid., 5. Conyers defines the nation-state as "political entities taking in large territories and uniting peoples heretofore politically unrelated."

These groups have their own purpose, authority structure, and internal discipline.[14] With the rise of nation-states, however, the influence of the natural associations is diminished in favor of more centralized authority. As this transpires, there is a concomitant development: a growing isolation of the individual. In the pre-modern period identity had been constructed in relation to a group. Now with the authority and the influence of the group eclipsed by the larger, more powerful state, identity is confused. Rather than necessary and generative to the life of a person, these associations are construed as voluntary and accidental. Under the new paradigm the question could be asked: which came first, the individual or the group? Or, put another way, does the individual give rise to the group or does the group give rise to the individual? According to Conyers, "the result was a powerful state and a lonely individual, two distinctive features of the modern period."[15]

While we tend to think of the world today almost exclusively in terms of large, diverse nation-states, this rather recent phenomenon brought with it significant changes to social, political, and religious life. In the modern nation-state the centralization of the government depends largely on the secularization of public life. As Michael Walzer has argued, in order to establish peace differences must be managed.[16] Generally, they are managed by a single, dominant group that organizes public life in such a way as to reflect and maintain its own culture. Unmanaged differences will inevitably "disturb the peace." Differences, especially religious differences with their ultimate claims, must be managed above all. So, there are three options: (1) insist that all have the same religion; (2) forbid religion from entering the public square; or (3) consign religion to the private sphere. Generally, it is options 2 and 3 that have characterized Western democracies. In France and Turkey, for example, the practice of laicism has effectively excluded religion from public life. In the United States and other Western democracies, freedom of religion may be guaranteed but ample social and legal strictures are present to consign religion effectively to the margins.

14. Bonhoeffer, *Ethics*, 147, thinks that there is inevitable tension that exists between the natural associations and the organized state. Governments and organizations may collapse but natural associations (e.g., family, friends, religious communities) tend to go on. Natural associations may be disrupted for a time but they generally survive. For that reason natural associations are ultimately more influential.

15. Conyers, *Long Truce*, 6.

16. Walzer, *On Toleration*, 25.

No doubt the religious wars that devastated Europe in the sixteenth and seventeenth centuries played a significant role in how modern philosophers and statesmen constructed their views of tolerance. But Conyers points out that the expansion of territories, the rise of powerful nation-states, and the growth of trade with its promises of wealth made Europe ripe for conflict without the stresses caused by religious differences. Clearly, religion was not the only factor leading to the horrors of the Thirty Years War, but it was partly to blame.

Conyers believes the modern doctrine of toleration has failed and will continue to fail because it bifurcates life into public and private spheres and assigns questions of ultimate concern a role only on the margins.[17] While the modern doctrine of tolerance pretends initially to support the idea of religion, it almost immediately will neutralize any sincere expression of religious conviction. With the one hand the tolerant democracy gives—and it can afford to give because it is a powerful, prosperous state—with the other it takes away. The wedding of tolerance with power will ultimately mean that toleration will give way to other kinds of intolerance.[18]

Reclaiming the Practice of Tolerance

Since the modern project of tolerance will likely fail, Conyers suggests that we must seek to reclaim the ancient practice of tolerance in order to meet the growing tensions apparent in our shrinking, global world. For those who are open to religion,[19] the practice of "high tolerance" or "authentic tolerance," as he refers to it, is natural inasmuch as it deals with ultimate questions of meaning and purpose. The modern strategy of tolerance, however, merely postpones those questions in order to privilege other, more manageable questions. But, according to Conyers, authentic tolerance must first be disentangled from the "questionable alliance with power and will to power."[20]

---

17. Conyers, "Rescuing Tolerance," 43–44, recognizes that the privatization of religion was intended not only to protect the state, but religious life as well. But this resulted in the assumption that public life belonged ultimately to the state.

18. Marcuse, "Repressive Tolerance."

19. For Conyers tolerance is a theological question. Modernity has worked hard to close the door on the transcendent nature of tolerance. Ultimately, understanding tolerance is for all insofar as any discussion about tolerance is a religious discussion.

20. Conyers, *Long Truce*, 229.

Conyers asks: Is there a practice of tolerance not based on indifference to the question of "the good"? Is there an authentic tolerance that does not privilege power and materialism over deeper, more abiding questions? Yes, he argues, and the answer is found in the central mystery of the incarnation. For Conyers "the powerful fact of the incarnation" provides a basis sufficient to reorder human existence and establish peace amidst difference.[21] Conyers is quick to point out, however, that he is not talking about "the doctrine of the incarnation"; for it is in the nature of doctrines to develop over time and doctrines may or may not be true. Rather he is speaking of the central conviction that God had become flesh in the particularity of Jesus of Nazareth and that He was in Christ to reconcile the world.[22]

As a "fact" or "conviction" rather than a doctrine, it is not necessary that we grasp the reality of the incarnation or can explain it in some systematic fashion. It is more important, according to Conyers, that the reality grasps us and reorients our lives essentially toward a more tolerant and open attitude toward others who share the same enfleshed existence. Incarnation then becomes the basis for hope. A life shaped by the vigorous conviction of the incarnation may well be aware that the world is filled with suffering (because of intolerance and other problems), but it also recognizes that it is not destined for suffering nor is it beyond hope. If God has entered our world and dwelt among us, then our world must be good and our future hopeful. This stands in stark contrast to the modern notion that the world is to be feared, subdued, and made safe for power and profit.

If the fact of the incarnation provides hope, then the purpose of the incarnation provides reconciliation. Initially, that means reconciliation between God and humanity; but it also means reconciliation between people for whom differences have proven hard and often insurmountable problems. Reconciliation in practice manifests itself in tolerance and openness to the other.[23] Conyers argues that the church is the "natural culture" for reclaiming an authentic practice of toleration despite the impulses that have led some to legitimate violence through religion. If God was in Christ reconciling the world (2 Cor 5:16), then the reconciliation of all things (*ta panta*) becomes the *raison d'etre* of

21. Ibid., 231–32.
22. Ibid.
23. Ibid., 241.

the church. Ultimately, the incarnation means that all things are interrelated. Therefore, all things must matter to God. And all things must include all people. In Christ, God loved the world. We are part of that world and so is the other.[24]

The incarnation also reveals something hitherto unknown regarding God and humanity. In Christ's self-emptying and death on the cross (Phil 2:5–11) his followers see a "lordly example" of humility and are called to imitate it.[25] Therefore, according to Conyers, the practice of the incarnation is first of all the practice of humility that manifests itself in listening to others. This does not mean listening for the sake of gaining advantage or seeking information; this is listening expectantly, waiting to hear the truth.[26] Conyers surveys the biblical evidence for toleration and defines it as: "a willingness to hear other traditions and learn from them."[27] Indeed the fundamental virtue necessary for tolerance to exist and flourish is humility. This kind of authentic tolerance reflects a depth to humility that is willing to set aside the self to attend to the voice of the other. Humility, then, for Conyers is what makes dialogue possible. Dialogue birthed in authentic tolerance is not content to dwell on similarities, agreements, and surface issues; it begins with commonalities but does not stop until it has engaged the most cherished and deeply held convictions of a group, even when those convictions differ considerably from people to people. And this kind of dialogue stands in sharp relief to the pseudo-toleration that makes "dialogue possible only so long as it conforms to certain 'rules' that preordain its result."[28] Conyers remarks:

> Just as pseudo-toleration answers power with power, it answers bigotry with bigotry. The hallmark of authentic tolerant practice should be the listening heart for which the wise king prayed and not the management of language and appointing itself the arbiter of all public discussions.[29]

Elsewhere Conyers refers to this tolerant disposition toward the other as *the practice of the open soul*. He writes:

24. Ibid., 234.
25. Hurtado, "Jesus as Lordly Example."
26. Conyers, *Long Truce*, 233.
27. Ibid., 33.
28. Ibid., 244.
29. Ibid. Most translations of 1 Kgs 3:9 indicate that Solomon prays for "wisdom," but the Hebrew phrase means literally "listening heart."

Such toleration reaches outward toward an ecumenical goal, with eternity as its ultimate horizon, because its practice is essentially the practice of the open soul. It springs not from the fear and self-protection that Thomas Hobbes was so sure animated all things in human society where life is naturally "solitary, poor, nasty, brutish and short," but it springs from a propensity toward magnanimity and a predisposition toward faith. The recovery of this *practice of toleration* would mark the reversal of a very old prejudice in the modern mind. It would reverse the deep-seated suspicion that undergirds much of modern thought, the suspicion that the world cannot be known, much less loved, and that it must be conquered in order to be made safe.[30]

The practice of the open soul is essentially the practice of hospitality. It involves welcoming the stranger and serving his/her physical, social, and spiritual needs. In any cross-cultural exchange both parties are strangers, aliens to one another. So hospitality involves not only giving but also receiving in a way that gives dignity and honor to the other. As Amy Oden has written, "Acts of inclusion and respect, however small, can powerfully reframe social relations and engender welcome."[31]

It is important to note that Conyers considers "high tolerance," as he refers to it, a recovery or reclaiming of what the church practiced in earlier days. He finds significant evidence that Christian believers in earlier centuries did exercise tolerance and openness, though not universally. He notes in particular the writings of Justin Martyr (d. 165), Clement of Alexandria (d. 215), and Thomas Aquinas (1225–1274). Justin, he notes, associated the *Logos* of Greek philosophy with the Christ and made possible a link from the earliest, pre-Christian philosophers to Christian theology. Similarly, Clement incorporated the best of Greek literature and philosophy into his own writings.[32] According to Conyers, Thomas Aquinas' *Summa Theologiae*—one of the greatest achievements in Christian thought and history—"would never have seen the light of day but for a strong sentiment for a certain openness toward thinkers from other faiths and other philosophies."[33] In particular on the question of truth (*Summa Theologiae, prima pars*, Q16, "On Truth") Aquinas draws from Christian, Jewish, Muslim and "pagan"

---

30. Ibid., 245.
31. Oden, *And You Welcomed Me*, 14. See too Pohl, *Making Room*.
32. Conyers, *Long Truce*, 34–36.
33. Idem, "Rescuing Tolerance."

teachers. But Aquinas does not draw on these thinkers is any sort of modern way. Conyers remarks:

> What are we to make of this unpretentious move by Saint Thomas, in a work of Christian theology, from the church fathers, to medieval Christians, to a Muslim, to a pagan? There is no self-conscious celebration of diversity here, not even the thought of it. Nor is there the resigned air of "everyone is entitled to one's own opinion, since no one can gainsay opinion." Just the opposite is the case, in fact, because there is the resolute pressing forward to an idea of truth that is common to everyone simply because it is *real* for everyone. It is inclusive not in the easy modern way that makes its claim before any effort has been expended to find common ground but in the more arduous medieval way.[34]

Conyers, of course, is not alone in this assessment. David Burrell suggests that the doctrine of God inherited by the enlightened west was already an achievement of interfaith dialogue.[35]

Conyers and Gülen

Although A. J. Conyers and Fethullah Gülen were shaped in different worlds culturally and religiously—and I find no evidence that one influenced the other—amazing resonance exists between them on this issue of tolerance. This resonance is located precisely in the vitality of their respective faiths. For both men, their deep religious commitment informs their unwavering commitment to tolerance.[36] Still, there are subtle differences between them based in large part upon the faith communities and worlds from which they come.

First, it must be acknowledged that both Gülen and Conyers are working from a similar definition of toleration. Gülen defines tolerance as embracing all people regardless of differences and having the ability to put up with matters we personally dislike by drawing upon the strength of convictions, conscience, faith, and a generous heart.[37]

---

34. Idem, *Long Truce*, 233.

35. Burrell, *Knowing the Unknowable God*, ix.

36. On the paradox of commitment and tolerance in Gülen, see Kurtz, "Gülen's Paradox."

37. Gülen, *Love & Tolerance*, 46.

One of the key concepts Gülen uses in discussions of tolerance is *hoshgoru* (*hosh* = good, pleasant; *goru* = view). Sometimes this word is translated into English as "tolerance," but conceptually it is probably best taken as "empathetic acceptance." For Gülen, tolerance involves identifying with and accepting others. But one cannot identify with others without first listening to them and understanding the world from which they come.

Conyers would agree with this construal of tolerance and go on to say that difference is what makes "high tolerance" possible. Unlike some moderns who may wish to eliminate differences and seek to assimilate minority groups into the powerful state, Gülen and Conyers argue that embracing differences ultimately serves the same goal and demonstrates respect for those who otherwise would be left out.[38] Furthermore, both Gülen and Conyers locate the resources necessary to create an atmosphere of tolerance precisely in the particularity of each faith community. For Gülen, the essence of Islam—like the word "islam"—involves surrender [to God], peace, contentment, and security. He cites a well-known episode from the life of the Prophet. When asked what practice of the faith is most beneficial, Muhammad remarks that feeding the hungry and offering *salaam* (the greeting of peace) to both friend and stranger are the most beneficial.[39] Essentially, the pursuit of peace and seeking to establish peace are fundamental to Islam. If "peace is better" as the Qur'an teaches (4:128), then the true Muslim will work toward peace. Conyers, likewise, from a Christian perspective, argues that the pursuit of peace via authentic tolerance is implicitly theological.[40] If the modern project of tolerance sets aside faith and ultimate questions about humanity, the world and God because these questions cannot be easily resolved, authentic tolerance deals precisely with these questions and embraces those who answer the questions differently.[41] The pursuit of peace is therefore an essential call for any Christ-follower as it is for any Muslim.

38. Ibid., 33. Other words for tolerance include "respect," "mercy," "generosity," and "forbearance." Tolerance is the "most essential element of moral systems."

39. Ibid., 58.

40. Conyers, *Long Truce*, 25.

41. Within the Christian tradition, for example, Jesus is known as the "Prince of Peace" based primarily upon the strength of an intertextual appropriation of Isa 9:6 to him. Likewise, Jesus teaches his disciples: "Blessed are the peacemakers for they will be called the sons of God" (Matt 5:9).

For Gülen, tolerance is ultimately rooted in the attributes of God. God is all-forgiving, all-merciful, all-compassionate. These attributes of God, while common to the teaching of all the messengers of the past, have been communicated most effectively through the Qur'an and the Sunna. In particular, the Qur'an calls all Muslims to engage in tolerance and forgiveness because of the nature of God (64:14). Although a true believer may defend himself from attack, God does not forbid showing kindness and acting justly to those non-Muslims who are willing to live in peace (60:8). True believers are called to forgive those who do not look forward to the Days of God (45:14). Likewise, they are to swallow their anger and forgive others when they have been harmed (3:134). Gülen cites these passages—along with many others—to show that the Qur'an is itself is "the source of leniency and tolerance."[42] Additionally, Gülen relates a number of episodes from the life of the Prophet and his companions to show that he was a man of peace and demonstrated peace in his relationships with friends, enemies, and People of the Book.[43] The negative statements about Jews and Christians in the Qur'an, according to Gülen, are not universal injunctions. They are sourced in contingent circumstances of doctrinal controversies or active hostilities. Clearly, the Qur'an does criticize certain beliefs held by Jews and Christians (e.g., claiming God has a son and granting certain powers to the clergy). However, these critiques are leveled against ideas and attitudes, not people. Furthermore, those verses that permit fighting are based on the active hostilities of particular Jewish, Christian or pagan groups against the nascent Muslim community. On the whole, according to Gülen, the Qur'an is balanced toward civilized, peaceful coexistence while preserving Muslim identity.[44]

One of the strongest points of connection between Gülen and Conyers on tolerance resides in their conviction that faith in the One God reveals the interrelatedness of all things. Gülen begins with the idea that love is the reason for creation and existence, and that everything in the world is God's handiwork. Accordingly, if you do not approach all humans, who are creatures of God, with love, then you hurt those who

---

42. Gülen, *Love & Tolerance*, 37–38. See the collection of Qur'anic passages cited by Gülen in Alp Aslandogan, "Interfaith Dialog and Tolerance."

43. Gülen, *Love & Tolerance*, 41–44.

44. I am grateful to Dr. Alp Alsandogan for helping me understand this point of Gülen's teaching.

love God and those whom God loves. Essentially, one cannot claim to love God without loving everything that God has made. Love, of course, is an essential pillar of tolerance.[45] Similarly, Conyers would agree with Gülen's teaching on love and the interrelatedness of all things. But once again, for him, the incarnation informs the discussion because it reveals God's love for all things and ultimately reconciles all things back to God. If all things are destined to be reconciled to God, then the believers' vocation in this age consists of joining God in "the ministry of reconciliation" (2 Cor 5:16–20).

The interrelatedness of all things leads Gülen to practice what Conyer's calls in his theology the "open soul." Gülen has famously said, "Be so tolerant that our heart becomes wide like the ocean. Become inspired with faith and love for others. Offer a hand to those in trouble, and be concerned about everyone."[46] For Gülen, faith in God and love for God's creation serve as twin pillars for a tolerance that makes one's heart as wide as the ocean. Practically, this is worked out in deeds of generosity, compassion, and hospitality directed to everyone, regardless of their need. Similarly, Gülen has said, "Applaud the good for their goodness, appreciate those who have believing hearts, and be kind to believers. Approach unbelievers so gently that their envy and hatred melt away."[47] Gülen does not limit the word "believers" to Muslims, but to People of the Book (Jews and Christians) and by extension all people. He bases this upon the Qur'anic injunction that calls Muslims to accept the earlier prophets and their books (2:2–4) and to act kindly and justly toward non-Muslims as long as they are not fighting against you (60:8). But such openness must also be balanced when it comes to oppressors. Gülen warns that there are limits to tolerance and dialogue when he writes, "Being merciful to a cobra means being unjust to the people the cobra has bitten."[48]

The practice of the "open soul" for both Gülen and Conyers depends upon humility. Humility for Gülen means judging "your worth in the Creator's sight by how much space He occupies in your heart and your worth in people's eyes by how you treat them."[49] We see in this

45. Kurtz, "Gülen's Paradox."
46. Gülen, *Pearls of Wisdom*, 75.
47. Ibid., 75.
48. Gülen, *Love & Tolerance*, 75–76.
49. Ibid., 31.

statement evidence of the spiritual side of Islam, a kind of mysticism typical of the Sufi tradition. The human heart is made for its Creator and is at its best (namely, humble and generous) when the All-Forgiving and All-Merciful One fills every corner. Gülen privileges the spiritual sphere of Islam over the institutional and political spheres. This means that one's commitment to vitality in his/her spiritual life manifests itself in treating others with compassion, forgiveness, love, and tolerance.[50] Such treatment will be noticed, appreciated and result in kind treatment in return.

As we saw earlier in this essay, Conyers also considers humility fundamental to any authentic practice of tolerance. But as a Christian, Conyers locates that virtue in the example of Christ and the call to "follow" him. Additionally, Conyers finds that the reality of the incarnation challenges every idea and practice of *exousia* ("power" or "authority"). In the New Testament Jesus is clearly a prophet with authority and he shares that authority with his disciples, yet the teaching here is "not simply one of power distributed from on high but power exercised as a cosmic exchange. It is not the love of power but the power of love: God has become man, and that man, the representative of the race of men, is indeed God, so that human beings can participate in all that God is."[51] For Conyers, the coming of Christ into the world is a powerful demonstration of God's love for us, a love that ultimately exalts those who are truly humble. As the Scripture says, "God opposes the proud, but gives grace to the humble" (James 4:6; quoting Prov 3:34).

For both Gülen and Conyers, the practice of tolerance—with roots firmly planted in their respective Scriptures and traditions—finds it *telos* in dialogue, what Conyers calls the "listening heart." But Gülen has been able to accomplish more than any leader or activist I know to inspire a generation of leaders who have taken the message of love, tolerance, and dialogue to the nations. In particular, Gülen has urged his followers to found organizations committed to dialogue and tolerance. He has recommended that tolerance awards be given to encourage leaders from a variety of faith communities to work toward peaceful coexistence. He has warned that tolerance and dialogue will be costly ventures that will take decades to change the social landscape.[52]

50. Kurtz, "Gülen's Paradox," 376–78.
51. Conyers, *Long Truce*, 238.
52. Gülen, *Love & Tolerance*, 54–57.

For Gülen interfaith dialogue involves people who are committed to their faith coming together and bearing witness to that faith for the express purpose of mutual understanding, empathy, appreciation, enrichment, and cooperation. Dialogue is not about proselytizing or attempting to convert others. It is not about debating the merits or various truth claims of each faith. It is not an attempt to unify all faiths or create a single world religion. It is also not about compromising one's own faith.[53] Those who approach dialogue with hidden agendas will find the engagement frustrating, polarizing, and ultimately a failure. Successes in interfaith dialogue will come slowly as sincere individuals share the stories that have shaped their lives. By learning the truth about others and their faiths, by respecting the differences that exist between all of God's creation, we find our own faiths enriched, our commitments deepened, and perhaps we will create a world where peace reigns.

Conclusion

While Gülen and Conyers share much in common in relation to their theology of tolerance, I find one significant difference between them. Gülen understands the crucial role that forgiveness and non-retaliation play in creating sacred spaces where tolerance can flourish. He refers to forgiveness as a great virtue that is paramount to tolerance. Forgiveness restores us and our world in ways that no other action can. To be forgiven is to be repaired. And yet one cannot seek forgiveness without forgiving others, for "the road to forgiveness passes through the act of forgiving."[54] But like tolerance, there are limits to forgiveness. To forgive "monstrous, evil" people who delight in suffering would be disrespectful to forgiveness itself. Furthermore, we have no right to forgive such people, for to forgive them is to disrespect the people who have suffered so much from them. Similarly, a person committed to tolerance must also be committed to non-retaliation. According to Gülen, tolerance will manifest itself in halting verbal attacks or abuse of unbelievers; true Muslims, he argues, must swallow their anger and forgive as the Qur'an teaches (3:134). Citing the Sufi leader Yunus, Gülen encourages those who have been attacked to act as if they had no hand or tongue with

---

53. Ibid., 42.
54. Ibid., 27–30.

which to strike back.[55] Clearly, for Gülen, forgiveness and a commitment to non-retaliation are foundational to tolerance.

I am unable to find an explicit discussion of forgiveness and non-retaliation relating to tolerance in Conyers' writings. While I think these two commitments may be implicit in his emphasis on humility, openness, and the reconciliation that comes through Christ, the fact is that Conyers does not mention them unambiguously in his attempt to reclaim the ancient practice. This may be credited to the insulated academic and ecclesiastical environments in which many European and American theologians have worked.

Gülen, on the other hand, has labored in a world where injustice and suffering are the ambient reality, where retaliation is natural, and where forgiveness is only a distant hope. Sadly, Gülen's teaching on peace, tolerance, and dialogue is not accepted by all Muslims. His voice is often muted—if not silenced—by political elements within certain Islamic communities that tend toward restricting freedoms and imposing more extreme versions of Islam on others. Still the Gülen movement represents a hopeful trend among moderate Muslims, a growing minority that is attempting to reform Islam from within.

If Conyers and Gülen had ever spent time together, I'm confident they would have come away from those conversations enriched, find in one another a friend and co-worker in the cause of peace. Both men, in my view, are effective advocates of dialogue and authentic tolerance precisely because of the strength of their faiths.

---

55. Ibid., 61.

Bibliography

Aslandogan, A. "Interfaith Dialog and Tolerance in the Contemporary World: Fethullah Gülen." Paper presented to the Southwest Commission on Religious Studies, Dallas, Texas, 2007.

Bonhoeffer, Dietrich. *Ethics*. Edited by Eberhard Bethge, translated by Neville Horton Smith. New York: Touchstone, 1995.

Burrell, D. *Knowing the Unknowable God: Ibn-Sina, Maimonides, Aquinas*. Notre Dame: University of Notre Dame Press, 1986.

Çetin, Muhammed. *The Gulen Movement: Civic Service without Borders*. New York: Blue Dome, 2009.

Conyers, A. J. *God, Hope and History: Jürgen Moltmann and the Christian Conception of History*. Macon, GA: Mercer University Press, 1988.

———. *The Long Truce: How Toleration Made the World Safe for Profit and Power*. Dallas: Spence, 2001.

———. "Rescuing Tolerance." *First Things* 115 (2001) 43–46.

Gülen, Fethullah. *Pearls of Wisdom*. Somerset, NJ: Light, 2000.

———. *Toward a World Civilization of Love & Tolerance*. New Jersey: Light, 2004.

———. *The Statue of Our Souls: Revival in Islamic Thought and Activism*. New Jersey: Light, 2005.

Helwys, Thomas. *The Mistery of Iniquity*. 1612. Reprint, London: Kingsgate, 1935.

Hurtado, L. W. "Jesus as Lordly Example in Philippians 2:5–11." In *From Jesus to Paul: Studies in Honour of Francis Wright Beare*, edited by P. Richardson and J. C. Hurd, 113–26. Waterloo, ON: Wilfrid Laurier University Press, 1984.

Kurtz, L. R. "Gülen's Paradox: Combining Commitment and Tolerance." *The Muslim World* 95 (2005) 373–84.

Locke, John. *A Letter Concerning Toleration*. New York: Liberal Arts Press, 1950.

Marcuse, H. "Repressive Tolerance." In *A Critique of Pure Tolerance*, edited by R. P. Wolff, B. Moore, and H. Marcuse, 95–137. Boston: Beacon, 1969.

McBeth, H. Leon. *The Baptist Heritage*. Nashville: Broadman, 1987.

Mullins, E. Y. *The Axioms of Religion*. Nashville: Broadman, 1978.

Oden, Amy G. *And You Welcomed Me: A Sourcebook on Hospitality in Early Christianity*. Nashville: Abingdon, 2001.

Pohl, C. D. *Making Room: Recovering Hospitality as a Christian Tradition*. Grand Rapids: Eerdmans, 1999.

Ünal, A., and A. Williams. *Advocate of Dialogue: Fethullah Gülen*. Fairfax, VA: Fountain, 2000.

Walzer, Michael. *On Toleration*. New Haven, CT: Yale University Press, 1997.

11

Fyodor Dostoevsky's *The Brothers Karamazov*
Resisting Pernicious Tolerance by Living the Iconic Life

Ralph C. Wood

WHEN I THINK OF CHIP CONYERS' CONTRIBUTION TO BAPTIST LIFE in particular and to the ecumenical church in general, I think of his steadfast avoidance of cliché. He refused to make the obvious still more obvious—as the wag has added—in perfectly obvious terms. A single example of Chip Conyers' originality of mind will have to suffice. It concerns the danger that our mutual friend David Solomon warns against when he says that we Southerners and Baptists who came of age in the 1960s cut our teeth on the easiest moral issue of the twentieth century: race. Once we discovered that segregation was a hideous denial of the humanity of our black brothers and sisters, we were then tempted to treat other ethical and theological questions as if they were equally simple.

As a native son of Georgia and a convert to Baptist tradition, Chip Conyers sought, in non-simplistic terms, to penetrate the evil that has so sorely vexed both his region and his religion. He saw that racism was not a uniquely Southern iniquity but the symptom of a much more pernicious disease afflicting the whole of modern life—namely, the commodification of our entire existence. Chip discerned that the real root of our troubles lies in the sixteenth and seventeenth centuries with the burgeoning of the means for production and conquest. As the rapid triumph of machinery drew the masses into the great industrial cities where the means of manufacture and trade were concentrated, governments also began to operate as impersonal machines backed by large armies, the better to manage their huge territories and to conquer new lands that would enhance their wealth.

In what may be the most enduring of his books, *The Long Truce: How Toleration Made the World Safe for Power and Profit*, Conyers argued that the Enlightenment ideal that seemed to offer religious freedom to us Protestants had, in fact, the deleterious counter-effect of producing the hegemonic nation-state and its close ally called untrammeled capitalism. With devastating clarity, Conyers came to see that this modern way of life no longer valued human beings as particular persons offering their unique and irreplaceable gifts to a communal enterprise. Rather did the Enlightenment make us into solitary individuals having equal rights because we are regarded as equally interchangeable parts in the gigantic machine of the commercial and martial state. We are little more than instruments of production and profit and warfare.

The masters of the market and the military are willing, in turn, to "tolerate" the religion of their drudges and minions only if it is reduced to the private sphere, where it remains essentially harmless. Far from being the regressive invention of benighted medievals, therefore, chattel slavery was what Conyers rightly called "the eldest child of modernity." For in the figure of the Negro slave we moderns created the ultimately autonomous person—one who no longer belongs to family and clan, to region and guild, to community and church and God, but only to oneself in the smallest sense: he is the servant of those who possess total political and commercial power. In offering his drastic critique of the slavery that once held black people in bonds, Conyers also revealed that here in "the land of the free" we also are enslaved to a culture of convenient tolerance and unrestrained consumption.

I cannot testify for sure that *The Brothers Karamazov* served as a life-marking book for Chip Conyers, but I suspect that it did. For Dostoevsky was deeply concerned with an issue that also agitated Conyers. Like Dostoevsky, he discerned that the Enlightenment project of liberalism had a canker at its core, and the worm eating at its heart was called "tolerance." For while liberalism could offer protections against common evils, it would have an increasing difficulty defining common goods. Among American Protestants, Conyers was among the first to recognize that liberalism would issue in an unprecedented secularism, rapidly displacing religion from the center of human life. The movement that began with the aim of setting people free would threaten, in fact, to empty the public sphere of those virtues that alone might prevent a return to the brute and slavish state of nature that Thomas

Hobbes envisioned: the "war of all against all." Yet before examining *The Brothers Karamazov* as a powerful literary treatment of the problem, we will do well to sketch the rise of the Enlightenment ideal that Chip Conyers was early to discern as a pernicious evil.

I.

Toleration is a subject that, almost more than any other, preoccupies modern mentality. Baruch Spinoza, John Milton, G. E. Lessing, Pierre Bayle, Roger Williams, and William Penn all devoted themselves to it. Yet it is John Locke's "Letter on Toleration" that still shapes the debate. Once the Protestant Reformation had finally exploded the already fissiparating unity of Europe, repression and even civil war soon riddled English life. Having been religiously exiled to the Dutch Republic, where a secular state had been founded in order to permit religious differences, Locke sought to bring a similar freedom from religious persecution to his own nation. As himself a deist perched high above the religious fray, he sought to judge it from an ostensibly neutral perspective that credited only those universal ethical norms that all people of good will could discern and affirm.

The key to Locke's notion of toleration lies in his clear division between the civil and the religious realms: "He jumbles heaven and earth together, the things most remote and opposite, who mixes these two societies."[1] Our civil interests, as Locke defines them, are these: life, liberty, health, and property. Such public goods are construed as being external and thus as the proper realm of the magistrate or civil government. As such, they may and must be preserved by use of force, which is the government's chief legitimate power. Our religious interests, by contrast, are internal and private, for they concern salvation in the afterlife. The state has no power, therefore, to rule in this realm—neither to mandate the articles of faith, to determine the forms of worship, or to adjudicate other religious disputes. For religion is not an outward and public but a private and individual matter. "The care . . . of every

---

1. All quotations from "A Letter Concerning Toleration" are taken from William Popple's 1689 translation of Locke's Latin original, *Epistola de Tolerantia*. Voltaire translated it into French five years later, though not without showing his witty contempt for religion: "[England] is the country of sects. An Englishman, as a freeman, goes to Heaven by whatever road he pleases."

man's soul," Locke peremptorily declares, "belongs unto himself and is to be left unto himself.[2] Though he assumed that Anglicanism would remain the established state church, Locke urged that other expressions of Protestant religion should to be tolerated, so long as they themselves remained tolerant. Yet two groups are not to be tolerated at all: atheists and Roman Catholics. Atheists deny the God who is the basis for the natural law that undergirds morality and the state.[3] Catholics are perhaps even more subversive to the commonweal of such a religiously pluralistic state, for they "deliver themselves up," Locke lamented, "to the protection and service of another prince."

The problem lies not with Locke's denial of state inducement of religious belief. As Locke rightly observes, God himself refuses to coerce people against their will. There are indeed religious requirements of both belief and practice that can be commanded by the churches.[4] The state, by contrast, has no such mandatory power over Christians. Such governmental force would prompt only empty outward conformity, not substantial religious obedience. Persuasion is the only legitimate means for inducing true faith.

Thus far, thus good. The real trouble with Locke comes, in my estimate, when he excludes Catholics from religious freedom because of their allegiance to "another prince." He refers, in the literal sense, to the pope as a political figure allied with the various Catholic monarchs of Europe for political no less than religious purposes. Hence the common charge, and thus the vile canard, that Catholics are "se-

---

2. Jefferson agreed: "The legitimate powers of government," he would add a century later, "extend to such acts only as are injurious to others. But it does me no injury for my neighbor to say that there are twenty Gods, or no God. It neither picks my pocket nor breaks my leg." Jefferson, "Notes on Virginia."

3. Locke's notion of natural law has but faint resemblance to its medieval predecessors. Hence Lord Herbert of Cherbury's rather thin Lockean formulation of the five reasonable propositions that, according to him, all people of all times have held, without regard to race or religion, except when obscured by the distortions and accretions of so-called revealed truth: (1) that God exists; (2) that he ought to be worshipped; (3) that virtue and piety are the chief part of worship; (4) that there must be repentance for crimes and vices; (5) that there are rewards and punishments in the life to come based on the ways we have acquitted ourselves in this earthly life.

4. Locke denies even *this* authority to the churches, regarding them as purely voluntary organizations whose sovereignty resides solely in their individual members acting collectively, not in their ministers or deacons, their presbyters or vestries, much less in their bishops and prelates who might claim to represent the authority of Christ himself.

cret agents of the pope." Yet despite the example of Guy Fawkes, very few orthodox Catholics, even in the late seventeenth century, would have regarded the papacy *primarily* as a political power unto whom they "deliver themselves up." On the contrary, they would have given the pope their allegiance as the earthly and religious representative of Another Prince. Indeed, *all* Christians put themselves under the primary "protection and service" of this same Prince who is not the monarch or president of any worldly regime but Lord of the church and thus of the entire cosmos. In the strict sense, therefore, Christians are subversive to *any* state that presumes to command the final loyalty of its citizens. For Locke, however, there can be no tournament of narratives, no hierarchy of loyalties between church and state, since heaven and earth constitute two societies that are inherently incomparable: they must not be "mixed."

Among the many problems arising from the Lockean idea of tolerance, William Cavanaugh has identified the single most acute and pernicious one. He argues that toleration emerged not so much as a political necessity for halting of the so-called religious wars of the seventeenth century, but rather as a political convenience for widening the scope of secular authority. According to Cavanaugh—and in complete agreement with Chip Conyers—these wars marked the birth pangs of the sovereign nation-state, with its massive growth in size and its increasing alliance with national and international markets. Political power was centralized, Cavanaugh argues, so as to provide "a monopoly on violence within a defined territory." Public discourse was deliberately secularized during the Enlightenment, Cavanaugh maintains, in order to save the state from the threat posed by the churches: "Christianity produces divisions within the state body precisely because it pretends to be a body which transcends state boundaries." The Enlightenment ideal of toleration thus excludes the communal body called the church, says Cavanaugh, "as a rival to the state body by redefining religion as a purely internal matter, an affair of the soul and not of the body."[5] In

---

5. Cavanaugh, "The City," 191, 189, 190, 192. The rise of the modern nation-state is premised on the elevation of this isolated and autonomous individual who is defined largely by his accumulation of privately owned goods. As essentially propertied creatures, individuals have relation to each other largely by means of self-protecting contracts. These contracts have a temporal duration, moreover, even as they are contingent upon the agreement of the contracting parties. Contracts can also be dissolved by limiting clauses or by mutual consent. No longer is there an unbreakable bond that unites

the name of an alleged inclusivity, therefore, a drastic exclusivity was promulgated. The state alone, not the church, can establish a true commonwealth, for religion now pertains chiefly to the private individual.

From such sentiments there emerges the modern individualism that values untrammeled liberty above all else—whether negatively defined as doing no harm to others, or else positively interpreted as constructing one's own life without let or hindrance. No longer is freedom understood as obedience to a *telos* radically transcending ourselves and thus wondrously delivering us from bondage to mere self-interest. Rather does liberty come to mean a life lived according to one's own individual construal of reality.[6] At its extreme, such individualism holds that we can make up our identity entirely out of whole cloth, that we can strip away all bothersome particularities that locate us within concrete narrative traditions, and thus that we can be free only as we rid ourselves of the troublesome commitments and obligations that we have not chosen entirely for ourselves. In sum, we may and must become autonomous selves immunized from all moral and social obligations except those that we have independently elected.[7]

Such privatizing and individualizing and subjectivizing of religion has a dreadful epistemological consequence. The feminist political theorist Wendy Brown identifies it succinctly:

> [T]hat which is most vital to individuals qua individuals—personal belief or conscience—is not only that which is divorced from public life but that which is divorced from shared Truth.

---

the entire body politic in devotion to common ends. The basis of such politics has indeed disappeared—namely, the indissoluble covenant between God and his people, as this bond is sealed through the sacraments. "It is not surprising," declares Cavanaugh, "that ... Descartes placed 'among the [antique] excesses all of the promises by which one curtails something of one's freedom,' that Milton wrote a treatise on divorce, or that Kant condemned the covenants that bind one's descendants" (190).

6. In *Planned Parenthood v. Casey*, the 1992 Supreme Court case upholding *Roe v. Wade*, the justices (Anthony Kennedy is rumored to be the actual author) confirmed this Enlightenment assumption by declaring that all Americans have the privilege of construing reality for themselves: "At the very heart of liberty is the right to define one's own concept of existence, of meaning, of the universe, of the mystery of life." Consider, by contrast, Abraham Lincoln's sharp riposte to Stephen Douglas's insistence that Southerners should have the right to choose slavery if they so wished and so voted: "No one has the right to choose to do what is so fundamentally wrong" (quoted in Miscamble, *Keeping the Faith*, 100).

7. This argument is made most convincingly by Michael Sandel, *Democracy's Discontents*.

> Tolerance of diverse beliefs in a community becomes possible to the extent that those beliefs are phrased as having no public importance; as being constitutive of a private individual whose private beliefs and commitments have minimal bearing on the structure and pursuits of political, social, or economic life; and as having no reference to settled common epistemological authority.[8]

There is also a drastic moral consequence inherent in this perspectival view of truth. Our late-modern notion of tolerance is usually advocated by those who have already attained such power that they can afford to "tolerate" their opponents—so long, it must be noted, as the tolerated abide by the rules laid down by the tolerators, thus offering no real threat to established authority. Tolerance usually reveals that someone has already won and someone else has already lost, and that the winners get to decide what is tolerable. Our much-vaunted American ideal of state neutrality in religious matters often means that the governmental principalities and powers have already adopted and enforced a particular notion of the good built largely on Enlightenment and procedural notions of utility and rights.[9] How, then, are those who hold to radically opposing construals of reality to deal with each other—especially when one acknowledges the triune God and the other does not—by some means other than a polite tolerance that obscures the power arrangements underwriting it?[10]

II.

The Enlightenment confidence in our own autonomous ability to answer such human quandaries confronted Dostoevsky most powerfully in the work of N. G. Chernyshevsky. In 1861, he published a novel called *What Is to Be Done?* The title itself exposes the author's confidence that a tempestuous restructuring of human life is at hand, that old ideas are to be swept out and a daring new vision of the future is to be ushered in. The central premise of Chernyshevsky's second-rate novel is that hu-

---

8. Brown, *Regulating Aversion*, 32.

9. Alasdair MacIntyre argues that, precisely because the contemporary state cannot be "evaluatively neutral . . . it cannot be generally trusted to promote any worthwhile set of values, including those of autonomy and liberty" ("Toleration," 213–14).

10. This section of the essay has previously appeared in Wood, "Hospitality as the Gift."

man life is not qualitatively different than animal life, and that just as animals can be trained to behave properly so can we humans be taught to live according to enlightened and mutual self-interest.

Like an early-day Ivan Pavlov or B. F. Skinner, Chernyshevsky denied that we humans possess any intrinsic freedom or dignity. On the contrary, we share with the other animals a fundamental urge to preserve our own health and happiness at all costs. We seek nothing other than our own material well-being. In an infamous analogy, Chernyshevsky insisted that there is no qualitative difference between Sir Isaac Newton seeking to fathom the law of gravity and a chicken pecking for a grain of corn in the dirt. They are both pursuing their own self-interest in ways that are at variance only quantitatively. What we desperately need, argued Chernyshevsky, is a new political system that will free us from the false conventions and institutions of society, thus enabling us to live according to our natural self-interests. Because we are rational animals, he argues, we can be taught to subordinate our merely private obsessions for the good of the whole. Human nature, it follows, is as malleable as hot iron: we can make of it what we want, hammering it into whatever shape pleases the mallet-wielder—the omnicompetent nation-state. For Dostoevsky, the chief anti-icon of such preening Enlightenment liberalism was the Crystal Palace, the world's first gigantic glass-and-iron structure. It was erected outside London as the grandiose center of the Great Exhibition of 1851, a kind of inaugural world's fair held in celebration of the Victorian triumph in all things mechanical and economic.

Yet the book that fired Dostoevsky's literary fury in response to such human arrogance was Chernyshevsky's *What Is to Be Done?* It made him livid with religious rage. Dostoevsky saw in this liberal ideal of absolute human autonomy a threat far worse than the tyranny of the czars. Whereas the czarist repression lopped off men's heads, this new secular liberty threatened to destroy their souls. Though it promised life, it denied what is far more important than life—namely, the God who gives life its meaning and value and hope. What this Enlightenment vision ignores is not only the self-revealing, self-defining God who is the source of all goodness but also the evil that is always opposed to it. In defiance of Chernyshevsky's naive notion that we are benign self-serving animals, Dostoevsky wrote a short novel called *Notes from Underground*.

Its thesis is that human self-will, far from being capable of socialist mutuality, is bent on a demonic autonomy wherein every man becomes a law unto himself. Humans are not determined merely to achieve their own self-interest, as Chernyshevsky thought. Our species is just as often bent toward self-injury. The anti-hero of the novel is called the Underground Man, a thoroughly nasty character who delights in wounding himself no less than others. He begins his confession with these words, "I am a sick man ... I am a spiteful man. I am an unpleasant man." Though he thinks his liver is diseased, he refuses to seek medical help. Why? Out of spite, out of the desire to be sick rather than healthy, in proof that he is not an animal who wants to adjust to his environment and satisfy his needs. On the contrary, the Underground Man despises the notion that human beings can be made content by filling their bellies and perfecting their habitat. Were such a robot's utopia ever established, he says, we humans would smash it to shards. Hence his screaming protest against the Crystal Palace of anthropoid contentment:

> And why are you so firmly, so triumphantly convinced that only the normal and positive—in short, only prosperity—is to the advantage of man? Is not reason mistaken about advantage? After all, perhaps man likes something besides prosperity? Perhaps he likes suffering just as much? Perhaps suffering is just as great an advantage to him as prosperity? Man is sometimes fearfully, passionately in love with suffering and that is a fact. There is no appeal to universal history to prove that; only ask yourself, if only you are a man and have lived at all. As far as my own personal opinion is concerned, to care only for prosperity seems to me somehow even ill-bred. Whether it's good or bad, it is sometimes very pleasant to smash things, too. After all, I do not really insist on suffering or on prosperity either. I insist on my caprice, and its being guaranteed to me when necessary. ... In the crystal palace [suffering] is even unthinkable; suffering means doubt, means negation, and what would be the good of a crystal palace if there could be any doubt about it? And yet I am sure that man will never renounce real suffering, that is, destruction and chaos. Why after all, suffering is the sole origin of consciousness. ... Consciousness, for instance, is infinitely superior to two times two makes four. Once you have two times two makes four, you have nothing to understand.[11]

---

11. Dostoevsky, *Notes From Underground*, 31.

The point of this perverse confession is that we human creatures live and move and have our being only in and through a certain *unease* with the world. It is in separation from animal contentment that our souls are born. This human self-transcendence of the merely natural opens the way also to terrible evils such as the Underground Man himself embodies, but at least he proves that we are not animals dwelling in a herd, not ants inhabiting a heap. We are suffering, sinning, believing, doubting human beings who live and die before God and our fellows. Any secular substitute for this God-ordained condition, and especially those placebos that claim to offer unlimited freedom, will end in unlimited despotism.

This paradox that absolute liberty leads to absolute tyranny is at the heart of the famous Grand Inquisitor scene in *The Brothers Karamazov*. There Dostoevsky envisions the ultimate utopian nightmare: a paternalistic government providing all the physical conditions of freedom while denying freedom itself, and the people in turn surrendering their liberty for totalitarian security. It was as if, forty years before the Russian Revolution, Dostoevsky saw the terror to come and prophesied vigorously against it. Nothing other than transcendent faith in the God of the gospel, he cried, could prevent this degradation of human life into animal conformity.

III.

Two recent books on Dostoevsky trench on these Enlightenment problems in Conyeresque ways, especially in their counter-interpretations of *The Brothers Karamazov*. For this greatest of Dostoevsky's novels is the center of their focus, since it is here, more than in any other place, that Dostoevsky most convincingly confronts the peril and promise of late-Enlightenment modernity. In *Dostoevsky and the Affirmation of Life*, Predrag Cicovacki, a professor of philosophy at the College of the Holy Cross, focuses on a single injunction that the novice monk Alyosha Karamazov gives to his brother Dmitri near the end of the novel. "Love life," Alyosha enjoins his troubled sibling, "more than its meaning."

Like many other readers of Dostoevsky, Professor Cicovacki regards Alyosha as a reliable spokesman for Dostoevsky himself. It is certainly true that Alyosha is warning Dmitri against the mistake made by their skeptical other brother named Ivan. Ivan is the Dostoevskian character who most fully embodies the soul-rending doubts that have become endemic to modern life. Citing the work of Isaiah Berlin, Cicovacki demonstrates that Ivan is wracked by the three most devastating Enlightenment "humiliations" of Christian tradition: (1) the denial that man is the purpose and center of creation, (2) the insistence that man is a but a creature of nature like all other animals, and (3) the discovery that reason is not autonomous and objective but subject to overt passions and covert illusions that radically distort its judgments.[12]

Stated overly simply, Cicovacki's argument is that Dostoevsky does not give typically Western answers to this devastating Enlightenment discrediting of Christianity. On the contrary, he regards Dostoevsky as an anti-rationalist who insists, with Alyosha, that it is not necessary to know the meaning of life as a condition for affirming it; on the contrary, it is actually impossible to have such a comprehension of reality. In this somewhat apophatic reading of Dostoevsky, the great Russian is seen as providing a helpfully Eastern vision of life over against a more Western outlook. The Eastern church, in Cicovacki's reading of Dostoevsky, provides the novelist a more intuitive and cyclical view of things than does the rationalist and linear West. Dostoevsky's Russian Orthodoxy is devoted to a mystical sense of the earth as being more our mother than our sister, and it is thus committed to the God who is more immanent than transcendent. Dostoevsky regarded life as too contradictory, Cicovacki argues, to be comprehended and lived on strictly rational grounds. As Dostoevsky himself confessed, "there is nothing more fantastic than reality itself."[13]

These essential contraries are voiced, as we have seen, by the surly narrator of *Notes from the Underground*, a man dwelling misanthropically and anonymously in his miserable "mousehole." On the one hand, the *repressive order* of man-managed nature is represented by the Crystal Palace, a triumph of such scientific skill and mechanical expertise that it portended the ultimate reduction of humanity to animality by means of a similar mastery and control. The *rationalistic systems of late modernity*, whether political or psychological, have frighteningly fulfilled the Underground Man's fear. On the other hand, his own advocacy of the *destructive freedoms of postmodernity* are no less terrifying. For he elevates will over reason, self-hurting over self-interest. To keep himself

12. Cicovacki, *Dostoevsky*, 17.
13. Ibid., 11.

free from the soul-deadening conformity of totalizing order (with its beehive insistence on predictability), he indulges in arbitrary acts of voluptuous self-will.

To have anticipated the various irrationalisms of postmodernity makes Dostoevsky exceedingly prescient. One needs only to inspect Benedict XVI's protest against the de-Hellenization of Christianity, in his Regensburg speech of 2006, to discern how fully Dostoevsky anticipated the advent of nihilistic rationalism:

> [O]nly the kind of certainty resulting from the interplay of mathematical and empirical elements can be considered scientific. Anything that would claim to be science must be measured against this criterion. Hence the human sciences, such as history, psychology, sociology and philosophy, attempt to conform themselves to this canon of scientificity. A second point, which is important for our reflections, is that by its very nature this method excludes the question of God, making it appear an unscientific or pre-scientific question. Consequently, we are faced with a reduction of the radius of science and reason, one which needs to be questioned.... [I]f science as a whole is this and this alone, then it is man himself who ends up being reduced, for the specifically human questions about our origin and destiny, the questions raised by religion and ethics, then have no place within the purview of collective reason as defined by "science," so understood, and must thus be relegated to the realm of the subjective. The subject then decides, on the basis of his experiences, what he considers tenable in matters of religion, and the subjective "conscience" becomes the sole arbiter of what is ethical. In this way, though, ethics and religion lose their power to create a community and become a completely personal matter. This is a dangerous state of affairs for humanity, as we see from the disturbing pathologies of religion and reason which necessarily erupt when reason is so reduced that questions of religion and ethics no longer concern it. Attempts to construct an ethic from the rules of evolution or from psychology and sociology, end up being simply inadequate.[14]

The Underground Man is wholly agreed. According to him, life cannot be both ordered and free, both just and happy, both "scientific" and religious. Hence his final despair.

---

14. Benedict XVI, "Faith, Reason."

The chief contention of Professor Cicovacki's book is to show that Dostoevsky overcomes this deadly antinomy by discerning that the Underground Man's irreconcilable opposites are in fact dialectical polarities that cannot be divided but must be united. Their union requires a subrational affirmation of life as the supreme gift. God grants us the drastic freedom either to ennoble or degrade this largest of all gifts. Dmitri Karamazov describes such ennoblement and such degradation when he declares that every human heart is imbued with the contradictory ideals of the Madonna, on the one hand, and of Sodom on the other—the utterly sacred and the utterly profane. Hence Dmitri's famous complaint: "Man is broad, even too broad, I would narrow him down."[15]

Though his argument is too complex for brief treatment, Professor Cicovacki argues that Dostoevsky refuses any such constriction of human life. Its troublesome breadth and incomprehensible variety are the source of its sustaining and invigorating vitality. Ivan Karamazov ends in cruelty and madness because he will not embrace such a harsh and contradictory world. He demands to *understand* why the universe is full of purposeless suffering before he will *embrace* it. Dmitri, by contrast, finds newness of life because he gradually discerns, with Alyosha's help, that God creates a partially indeterminate cosmos in order to leave room for human freedom. Authentic faith is the willingness to affirm the complementarity of good and evil—indeed, to embrace the God "who lacks any discernible essence and who is the God of existence, the God of the mysterious flow of life":[16]

> Dmitri does not search for the meaning of life but the experience of being alive. He does not ask what the meaning of life is but senses that it is he who is being asked. Dmitri understands that he is being questioned by life and that he must answer with his own life. His answer consists in reverence and awe for life—he serves this life without any demands for rights, or pretensions of greatness. Dmitri is the incarnation of the affirmation of life, even in the face of evil. If there is a hero in *The Brothers Karamazov*, Dmitri is it.[17]

15. Cicovacki, *Dostoevsky*, 257.
16. Ibid., 332.
17. Ibid., 311.

In his *Dostoevsky: Language, Faith, and Fiction*, Rowan Williams, Archbishop of Canterbury, also regards Dmitri as the hero of the novel, but for radically opposed reasons. Dostoevsky, in his view, does not respond to the challenges of the Enlightenment with an apophatic-existentialist appeal to love life apart from its meaning. The Anglican bishop-theologian confesses that Dostoevsky does not make his counter-argument easy. For the great Russian writer notoriously proclaimed that if he were pressed to choose between Christ and the truth, he would not hesitate to choose Christ. Yet Williams demonstrates that by "truth" Dostoevsky does not refer to the veracity or trustworthiness of being itself, but rather to the modern conception of a closed universe where every effect is inevitably produced by its antecedent cause, where human nature and desire become mechanisms that can be controlled by the powerful, and thus where arbitrary will is all that finally matters. Dostoevsky was right, Williams argues, to reject such a pernicious notion of "truth."

Williams's basic thesis is that, for Dostoevsky, love is always a difficult and often deceptive thing, never something obvious and uncomplicated. On the contrary, it's the demonic that would make life horribly easy. Ivan Karamazov's famous claim that "if God is dead, then all things are permitted" is much more satanic than the traditional reading indicates. He is not simply stating the rather obvious notion that if there were no afterlife to guarantee justice for the good and punishment for the evil then everyone would eagerly serve their own wills, all restraint being lifted, all crime becoming legitimate. What he really and terribly means is this: if God is dead, then the ego must occupy his vacant place. In the absence of God, there is no transcendent order for determining the difference between atrocity and beauty, between love and hatred of neighbor, between virtue or and vice—except as the solitary self decides. No wonder that Nietzsche, the apostle of autonomous will, declared God to be dead at virtually the same time Ivan was making his own pronouncement.

It follows that Dostoevsky's devil is not, like Goethe's Mephistopheles, a friendly "spirit who negates," a naughty "imp of the perverse" who keeps life from becoming an endless Sunday school picnic of tedious yea-saying. He is, instead, the deceptive specter who leaves us in suspense concerning his own reality or unreality: "We do not know," Williams declares, "what it is that emerges from our own intelligence [as hallucination] and what is given to us and required of us from beyond ourselves—both the vision of God and the vision of total meaninglessness." Yet there is hope for Satan's final defeat and thus our own undeception. The arch dissembler cannot dwell forever, Williams writes, because "he is locked out from the self-commitment of bodily and temporal life and thus from the self-risking of love."[18] Though Ivan Karamazov ends in demonic insanity, he at least retains the miserable integrity of his unbelief. Dostoevsky might have enabled him (if he had lived to write his sequel to *The Brothers Karamazov*) to become a holy fool in the Orthodox tradition—a man who, like St. Basil of Moscow, so totally abandoned himself to God that he didn't bother to wear clothes.

Such a serious estimate of the devil reveals that Dostoevsky may be our profoundest Christian artist. In his fiction, the path toward goodness and salvation is not easily traversed. It's not a matter of discerning the inherent order of the universe and then ordering our lives according to it, in rigorous medieval fashion. Our age faces new possibilities for both good and evil. Dostoevsky is the most convincing modern writer because he engages these new chances and changes, acknowledging rather than avoiding the world's troubling ambiguity and inherent disorder. He refuses to make God into a tyrant who constantly slaps the world into shape. He is the God of love—not in *spite* of his refusal to overrule human freedom, but rather *because* he works chiefly through personal agency. "Faith moves and adapts, matures and reshapes itself, . . . by the relentless stripping away of . . . egoistic or triumphalistic expectations."[19] If God were to make faith a matter of assured and relentless progress, then he would not be the self-emptying God but the sovereign Manager of the universe, a divine monster akin to the devil himself.

Secular interpreters have often made the opposite case. They have argued that Dostoevsky seeks to be a Christian novelist but in fact fails, as his work finally succumbs to the world's endless ambiguity and uncertainty. As Blake famously said of Milton, so do they say of Dostoevsky: he was "of the Devil's party without knowing it." Such skeptics insist that the conflicting narrators and contradictory characters and opposing scenes reveal that Dostoevsky did not succeed in giving fictional embodiment to his Christian convictions. Rowan Williams turns these

---

18. Williams, *Dostoevsky*, 43.
19. Ibid., 10.

critics on their head. Dostoevsky is all the more persuasively Christian, he argues, for refusing "any obvious strategy of closure in the narrative."[20] Dostoevsky's inconclusiveness places the real burden on the *reader* to decide whether Christian faith can offer a lasting reconciliation of life's seemingly insuperable antagonisms. Never does Dostoevsky make the gospel into a proposition that offers ready dictates or easy resolutions. It is truly good news in its very oddity, its peculiar refusal to take its place as one among many means to a noble life, as yet another instrument for achieving virtue and avoiding vice. Its truth is singular, paradoxical, strange, unfinished.

Williams's most revolutionary discovery is that Dostoevsky's fiction is open-ended and unfinished *because* it is Christian. His novels are inconclusive (though not relativistic) in ways that reflect God's own inconclusive action in the world:

> The Dostoevskian novel . . . enacts the freedom it discusses by creating a narrative space in which various futures are possible for characters and for readers. And in so doing it seeks . . . to represent the ways in which the world's creator exercises "authorship," generat[ing] dependence without control.[21]

Hence the subtitle of Williams's book and one of its central insights: "faith and fiction" are profoundly linked. They are both practices that stand over against a world of ordinary giving and getting, of hurting and being hurt. Faith is a free response to God's own freedom as we unexpectedly and undeservedly encounter it within the knotty resistances of the world. Dostoevskian fiction is similarly gratuitous. It narratively reveals that no human situation can be finally hopeless and finished. Death is rarely the conclusion of most Dostoevsky novels. His belief in immortality makes him concerned not primarily with what happens in the afterlife but rather with the unprecedented worth of every human being, no matter how seemingly valueless.

This means that the Lord of freedom values his creation so profoundly that he permits his creatures the liberty to refuse both acceptance and understanding of his world, even if such freedom ends in slavery. Ivan Karamazov is the most notable example, as we have seen. Ivan assails God, in agonizing protest, for allowing innocent children to

20. Ibid., 8.
21. Ibid., 12.

suffer unspeakable evils. Nowhere does Dostoevsky provide a vision of cosmic harmony as an answer to this most unanswerable of questions. Yet neither does he despair of all resolution. His fiction contains no irrationalist resignation to the final untruthfulness of things. Nor does he make Christ into a stark sign of absolute contradiction to the world, an unworldly savior who transports his disciples into blissful acceptance and undoubting faith.

Dostoevsky has his characters learn, instead, how to dwell amidst wrenching tensions and contradictions. He will not let them escape into a bland all-embracing tolerance. Among the many paradoxes at work in Dostoevsky's fiction, Ivan's protest is perhaps the most obvious. Without an ultimate order of significance, his outcry would have no meaning, his care for children no substance, his love for "the sticky little leaves in spring" no validity. Yet this transcendent order is immensely complex and often uncomforting. Dostoevsky's Christ does not merely confirm and re-establish the world's best impulses. He introduces radically new possibilities and realities. He *interrupts* closed systems of thinking and destructive ways of desiring. He refuses to leave us alone in our joylessness and lovelessness. Yet he never coerces. For then he would become just another force of nature, and the church would be just another product of culture:

> Christ is apprehended when something not planned or foreseen in the contents of the world breaks through, in an act or event that represents the *gratuity* of love or joy. Such an event alters what is possible by offering to the will what might be called a "truthful" or appropriate direction for its desire. Christ does not compel and thus cannot be treated in the framework of causes and effects; if his possibility is not "caught," nothing can make it.[22]

To "catch" the gospel is the greatest of all gifts, and to keep hold of it is the greatest of all privileges. But such a life in Christ entails no promise of happiness or security. There is no guarantee that the world will be healed or that we ourselves shall be spared immense suffering. On the contrary, to be immersed in the viscous reality of the world by making choices and reaping their consequences is inevitably to be burdened with both hurt and guilt. The opposite of tolerance is not bigotry, therefore, but engagement and responsibility. This explains

22. Ibid., 30.

why Williams finds Prince Myshkin, the protagonist of *The Idiot*, to be disturbingly un-Christlike. Myshkin causes inadvertent harm, in fact, because he remains so "innocent," so cut off from a suffering solidarity with other human beings, so "free" of guilty responsibility for them.

Neither is Alyosha in *The Brothers Karamazov* a figure of unalloyed goodness. His refusal to condemn evil makes him perniciously tolerant. Hence Father Zosima's insistence that Alyosha leave the monastery and enter the world. Without learning to give and to receive both blessing and injury, he would become a dangerously tolerant monk. Even the holiest of Dostoevsky's characters, Zosima himself, makes his ringing affirmations about love and joy and the goodness of the world only after he has first confronted the cost of Christlikeness, precisely as Williams describes it:

> For Jesus to be human at all ... is for him to be faced with choices not simply between good and evil but between options that *might* arguably be good but also bring with them incalculable costs. The options that confront actual historical agents are not like self-contained items on a shelf or rack awaiting buyers; they are part of a continuum of human policies that may be flawed and damaging, and they will already be constrained by what has happened [in the past]. This is the concrete meaning of embracing the consequences of fallenness.[23]

Perhaps the most remarkable of the archbishop's claims is that Dostoevsky's fiction is most faithfully Orthodox (in the Eastern sense) because it is most uncompromisingly apophatic. This technical term refers to the inability of all human categories to conceptualize God. Rather than assigning human attributes to God that threaten to make him an infinitely large version of ourselves, we do better to say what God is not—"immortal, invisible, God only wise," as the old hymn declares, "in light inaccessible hid from our eyes." Dostoevsky's fiction finely embodies this "negative theology" by holding to "the principle that whatever is specifically said of God has also to be un-said as soon as it seems to offer the seductive prospect of a definition of the divine essence."[24]

> There is, for Dostoevsky, no form of words about faith that is beyond criticism; sincerity is not enough.... To refuse to [admit the relativity of one's faith] would be to suggest that a point had

23. Ibid., 57.
24. Ibid., 59.

been reached where there was nothing more to be said—which would be to take refuge in the escape from time which undermines true faith.... There is nothing sayable that cannot be answered or contradicted or qualified in some way or another. ... [E]very new statement of faith has to issue into a linguistic world where it may be either contradicted, ignored, parodied or ... trivialized as a cliché.[25]

In a brilliant final chapter on icons and iconic characters, the Archbishop of Canterbury argues that icons reveal the mystery they portray. They are a *presence* more than an action. They disclose "what is hidden in the person who is confronted by [them]. The more depth and fullness in the depiction, the more the capacity to unveil the beholder."[26] It is not surprising that Williams should regard Father Zosima as an iconic figure in this precise sense: everyone in *The Brothers Karamazov* finds fulfillment or frustration in relation to him. It is this holy man—not an abstract theodicy that requires unbelievers to justify and accept the undeserved suffering of children—who is the answer to Ivan and the Grand Inquisitor.

Yet it is Dmitri, the brother who is blamed for the murder of his father, though in fact he is technically innocent, who becomes the iconic hero of the novel. Ever so gradually and reluctantly, he learns to practice the celebrated teaching of Father Zosima that "all are responsible for all." Dmitri takes responsibility for having wished and longed for his father's death. He accepts his undeserved imprisonment in the conviction that he cannot receive God's mercy except through what Williams calls "an appalled longing for expiation."[27] Dmitri reveals, above all, that Dostoevsky does not compel a choice between Christ and the truth. Christ *is* the Truth because he is "the primordial Icon, the eternal image of God."[28]

This Christ of the gospel is no obvious or manageable image. In accord with the Christian East, Dostoevsky discerns a deeply kenotic, self-emptying quality in the incarnate Christ. He both reveals and withholds himself. His loving presence is known through his voluntary absence. He creates both "understanding and not-understanding, reverence and

25. Ibid., 45.
26. Ibid., 206.
27. Ibid., 219.
28. Ibid., 207.

contempt." It is not that these opposites are equal and self-cancelling, but that Christ enables and requires his disciples to live within their tension, as he himself supremely occupied this contested realm. "Even the eternal, finally authoritative image, when it is manifested in history, is subject to rejection and disfiguring; the Word of God is not naturally and visibly the last word in history."[29]

Evil, by contrast, seeks the absolute finality that faith foregoes. It wants to be uncontradicted and unqualified. It does so, Williams argues, by refusing to occupy space and time, to inhabit bodies and histories and limits. Satan is the discarnate emperor of Nothing, a figure for whom all moments and choices and persons are equally null and thus equally interchangeable. No wonder that Dostoevsky's nihilistic characters often end in suicide, the choice to end all choices. By contrast, the figure in the face of an icon engenders new life. It comes forth to meet the viewer with "an otherness that is ultimately quite inaccessible to me and resistant to my control," Williams observes. "[I]t is an otherness that seeks itself in me, and enables me to seek myself in it, not a diminution of my own solidity but the condition for it."[30] Icons invite us to live with transformed if also troubled faces. Anti-iconic figures who have not been thus transformed are always shown in profile, for not to have a full face is not to be fully human. "When souls start to break down," declared Dostoevsky's contemporary Nicholai Gogol, "then faces also degenerate."

Ours is a faceless and demonic time because so many of our political and economic regimes have had an anti-iconic estimate of human beings, regarding us not as images of God but as undifferentiated and dispensable units to be used for placeless and timeless projects of manipulation and control. Thus is ours the Age of Ashes, the time of the Gulags and the Treblinkas, the Dresdens and the Hiroshimas, the reduction of human life to cinders. In cultures such as ours, where there are few convincing declarations of the gospel and still fewer human icons of Christ in the world, the command to "love God" hardly registers. It has little if any greater force than "eat Wheaties," as Thomas

---

29. Ibid. It is not too far-fetched to suspect that the Archbishop of Canterbury may have been thinking here of the Islamic terrorists who will not "tolerate" any desecration of the image of Mohammed. Their willful hatred and violence are not so much anti-Islamic, therefore, as postmodern and anti-iconic.

30. Ibid., 208.

Merton sardonically observed. Thus does Williams's description of the life-world depicted in Dostoevsky's novel *The Devils* also describe our own late hour:

> There are no narrative icons around, and so the cultic icon [employed in worship] is in danger of being seen as equally an empty sign, without power. And when the image, in painted wood or flesh and blood, is experienced as vacuous and ineffectual, the potential for realizing the image of God in actual human beings disappears: no icon, no human compassion or self-questioning.[31]

• • •

Rowan Williams's book on Dostoevsky is the profoundest theological and literary treatise I have read for many years. He demonstrates that Dostoevsky is the greatest of all modern Christian writers because he remains at once profoundly Eastern *and* Western, both traditional *and* contemporary. He shares the anguish of Western self-consciousness, even as he engages it with an Eastern iconic imagination. He beckons us not to denigrate but rather to integrate authentic doubt with iconic holiness of life. Williams's work thus forms a fitting tribute to our dear departed friend, A. J. "Chip" Conyers. For this remarkable man lived the iconic life in Dostoevsky's precise sense: he confronted the fiercest but perhaps least obvious challenge to Christianity in our time—the seemingly benign but in fact pernicious toleration that would eliminate all icons of Christ.

Yet this gentle radical, this revolutionary conservative, this quietly dissident theologian, was not a nay-sayer. His final word was not Nay but Yea, not angry admonition but joyful summons. He called us neither to a Luddite smashing of our machines nor to an agrarian rejection of the wondrous technics which, as he gratefully confessed, had kept him alive for a decade. He urged, instead, that we live in communities of mutual trust and glad obligation, in places that honor an endearing smallness of scale as well as the gritty particularities of history. Such transcendent unity in community—achieved only through such iconic living—is the theme of Conyers' final book, *The Listening Heart: Vocation and the Crisis of Modern Culture*. The following sentences from it were read at Chip's funeral. Here he seeks to address the clamant late-modern obses-

---

31. Ibid., 218.

sion with diversity and difference and tolerance. Rather than divinizing them in the name of a bland universalism, or else demonizing them by way of a vicious tribalism, he defines the way God intends our variety to constitute a splendid symphonic and iconic unity:

> It is not only a relief, but positively good news, in the light of a vocational understanding of life, that differences are good also. It is true that in a fallen world they are occasions of distrust, envy, misunderstanding, animosity, and shame. But this comes from the failure to discern that differences are gifts for others, not occasions for animosity. In this they do not isolate us but unite us. Races, genders, language groupings, and the like, are classically [the occasion for] misunderstanding and conflict. But they also represent the way we grasp the world differently, through different cultures and sentiments, through various metaphors and [patterns of] syntax. As such, each of these human differences can be the basis for understanding existence in a valid, albeit partial, way. Thus with our insights, shaded toward different emphases, enjoying and using the world in our slightly different ways, we are enabled to enrich the greater community. While giving expression to what is temporally divided, we begin together to give witness to what is finally united. For the end of all things is the God who calls us, in whom we find rest, by whose one light we find our separate ways toward that city "not made with hands, eternal, in heaven." Those [on pilgrimage] toward that ultimate goal, even while they are separate, and [while] acknowledging that their experiences and ways are distinct, can yet give living witness to the fact that, in the mystery of God's calling, they are one.[32]

The aim of icons is worship through obedient faithfulness, for they reveal to our unspiritual and mundane eyes the invisible and spiritual Realities. They offer us theophanies, divine self-disclosures, windows into eternity. Chip Conyers was such an icon, calling us still and always to that unity-within-community which is the iconic life of the triune and incarnate God himself.

---

32. Conyers, *Listening Heart*, 192.

Bibliography

Benedict XVI. "Faith, Reason and the University: Memories and Reflections." Lecture delivered September 12, 2006. Online: http://www.vatican.va/holy_father/benedict_xvi/speeches/2006/september/documents/hf_ben-xvi_spe_20060912_university-regensburg_en.html.

Brown, Wendy. *Regulating Aversion: Tolerance in the Age of Identity and Empire.* Princeton: Princeton University Press, 2006.

Cavanaugh, William T. "The City: Beyond Secular Parodies." In *Radical Orthodoxy*, edited by John Milbank, Catherine Pickstock, and Graham Ward, 182–200. New York: Routledge, 1999.

Cicovacki, Predrag. *Dostoevsky and the Affirmation of Life.* South Bend, IN: St. Augustine's Press, 2009.

Conyers, Chip. *The Listening Heart: Vocation and the Crisis of Modern Culture.* 2006. Reprint, Waco, TX: Baylor University Press, 2009.

Dostoevsky, Fyodor. *Notes from Underground.* Translated by Ralph E. Matlaw. New York: Dutton, 1960.

Jefferson, Thomas. "Notes on Virginia." 1782. Online: http://www.nobeliefs.com/jefferson.htm.

Locke, John. *Epistola de Tolerantia.* Translated by William Popple. Online: http://www.constitution.org/jl/tolerati.htm.

MacIntyre, Alasdair. "Toleration and the Goods of Conflict." In *The Tasks of Philosophy: Selected Essays on Ethics and Politics*, vol. 2. New York: Cambridge University Press, 2006.

Miscamble, Wilson D. *Keeping the Faith, Making a Difference.* Notre Dame, IN: Ave Maria, 2000.

Planned Parenthood of Southeastern Pa. v. Casey (91-744), 505 U.S. 833 (1992). Syllabus online: http://www.law.cornell.edu/supct/html/91-744.ZS.html.

Sandel, Michael. *Democracy's Discontents: America in Search of a Public Philosophy.* Cambridge, MA: Harvard University Press, 1996.

Williams, Rowan. *Dostoevsky: Language, Faith, and Fiction.* Waco, TX: Baylor University Press, 2008.

Wood, Ralph C. "Hospitality as the Gift Greater than Tolerance: G. K. Chesterton's *The Ball and the Cross.*" *Logos* 12.4 (Fall 2009) 258–85.

12

Post-Consensus Ethics, the Natural Law, and Civil Society

J. Daryl Charles

We should let ourselves be guided by what is common to all. ... To be wise[1] is the greatest virtue. Wisdom consists in speaking and acting the truth, giving heed to the nature of things. ... Although intimately connected with the Logos, men keep setting themselves against it.

—Heraclitus[2]

But if the principles of Justice were founded on the decrees of peoples, the edicts of princes, or the decisions of judges, then Justice would sanction robbery and adultery and forgery of wills. ... But in fact we can perceive the difference between good laws and bad by referring them to no other standard than Nature; indeed, it is not merely Justice and Injustice which are distinguished by Nature, but also and without exception things which are honourable and dishonourable. For since an intelligence common to us all makes things known to us and formulates them in our minds, honourable actions are ascribed by us to virtue, and dishonourable actions to vice; and only a madman would conclude that these judgments are matters of opinion, and not fixed by Nature.

—Cicero[3]

---

1. The word used here is σωφρονεῖν. The translation I am using (see n. 2) renders it "to be temperate"; however, the proper sense is *thinking* properly, thereby suggesting *being wise*.

2. Fragments 2, 10, 64, reproduced in *Heraclitus*, pp. 19, 68.

3. *Laws* 1.16 (LCL, 345–47).

Introduction: The Problem of Consensus

Long ago and far away, a strange belief persisted. It was the belief that all human beings shared moral common ground by reason of a shared moral nature. This notion, however quaint, would have been held by most people, with relatively few exceptions. In fact, theologians, legal theorists, statesmen, or political philosophers could press the argument, without noticeable dissent, that the rudiments of the moral life are the same for all people at all times and at all places.[4] Again, long ago and far away.

But that was then and this is now. A different storyline is dominant in our own time.[5] As one social critic has observed, anyone who makes it his or her vocation to teach in the so-called "moral sciences" these days is bound to encounter a primate who protests that "there is no [normative] truth."[6] On this newer account, the principles of right and wrong, we are reminded *ad nauseum*, are *not* the same for all people everywhere. Rather, "right and wrong," "good and evil," "just and unjust" are categories that are properly understood to be sociocultural, procedural, situational, or adaptational. All that we *can* know for certain is that there is *no* moral common ground among all people in a universal sense, and the sooner we are freed from this illusion or backward way of thinking, the better.

A particularly poignant index of the present state of moral affairs came in the form of an address by former Princeton University President Harold Shapiro at Cornell some years back.[7] The timing of this speech was dramatic because Shapiro was addressing the matter of the university's role in moral education at precisely the time that Princeton was offering an endowed chair to a controversial ethicist and animal-rights activist who had distinguished himself for his forthright

---

4. In books 2 and 5 of *Nichomachean Ethics*, Aristotle maintains this with regard to the character of justice: it is uniform for all people everywhere. See as well Aquinas, *Summa Theologica* I-II Q. 94, a. 4.

5. None has captured the jarring contrast between past and present more deftly than Budziszewski, *What We Can't Not Know*, 3–15.

6. Arkes, *First Things*, 51. Of course, it is only proper to respond by asking whether the proposition "there is no truth" is indeed true.

7. Shapiro, "Liberal Education."

and forceful advocacy of euthanasia and infanticide, and, perhaps less known—since 2001—for his consent for bestiality.[8]

The question raised by Shapiro was this: Can—and should—the university teach its students to be better citizens and better people? And if so, then on what basis? In the address Shapiro considered the possibilities for moral education against the backdrop of liberal education as he understood it. Shapiro identified three elements that are thought to anchor liberal education: the need to (1) "provide an understanding of the great traditions of thought"; (2) "free our minds from unexamined commitments and unquestioned allegiances"; and (3) "prepare us for an independent and responsible life of choice."

Let us take stock of Shapiro's language. What might Shapiro have in mind when he calls us to "free our minds from unexamined and unquestioned commitments and allegiances"? What specifically might these unexamined commitments and allegiances be? We should note here that when he speaks of "independent and responsible lives of choice," Shapiro is assuming, and asserting, that (a) it is responsible to be independent rather than to be communal, consensual, or subordinated to the common good; and (b) "choice" needs no moral qualification, since "choice" unfettered represents a moral good.

In further elaborating these three points, Shapiro made the rather remarkable statement that these tenets are especially important in a world where we increasingly need to replace—and I quote Shapiro—"rigid kinship rules, strict religious precepts, and other aspects of totalitarian rule that have traditionally imposed order on society."[9] Notice, again, the vocabulary. For Shapiro, "kinship rules" and "religious precepts" are to be viewed as "rigid," "strict," even "totalitarian." One wonders whether there was any reaction in the audience at Cornell to these particular comments. Such a view of moral education, I submit, at worst is frightening and at the very least should give us pause. But it

---

8. It will be recalled that Shapiro, who had chaired President Clinton's National Bioethics Advisory Commission, appointed Peter Singer to the DeCamp Chair of Human Values at Princeton. As an animal-rights activist, Singer went public in 2001 on bestiality, the final sexual taboo. He did so in a review of the book *Dearest Pet: On Bestiality* (New York: Verso, 2000), authored by Dutch biologist and naturalist Midas Dekkers, that appeared in the online magazine Nerve.com. Singer's conclusion was that "sex across species barriers" in fact "ceases to be an offence to our status and dignity as human beings."

9. Shapiro, "Liberal Education," 19.

does explain why a prestigious American university, with relatively little protest, can present an endowed chair to an activist-ethicist who has argued at great length in favor of rights for animals while denying those same rights to the neonate handicapped and the dying.

Contra Shapiro, "kinship rules" and "religious precepts" are neither "rigid" nor "totalitarian," despite what the intractable nihilism and secular fundamentalism of our day rigidly maintain. Rather, they are evidence of common moral ground shared by all—common ground that is verified *communally and consensually*, and *not* as individuals who exercise "choice" independently of the community. What's more, all human beings, regardless of sociocultural location, have a rudimentary knowledge of what that common moral fund is. All people *do* in fact know that murder, theft, defrauding one's neighbor, adultery, treachery, dishonoring parents, slander, and so forth are *intrinsically* wrong. Whence comes this awareness? Such is owing neither to genetic adaptation, nor to insights from cultural anthropology, nor to religious sentiments inherent specifically in Eastern or Western culture, nor to majoritarian opinion. These behaviors are quite simply universally forbidden. Period. Their wrongness corresponds to a prior moral "law"—a law that we did not create or manufacture but which we "discover" and in which we continually find shelter.[10]

Nevertheless, to suggest today—whether in academic, legal, or popular culture—that there exist universal norms regarding matters of right and wrong, good and evil, is itself considered perverse—the very height of presumption, bigotry, intolerance, and moral colonialism. Such, alas, is the cultural climate. Truth be told, there exists around us *no cultural consensus* as to what is right and wrong, acceptable and unacceptable; consequently, we sit one step removed from moral-social anarchy. And because there is permitted to exist no consensus regard-

10. Of course, this sort of suggestion is what so outraged Senators Biden, Kennedy, and company almost two decades ago on the occasion of the Clarence Thomas Supreme Court hearings, and it continues to outrage our contemporaries. The fact that Judge Thomas was indebted to a more classical understanding of natural law, an understanding that assumes and seeks to respect the moral foundations of law and politics, was supremely vexing—and in the end, unacceptable—to Biden. The result was the Senator from Delaware, a professing Catholic, waxing rather self-righteous as he proceeded to lecture both Thomas and the American public that natural law is a "dangerous doctrine." What especially infuriated Senator Biden was Judge Thomas' insinuation that there are "moral predicates" of an enduring nature—viz., good and evil, justice and injustice—that undergird law.

ing moral basics, we shall therefore need to rethink, reformulate and reassert the moral underpinnings of human culture—and notice that I do not say *Western* culture, nor do I say *Christian* culture. That is, we shall need to reformulate what moral thinkers of past generations understood to be "the permanent things."[11] For indeed what we might call moral "first things" or "necessary truths"[12] help furnish a moral consensus on which civil society—*any* society—must be founded and which must continually be reaffirmed.

But we are not the first to wrestle with the dilemma of a "moral consensus," even when the matter is heightened in the present post-consensus environment in which breathtaking biogenetic and biotechnological developments press upon us. Several generations removed from us, writer-thinkers discerned—and sought to forestall—what currently is in full bloom. Consider, by way of example, the trenchant social criticism of theologian John Courtney Murray. Murray observed that "civil society" presupposes a wider consensus—a consensus that, yes, is constitutional, legal, and political, but which, at its base, is moral. People, he argued, do not arrive accidentally at this consensus, but rather deliberatively, by way of reason and reflecting on our common experience based on the *imago Dei*. At the core of this moral discernment, he insisted, is lodged "an ensemble of substantive truths," i.e., "elementary affirmations that reflect realities inherent in the order of existence."[13] These correspond to what has been called *patrimonium generis humani*, a heritage of essential human truths that sustain and furnish the substance of civil life at all times. As Murray was keenly aware, these essential truths are both classical and Christian in their derivation,[14] refined

---

11. T. S. Eliot, who is often credited with introducing the expression "the permanent things," wrote in *After Strange Gods*, 33: "The number of people in possession of any criteria for discriminating between good and evil is very small; the number of the half-alive hungry for any form of spiritual experience, or what offers itself as spiritual experience, high or low, good or bad, is considerable. My own generation has not served them very well. Never has the printing press been so busy, and never have such varieties of buncombe and false doctrine come from it." He well could have been describing our own time.

12. So Arkes, *First Things*, esp. chs. 2 and 4.

13. Murray, *We Hold These Truths*, 9.

14. That is to say, wisdom is a repository of not only Christians but all who seek it; wisdom is universally accessible.

and developed in our particular cultural heritage as a result of Christian conviction—even when they now stand neglected or rejected.

Ponder for a moment what patrimony or heritage entails. It is something bequeathed and received, not created or constructed. The fact of a *received* consensus is the whole premise of *public* argument, debate and discussion, for if society is to be civilized and civilizing, that consensus is not negotiable over time, since it is enduring. When we speak of an "ensemble of substantive truths" or a "heritage of essential truths," we refer to what might be called *necessary* truths, that is, truths that must be comprehended before we can comprehend anything else. That there exists an essential rightness or wrongness to particular human behavior is intuited prior to human experience and experiment.[15]

Thus, the framers of this nation's charter documents could utter statements such as "These are the truths we hold," and they could speak publicly and formally of "self-evident truths," the "laws of nature," and "nature's God." Clearly presupposed was a general consensus regarding moral reality and necessary truths, regardless of the deistic or theistic metaphysic to which they may have ascribed. Therefore, if we who are perched near the cusp of the twenty-first century are convinced of objective norms that are universal in scope and nature, a conviction shared by moral thinkers ranging from Aristotle to St. Paul to Aquinas to Murray to Benedict XVI, then we shall need to contend for this consensus in the public sphere. After all, a moral-social consensus is not guaranteed over time; it can erode, be forgotten, and even be virulently suppressed, as is presently the case.

By contending in public life that a moral consensus about human nature and human affairs is real, we counter the cultural *Zeitgeist* by declaring that everything is *not* in doubt, relative, or up for grabs. The moral consensus that we affirm, it needs emphasizing, is true not because we—or anyone else—might believe it; rather, we believe it because it is true, which means that it is true for *all human beings*, irrespective of their location in human civilization. Hence, C. S. Lewis

---

15. The notion that "all men are created equal" might be described as moral preknowledge, a necessary truth that is intuited by all people, regardless of their social-cultural location. So, for example, "[w]hen people are rewarded or punished not for their own acts, but for the accident of their racial background, they are not praised or blamed for anything that it was in the power to affect, and they are treated, therefore, as though they did not possess the freedom or autonomy of moral agents . . . therefore it must be said that racial discrimination is wrong *of necessity*" (Arkes, *First Things*, 53).

could write: "This thing which I have called for convenience the Tao, and which others may call Natural Law ... is not one among a series of possible systems of value. It is the sole source of all value judgment. If it is rejected, all value is rejected."[16] Precisely for this reason, then, such consensus must undergird our public philosophy.[17]

The moral realist is cognizant of the fact that the consensus erodes over time. It requires reaffirmation in successive generations and needs to be preserved from the effects of the moral "barbarian."[18] As we have learned in recent history, moral barbarism is able to take on a sophisticated and inevitably duplicitous cast. Even the holocaust of the unborn, which we are presently witnessing, can be not only denied but blessed as wise public policy. At the most basic level of discourse, however, when rational standards of moral judgments are undermined or denied, the result is a "lack of reasonable conversation according to reasonable laws," regardless of "the surface impressions of urbanity."[19]

Anatomy of a Post-Consensus Cultural Climate

But to speak of a pervasive climate of skepticism, nihilism, absence of reasonable conversation and debate, or a lack of civility is to describe

16. Lewis, *Abolition of Man*, 56.

17. This, in my view, is the broader significance of John Paul's 1993 encyclical *Veritatis Splendor*.

18. This is the description used by Murray, *We Hold These Truths*, 12. The "barbarian" is one who "makes open and explicit rejection of the traditional role of reason and logic in human affairs" and who "reduces all spiritual and moral questions to the test of practical results or to an analysis of language or to decision in terms of individual subjective feeling." It is perennially the work of the barbarian "to undermine rational standards of judgment, to corrupt the inherited intuitive wisdom by which ... people have always lived, and to do this ... by creating a climate of doubt and bewilderment in which clarity about the larger aims of life is dimmed and the self-confidence of the people is destroyed, so that finally what you have is the impotent nihilism ... now presently appearing on our university campuses" (ibid.). It is interesting that these words were penned fifty years ago.

19. Ibid., 12–13. Society becomes barbarian "when men are huddled together under the rule of force and fear; when economic interests assume the primacy over higher values; when material standards of mass and quantity crush out the values of quality and excellence; when technology assumes an autonomous existence ... without purposeful guidance from the higher disciplines of politics and morals ... ; when the state reaches the paradoxical point of being everywhere intrusive and also impotent ... ; when the ways of men come under the sway of the instinctual, the impulsive, the compulsive" (ibid. 13–14).

symptoms of an eroding moral consensus and not the root problem itself. The waxing of a secular fundamentalism plus the emergence of an unprincipled ideological pluralism, exacerbated by the inability of people of faith to articulate an integrated world- or life-view that possesses a robust public philosophy—these together help to foster a cultural climate that we presently encounter, even when one might well argue that the process of cultural decomposition was well underway long ago or that the deconstructive process is more advanced in Europe than in the U.S. Such reservations or objections notwithstanding, these particular elements—a deeply ensconced secularism, unprincipled pluralism, and philosophical impotence—require further comment.

We might respond to the first—the entrenchment of a "fundamentalist" secularism—that, against conventional wisdom and the contemporary *Zeitgeist*, there indeed *is* a place for religious arguments in the public square. Thus, despite considerable cultural "drag" we shall need to counter rigorist secularists of our day with some forcefulness when they argue that religious beliefs are inherently irrational or that there is no place for religious conviction in public conversation and debate.[20] The exclusion of so-called religious arguments from the public arena is a relatively recent development. What's more, the fact is that the common good of society is preserved by moral principle, and moral principle is indebted to religious conviction, the protests of the new biologists and evolutionary psychologists notwithstanding. Furthermore, even the secularist's construal of ultimate reality is "religious"[21] in nature, since it too has (1) an ultimate authority, (2) a cosmology and metaphysics, (3) a particular anthropology, (4) a framework for ethics, and (5) a plan for organizing society.

---

20 The task is complicated by religious commentary that, wittingly or unwittingly, relegates religious conviction to the private sphere; thus, for example, Derek H. Davis, who argues that "it is the nonpublic [i.e., private] sphere that must be respected as the domain of religion and that will supply ... the morality and virtue so essential to the successful functioning of democratic government" ("Classical Separation Perspective," 101). Precisely this—the privatization and marginalization of religious belief—is what is so deeply problematic today. A welcome antidote is Brendan Sweetman, in *Why Politics Needs Religion*, who argues for the place of religious arguments in public discourse with precision and accuracy.

21. The term "religious" derives from the Latin *religare*, "to bind together," and thus, by extension, to give coherence to one's view of ultimate reality, whatever that view might be.

Intellectual honesty, then, requires our acknowledgement that every world- and life-view is "religious" to the extent that it is bound together by certain theological, metaphysical, ethical, anthropological, and social assumptions. Consequently, we are left to concede that *there is no such thing* as moral "neutrality" in the public sphere. Alas, *all people* draw the line at some point between right and wrong, between acceptable and unacceptable. What differs is the point at which people draw the line. In the end, *someone's* ethics will become public policy; indeed, *someone's* ethics will become law.[22]

At the same time, we must also acknowledge that religious conviction need not be clothed in religious language, since many of our contemporaries *do not speak that language*. Nor should we assume that in a "post-Christian," post-consensus cultural climate they *understand* that language. One thinks, for example, of the strategy adopted by St. Paul, the "apostle to the Gentiles," in Athens, recorded in Acts 17, both in the marketplace and in his address to the Council of the Areopagus. Significantly, the Council was an esteemed presidium consisting of thirty highly-educated and influential Athenians of Stoic or Epicurean philosophical bent, who worked "in committee" as it were on diverse educational, legal, and social issues of the day.[23] Already by St. Paul's day, the Areopagus Council had a rich history, having been in existence for over three hundred years. The apostle's strategy is worth noting: he addresses his highly cultured and broadly pantheist audience on the basis of natural-law assumptions and the created order (utilizing what theologians might call "general revelation" or "common grace"). Only after he has built a bridge to the thought world of his audience does he introduce the uniqueness of the Christian message.[24] The lesson here,

---

22. This point has been argued cogently by J. Budziszewski in *The Revenge of Conscience*; *True Tolerance*; and "Illusion of Moral Neutrality."

23. For example, Cicero served on the Areopagus Council one hundred years before St. Paul addressed the esteemed body. Writing in the mid-first century BC, Cicero could observe that in spite of its decline in political power, Athens still enjoyed "such renown" that "the now shattered and weakened name of Greece is supported by the reputation of this city" (*Pro Flacco* 26). Perhaps the best English-language resource on the background of the Areopagus Council is Bert Gaertner's *The Areopagus Speech and Natural Revelation*.

24. Elsewhere I have examined St. Paul's strategy in Athens and in his Areopagus address in "Engaging the (Neo)Pagan Mind," a modified version of which appears in ch. 6 of *The Unformed Conscience of Evangelicalism*; additionally and more recently, see "Paul before the Areopagus" and *Retrieving the Natural Law*, 45–54.

I think, is worthy of emulation: we meet our secular or agnostic contemporaries at their level philosophically, out of respect for our shared humanity (i.e., based on the *imago Dei* and neighbor-love), and it is possible to do this without sacrificing our convictions.[25]

As to the second element, unprincipled ideological pluralism, we shall need to purify terms such as "tolerance," diversity," and "compassion" and restore to them their proper meaning. This, of course, will not be easy, given the ideological and linguistic prostitution to which these (and like) terms have been subjected in our own generation. Someone has observed that when a revolutionary group wishes to wage war on human decency, the first—and most effective—strategy is to co-opt language in the service of the cause. Thus, it is not surprising that homosexual activists and proponents of physician-assisted death, to cite but two examples, routinely speak in terms of "compassion," "mercy," "dignity," and "civil rights."[26] Subsequently, as they seek to expand their program both on a popular level and in the context of policy debates, the rhetoric of "compassion" and "rights," which is necessary to broad-based popular support, allows them to capture the moral high ground.[27] It is precisely this sort of verbal sleight-of-hand that George Orwell had in mind as he penned in 1947 a brief but highly important essay titled "Politics and the English Language." What Orwell found in his own day is all the more applicable to our own:

> One ought to recognize that the present political chaos is connected with the decay of language.... Political language—and this is true of all political parties, from Conservatives to Anarchists—is designed to make lies sound truthful, and

---

25. This, by the way, is precisely the rhetorical tactic taken in the essays that comprise C. S. Lewis' *Mere Christianity*. The book begins with "Right and Wrong as a Clue to Meaning in the Universe"—a discussion that clearly has the skeptic or unbeliever in view—and only later in the volume are the distinctives of Christian faith enunciated, *after common ground with the readership has been established.*

26. The "linguistic turn" (read: perversion of language) in preparing the social climate for ethical shifts is conveniently (when blatantly) illustrated by relativist Joseph Fletcher: "Christian Europe started moving from *pagan Rome's compassionate regard* for the dignity of free persons to the *savagery of an indiscriminating condemnation of all suicide* in the Middle Ages" ("Defense of Suicide," 237–38; emphasis added).

27. We must treat these activists, even in their morally obtuse state, charitably insofar as they themselves remain a mirror of the image of God. Charity, however, which is wedded to truth and moral reality, does not permit them to determine the norms of moral discourse or policy prescription.

murder respectable, and to give an appearance of solidity to pure wind.[28]

Orwell rightly saw the connection between our moral vocabulary and sociopolitical upheaval, which proceeds in the interest of "reality-control."[29] Orwell feared that a society's emasculation and manipulation of language could render its citizens truly powerless to say that anything was right or wrong. In this moral state of affairs, nothing is certain, nothing can be maintained as good and true, and nothing can be denied as false and evil or undermining the common good. Such a moral-political climate leaves us amputated. In the words of Jean Elshtain, "Cut off from the bonds that help us to hold our 'selves' intact, we are more readily ground down to become the generic mulch of the order."[30] Surely, Orwell would have much to say about current debates over governmental "bailouts," bioethical and healthcare issues, and human sexuality. Alas, many public issues, to a large extent, are strikingly battles over words and their meanings and not discussions about underlying moral truth.

Hence, one of the most important tasks for Christian citizens is to insist that as a culture we engage in truth-telling and that we name things accurately and appropriately. In this vein, Elshtain painfully reminds us of "what happened when totalitarian regimes had the power to control language and to cover mass murder with the rhetoric of 'improvement

---

28. Orwell, "Politics and the English Language," 4:136.

29. While the essay "Politics" gives theoretical explanation to this linkage, the novel *1984* serves as a graphic illustration thereof. Vocationally, Orwell was a journalist, not a moral philosopher; moreover, he wrote as a religious agnostic. Nevertheless, his insights into the relationship between language and "worldview" were prescient.

30. Elshtain, "Relationship," 52. For this reason, Elshtain observes, Orwell's target audience consisted of "friends of totalitarianism," whether politically leftist or rightist (ibid.). Why was Orwell so concerned to target the intellectual? In offering an explanation, Elshtain states a truism: "Fearful of offending the public opinion within his own group, the intellectual lives in dread of being tagged with a label . . . and trims his thought and words energetically in order to conform and stay in good graces with the group" (ibid.). This condition, I think, is continually validated in the academy and increasingly in public discourse. In a certain sense, much of the professoriate—politically and ideologically—remains "friends of totalitarianism." To illustrate, one only need observe the backlash against orthodox Christians not only in the culture but especially in the academy for their opposition to homosexual proclivities, a reaction that is nothing short of vicious.

of the race' and even 'mercy and compassion.'"[31] Thus, for example, in countering the homosexual activist, we shall need to affirm, with R.V. Young, that "compulsive behavior arising from peculiar inclinations is not an adequate basis for establishing social institutions, much less for threatening those upon which society has long depended."[32]

A bit of history, however, might be helpful in adjusting our sight and coming to our aid.[33] In our own cultural tradition, "tolerance" emerged as a political and social virtue and possessed meaning against the backdrop of the European experience, as mirrored *inter alia* in the writings of John Locke. As a social and political virtue, tolerance has foremost public or communal (over against private) dimensions. In principle, while we may disagree with another's opinion, vice, or lifestyle, we extend that person's personal "right" to a specific opinion or behavior that we may find objectionable. Christians and non-Christians of *all* varieties tolerate one another's differences because of what they *all* share in common—the laws of nature, inalienable rights, and human dignity that inheres in personhood. When, however, a person—in the name of "tolerance"—is making claims on the *public square* and wishing to normalize what is abnormal, extending so-called "rights" to broader society to engage in and advance what is morally abhorrent and unnatural, tolerance must then cease, for we tolerate what we dislike *until it begins making claims on the wider community in a way that undermines the common good*. Thus, moral seriousness compels us to draw a strict distinction between the freedoms of an individual, practiced "in private," and the needs of the community, of which we *all* are contributing parts. This distinction is not necessarily owing to Christian insight, for Locke himself makes the basic political observation—an important one for contemporary Americans—that a great deal of difference can be tolerated *provided that it does not endanger social cohesion*. We shall have more to say about tolerance below.

31. Idem, *Who Are We?*, 128.

32. Young, "Gay Invention." In affirming the inviolable relationship between human nature and public policy, Young insists: "the peculiar use of a natural organ or faculty does not change its nature. A man can walk around on his hands, but that does not turn hands into feet; and society ought not to be obliged to redesign sidewalks and staircases to accommodate compulsive 'handwalkers' . . . , even if they are born with the inclination" (ibid.).

33. Precisely here, Chip Conyers spent much time reflecting on our present cultural condition. See his wonderfully informative work *The Long Truce*.

In regard to the third element, philosophical impotence, we shall need to be prepared to offer a spirited and philosophically robust public defense of our positions. And this, naturally, presumes a willingness on our part to engage our contemporaries in a manner that is simultaneously *winsome yet insistent that some moral truth can be apprehended.* "Now more than ever," notes one social critic, "Christians as citizens must be defenders of human reason, insistent that epistemological questions cannot be severed from ontological concerns."[34]

Difficult as this task may be, we are not without adequate resources. It is perhaps not incidental that John Paul II's last major encyclical, in 1998, was *Fides et Ratio*, by which the former pontiff reminded us that because of *human nature*, faith and reason may not be divorced.[35] Reason unsubordinated to a higher authority leads to various philosophical distortions (e.g., rationalism, empiricism, scientism, and nihilism) while a faith that does not seek understanding (e.g., fideism) is a denial of the image of God in us. Faith and reason have a symbiotic relationship in their common pursuit of truth.[36]

Undergirding *Fides et Ratio* as well as the very important 1993 encyclical *Veritatis Splendor* is John Paul's assumption—an assumption amply supported by the historic Christian tradition—that there are basic truths intuited by all human beings by virtue of their being

34. Elshtain, *Who Are We?*, 137–38.

35. John Paul's emphasis in the encyclical on "nature" and "seeking the truth" allows several broader themes to emerge: (1) reason is by nature oriented to truth and thus equipped with the means necessary to arrive at truth (no. 49); humans are by nature truth-seekers, given their inclination to reflect on why things are as they are (no. 3); and (3) humans seek to know the truth about their own existence, about life, and about the Creator (nos. 4, 5, 15, 20, 26, 53, 80). John Paul, however, is under no illusion about the devastating effects of sin, for sin has "wounded," "impaired," and "alienated" reason (nos. 22, 80, and 107). Nevertheless, he believes, reason's limitations are *not* grounds for *abandoning* reason. Right use of reason, which apprehends the natural law, is properly *rational, not rationalistic*.

36. Benedict XVI has continued this notable emphasis, as evidenced by his highly controversial address at the University of Regensburg in September of 2006. In this address, titled "Faith, Reason and the University: Memories and Reflections," Benedict combined personal reflections on teaching theology at the University of Bonn several decades prior with his own assessment of the state of contemporary academic discourse. Particularly "in the face of such radical skepticism" as is prevalent today, Benedict continues, "it is still necessary to raise the question of God through *the use of reason*, and to do so *in the context of the tradition of the Christian faith*" (emphasis added). This, he reminded his German audience, though currently unfashionable was "accepted without question" several decades ago within the university as a whole.

created in the image of God. In the words of St. Paul, even the Gentiles, i.e., those without special revelation or the "law," "instinctively do what the law requires." Thereby they demonstrate that the law is "written on their hearts" (Rom 2:14–15). *This* is the natural law, which, according to Aquinas, reduces in its essence to "Do good and avoid evil," from which all other moral principles extend. Thus, we are in need of a new generation of philosophers—moral, legal, and political—to emerge out of the post-consensus morass for the purposes of instructing us in the way of wisdom and undergirding our cultural witness.

Contending for Moral First Things in Public Debate

Apart from the reference point of moral "first things" anchored in natural-law reasoning, it will be difficult—if not impossible—to take part responsibly in the great ethical debates of the day and to contribute meaningfully to a reshaping of any sort of baseline cultural consensus about moral reality. Several broader ethical categories might serve to illustrate, only in cursory fashion, the need for cultural consensus. In what follows, I have chosen three spheres that are intended simply to be illustrative. But first a word about our *mode* of engaging the surrounding culture.

In the American context, we are routinely treated to caricatures of the religiously orthodox (read: "fundamentalists") that are damning. Those who would dare take their Christian confessional commitments seriously and interject them in the public sphere are characteristically stereotyped as moral imperialists—bigoted, judgmental, and hopelessly inhumane. In a pervasively *non-judgmental* social climate, we are expected to tolerate all things, even the morally intolerable, and do this in the name of tolerance, of course. What we *dare not* tolerate, however, is the person who would make moral judgments and bring them into the public realm. This intrusion into our social space, after all, is most unwelcome, since it will lead to various forms of confrontation.

This negative stereotype of the confrontational, judgmentalistic Christian sets the stage for a recent collection of intriguing essays published under the title *Mutual Treasure*. As suggested by the subtitle, *Seeking Better Ways for Christians and Culture to Converse*, the volume calls the reader away from "confrontational" approaches in interfacing with the culture and toward a "dialogical" method of interaction.

In the preface to the volume, the editors write: "We are appalled at the confrontational nature of much public discourse.... Christians are not immune from this prevailing culture of confrontation."[37] The "better" way, accordingly, is to "build relationships of mutual trust" with those who oppose you. "You then talk respectfully about your differences in the spirit of being open to finding some 'treasures' in their contrary position, hoping that they will likewise find some treasures in your point of view."[38]

Four essays in this volume do a commendable job of demonstrating how Christian witness through dialogue shows itself to be most effective and enduring. These four, respectively, discuss Christian involvement in the art of filmmaking, in the political process, in aiding victims of violent crime, and in conversations within the academy.[39] The respective authors argue for creative and deliberately incarnational ways of clothing Christian conviction in the public sphere. To be sure, "building relationships" through our respective callings remains unquestionably *the* human—and thus the "better"—way to engage fellow human beings; Christian charity demands no less. At the same time, what is noticeably absent from many of the contributions to this volume is the possibility that (a) our commitment to the permanent things, i.e., to "necessary truths," might on occasion impede "building relationships"; (b) faithfulness to divine revelation (based on moral integrity) rather than "openness" to the "other" might be the higher virtue; and (c) the collision between truth and error, particularly as error makes comprehensive claims on the public square, may result in "confrontation." While charity surely can take the shape of "being a good listener" and "cultivating mutual understanding," one wonders how St. Paul, who himself was known to theorize on charity in his epistolary writing, might greet the openness/"mutual treasure" thesis as an "apostle to the Gentiles."[40]

---

37. In Heie and King, *Mutual Treasure*, 15.

38. Ibid.

39. The essays are: Hafer, "Changing the Culture, One Film at a Time," 110–24; DeWeese, "Personalism in Politics: Finding Common Ground in the Legislature," 54–72; Krause, "A Restorative Alternative to an Adversarial Criminal Justice System," 161–75; Thomas, "Roundtable Conversation: Hospitality in the Academy," 93–109.

40. One contributor to *Mutual Treasure*, for example, proposes a Gadamerian philosophical hermeneutic as a means by which the Christian community might view homosexuality as "an arena for mutual understanding," since "prejudices delimit my horizon" (King, "Conversations on Homosexuality as a Way to Love Enemy Preferences,"

My own sense of Christian history and obedience to the faith leads me to suspect, notwithstanding the good intentions of *Mutual Treasure*'s editors and contributors, that the Christian community, *if* she takes issues of human life and personhood seriously, will need on occasion to be "confrontational," even when this means being misinterpreted by the culture (as well as the publishing industry). Ethical issues such as human trafficking, genocide, terrorism, violent crime, as well as abortion, sexuality, and related bioethical dilemmas—all of *which* vex and oppress human culture in varying degrees—will require of us that we marry, rather than divorce, charity and truth.[41] And it is well possible that these issues might preclude the possibility of "dialogue" in the formal and temporal sense. Alas, they may require "confrontation," despite the supremely "non-judgmental" cultural *Zeitgeist* that envelops (and wishes to silence) us.[42]

A remarkable—and eminently helpful—example of how "dialogue" might actually foster what is substantively *immoral* can be seen in the events surrounding the May 2009 commencement exercise at the University of Notre Dame. Considerable controversy among Roman Catholics surrounded Notre Dame's decision to invite President Obama

---

146). Reading this essay conveys the impression that "mutual understanding" is *an end in and of itself*. Nowhere does the essay even mildly suggest that homosexuality is a contradiction of (a) Christian faith, (b) the Church's historic teaching, (c) the Christian moral tradition, and (d) biological and psychological realities of human nature based on the *imago Dei*. The reader is only left to ponder what churches and denominations might look like if we pursued "alternatives to battling over homosexuality" (ibid., 158). Perhaps, the author suggests, rather than "battling" over the issue, the church might benefit from "faithful dissent" offered by those advocating gay-lesbian spirituality (ibid.). Avoiding confrontation, alas, and not faithfulness to Christ and moral integrity, would seem to constitute the higher virtue.

41. Let us be clear: truth will *always* uphold what is morally right and virtuous, never compromising its integrity; at the same time, charity will *always* uphold what is true and right, even as it seeks a humane and accommodating expression in the awareness that fellow human beings bear the image of God. These two elements are *not* in opposition; rather, they represent two sides of the same ethical coin. It is sadly characteristic of contemporary approaches to ethics—and, all the more sadly, representative of many Christian ethicists—that truth and charity are construed as opposites, standing in a sort of adversarial relationship.

42. An interesting pattern invites serious scrutiny: when the "religious right" (so-called) is counter-cultural, this is typically blasted as bigoted, reactionary, narrow-minded, and "fundamentalist." When, by contrast, those on the left of the political spectrum decry culture or the political establishment (or the "religious right"), this is perceived as thoughtful, nuanced, even "prophetic."

to speak and to bestow upon him an honorary degree. And consider the context: given the President's radicalized stance on life issues (the most radical of any U.S. president ever), not the least of which is Obama's personal stance on abortion and abortion providers,[43] as of one week before the commencement, seventy-four Catholic bishops had publicly censured Notre Dame for its decision to present the President with an award.[44] It was for this reason that Bishop John D'Arcy—bishop of Ft. Wayne-South Bend at the time and the local bishop over Notre Dame's president, Father John Jenkins—to his great credit sorrowfully declined to attend. In his public statement, D'Arcy avowed: "Even as I continue to ponder in prayer these events, which many have found shocking, so must Notre Dame. Indeed, as a Catholic university, Notre Dame must ask itself, if by this decision it has chosen *prestige over truth*."[45]

Nevertheless, what was heartening, despite Notre Dame's insistence on thumbing its nose at the church and its historic teaching on protecting the unborn, is the sheer number of people from *within* the Notre Dame community—the number has been estimated at between 2,500 and 3,500 people, both students and faculty[46]—that protested the event by not attending commencement but rather meeting alternatively on the University's South Quad for the purpose of celebrating Mass, worship, prayer, and singing.

What placed Obama's invitation to Notre Dame in a particularly dramatic (and proper) relief was the decision of Prof. Mary Ann Glendon, Learned Hand Professor of Law at Harvard Law School and U.S. Ambassador to the Vatican from 2007 to 2009,[47] to inform Father

43. Obama's refusal during the 2008 presidential campaign to answer the question of when life begins and his related response—such an issue is "above my pay grade"—is inexcusable and cynical but also supremely telling. In this regard, see William McGurn's comments on Obama's promise to Planned Parenthood observed in n. 53 below.

44. These included Archbishop Donald Wuerli of Washington (DC), Justin Cardinal Regali, Archbishop of Philadelphia, and Francis Cardinal George, Archbishop of Chicago and President of the U.S. Conference of Catholic Bishops (hereafter "USCCB").

45. D'Arcy, "Bishop D'Arcy laments" (emphasis added). D'Arcy described this development as a "terrible breach between Notre Dame and the Church."

46. This estimate comes from several Notre Dame faculty members and personal acquaintances who attended the mass and worship service rather than the commencement. It refutes reports by the *New York Times*, the *Washington Post*, CNN, and other news outlets that only several hundred people total attended the protest service.

47. Glendon is also the current president of the Pontifical Academy of Social Sciences.

Jenkins that she had decided to decline receiving the coveted Laetare Metal, Notre Dame's highest honor, at the University's commencement ceremonies. (It should be noted that in 1996 Glendon had received an honorary degree from Notre Dame.) As a "longtime consultant to the U.S. Conference of Catholic Bishops,"[48] she expressed regret to Jenkins that he seemed prepared to use her to soften criticism of Obama's invitation to speak at the University's commencement exercise and to receive the award.[49]

What Glendon found lamentable in Jenkins' decision was the fact that Obama stands "in disregard of the settled position of the U.S. bishops—to honor a prominent and uncompromising opponent of the Church's position on issues involving fundamental principles of justice [i.e., issues of human life]." Here Glendon was referring to the 2004 declaration by the USCCB that institutions "should not honor those who act in defiance of our fundamental moral principles" and that such individuals "should not be given awards, honors or platforms which would suggest support for their actions."[50] Glendon ended her communiqué to Jenkins by stating, "I am at a loss to understand why a Catholic university should disrespect it [the USCCB mandate]." "I am concerned," she reiterated, "that Notre Dame's example could have an unfortunate ripple effect."

In the end, Prof. Glendon's action was both charitable *and* confrontational; her charity permitted—indeed, it demanded—that she con-

---

48. In her declining the Laetare Metal at Notre Dame's 2009 commencements exercises, Glendon chose to issue an open letter to John Jenkins. See Glendon, "Declining Notre Dame."

49. Some will remember another morally significant event in Notre Dame's recent past (2006), in which fifty bishops censured Father Jenkins for his refusal to cancel *The Vagina Monologues*.

50. This, it needs reiterating, is wholly aside from (a) the apostolic document *Ex Corde Ecclesiae*, which stressed the critical importance of Catholic universities affirming the Church's teaching, and (b) what is unambiguously and authoritatively taught in the *Catechism of the Catholic Church* (nos. 2270–71): human life must be respected and protected absolutely from the moment of conception. From the first moment of his existence, a human being must be recognized as having rights of a person—among which is the inviolable right of every innocent being to life ... "Before I formed you in the womb I knew you, and before you were born I consecrated you ... Since the first century the Church has affirmed the moral evil of every procured abortion. This teaching has not changed and remains unchangeable. Direct abortion, that is to say, abortion willed either as an end or a means, is gravely contrary to the moral law ... You shall not kill the embryo by abortion and shall not cause the newborn to perish ..."

front the source of ethical non-negotiation while exposing the source of moral compromise. And in the end, regarding the issues Glendon sought to raise, there is *no moral common ground*, as Anthony Esolen has rightly noted.[51] Accordingly, her decision was the expression of great moral courage, serving as a model for the wider Christian community. Despite the glee with which a number of religious "centrists" supported Obama in the 2008 presidential campaign, at the time castigating religious conservatives for their "obsession" with the abortion question, not a few social critics—properly, in my view—have framed the abortion question as the civil rights issue of our time, given two crucial factors. At one level, it concerns the exclusion of the most fundamental human right—the right to live—from millions of unborn humans.[52] At another level, it gives entrée to all "right-to-life" issues that emanate from the question of personhood. The moral atrocity of abortion surely ranks as high or higher than the denial of civil rights to African Americans. As one Notre Dame faculty member noted who attended the Sunday Mass/worship service rather than the commencement, can anyone imagine Martin Luther King Jr. saying, "We disagree deeply about our differences but the important thing is that we learn to talk about them charitably"?[53]

---

51. Esolen, "Notre Madame et le President." See as well the devastating critique of so-called "centrist" and "moderate" voices in George, "Obama's Abortion Extremism."

52. And if the unborn are not persons, then it needs to be asked, *why* should Obama and other pro-abortion activists be concerned with *getting the numbers of abortions down*?

53. In the end, the Christian simply cannot avoid confrontation on the things that really matter. On occasion, we will need to *demand justice and change* (albeit utilizing diverse strategies), even at the risk of being falsely stereotyped. The day after Obama spoke at Notre Dame, William McGurn, writing in the *Wall Street Journal*, conceded that "We cannot blame the president [i.e., Obama] for this one," since he spoke openly in the 2008 presidential campaign about his aggressively pro-abortion views, assuring groups such as Planned Parenthood that he was "about playing offence," not defense. No, McGurn insisted, this invitation fits a pattern at Notre Dame, which is "rich enough that it can safely thumb its institutional nose at the 70 or so bishops who publicly challenged the university for flouting their [USCCB] guidelines on such invitations." In the Smithsonian, McGown noted in closing, there hangs a moving photograph of then President Theodore Hesburgh linking hands with Martin Luther King Jr. at Soldier Field in Chicago. "Today," McGurn lamented, "nearly four decades and 50 million abortions after *Roe v. Wade*, there is no photograph of similar prominence of any Notre Dame president taking the lead at any of the annual marches for life."

Personhood and the Human Consensus: Sanctity or Quality of Life?[54]

Virtually all pressing bioethical questions of our day revolve around the issue of personhood. If defining human personhood is a morally relevant question,[55] then as a society we shall need to probe what constitutes human *nature*. To identify and amplify human "nature" is to identify and underscore an *abiding consensus* about personhood. Not a few bioethicists, theorists, and social activists in our day call into question the very notion of personhood based on social utility, functionality, or productivity; hence, the standard language of "quality of life."[56] When

---

54. An extended discussion of personhood and human sanctity is found in Charles, *Retrieving the Natural Law*, 195–208.

55. Lest we assume categorically that personhood *is* in fact morally relevant, Peter Singer would instruct us: "Taken in itself ... membership of the human species is *not* morally relevant.... Whatever criteria [for personhood] we choose ... we will have to admit that they do not follow precisely the boundary of our own species.... There will surely be some non-human animals whose lives, by any standard, are more valuable than the lives of some humans. A chimpanzee, a dog, or pig, for instance, will have a higher degree of self-awareness and a greater capacity for meaningful relations with others than a severely retarded infant or someone in a state of advanced senility" (*In Defense of Animals*, 4, 19). Similarly, Michael Tooley announces that "it is clear that the development of human form is not in itself a morally relevant event" ("Abortion and Infanticide," 433). And Stan van Hooft insists: "If there are differences in moral status between human beings and other animals, they do not arise from the mere fact of species membership... So I propose that we cease using the terms 'human' or 'human beings' as any but classificatory terms. Such terms do not designate metaphysical essences that ground moral status, and they contribute nothing to the solution of ethical problems in health care settings" (*Life, Death, and Subjectivity*, 41–42).

56. In his chapter "Conferring Moral Status on an Embryo," in *The Ethical Brain*, Michael S. Gazzaniga, director of the Center for Cognitive Neuroscience at Dartmouth College, argues that a human fetus is not "one of us" until roughly twenty-three weeks, when life is "sustainable" and the brain is sufficiently developed. At that point, according to Gazzaniga, the fetus becomes protected from abortion. Because "it is hard to ascribe the sense of what is happening to the uniqueness of the 'individual' or 'soul' that is supposedly being formed," therefore "assigning ... moral status to a fourteen-day old ball of cells and to a premature baby" is "conceptually forced," and at the level of neuroscientific knowledge, "nonsensical." Gazzaniga acknowledges that the implications of assigning moral status are "far-reaching" and "affecting abortion, in vitro fertilization, biomedical cloning, and stem cell research." "The *rational* world," he informs us, "is waiting for resolutions of this debate" (ibid., 6–12; emphasis added). In similar fashion, noted bioethicist Tom Beauchamp argues in the *Kennedy Institute of Ethics Journal*: "If nonhumans turn out to possess significantly more advanced capacities than customarily envisioned, their moral standing would be upgraded to a more human level.

philosophers and scientists are accustomed to speak of the human being as a "rational animal," they invite qualification. At a rudimentary level, rationality is understood to convey sentience, self-conscious awareness, and the ability to reflect. Hereby humans distinguish themselves from other animals—in their aspirations, in their creativity, in their moral imagination, and in their pursuit of what is good. This "consensual" understanding of human nature did not arrive yesterday, even when today it is being vigorously challenged. It is affirmed by both ancients and moderns, and as a consensus it exists irrespective of culture and social location.

Illustrative of this abiding "consensus" regarding human nature is Aristotle's well-known example of the oak in his *Physics*, which distinguishes between essence or nature and outward form. Resident within the acorn is all of the potential that distinguishes the genus oak. This potential furnishes a sufficient explanation of both the diversity and sameness within the genus, and it offers an adequate description of the nature of the oak, at whatever stage of the oak's development along the way. This description of "nature" has nothing to do with how the genus oak functions, how it may be used, the strength and characteristics of its wood, how large it may eventually grow, or how it may weather the elements throughout its growth process. Nor does this understanding vary among Asians, Africans, Europeans, or North and South Americans. Rather, it corresponds narrowly yet precisely enough to what the oak is *in its essence*.

John Paul II's important 1995 encyclical *Evangelium Vitae* ("The Gospel of Life") serves as a helpful reminder of what shape a natural-law response might take as it refracts on human "nature." Even if the presence of a spiritual soul cannot be proven by empirical data, John Paul cautions, the very results of scientific research on the human embryo provide a strong indication of the presence of a person "at the moment

---

However, this possibility remains speculative and may be less important than the thesis that because many humans lack properties of personhood or are less than full persons, they are thereby rendered equal or inferior in moral standing to some nonhumans. If this conclusion is defensible, we will need to rethink our traditional view that these unlucky humans cannot be treated in the ways we treat relevantly similar nonhumans. For example, they might be aggressively used as human research subjects and sources of organs ("Failure of Theories of Personhood," 320).

of the first appearance of a human life."[57] The conclusion is difficult to avoid: "How could a human individual not be a human person?"[58]

What is being developed by John Paul in *Evangelium Vitae* is a consistent "life" ethic, one that offers a moral rationale for *why* there is *a continuum from embryo to the grave*. This ethic stands in contrast to what he has referred to as a "culture of death." For this reason he finds it necessary in the encyclical to emphasize "the entire unified process of human existence."[59] Developing a moral rationale, in John Paul's view, is critically urgent in our day: "With the new prospects opened up by scientific and technological progress there arise new forms of attacks on the dignity of the human being.... Broad sectors of public opinion justify certain crimes against life in the name of the rights of individual freedom..."[60] And as John Paul well understood in his lifetime, the root of modern totalitarianism is the denial of the transcendent dignity of the human person that inheres in the natural law.[61]

If, with John Paul, we are informed by natural moral law, our intrinsic human *nature* can be understood to account for what all people hold in common, while human *personhood* gives expression to that which makes the human species utterly unique and separate from the rest of the created order. Nature and personhood together bequeath human dignity,[62] and hence, life's sanctity. Both elements exist *irrespective* of the degree to which non-perfected human beings function or the extent to which they are thought to be socially useful. In the words of Karol Wojtyla, before he became John Paul II, a human being represents "the kind of good that does not admit of use and cannot be treated as

57. *Evangelium Vitae* [hereafter *EV*] no. 14.
58. Ibid.
59. Ibid., no. 2.
60. Ibid., no. 4.
61. *VS* no. 99.
62. Perhaps it is necessary to qualify the word "dignity," since there are several ways in which the term is used. By "dignity" we do not signify how one feels, such as when one's "sense of dignity"—i.e., one's sense of self-worth or self-esteem—is threatened. Nor is dignity a property or quality that we know merely through "intuition," since some humans have a sense of dignity while others do not. It is rather something that is intrinsic to the person, an endowment, an objective essence that merits respect and consideration from other persons. Comparatively, it can be appreciated by the fact that it distinguishes us from animals, since we are by nature rational, moral agents. Most importantly, it follows that dignity cannot be lost or diminished by reason of social utility, functionality, or personal productivity.

an object of use and as such a means to an end."[63] Human dignity and sanctity are such that a human being is "a good toward which the only adequate response is love."[64]

Moreover, the *mere probability* that a human person is involved would suffice to justify an

> absolutely clear prohibition of any intervention aimed at killing a human embryo. Precisely for this reason, over and above all the scientific debates and those philosophical affirmations to which the magisterium has not expressly committed itself, the church has always taught and continues to teach that the result of human procreation, from the first moment of its existence, must be guaranteed that unconditional respect which is morally due to the human being in his or her totality and unity as body and spirit . . .[65]

The Common Good and Civil Society[66]

Important as abstracting at the philosophical level may be for the Christian community and Christian scholars in particular, moral principle must find application to society's moral quandaries in ways that do not reduce to mere philosophical abstraction. This application will occur relationally and in community, since humans are *by nature* social beings. But what precisely do we as people of faith propose for society as a whole? What principles inform the Christian's view of society, given the fact that most people in society reject Christian faith, and by what strategies do people of faith attempt moral persuasion? Aside from the work of evangelism, narrowly construed, are there other aspects of the church's witness to the culture? For some, at the most fundamental level, it is unclear, perhaps even dubious, whether Christians have a stake in how society operates. And if we do not propose a "Christian society" *per se*, how do we leaven culture, bringing moral truth to bear without

---

63. Wojtyla, *Love and Responsibility*, 41.

64. Ibid.

65. *EV* no. 60, which references *Donum Vitae* (1987), a document declaring the respect for human life and the dignity of procreation; cf. also *Dignitas Personae* ("The Dignity of a Person"), Vatican instructions on bioethics issued in 2008.

66. An extended discussion of the common good is found in Charles, *Retrieving the Natural Law*, 232–48.

succumbing either to the theocratic, the isolationist, or the accommodationist distortions?

At the most basic level, the Christian community enters into voluntary yet open-hearted engagement of the culture in all aspects of social interchange. It is necessary that all participate, each in various ways according to his or her abilities and role, without which it is impossible to promote the common good of the culture.[67] This obligation inheres in the very *dignity of the human person*,[68] a linkage of which theological and cultural separatists need reminding.

Christians begin, then, by establishing what is the common good of the culture. The common good, as I am using the expression, might be defined as the sum total of social conditions that allow people, whether as groups or as individuals, to reach their fulfillment as human beings within society and allow them at the same time to be protected as human beings. We do this in the awareness that people are created in the image of God. The *Catechism of the Catholic Church* helpfully identifies three components that comprise the common good. First, the common good presupposes respect for the person as such. In the name of the common good, public authorities are bound to respect the fundamental and inalienable rights of the human person.[69] Second, the common good requires the social well-being and development of the group itself; development, after all, is the epitome of all social duties. At the most basic level, society must safeguard what is needed to lead a truly human life; these needs include food and clothing as well as shelter, health, opportunities for work, education and cultural growth, the right to establish a family ("family" as informed by the cultural history), and the basic freedoms of worship and speech.[70] Finally, the common good requires peace, that is, the stability and security of a just order. It presupposes that authority should ensure by morally acceptable means the security of society and its members, providing an environment in which human beings might flourish. Hereby the *Catechism* is underscoring the basis of the right to legitimate personal and collective defense.[71]

---

67. *CCC* no. 1913.
68. Ibid.
69. Ibid., no. 1907.
70. Ibid., no. 1908.
71. Ibid., no. 1909.

In his important encyclical *Veritatis Splendor*, John Paul II argues for the necessity of objective moral norms. Without such recognition, he insists, freedom and a "genuine democracy" are illusory, and in time this "tyranny of the majority" becomes oppressive. John Paul is adamant that there can be "no freedom apart from or in opposition to the truth,"[72] for "as history demonstrates, a democracy without values easily turns into open or thinly disguised totalitarianism."[73] Only through "obedience to universal moral norms does man find full confirmation of his personal uniqueness and the possibility of authentic moral growth."[74]

Because human rights belong to *persons*, any discussions of "rights" are meaningless apart from a non-fluid, i.e., objective, understanding of personhood. And because one's understanding of "the common good" depends on one's view of rights, the common good in a society stands or falls on society's views of personhood and rights. It follows, then, that where universal moral truths are not acknowledged, persons and human rights will suffer, a fact that recent human history more than adequately confirms.[75] Human "persons," as we have sought to define them, possess inalienable rights due to the fact of their dignity. This conviction, of course, stands at odds with contemporary construals of "rights"—for example, First Amendment rights, abortion rights, privacy rights, gay marriage rights, and the right to die—which are vying for public sanction. But can Christians enter into public debate and require that "rights" be not only defined but also *substantiated*?

Freedom, John Paul warns, does not extend to the toleration of intrinsic evil, and where the denial of universal moral truth is permitted to exist, the result is that "law" is reduced to a function of "raw, totalitarian power."[76] If there is "no ultimate truth to guide and direct political activity," he cautions, then ideas and convictions can easily be manipulated for reasons of power.[77] These observations, it seems to me, need particular reinforcement in our own day.

---

72. *VS* no. 96.

73. In *Centesimus Annus* no. 34, John Paul restated this burden.

74. Ibid.

75. See n. 88 for a statistical estimate by cultural historians of the horrors that, in the twentieth century alone, human beings have imposed on other human beings.

76. Ibid., nos. 96 and 99.

77. Ibid., no. 101.

Rethinking Tolerance: From Unchaste "Moral Neutrality" to a Chastened and Principled Pluralism[78]

As we noted earlier, the character of tolerance, properly construed, is that we endure particular customs, behaviors or habits—sometimes even (relatively) bad habits—of people in the interest of preserving a greater social unity. In the Lockean context, tolerance was advocated for religious non-conformists. Never was it understood to imply—much less to sanction—*morally questionable behavior*. Notice: a public virtue in its prior state can become a vice if and when it (a) ceases to care for truth, (b) ignores the common good, and (c) disdains the values that uphold a community. The culture of "tolerance" in which we presently find ourselves, at least in the Western context, is a culture in which people believe nothing, possess no clear concept of right and wrong, and are remarkably indifferent to this precarious state of affairs.[79] The challenge facing us, especially people of faith, is learning how to purify "tolerance" so that it remains a virtue without succumbing to the centripetal forces of relativism.

Any discussion of the notion of tolerance must first presuppose a context of pluralism. But we encounter problems. Pluralism can be understood in multiple ways; therefore, how we define pluralism is critically important. On the one hand, it can simply signify the phenomenological reality of differing cultures, ethnic groups and traditions, as well as the social structures and mechanisms that order a society. These cultural phenomena and mechanisms are a social fact of life. It is out of this "structured"[80] form of pluralism that the American experience emerged; hence, our nation's motto *E pluribus unum* ("Out of many, one").[81] Herein different communities, different identities, different eth-

---

78. An extended discussion of tolerance, moral neutrality, and principled pluralism is found in Charles, *Retrieving the Natural Law*, 248–57; and idem, "Truth, Tolerance," esp. 211–18.

79. Syndicated columnist David Warren quips that tolerance is one of those ideas "loosely hatched" during the Enlightenment but carried forward today by postmodernists "into the realm of dementia"; see his commentary "Tolerance/Forgiveness." It is hard to disagree with Warren.

80. "Structured pluralism" is what James W. Skillen (*Recharging the American Experiment*, 83–95) uses to describe "the diversity of organizational competencies and social responsibilities" in society.

81. Ethicist Ian Markham, in *Plurality and Christian Ethics*, 5–6, prefers to use the term "plurality" in order to distinguish social-cultural diversity from religious or philosophical pluralism.

nic traditions agree to coexist; they do so because of a commitment to an over-arching and principled common cause.

On the other hand, pluralism can operate under the assumption—spoken or unspoken—that among competing ideological viewpoints, worldviews, or religious understandings of reality, none has (or is permitted to have) a privileged place as a framework for interpreting reality. On this view, all religious or philosophical positions possess an essential unity and all religious viewpoints stand on equal terms. Pluralism thus construed has a leveling effect. Hence, to argue for the authority and supremacy of Christianity, we are told, amounts to religious and cultural imperialism. This allegation, of course, places pluralism intrinsically at odds with Christian truth-claims, which are uncompromising in their assertion that the Creator has revealed himself definitively. Ideological pluralism, then, calls for discernment, since its apologists demand that we "tolerate" alternative explanations of reality, while at the same time pressuring us to negotiate—and abdicate—claims to ultimate truth. In American culture, a shift in understanding "tolerance" has occurred—a shift that calls for vigilance. "Tolerance" has devolved into an indifference toward truth, often belligerently and intolerably so; the result is a baneful permissiveness toward all manner of evil. Thereby a virtue has been transmuted into vice.[82]

Therefore, we must expose the falsehood of the philosophical and sociological notion that a pluralistic society can be neutral on moral matters, since this thinking inevitably leads to the establishing of the most secularized, materialistic, and hedonistic elements of the population. Let us, then, acknowledge that, ultimately, *someone's* morality will be legislated.[83] Two examples may suffice to illustrate. If someone claims the right to die, society is morally constrained to respond on the basis of the natural law: as an objective good, human life has intrinsic value that must be protected by the state (if the state is legitimate), whose principle function under heaven is to guard the social order (i.e., to reward

---

82. Francis Canavan has commented on one aspect of the dilemma this way: "it is an old half-truth that you cannot legislate morality. The other and more significant half of the truth is that a society's laws inevitably reflect its morals and its religion. As a society's religious and moral beliefs change, then, so will its laws" ("Pluralism and the Limits of Neutrality," 158). Indeed, this change has been long under way.

83. Relatedly, Canavan writes: "If we are a plurality of communities, [the right] to maintain and transmit the community's beliefs and values is at least as important as the right of the individual to live as he pleases" (ibid., 160–61).

the good and punish evil). Neutrality therefore is not an option, permitting right-to-die advocates—or the state, for that matter—the luxury of finding a constitutional right to privacy. Likewise, in response to homosexual activists who insist on gay marriage as a civil right on par with heterosexual marriages, we might argue that neither government nor the public can seek refuge in a purported "neutrality," since there exist a particular "nature" and a particular function of human activity that are consensually demonstrable throughout human civilization. Overthrowing that human consensus is neither good science, nor just law, nor healthy sociopsychology, nor moral-intellectual honesty.

No moral "neutrality" was envisioned by the framers of this nation's charter documents, who believed that rationally discerned moral norms will inform a society's understanding of rights, justice, good, and evil—norms that guard against tyranny of *both* the minority *and* the majority. In the interest of all of society, particular "goods" will need to be defended. Otherwise, the cannibal has the "right" to be "different," pedophilia is defensible "self-expression," and one man's mugging is simply another man's good time.

Hence, the public nature of the marketplace (of both ideas and goods), then and now, as well as of social institutions, coupled with the very public nature of Christian witness (then and now), compels people of faith to work for the common good using any and all means, so long as democratic pluralism resists the centripetal slide into a soft form of totalitarian statism.[84] For those of us who tend to shy away from confrontation, the hard truth is this: a society that wishes to remain civil and civilizing will need to be intolerant of vice. Indeed, it

> cannot function well, cannot survive, and cannot protect the innocent . . . from harm and evil, without a large measure of intolerance. Yes, intolerance – of theft, burglary, cruelty, classroom hooliganism, disrespect for parental authority, and violent crime of all sorts; of substance abuse, infidelity, illegitimacy, perver-

---

84. In response to the potential objection that a balance of power—namely, judicial, executive and legislative—excludes the possibility of political tyranny of various degrees in the U.S., I would simply pose the following question: What if all three branches of "democratic" government, mirroring the values of elitist but amoral culture, are (more or less) committed to a bleaching of the religious viewpoint and an eradication of Christian participation in the moral, legal as well as political process? And more seriously, what if a sizable number of "Christians" have been co-opted by the prevailing socio-political forces, given their desire for cultural and academic respectability?

sion, pornography, rape, and child molestation; of fraud, envy, covetousness, and knavery; of sloth, mediocrity, incompetence, maleducation, improvidence, irresponsibility and fecklessness. A society tolerant of those things would soon find itself in serious trouble, even facing dissolution, and many people in that society would be in peril of their lives.[85]

Indeed, many people in that society would be in peril, even when they would be *blissfully unaware* of their perilous condition.

Everyone has claims on the public square, including people of religious faith. While it is not a given that everyone's claim will be "tolerated," tolerance properly understood mirrors a strong and principled commitment to promote moral truth and work for the common good.[86] Purging an adulterated term like "tolerance" will not be easy,[87] but it must be done in our day.

Concluding Reflections

Earlier in this essay several constitutive elements of the common good were identified—notably, a respect for persons and their rights based on human dignity, social well-being that extends into social duty, and the environment of peace and stability in which people can flourish. Aggressively undercutting these essentials in our world at present are several generic (though related) perversions of the common good that undermine the very constitution—and hence preservation—of "civil society" as we know it. One is more overtly totalitarian thinking (whether secular or religious), with its dehumanizing of personhood, oppression of the human spirit, and obliteration of justice and human rights. This may take the form of overtly *political* forms of totalitarian rule, which have caused historians to denominate the twentieth century as the bloodiest on human record.[88] Or, in its religious form, it may express

---

85. Attarian, "Dispraise of Tolerance," 22.

86. See, in this regard, Ratzinger (Benedict XVI), *Truth and Tolerance*.

87. The evolution and devolution of the notion of tolerance, of course, was a subject about which Chip Conyers wrote with considerable elegance and passion, most forcefully in *The Long Truce*.

88. Ponder, for the moment, the mind-boggling statistics that serve to illustrate the disappearance of evil and good in twentieth-century regimes. In his introduction to *The Black Book of Communism*, published in 1999 and causing an uproar in France at the time, French historian Stéphane Courtois breaks down according to individual

itself in the totalitarian tendency of jihadic Islam, with its theocratic and at times violent commitment to impose *shari'a* law on society and which, by all accounts, is on the rise. But it may also be a "creeping" form of tyranny—what John Paul II called a "veiled" or "thinly-disguised" totalitarianism[89]—which plagues much of contemporary Western culture and is characterized by a disintegration of the moral-social order. Animating this "veiled" totalitarian mindset is a conspicuously *materialist metaphysic* that insists, along with the political totalitarian, on *bleaching* the human mind, the human experience, and human culture of the religious-spiritual component.[90] Both the political as well as the democratic-liberal expressions of totalitarianism issue out of a material understanding of human nature; both, regardless of whether they are in the global South or North, East, or West, quench and indeed oppress the human spirit.

In the democratic-liberal context (in which I write), the perversion of the common good requires our vigilance. Increasingly therein, freedom is divorced from rather than tethered to truth; that freedom is understood to be unbridled, unsubordinated to any authority higher than personal experience. While the natural law does not require that democratic pluralism be the sole possible means of organizing society, it does acknowledge that politics, law and our social arrangements must reflect a moral universe whose existence is owing to norms that transcend the self. Thus, the question is not whether relatively "free" societies will remain free but rather whether they will remain *just*. Without fixed moral norms that depend on transcendent moral references, a society can remain neither just nor free. It can only descend over time into various forms of barbarism and moral-social chaos, out of which the imposition of power always and everywhere must proceed

---

nation-states the total numbers of victims who were sacrificed to Communist ideology. The estimate given by Courtois is in the neighborhood of one hundred million. By contrast, the estimate of military historian Robert Conquest, in *Reflections on a Ravaged Century*, is in the range of one hundred seventy million. Regardless of our metric, these rough estimates, in any case, dwarf Nazism's remarkable record within a much shorter span of years.

89. *Centesimus Annus* nos. 34 and 88; *VS* nos. 96 and 101.

90. The materialist metaphysic, with its implications, is critiqued in Charles, "My Criminal Brain." In the Western context, where the religious viewpoint *is* tolerated, it is relegated to the *private* domain and is not permitted to express itself in the public sphere. A sturdy antidote to this privatization is offered by Sweetman, *Why Politics Needs Religion*.

(as surely as water always finds the lowest spot). Rightly has John Paul argued that there can be "no freedom apart from or in opposition to the truth."[91] Without such recognition, freedom and a "genuine democracy" are illusory, and in time a "democratic" tyranny of the majority becomes oppressive and inhumane.[92]

Every generation, writes legal scholar Russell Hittinger, finds a new reason for the study of the natural law.[93] For a generation past—in the mid-twentieth century, for example—totalitarianism provided the occasion. Hittinger sees parallels between the moods that dominate the cultural West today and the "pessimistic resignation" and agnosticism of German society in the 1930s, dispositions that left the German legal profession intellectually defenseless in the face of changes in German society. Whether or not one agrees with Hittinger's legal and cultural prognosis, the challenge before us is to rediscover the "moral predicates" of law, politics, and human social arrangements, without which democratic institutions and civil society as we know them cannot long survive.[94] When these "moral predicates," or "first things," are challenged, obscured, or denied, it becomes once again necessary to assert both their reality and their place in the culture.[95]

Such a time, I would argue, is upon us.

---

91. *VS* no. 96.

92. Ibid. no. 101.

93. From the introduction of Rommen, *Natural Law*, xii.

94. In Hittinger's more recent book, *The First Grace*, the implications of natural-law thinking for civil society are developed in a compelling manner.

95. If perchance the reader is bothered by my supposedly "morally rigorist" tone, my concluding question is simply this: As Christian stewards, what sort of world do we bequeath to our children and their children? And what sort of parents are we?

Bibliography

Aquinas, Thomas. *Summa Theologica*. Translated by the Fathers of the English Dominican Province. 5 vols. New York: Benziger, 1947.

Aristotle, *Nicomachean Ethics*. Translated by Terence Irwin. 2nd ed. Indianapolis: Hackett, 1999.

Arkes, Hadley. *First Things: An Inquiry into the First Principles of Morals and Justice*. Princeton: Princeton University Press, 1986.

Attarian, John. "In Dispraise of Tolerance, Sensitivity and Compassion." *Social Critic* (Spring 1998) 14–23.

Beauchamp, Tom L. "The Failure of Theories of Personhood." *Kennedy Institute of Ethics Journal* 9 (1999) 309–24.

Benedict XVI, "Faith, Reason and the University: Memories and Reflections." Online: http://www.vatican.va/holy_father/benedict_xvi/speeches/2006.

Braaten, Carl E. "Natural Law in Theology and Ethics." In *The Two Cities of God: The Church's Responsibility for the Earthly City*, edited by idem and Robert W. Jenson, 42–58. Grand Rapids: Eerdmans, 1997.

Brunner, Emil, and Karl Barth. *Natural Theology*. Translated by P. Fraenkel. 1946. Reprint, Eugene, OR: Wipf & Stock. 2002.

Budziszewski, J. "The Illusion of Moral Neutrality." *First Things* (August–September 1993) 32–37.

———. *The Revenge of Conscience: Politics and the Fall of Man*. Dallas: Spence, 1999.

———. *True Tolerance: Liberalism and the Necessity of Judgment*. New Brunswick, NJ: Transaction, 1992.

———. *What We Can't Not Know: A Guide*. Dallas: Spence, 2003.

Calvin, John. *Institutes of the Christian Religion*, edited by John T. McNeill, translated by F. L. Battles. Louisville: Westminster John Knox, 2006.

Canavan, Francis. "Pluralism and the Limits of Neutrality." In *Whose Values? The Battle for Morality in Pluralistic America*, edited by Carl Horn, 153–65. Ann Arbor: Servant, 1985.

Catechism of the Catholic Church. Washington, DC: United States Catholic Conference, 1994.

Charles, J. Daryl. "Engaging the (Neo)Pagan Mind: Paul's Encounter with Athenian Culture as a Model for Cultural Apologetics." *Trinity Journal* 16 (1995) 7–62.

———. "My Criminal Brain Made Me Do It: Biogenetics and the Loss of Moral Responsibility." *National Catholic Bioethics Quarterly* 9 (2009) 485–515.

———. "Paul before the Areopagus." *Philosophia Christi* 7.1 (2005) 125–40

———. *Retrieving the Natural Law: A Return to Moral First Things*. Critical Issues in Bioethics. Grand Rapids: Eerdmans, 2008.

———. "Truth, Tolerance and Christian Conviction: Reflections on a Perennial Question—A Review Essay." *Christian Scholar's Review* 36.2 (2007) 185–218.

———. *The Unformed Conscience of Evangelicalism*. Downers Grove, IL: InterVarsity, 2002.

Cicero. *De Re Publica, De Legibus*. Translated by C. W. Keyes. LCL. Cambridge: Harvard University Press, 1927.

———. *Pro Flacco*. Translated by C. Macdonald. LCL. Cambridge: Harvard University Press, 1927.

Conquest, Robert. *Reflections on a Ravaged Century*. New York: Norton, 2000.
Conyers, A. J. *The Long Truce: How Toleration Made the World Safe for Power and Profit*. Dallas: Spence, 2001.
Courtois, Stéphane, et al. *The Black Book of Communism: Crimes, Terror, Repression*. Translated by J. Murphy and M. Kramer. Cambridge: Harvard University Press, 1999.
Davis, Derek H. "The Classical Separation Perspective." In *Church, State and Public Justice*, edited by P. C. Kemeny, 81–113. Downers Grove, IL: InterVarsity, 2007.
D'Arcy, John. "Bishop D'Arcy laments 'terrible breach' between Notre Dame and the Church, critiques recent Jenkins comments." April 23, 2009. Online: http://www.catholicculture.org/news/headlines/index.cfm?storyid=2691.
Dignitas Personae. Instruction of the Vatican's Congregation for the Doctrine of the Faith. Online: http://www.usccb.org/comm/Dignitaspersonae/index.shtml.
Dworkin, Ronald. "The Illusive Morality of Law." *Villanova Law Review* 10 (1965) 631–39.
Eliot, T. S. *After Strange Gods*. London: Faber & Faber, 1933.
Elshtain, Jean Bethke. "The Relationship between Political Language and Political Reality." In *Real Politics: At the Center of Everyday Life*, 47–55. Baltimore: Johns Hopkins University Press, 1997.
———. *Who Are We?: Critical Reflections and Hopeful Possibilities*. Grand Rapids: Eerdmans, 2000.
Esolen, Anthony, "Notre Madame et le President." *Touchstone* (July–August 2009) 3–4.
Fletcher, Joseph. "In Defense of Suicide." In *Suizid und Euthanasie*, edited by A. Eser, 237–38. Stuttgart: Enke, 1976.
Gaertner, Bert. *The Areopagus Speech and Natural Revelation*. ASNY 21. Uppsala: Almquist, 1955.
Gazzaniga, Michael S. *The Ethical Brain: The Science of Our Moral Dilemmas*. Washington, DC: Dana, 2005.
George, Robert P. "Obama's Abortion Extremism." The Public Discourse, October 14, 2008. Online: http://www.thepublicdiscourse.com/2008/10.133.
Glendon, Mary Ann. "Declining Notre Dame: A Letter from Mary Ann Glendon." *First Things* blog "First Thoughts," April 27, 2009. Online: http://www.firstthings.com/blogs/firstthoughts/2009/04/27/declining-notre-dame-a-letter-from-mary-ann-glendon.
Heie, Harold, and Michael A. King, editors. *Mutual Treasure: Seeking Better Ways for Christians and Culture to Converse*. Scottdale, PA: Herald, 2009.
Hittinger, Russell. *The First Grace: Rediscovering the Natural Law in a Post-Christian World*. Wilmington, DE: ISI Books, 2003.
Hooft, Stan van. *Life, Death, and Subjectivity: Moral Sources in Bioethics*. New York: Rodopi, 2004.
John Paul II. *Centesimus Annus*. Online: http://www.vatican.va/holy_father/john_paul_ii/encyclicals/documents/hf_jp-ii_enc_01051991_centesimus-annus_en.html
———. *Evangelium Vitae*. Online: http://www.vatican.va/holy_father/john_paul_ii/encyclicals/documents/hf_jp-ii_enc_25031995_evangelium-vitae-en.html.
———. *Fides et Ratio*. Online: http://www.vatican.va/holy_father/john_paul_ii/encyclicals/documents/hf_jp-ii_enc_15101998_fides-et-ratio_en.html.

———. *Veritatis Splendor*. Online: http://www.vatican.va/holy_father/john_paul_ii/encyclicals/documents/hf_jp-ii_enc_06081993_veritatis-splendor_en.html.

Lewis, C. S. *The Abolition of Man*. New York: Macmillan, 1947.

———. *Mere Christianity*. Rev. ed. New York: Macmillan, 1960.

———. "On Ethics." In *Christian Reflections*, edited by Walter Hooper, 44–56. Grand Rapids: Eerdmans, 1967.

Markham, Ian. *Plurality and Christian Ethics*. Rev. ed. New York: Seven Bridges, 1999.

McGrath, Alister E. "The Challenge of Pluralism for the Contemporary Christian Church." *Journal of the Evangelical Theological Society* 35.3 (1992) 361–73.

———. *A Passion for Truth: The Intellectual Coherence of Evangelicalism*. Downers Grove, IL: InterVarsity, 1996.

McGurn, William. "Obama Scored Big at Notre Dame." *Wall Street Journal*, May 19, 2009. Online: http://online.wsj.com/article/SB124269063343832561.

———. *Miles to Go*. Cambridge: Harvard University Press, 1996.

Murray, John Courtney. *We Hold These Truths: Catholic Reflections on the American Proposition*. New York: Sheed & Ward, 1960.

Orwell, George. "Politics and the English Language." In *The Collected Essays, Journalism and Letters of George Orwell*, edited by S. Orwell and I. Angus, 4:156–70. New York: Harcourt, Brace, 1968.

Ratzinger, Joseph Cardinal (Benedict XVI). *Truth and Tolerance: Christian Belief and World Religions*. San Francisco: Ignatius, 2004.

Robinson, T. M. *Heraclitus: Fragments*. Phoenix Supp. 22. Toronto: University of Toronto Press, 1987.

Rommen, Heinrich A. *The Natural Law: A Study in Legal and Social History and Philosophy*. Translated by T. R. Hanley. Indianapolis: Liberty Fund, 1998.

Shapiro, Harold T. "Liberal Education, Moral Education." *Princeton Alumni Weekly*, January 27, 1999, 16–21.

Singer, Peter. *In Defence of Animals*. Oxford: Blackwell, 1985.

———. Review of *Dearest Pet: On Bestiality* by Midas Dekkers. *Nerve.com*. Online: http://www.nerve.com/Opinions/Singer/heavypetting/main.asp.

Skillen, James W. "Natural Law and the Foundations of Government." *Public Justice Report*, November 1991. Online: http://www.cpjustice.org/stories/storyReader$1012.

———. *Recharging the American Experiment*. Grand Rapids: Baker, 1994.

Sweetman, Brendan. *Why Politics Needs Religion: The Place of Religious Arguments in the Public Square*. Downers Grove, IL: InterVarsity, 2006.

Tooley, Michael. "Abortion and Infanticide." In *Ethical Theory: An Anthology*, edited by Russ Shafer-Landau, 428–38. Oxford: Blackwell, 2007.

Young, R. V. "The Gay Invention: Homosexuality Is a Linguistic as Well as a Moral Error." *Touchstone* 18.10 (December 2005). Online: http://www.touchstonemag.com/archives/article.php?id=18-10-036-f.

Warren, David. "Tolerance/Forgiveness." *Sunday Spectator*, December 4, 2005. Online: http://www.davidwarrenonline.com/index.php?artID=546.

Weigel, George. "Obama and the 'Real' Catholics: The President Inserts Himself into a Religious Debate." *National Review Online*, May 18, 2009. Online: http://www.nationalreview.com/articles/227531/obama-and-real-catholics/george-weigel?page=1.

Wojtyla, Karol. *Love and Responsibility*. Translated by H. Willetts. New York: Farrar, Straus & Giroux, 1981.

13

What Sort of Community?

The Catholic Vision of the Church after Toleration

Coleman Fannin

THE CHRISTIAN CULTURE, SUCH AS IT WAS, OF WESTERN EUROPE AND North America has been supplanted by pluralism even as Christianity has grown exponentially in the global South. The origins of this transformation are manifold and complex, but the rise of toleration in the seventeenth century is as fitting a point as any at which to begin. Although it predated American non-establishment and European disestablishment by more than a century, toleration facilitated these and subsequent developments that together produced what H. Richard Niebuhr called the "enduring problem" of Christ and culture in the modern world. The work of the late theologian A. J. Conyers is worth revisiting for this reason alone. Yet it holds additional insights that may not be apparent at first glance, for Conyers is one of a small but significant number of Baptists who have recently sought a path away from individualism and Americanism and toward community and catholicity.

In *The Long Truce* and its sequel, *The Listening Heart*, Conyers presents a two-part catholic vision: first, he diagnoses the problems engendered by the way toleration came to be understood in modernity; and second, he argues that in the midst of pluralism the church must embody an alternative model of toleration grounded in a sense of vocation. In this essay I highlight benefits of Conyers' vision for contemporary theology, particularly Baptist theology in the United States. I also consider it alongside the work of other scholars, including James McClendon, a Baptist who outlines a "catholic baptist" ecclesial vision, and William Cavanaugh, a Catholic who identifies the church as its own politics. Conyers shows that whereas the modern doctrine of toleration is violent and fractures community, the pre- and postmodern practice of toleration is nonviolent and enables catholicity. McClendon and Cavanaugh demonstrate that such an alternative must be grounded in a robust ecclesiology and the ongoing practices of communities sustained by tradition. Both are required to sustain the sort of moral formation that enables Christians to live together, dialogue with those with whom we disagree, and follow the way of the cross rather than acquiesce to the security of the state.

Whose Vision? Which Toleration?

Conyers' chief contribution in *The Long Truce* is to set forth a parallel between the emergence of toleration and that of the nation-state, a parallel anticipated and affirmed by thinkers such as Pierre Bayle, John Locke, John Stuart Mill, and John Dewey. The governments that emerged from the so-called "Wars of Religion" that destabilized Europe propagated the notion of toleration as a preventive measure: in exchange for political and economic sovereignty, they would remain indifferent to other loyalties and values. Although it brought a measure of relief to religious minorities, this transaction obscured other motives and conditions, especially the state's desire to marginalize rivals by setting the limits of toleration. As modernity advanced the state relentlessly consolidated power while slowly dissolving the local authorities—congregations, families, churches, and trade associations—of which society had long been composed, all in the name of the "public virtue" or *doctrine* of toleration. The truth claims of such groups came to be viewed as subordinate to "the will of the people" expressed through the mechanisms of the state. As Conyers explains, "If the *telos* or the multiple goals that govern our actions are fundamentally artifacts of our imagination and will, rather than disclosures to us of what is authoritative, then natural, timeless, and informal associations have no *necessary* authority in human lives." Once these authorities are diminished in the consciousness of the people, "the state proves to be the benefactor."[1] Human persons were reduced to citizens and consumers, retaining only instrumental value in pursuit of what Conyers names "power and profit"; thus the West came to be defined by a "bipolar vision" of individual and state.

---

1. Conyers, *Long Truce*, 190.

People began to think of themselves not so much in terms of their social setting, or their families, or their churches, but as autonomous free agents. They viewed their associations with others as accidental and volitional, not necessary and obligatory. Therefore, the identity of the individual was less and less to be found in his primary relationships in the community. It appeared theoretically possible—though it was still not practically so—that the individual could choose his group identity. It seemed, therefore, (again, more on the level of theory than practice) that the individual gave rise to the group rather than the group making the life of the individual possible. At the same time, as his primary associations faded, his identity with a "nation" became more pronounced: more and more, he became American, or German, or Italian, or French. The result was a powerful state and a lonely individual, two distinctive features of the modern period.[2]

The assertion that the group is prior to the individual cannot be examined closely here, but if we acknowledge the prevalence of a bipolar vision, it is not difficult to see which pole is dominant. Conyers rightly insists that in a pluralist world toleration is "an indispensable point of departure from which to discover a common humanity and a common destiny."[3] However, its goodness depends on whether it serves a good purpose, and a "powerful state" in which individuals share only "identity with a 'nation'" does not qualify. The state offers toleration for the sake of its own authority and ends, not those of religious or other groups. "And if we consider that groups exist with their own peculiar sense of social ends and their own system of authority," Conyers says, "then we find that the central power makes peace with groups by detaching them from their spiritual essence and then testifying to its respect for the dispirited remains of what was once both the body and soul of a culture."[4] That is, the state is not neutral toward religious goals and values, and those it cannot absorb it renders private. Again, the assertion that a group necessarily has its own ends that may be incompatible with those of other groups must be granted at this point. If we do

2. Ibid., 5-6.
3. Ibid., xiii.
4. Ibid., 10.

so, understanding the implications of the modern doctrine necessitates "our inquiring *what sort of community this virtue serves.*"[5]

Conyers starts by tracing the "feeling of uncertainty" that arose in the early seventeenth century and the quest for certainty and universality that followed. Philosophers from René Descartes forward sought a secure foundation for rationality, a quest manifested in a preference for the abstract and theoretical over the concrete and practical. The problem, in a word, is that unlike mathematics or empirical science, economics and politics are "fraught with uncertainties." Thus, while everyday life remained chaotic, philosophy and theology escaped into an *emotional* certainty. Here Conyers challenges Stephen Toulmin's reading of this development as leading to "intellectual and cultural rigidity," as this was also the period that "the case [was] made, for the first time in history, that 'toleration' is a necessary public policy." Further, he argues that the fears of early moderns drove them not toward metaphysics but "toward justifying and strengthening authoritarian regimes and giving philosophical weight to the organizing of society *against* the kind of speculation that had been the occasion for religious wars." The insidious part of the story is that toleration was about more than preventing conflict; it was also about "a new sense of opportunity—unparalleled in any time since the rise of the Roman Empire—for the growth of economic and political influence."[6] The spirit of modernity is about not so much rigidity of thought and belief as displacement of authorities and actions that threaten sovereignty, the other "widespread preoccupation" (along with toleration) of the new era. In withdrawing into theory philosophy and theology vacated a space filled by the sheer power of the secular state.

Demonstrating the connection between toleration and sovereignty would require another book; Conyers only points out that "toleration is most valued in large-scale Western societies, where cultural conquest has been most successful and economic expansion most obvious."[7] However, he does closely examine two other forces transformed by bureaucracy and the bipolar vision: economics and war. Both are important, but the key to recognizing the failure of toleration is the violence that has accompanied the modern state since the early seventeenth

---

5. Ibid., 44.
6. Ibid., 48–49.
7. Ibid., 51.

century. As Conyers explains, "War that had broken out over religious rivalries stood in a double relationship to that new secular power: it was both the means by which a sovereign authority expanded its power, and it constituted the emergency that justified such power."[8] Although war disrupts every structure and habit of society, it also reorganizes society according to a logic entirely determined by its "imminently practical goals." European nations exploited religious wars to justify a secular vision of society based on the superiority of the claims of the state over those of the church. They also dispersed responsibility so widely that individuals could no longer see the results of their discrete decisions. This logic would be horrifically exemplified by the Holocaust, but it began with the bureaucratization of military administration in which the natural distinctions among soldiers were dissolved into the "newly created machine of war." According to Conyers, "An army, under the pressure of war, discovering the usefulness of 'bureaucratized violence,' becomes a microcosm of society, turning (much more gradually) from its sacred identity—from its blood, its soil, its temples, and its gods—to the secular exigencies of utilitarian purposes." The result was "a standing army perpetually in readiness for conflict," conflict that came quickly and regularly in service to Western expansion.[9] Ultimately, then, the community *served by* the modern doctrine of toleration is one that *serves* power and violence; that is, it is no community at all.

Conyers does not merely critique the modern doctrine; he proposes an alternative: the ancient, pre-Reformation model or *practice* of toleration. Although related to true virtues such as humility, patience, and prudence, genuine toleration is not itself a virtue because it has limits; instead it is a strategy that is always subordinate to the higher goal of harmony. "As an ancient practice [toleration] makes possible the catholic vision of life together, so that the different associations both reinforce and give balance to one another, and so that there is on the horizon a view of the whole world and all of humanity as an interlinking community."[10] At this point several questions arise. Conyers clearly intends "catholic" to connote the broader meaning "universal." Still, he could use another term, so what does he mean by a *catholic* vision, and how does he reconcile it with dissent from the state without retreat

8. Ibid., 50.
9. Ibid., 60.
10. Ibid., 12.

from pluralism? What sort of community does *this* approach to toleration serve? Or, given that the latter could not precede the former, what sort of community makes catholicity possible?

Baptists at the End of Modernity

Before answering these questions we must pause to consider a concern. One could read Conyers as just another conservative or libertarian critic of liberalism and advocate of restoring "Christian values," if not establishment. Indeed, comfort with the notion of Western culture adds a troubling air to his suggestion that "the church founded by Jesus Christ might be the natural culture for an authentic recovery of toleration."[11] Conyers also invokes not only an idealized premodern Christianity but also a bygone time when American society was grounded in "a federal or covenantal understanding of political relationships among distinct communities," while providing little evidence of its demise.[12] Such comments, though infrequent, can give the impression that the resuscitation of Christendom is his goal. Insofar as this is true, it is a caveat added to the potential of his theology. However, I am convinced that Conyers does not fall into this trap and that his arguments ought to confound conservatives as well as liberals.

I am also convinced that while he draws on premodern sources and scorns postmodernism, he makes a postmodern case, albeit an unconventional one, for catholicity. Paradoxically, perhaps, understanding what he means by "catholic" requires reading him *as a Baptist*. On one hand, Conyers has a thoroughly Baptist background; after converting from Methodism he earned degrees from two Southern Baptist seminaries, served as pastor of several Baptist churches, chaired the religion department at a Baptist college (Charles Southern University), and spent the final decade of his career teaching at a Baptist seminary he helped found. On the other hand, he is not forthcoming about this identity; the word "Baptist" is virtually absent from *The Long Truce* and *The Listening Heart*. Still, the respective topics of these works are clues that Baptist history and the dilemma of contemporary Baptist life animate his theology.

---

11. Ibid., 234.
12. Ibid., 19.

After all, Baptists were among the direct beneficiaries of the English Act of Toleration and championed not only the right to dissent from established churches but also the shift from toleration to religious liberty, which, not coincidentally, enabled the phenomenal growth of their marginal sect after the American Revolution. Alas, gratefulness for the First Amendment made them too much at home in the U.S., especially in the South, a reality chronicled as early as the 1960s by historians such as Rufus Spain and John Lee Eighmy.[13] In Conyers' terms, "more and more," Baptists became American or Southern; slavery and civil rights are only the most obvious examples of cultural captivity. Meanwhile the Southern Baptist Convention (SBC), like nearly every denomination, slowly fractured along political lines, culminating in the conservative-moderate "holy war" of the 1980s. The "true" Baptist position on religious liberty was bitterly contested during this controversy, and Barry Hankins has shown that disagreement with moderates' understanding of separation of church and state was a strong motivation for the conservative cause.[14]

Conyers found himself on the losing (moderate) side, but his work on toleration and vocation is an implicit critique of his Southern Baptist tradition, including both parties who claim its fragments. Indeed, he calls the SBC conflict "petty" and observes that "neither side has acquitted itself admirably or with much integrity."[15] By and large, Baptists traded in their radical critiques for the bipolar vision, adopting an individualistic faith, narrowing their conception of politics, and reserving their concerns about religious liberty to "papists." The conservative party was awakened from slumber by the social turmoil of the 1960s and early 1970s and has joined other evangelicals in resisting pluralism, secularization, and the decline of Christian America. In contrast (and in response), the moderate party has extolled these trends as a vindication of soul competency, the view that the individual conscience can choose his or her faith and community as well as interpret the Bible for him- or herself. Similar ideas have long been present in Protestantism, but moderates—heirs to the strains of Scottish Common Sense Realism that influenced heroes such as James Petigru Boyce and E. Y. Mullins

13. Spain, *At Ease in Zion*; Eighmy, *Churches in Cultural Captivity*. The reason why Conyers mentions only toleration and not religious liberty remains a mystery.

14. Hankins, *Uneasy in Babylon*, 15–17, 107–38.

15. Conyers, *Listening Heart*, xiii.

and convinced they are facing fundamentalists who are papists in disguise—have taken them in a particularly atomistic direction, thereby grounding their theology in the very convictions Conyers decries.

Additional distinctions and qualifications can be made, but the point is that while Baptists in the South may be theologically and politically at odds, they agree that Christianity and the American state, rightly understood, are fundamentally compatible. The First Amendment ensures that individuals can pursue their own religious desires, and the market ensures that they have many options. The only debate is over who will win the "culture wars" and, more important, who will control the levers of power. Conyers' analysis of toleration, however, attests to the reality that these Baptists are bound ever more tightly to the state. While secularism spread and Protestantism fractured, a stubborn veneer of Christianity allowed Christians the luxury of individualism. Now, Conyers notes, "that period of relative isolation is now quickly coming to an end" and the veneer has all but vanished. "While for most of the second millennium the culture of Christendom was relatively secure in its adoptive homelands, it appears that the first and third millennia will prove to be the times of testing in the crucible of plurality."[16] Those immersed in Southern culture and a Baptist subculture have belatedly become aware of this transition but have yet to grasp how their theology renders them incapable of halting the hemorrhage to generic evangelicalism, personal spirituality, and simply "none."

Conyers addresses several of these issues in "The Changing Face of Baptist Theology," written as he prepared *The Long Truce*. The article is structured by three "fronts"; the first is the debate over Baptist origins that has resurfaced in response to a resurgent Calvinism among conservatives and an attempt to reclaim Anabaptist roots by several moderate theologians, notably James McClendon. McClendon includes other groups who share marks of the Radical Reformation in a "baptist" (with a small b) tradition—the "believers church" by another name. Conyers acknowledges that McClendon's is the best contemporary Baptist theology but regards appeals to Anabaptists as "strained" and "contrived" in light of evidence of English Baptists' connections to Calvinists. This colors his assessment of McClendon, who is an ally otherwise. Still, Conyers is interested not so much in authenticating Baptists' origins as in identifying their contributions, which are more readily apparent in

---

16. Idem, *Long Truce*, 34.

the Reformed tradition, and their future, which will not be found in a "Calvinist revival."

> Instead it will likely be found in a Reformed theology so articulated that it gives adequate place to human experience and, at the same time, serves to underline the false strategems of modern culture as well as to affirm what is worthy in that culture. A theology of this type must accommodate the Baptist conviction that (to use Mullins' term) the soul is "competent" to respond to God's gift of himself in Jesus Christ. At the same time, it must recover the communal implications of a church composed of those called out by Christ and freely consenting to his yoke of obedience.[17]

This is one of Conyers' more tantalizing comments about the sort of community he envisions. Clearly such a theology is distinct not only from the Baptist holy war but also from the Arminian-Calvinist debate that polarizes evangelical Christianity and risks either Pelagianism or Gnosticism. Conyers thinks Baptists, at their best, have transcended this polarity by affirming both free will—part of the goodness of God's creation—and a form of natural theology. At this point, at least, he also thinks these affirmations (and their "communal implications") are more characteristic of the Reformed tradition than the Anabaptist tradition.

The second front of Baptist theology, then, is that of responding to the "strain" within Western culture. Conyers recognizes that "Baptist convictions about freedom and individualism (i.e., 'soul competency'), as well as their democratic mode of church polity, make Baptists unalterably children of their modern age."[18] Thus he appreciates the critiques of "modern habits of mind" by Baptists such as McClendon, Nancey Murphy, and Stanley Grenz. Yet he finds their postmodern sympathies troubling because he understands the discarding of foundationalist epistemology to imply "theology without logic—or, in other words, without some axiomatic ordering of concepts at the level of method."[19] He also understands postmodernism to imply adopting the "aggressively anti-Christian" skepticism of the Enlightenment that endures in, for example, Jacques Derrida and Michel Foucault. Suffice it to say that neither worry is justified, but both inform Conyers' consideration of the

---

17. Idem, "Changing Face," 28.
18. Ibid., 28.
19. Ibid., 32. For a critique of postmodernism, see Conyers, "Can Postmodernism."

third front: that of contributing to a new ordering task in the church and society at large. "As the world necessarily searches for a means of creating order out of its long engagement with twentieth-century war and social conflict," he asks, "will it turn to new authoritarian regimes, or will it turn to the kinds of mediating, local institutions, founded on transcendent rather than secular hopes, hopes that spring from the kind of theology that Baptists can, if they will, articulate?"[20]

According to Conyers, McClendon and company construe the Enlightenment too narrowly by focusing on Descartes and Locke, leading them to throw out the baby with the bathwater, so to speak. As Gerhart Niemeyer, Leo Strauss, and Eric Voegelin—all of whom he discusses in *The Long Truce* and *The Listening Heart*—have shown, "the underlying impulse of modernity was to reject the 'givenness,' the irreducible limits and obligations of human life." More than simply individualism or rationalism, this impulse descends from "the ancient hope to be delivered from necessity and to be free in the sense of one who is autonomous (a law unto oneself) and thus self-created."[21] So, while Baptists are right to seek an alternative, they will find it not so much in the postmodern present as in the past.

> Baptists are in a position to aid the awakening because, in a very real sense, they are products of the modern age, since their beginnings are roughly contemporary with Locke, Hume, and Thomas Hobbes. Yet at the same time, Baptists represent a brand saved from the ashes of a rapidly secularizing culture that is becoming disoriented and forgetful of its goal. Like the moderns, Baptists affirmed the dignity of the individual; but unlike the heart of the modern age, they found this new theme of freedom and human dignity not in Promethean dreams of a powerful new role for humanity, but in the transcendent truths of a house "not made with hands, eternal in the heavens" (1 Cor. 5:1). As in the Hebrew prophetic movement's recovery of the covenants, and the Reformation's returning to scripture, the progress of the gospel among Baptists will come from the recollection of those things that were neglected.[22]

The claim that Baptists have been "saved from the ashes" is tenuous at best, but the overall message is timely. Baptists must revisit not

---

20. Conyers, "Changing Face," 21.

21. Ibid., 34.

22. Ibid., 36.

only their own origins but also other parts of the Christian tradition, the purpose of which is not only to mine usable material but also to be reminded that the church is necessary for faith as well as "an authentic recovery of toleration." Without a catholic vision Baptists are unable to counter the bipolar vision of individual and state, so we must investigate how a Baptist theology can be connected to a catholic vision.

Baptist Vision

Whereas Conyers begins with the "magisterial reformers" because he is wary of the dangers of separating from culture, McClendon begins with the Anabaptists because he is wary of compromises with culture. In this regard McClendon was influenced by Mennonite theologian John Howard Yoder. Yoder rarely engaged Southern Baptists directly, likely because they rejected the mainline ecumenical associations in which he was involved. However, in a 1970 essay entitled "A Non-Baptist View of Southern Baptists" he praised them for not relinquishing their distinctive positions, as though they "must evolve into the kind of mainstream pluralist tolerance which is characteristic of the American 'religious establishment.'"[23] At the same time, he charged them with adopting "provincialisms which put the distinctive identity of a Christian body at the wrong place." Baptists had so closely identified themselves with the structures, values, and assumptions of America and the South that their Christianity had been thoroughly domesticated. That is, Southern Baptist culture was but another form of "Constantinianism." Yoder writes:

> Such an arrangement is not like that of Constantine in the strict sense of a structure linking Church and State, but it has the same mood and tone; the Church is linked with the centers of power and prestige in a given society. She lays her moral claims upon the whole population with the "establishment" mentality reinforcing the call to personal decisions. The individual perceives the call which the Church addresses to him as a call to line up with things as they are; God and the established order are closely linked.[24]

23. Yoder, "Non-Baptist View," 220.

24. Ibid., 222. For a description of "Constantinianism," see Yoder, *Royal Priesthood*, 53–64.

Yoder pinpoints two distortions of Baptist convictions that flow from the establishment mentality: a "frontier revivalism" that construes baptism in individualistic terms, and the notion of the exclusivity (autonomy), rather than the priority, of the local congregation. Baptists came to emphasize personal spiritual experience and theological affirmations in baptism, leading to a gradual lowering of the acceptable age for children to be baptized. As a result, they no longer grasped that joining the church is "a commitment of one's total future personality to the standards and the discipline of the Christian community and to costly obedience to Christ as Lord."[25] Baptists simultaneously over-emphasized the local church in theology and under-emphasized it in practice; thus it is little wonder that they have been largely uninterested in Christian unity and ecumenical labor.

Yet McClendon and Yoder remained optimistic about the Baptist vision. Two decades later they collaborated on an article in the *Journal of Ecumenical Studies* in which they claim all Christians have a fundamental duty to achieve unity that "must consist not merely in common acknowledgment of 'one *Lord*' but also in 'one *faith,* one baptism.'" Strikingly, they also claim "the believers church or 'baptist' style of Christian life makes for just such unity."[26] In his *Systematic Theology* McClendon notes that baptists have "failed to see in their own heritage, their own way of using Scripture, their own communal practices, their own guiding vision, a resource for theology unlike the prevailing tendencies round about them."[27] Elsewhere, and again echoing Conyers, he argues that Baptists' emergence alongside modernity left them ill-prepared to avoid pitfalls such as the Calvinist-Arminian debate. "Baptists (large or small b) might by the grace of God survive the modern era, 1650 to our own time, but only with great difficulty could they be baptists in it."[28] Although he laments the omission of Anabaptist contributions in Baptist historiography, McClendon, like Conyers, is not primarily concerned with origins. Further, he notes that, taken

25. Ibid., 222.//
26. McClendon and Yoder, "Christian Identity," 561–62.//
27. McClendon, *Ethics*, 26.//
28. McClendon, "Believers Church," 315. Here McClendon identifies three tendencies of the modern world: "(1) a new sense of the self, called *individualism,* (2) a new, science-oriented way of construing human speech that among other effects *segregated religious utterance,* and (3) a new way of doubting much that we know, retrospectively dubbed *foundationalism.*"

alone, none of the marks of the believers church "can provide a genuine organizing principle for a baptist theology"; only the biblical narrative can do so.

> Scripture in this vision effects a link between the church of the apostles and our own. So the vision can be expressed as a hermeneutical principle: *shared awareness of the present Christian community as the primitive community and the eschatological community.* In a motto, the church now is the primitive church and the church on judgment day; the obedience and liberty of the followers of Jesus of Nazareth is *our* liberty, *our* obedience, till time's end.
>
> This is not meant as a denial of the facts of history, nor a rejection of their significance; it *is* a claim for the historical significance of *this present time* in the life of the church and therefore by implication of *every other* present time in its life. So far from rejecting the church's history ..., this baptist vision claims importance for every chapter of it.[29]

The baptist vision is historical but is not tied to a visible succession—Anabaptist, Reformed, or otherwise. Rather, it is grounded in the shared memory of having descended from communities that share certain marks and a "this is that" relationship to the New Testament church. McClendon and Yoder acknowledge that this vision is easily taken to be "amorphous and ill-defined," even deficient, but they insist that it "lays legitimate (though not uncontested) claim to the legacy called catholic$_1$," the earliest of three "catholic" senses and a quality "of being whole or well-rounded or typical as opposed to being one-sided or partial." Moreover, it is inherently traditional. "What is 'the baptist vision' itself if it is not tradition, and tradition as it works in Scripture and in the ancient catholic church$_1$, namely, by linking together into one the whole story of God's dealing with God's people?"[30] McClendon and Yoder are not content with catholic$_1$; the goal is always catholic$_2$: visible church unity accomplished in the enactment of certain practices.[31] Therefore the proper dialogical question is not "Who has the

---

29. McClendon, *Ethics*, 30–31; for a discussion of the marks, see 26–34.

30. McClendon and Yoder, "Christian Identity," 572.

31. The five practices are fraternal admonition (binding and loosing), the universality of charisma and the multiplicity of gifts, the Spirit's freedom in the open meeting, breaking bread (Eucharist), and induction into the new humanity (baptism). Yoder, *Royal Priesthood*, 370. For a more detailed exploration, see Yoder, *Body Politics*.

truer deposit of faith?" but "How shall we proceed in the search to locate the church catholic$_2$ that we confess?" All Christian communities face the same tests of authenticity in light of Scripture and tradition, of which the most important is whether they "[are] prepared to accept the Constantinian compromise of church and state with its insertion of state authority between believing communities and their rightful Lord and its recurrent persecution of those the state finds inconvenient for its purposes."[32] Though less stark in his rhetoric, Conyers has similar concerns. For McClendon and Yoder, recognition that war is not a "legitimate option" for Christians is the crux of the matter. As we will see, violence is at the center of Conyers' critique as well.

Catholic Substance

Conyers and McClendon share the conviction that the Baptist tradition has forgotten its natural catholicity but can recover it by looking to its own history *and* that of other traditions. Curiously, though, both mention Catholicism only occasionally. McClendon taught at Catholic institutions and initiated dialogue between Baptist and Catholic theologians. However, although Conyers spent a semester at Notre Dame in the 1970s, one may wonder if he has "Catholic" (with a big "C") in mind at all. One clue is his use of sources such as Thomas Aquinas and Flannery O'Connor and terms such as *subsidiarity, virtue,* and *vocation*. Another is an earlier article entitled "Protestant Principle, Catholic Substance" in which he asks, "Is there something in Protestant thought itself that, doing the work of a computer virus, finally renders impotent even the best of the Protestant intellectual tradition?"[33]

He answers this question by investigating how Protestantism, though right to object to intellectual elitism and call for a greater degree of democracy in the church, went wrong. Briefly, the success of the natural sciences convinced many Protestants that the scientific method was applicable to knowledge of any kind, including Scripture, which they came to see as a repository of unmediated *facts* rather than the revelation of a transcendent God. When these facts were called into question, some turned to experience as a source of truth, others to "progress." In rejecting scholasticism, then, Protestants rejected a way of thinking in

---

32. McClendon and Yoder, "Christian Identity," 576.
33. Conyers, "Protestant Principle," 15.

which facts are *accidents* that participate in but are subordinate to essential truths. "Struggling to give revelation its proper place, they also lost (not at first, and never altogether, but at length) fifteen hundred years of Catholic intellectual tradition."[34] Now the landscape has changed and the Reformation must be reconsidered in one of two ways. The first is to view it as a rediscovery of an essential truth that "must be defended at all costs against every competing idea"; the second is to view it as "a correction made in the nick of time, at great cost" and to acknowledge that the time has come to "correct the correction" and "[recover] the task that made the separation necessary in the first place: the safeguarding of a truly catholic vision of the world and its redemption."[35]

Conyers is not quite clear about what a "truly catholic vision" entails, but it involves a visibility that is an antidote to the interiorization of faith as experience or a set of propositions. It also makes possible the enjoyment of life together. In *The Long Truce* he argues that "the sense of vocation or purpose that animates all kinds of groups, but which in the church claims a loyalty that transcends other loyalties, is both necessary to social cohesion and, at the same time, an explosive ingredient."[36] Once Christians could no longer agree about which church merited loyalty and resorted to violence, toleration was proposed as a way to replace vocation with a state-centered unity. Toleration became a "secular virtue" based on individuals' preferences, and in lessening communal authority it no longer aided the fulfillment of their deepest need: understanding the meaning of their existence. By requiring greater external organization and authority "as well as emphasizing the protection of abstract 'rights' that are divorced from what the living community calls the 'good,'" it aided only the consolidation of power, becoming an ironic enemy of true freedom.[37]

Although it has a particular origin, Christianity also has an inherent "ecumenical impulse" or "catholic sentiment" that has been tested by the crisis of modernity. One problem with the modern strategy is that metaphysical and theological questions can never really be private, for even postponing them "says something about God, and about what we think in reference to God." Therefore Conyers believes it fair

34. Ibid., 16.
35. Ibid., 17.
36. Idem, *Long Truce*, 64.
37. Ibid., 226.

to ask "whether the *modus vivendi* provided in a life shaped by theology has not a *better* chance of achieving the practice of tolerance than otherwise."[38] However, another problem is that the strategy worked, to a point. Religious conflict declined and the new nation-states functioned remarkably well. This remained true of the United States even as Europe was torn apart by war and declined in population and influence. Conyers' explanation recalls that of John Courtney Murray four decades earlier: "There was a large residue of assumptions about the nature of human life and human destiny upon which the culture could unconsciously depend, and which had been placed there by a millennium of what Kierkegaard would call 'training in Christianity.'"[39] However, Conyers is less optimistic than Murray; like Alasdair MacIntyre, he argues that a new moral philosophy has emerged. "The new moral order naturally mimics the old one. It does not and cannot invent the moral sensibilities of people, but it can distort; it can mistake strategy for virtue."[40]

These are broad claims, to be sure. However, if we find them convincing, then acknowledgment of residual assumptions is pivotal. First, it presents questions about how long these assumptions will last and what will replace them. Second, it differentiates those who seek to knit Western culture back together from those who seek to reconstitute a pilgrim church. If we imagine this as a continuum, at one end is an establishmentarian approach, at the other a sectarian approach. Yet there are alternatives. For example, Conyers advocates a form of tolerant practice in which many communities live out their respective *teloi* or vocations while overlapping one another in a truly open society. Third, then, it demands that Christians consider the ways in which such assumptions have shaped their theology, especially how they make moral arguments. For example, Southern Baptists could proclaim a radical individualism only because they could count on social reinforcement of basic convictions. Of course, that basic convictions about race turned out to be wrong is but one indication that a critical evaluation of the old moral order is required. If we cannot blame the intrinsic errors of the West on Christianity per se, then we must not too easily blame them, as McClendon and Yoder do, on the "Constantinian compromise." Nonetheless, while modernity asserts a false catholicity through

---

38. Ibid., 242.
39. Ibid., 64.
40. Ibid., 20. See MacIntyre, *After Virtue*.

toleration, so too did Christendom assert a false catholicity through establishment.

One burden of Conyers' argument is to show how fundamental conflicts between social groups might be resolved without resorting to coercion. In *The Long Truce* he claims that the chief political virtue of Christians must be humility, which is rooted in the incarnation. Authentic toleration serves the interest not of the love of power but of the power of love: "God is become man, and that man, the representative of the race of men, is indeed God, so that human beings can participate in all that God is."[41] The incarnation announces that God and humanity are reconciled; therefore creation is indeed good and we can grow in knowledge of it, not to gain power but in order to love more fully and live together as friends.

> What I am distinguishing as the *practice* of toleration, over against the *doctrine* that emerges from development of democratic liberalism, is the logical result of a recognition that our imperfections oblige us to listen to the insights of others. We are utterly dependent upon the gifts of society and tradition—even traditions other than our own. It is toleration that recognizes not the implied self-sufficiency of the individual or of various idiosyncratic groups in a supposed pluralistic world but the insufficiency of these limits and the ultimate need for a catholic vision. Even as the doctrine of toleration promotes isolation, the practice of toleration gently nudges us into community. Therefore, authentic toleration serves, and does not hinder, the forming and functional life of groups within society. It does not hinder in that it does not discourage the quest for ultimate meaning that is the inner light and life of any social group of any lasting importance.[42]

This is a compelling description, but it leaves many questions unanswered. For example, how is such a community formed in the midst of cultural fragmentation? What ought we do when confronted by those who *have* power and are uninterested in dialogue?

---

41. Conyers, *Long Truce*, 238.
42. Ibid., 242–43.

A Community of Peace

At the end of *The Long Truce* Conyers claims that "the hallmark of authentic tolerant practice should be the listening heart for which the wise king [Solomon] prayed and not the management of language and appointing itself the arbiter of all public discussions."[43] He unpacks this claim in *The Listening Heart* by considering how a theology of vocation provides an alternative to the Western ideology of "choice." In doing so he moves away from any romantic notion of Christendom and toward the construction of the sort of community necessary to negotiate its ruins. By "vocation" he means neither an occupation nor religious vows but a fundamental orientation embodied in a community of shared goods. Vocation "is a view in which human life is drawn toward some purpose that is greater than the individual, one that stands above national interests, that invests life with nobility and beauty, and creates 'room' for the common life."[44] Conyers looks back to organic models in which each person understood herself as contributing to the good of the community. In turn, the community understood that its legitimacy and order were based not on power but on grace. Granted, the reality often fell short, but such models facilitate imagination of a different sort of social life or ecclesiology. Indeed, "vocation" is derived from the Latin *vocatio*, which means "call," and parallels the Greek *klēsis*, the root of *ekklēsia*, the New Testament term for "church."

The Enlightenment, however, substituted "choice" for vocation. By "choice" Conyers means that quality of society that emphasizes not relationship and attraction to the good but the primacy of the will, in which the central question facing the individual becomes something like "What do I want out of life?" This view rests on the fiction that groups are not natural but created by choice and "have no hold upon the individual beyond his voluntary participation."[45] In contrast, vocation implies an external agent whose call requires a free *response*. Although such a summons is often *against* the will of the person being summoned, vocation is hardly anti-rational. According to Conyers, "The specific way in which the Enlightenment used reason was *as a replacement for the idea of vocation*. One could then make *reasoned choices*. The true lo-

---

43. Ibid., 244.
44. Idem, *Listening Heart*, 7.
45. Ibid., 105–6.

cus of personal decisions was to be found in the individual who 'thinks for himself,' as Kant would put it, and who declines to depend upon the 'guidance of another.'"[46] Yet the consequences of the elevation of choice as an organizing principle are myriad: the dissolution of families, the decline of intermediate associations, abuse of the environment, unprecedented violence, and so on. We are left with a sort of schizophrenia: we believe in self-determination but long for authentic relationships. "Thus stand side by side, in unmistakable opposition, two ideas of the way one lives in the world. One is that of attentive listening to the guidance of another, whether of a wise guide, or tradition, or of God. The other is the notion of the self-determined 'free' man, who without listening to another, becomes the master of his own soul."[47]

Whereas in an organic society each person is indispensable, in modern society persons are *organized* according to their usefulness in production and conquest, thereby becoming interchangeable. That is, through technology and bureaucracy social organization came to resemble that of machines. According to Conyers, the shift toward urban centers belied a radical loss. "Formerly one could say that men thought of themselves as 'belonging' to the land, which exercised a benevolent and relatively predictable influence over their lives. Later they would belong to a company, or to a standing army, or to the state ... gradually reaching an apogee in the twentieth century, when it was possible to view the individual as belonging wholly to a totalitarian state." Contrary to the natural variety of attachments to church, region, and so forth, in these affiliations the person is subject only to the will of those in power. This reality colors what Conyers rightly names "perhaps the most important achievement of modern times," the recognition of the dignity of the individual. "Where such a development was balanced, it recognized that without the value of the person there is no real possibility of community. But where the emphasis on the individual was unbalanced by the fanciful dreams of Renaissance and Enlightenment thinkers and social movements, it becomes a detriment to community. That, unfortunately, is where we find ourselves at the moment."[48]

Here Conyers, intentionally or not, describes the Baptist predicament, a connection deepened by his contention that interchangeabil-

46. Ibid., 14.
47. Ibid., 17.
48. Ibid., 36–37.

ity—reinforced by such terms as "equality" and "independence"—is only fully apparent in the quintessential modern institution of slavery. Conyers was raised in a segregated culture endorsed by the Southern church. Like many white scholars of his generation, he attempts to discern how an evil so contrary to the gospel could have penetrated so deeply into the hearts and minds of his fellow Christians. What he finds is that racism was only the most obvious and horrifying manifestation of the subordination of life to the drive for conquest and production controlled by the state. Slavery transforms the human person into an autonomous individual. The slave is "freed" from place, family, community, and religion in order to be reduced to an instrument for the use of those in power, and not only slave-owners. As Conyers states, "It is no wonder that early modern leaders of the Enlightenment nearly always defended and promoted slavery."[49] The influence of the church had nearly eliminated slavery by the thirteenth century, only to see it return in modernity. In a sense, then, every modern person is a slave. This is not to ignore the special evil of chattel slavery or of what Conyers, citing Jürgen Moltmann, calls the "submodern" virtual slavery of much of the Third World in relation to the West.

Conyers opens *The Listening Heart* by inquiring into two troubling developments. The first is the difficulty of creating and sustaining "humane communities," the second the fact that the twentieth century saw more persons displaced and killed in war and genocide than all of earlier history combined, with no sign of slowing down in the new century. As noted above, the justification of standing armies requires their regular deployment. "From its rhetoric, one would think that the modern state is about peace; but from its actions, one can be certain it is organized for war."[50] Further, government control of economic interests as well as vast territories made conflict inevitable. "Sooner or later violence overtakes a society that functions chiefly on the basis of the rivalry of competitive desires, on the basis of choice, or on the basis of 'freedom' defined as the unhindered will. Modern secular society is the longest experiment in history attempting to elevate 'choice' or this kind of freedom to the level of a basic social principle. It should not be surprising, though I think to many the awareness of this has not surfaced, that modern life is also the

---

49. Ibid., 41.
50. Ibid., xii.

most violent period in the history of mankind.'"[51] Conyers is correct, of course; such awareness is not widespread, which goes far in explaining the frustration of seeking to build community in our age. Baptists tend to see the United States as a flawed but effective guardian of liberty and peace. However, toleration and religious liberty were justified on the basis of their being able to prevent violence.

One positive development is that the horrors of the twentieth century gave rise to new theories about the sources of violence, of which Conyers notes those of Hannah Arendt, René Girard, and Eric Voegelin. Their reflections on the connection between the outbreak of violence and the failure of community converge at a critical point: "Human beings naturally reach for meaningful action, and not finding it, resort to irrational and destructive action."[52] Conyers argues that in a world motivated by "egocentric desires, competing ambitions, autonomous freedom, or the freedom to choose," the only solution is the "contrary motivation" of vocation, which requires another sort of community. He asks:

> Is there a model for life that would help the recovery of real fellowship, of genuine life together? Can it be that the church is such a model when she has not, herself, succumbed to the prevailing anti-culture of late modernity? Is there a reason that the community with the most far-reaching common vision, an ecumenical vision, began with a Man who claimed nothing for himself, but answered to a call that ultimately meant his death?[53]

Toward a Baptist and Catholic Vision

Conyers' tone changes subtly but remarkably in *The Listening Heart*. Perhaps the Iraq War, which he opposed, influenced his thinking; indeed, he dedicates the project "to my students who wish to understand the gospel of peace in a world that, both near and far, rings loud with the tocsins of war."[54] Still, he maintains that "power as coercion has its place because the world is fallen. The power of affection or love has its

51. Ibid., 4–5.
52. Ibid., 5–6.
53. Ibid., xii.
54. Ibid., xiv.

place because the world longs for redemption. Yet they are competing options, and each appeals to us with ecumenical designs; both are ambitious in an empire-building way, seeking to complete itself with world domination."[55] If Conyers were more open to Anabaptist perspectives, he might find it easier to reconcile the "ecumenical designs" of love with life in a fallen world. After all, that toleration came coupled with a violent politics was a horrible twist on the Radical Reformation, a tradition he knew well from his engagement with Moltmann.[56] Similarly, if he were more open to postmodern perspectives, he might find it easier to reconcile Christianity's catholic claims with its loss of social sway. As it stands, though, *The Listening Heart* shows that the premodern notion of vocation must be recovered in order to inaugurate a truly postmodern age. "Now that the limits of modernity have become apparent to almost everyone, now that modernity has lost that 'self-evident' justification it once possessed, and now that people are willing to think in terms of 'post-modernity,' the question is open once more, 'Shall we heal a broken society through love, or through power?'"[57]

The choice between state and church need not be absolute, although portraying it as such can be rhetorically effective. How might Christians learn to give their *primary* allegiance to the church rather than the state? They must recognize several things, of which Conyers uncovers at least three: first, the state is not the keeper of the common good; second, the state is incapable of social unity because it is fundamentally violent; and third, discerning when to cooperate with or resist the state requires a catholic church able to exercise authority (not coercion) and create a space in which to pursue an alternative politics. Conyers' catholic vision is compelling but still distant from the practices of actual communities, and McClendon's baptist vision is helpful in this regard but still unable to account for any *visible* connection between such communities. That is, their accounts of catholicity will not do the work they want them to do. For these and other reasons, those persuaded by their arguments must dialogue with Catholic theology. At this juncture I can only suggest a few connections between Conyers' work and Catholic thought.[58]

---

55. Ibid., 32.

56. Conyers met Moltmann while studying at Tübingen and later examined his theology at length. See Conyers, *God, Hope, and History*.

57. Conyers, *Listening Heart*, 12.

58. For a more detailed explication of several of the following ideas, see Fannin,

Recent years have seen a revival of "common good" language in support of either the responsibility to seek social justice or the function of capitalism in the creation of wealth. While they differ in several ways, both views take for granted that the common good is the province of the state, a radical departure from how it was understood for most of history. The notion of the common good originated with philosophers who assumed a *polis* with shared convictions about the nature of the good. Likewise, theologians who developed this notion after Constantine assumed a harmony of church and society. All insisted that civic activity presupposes a web of tacit agreements. That is, economics and politics do not govern themselves but stand under the judgment of a moral framework that enables discussion of the correlation between the interests of individuals and those of families, churches, and other associations. In contrast, early liberal theorists insisted that the state be organized on the basis of the natural rights of the individual to pursue his or her own good, albeit in accordance with the moral or natural law. For *this* purpose individuals enter into a social contract bound by reason and the rule of law. Thus the Declaration of Independence declares that the role of the state, derived "from the consent of the governed," is to secure "self-evident" rights. Today the common good is typically equated with economic prosperity or respect for a broad spectrum of rights. Particular moral frameworks contribute to it insofar as they contribute to these goals and can be regulated by a neutral conception of justice that prevents the distortions they bring to public life. Advocates of the common good—libertarian, communitarian, or otherwise—tend to minimize the scope of moral agreement, dissociate it from intermediate groups, and locate it in the state, the defender of the common good against enemies foreign *and* domestic.

This rough summary is not meant to imply that the classical view of the common good is unproblematic for Christians or anyone else. Further, Catholics have been little better than Protestants in negotiating a society in which they have no built-in moral authority. It took them more than a century to be at home in America, culminating in the adoption of the Declaration on Religious Freedom (*Dignitatis Humanae*) by the Second Vatican Council. John Courtney Murray, the Jesuit vindicated by the Declaration, is the hero of this story to conservative and liberal Catholics alike. Murray well understood the erosion

---

"Religious Liberty."

of the American consensus by voluntarism and was convinced it was left to Catholicism to preserve the natural law tradition that was the nation's inheritance. Although Murray expected more than a minimum of morality in society, he recognized the limits of what could be infused by a juridical state and instead saw the church as having the primary, though not sole, responsibility for the common good and the state as having the limited responsibility of public order.[59] Yet the subculture Murray took for granted would soon collapse, and Catholics eager to fit in and succeed became willing to default to the state and culture on economic, political, and moral matters even as they became bitterly divided over them. Sociologically speaking, Catholics are now the same as their neighbors.

Despite this less-than-encouraging narrative, there are signs that Catholicism retains resources that can be utilized to reframe the common good. One example is the work of William Cavanaugh, an invited speaker at a Baylor University symposium on *The Long Truce*. The cover of the book is Joseph Nicolas Robert-Fleury's "St. Bartholomew's Day Massacre," which depicts Protestants dying at the hands of Catholics during the French Wars of Religion, and Conyers affirms the standard line that these wars were the impetus for toleration and the secular state. In reality, Cavanaugh explains, the paramount concern was the creation of the notion of "religion" as a universal yet individual impulse, "a set of beliefs which is defined as personal conviction and which can exist separately from one's public loyalty to the State."[60] In the early modern period, the common understanding of faith shifted from one inseparable from community and tradition to one defined by a criterion of propositions or experience. With this development, "Religion is no longer a matter of certain bodily practices within the Body of Christ, but is limited to the realm of the 'soul,' and the body is handed over to the State."[61]

It served the political and economic interests of the emerging Western states to grant rights in exchange for sovereignty and protection from those who would take them away. According to Cavanaugh, "The state itself created the threat and then charged its citizens for its reduction." It also had to coerce those citizens, but this was either hidden

---

59. Murray, *We Hold These Truths*, esp. 186–90.
60. Cavanaugh, "Fire Strong Enough," 403.
61. Ibid., 405.

or seen as necessary. "What separated state violence from other kinds of violence was the concept of legitimacy, but legitimacy was based on the ability of state-makers to approximate a monopoly on violence within a given geographical territory. In order to pursue that monopoly, it was necessary for elites to secure access to capital from the local population, which was accomplished in turn either by the direct threat of violence or the guarantee of protection from other kinds of violence."[62] Individuals had to be made to serve the state alone; thus religion had to be seen as an individual preference and the church as a voluntary association. With the latter domesticated, it was comparatively easy for the state to detach individuals from other groups. As Conyers shows, toleration was the "solvent" that made this possible. However, the state is the most intolerant of institutions, for it decides what voices to privilege on the basis of instrumental calculations of individual preferences, particularly those backed by political and economic power.

In contrast, local communities are more capable of fostering mutual respect and exercising prudence in determining which voices are "irrational, irrelevant, or intimidating" without violating their dignity. Modern toleration undermines just this sort of community, and the relentless drive of a capitalist economy and the pervasive influence of consumerism, including in the church, deepen the problem. "The motor of such an economy is said to be 'demand.' What is produced and in what quantity depends on what is demanded, and not on any conception of what the goods of human life are," Cavanaugh states. "Furthermore, for production to increase, it does not especially matter what is demanded, only that there is demand, that is, preferences and the money necessary to satisfy those preferences." Thus toleration and consumerism are perfect companions and necessitate "the radical disengagement from attachments which transcend mere choice." Paradoxically, the limitless diversity of choices results in a "stifling homogeneity" of culture—we all consume the same products produced by the same corporations—as well as the enforcement of the imperative of choice itself, whether in the "right" to take unborn life or wars undertaken to defend "freedom."[63]

---

62. Idem, "Killing for the Telephone Company," 249–50.

63. Cavanaugh, "Ecclesiology and Toleration." He adds that "the [Southern] Baptist boycott of Disney was laughed off by the national media, not on the basis of any substantive goods embodied in Disney products, but simply because Disney is unavoidable. Resistance is futile."

Conyers correctly gleans that the imperative is to create catholic communities guided by an incarnational theology of vocation. However, he does not discern how such communities come about or that the church is not simply another participant in a localized politics but is *itself* a politics. Christians cannot be expected to deny the sovereignty of the state without being able to point to another sovereignty. For example, until recently Christians in America have accepted the nation's military endeavors without question. As Conyers recognizes, "None competes with governmental power so effectively as does the authority of religion. The first line of resistance to government authority will naturally be the authority of the church."[64] This was the case in the early modern period, but the church and its authority were divided and largely ineffectual. Similarly, no non-peace church objected to an American conflict until Vietnam. Of course, many Americans objected to the Iraq War, but not because the leaders of the Catholic Church and every mainline denomination did so; indeed, there was a high correlation between church attendance and *support* for the war.

Beginning with Vatican II, no group has considered Christianity's response to violence more carefully than the Catholic Church. Ronald Musto elucidates the point that in affirming religious liberty the council "divorced itself from any one social, political, or economic system," including the Constantinian alliances of Europe. "The scriptural tradition replaced the un-Christian traditions of Roman law, natural law, or Aristotelian logic. This change opened the door for a gradual discarding of the just-war tradition."[65] Perhaps this is too optimistic. Nonetheless, John Paul II offers glimpses of a different way of thinking about war, notably in *Centesimus Annus*, in which he declares "no, never again war," and *Evangelium Vitae*, in which he preserves self-defense in theory but recognizes the legitimacy of *not* defending oneself "according to the spirit of the Gospel Beatitudes."[66] In the former the late pope sounds like Conyers when, in addition to affirming the principle of subsidiarity, he observes, "If there is no ultimate truth to guide and direct political activity, then ideas and convictions can easily be manipulated for rea-

---

64. Conyers, *Listening Heart*, 72.

65. Musto, *Catholic Peace Tradition*, 193.

66. John Paul II, *Centesimus Annus*, §52; *Evangelium Vitae*, §55.

sons of power. As history demonstrates, a democracy without values easily turns into open or thinly disguised totalitarianism."[67]

The current pope, Benedict XVI, has devoted considerable time to reflecting on the decline of Christianity in Europe, a land scarred by totalitarianism and religious division. In *Without Roots*, written prior to his election, he responds to philosopher Marcello Pera's proposal for a non-denominational civil religion by asserting that the "Christian consciousness" of the United States is due to the free churches—with help from Catholics—and a positive conception of the separation of church and state. "The private sphere has an absolutely public character. This is why what does not pertain to the state is not excluded in any way, style, or form from the public dimension of social life."[68] In Europe, however, separation proceeded from conflict between state churches and the Catholic Church. In playing up the contrast Benedict fails to consider whether the American state really is "little more than a free space." Regardless, in *Deus Caritas Est* he sharply criticizes the "mere bureaucracy" of the state without love. In contrast, a rightly ordered state "generously acknowledges and supports initiatives arising from the different social forces."[69] That is, the renewal of cultural "roots" falls to entities that inhabit complex space. In *Caritas in Veritate* he argues that whereas Marxism *and* capitalism tend to reduce the human person to an economic unit, Christianity demands space for development of many communities and institutions in civil society. He uses the term "vocation" twenty-eight times, often in quoting past encyclicals. According to Benedict, "To regard *development as a vocation* is to recognize, on the one hand, that it derives from a transcendent call, and on the other hand that it is incapable, on its own, of supplying its ultimate meaning."[70]

Benedict recognizes that Christianity is a majority only in number, so he borrows the concept of "creative minorities" from historian Arnold Toynbee to describe the approach the Church must take. "Such minorities are formed when a convincing model of life also becomes an opening toward a knowledge that cannot emerge amid the dreariness of everyday life.... There is nothing sectarian about such creative minorities. Through their persuasive capacity and their joy, they reach other

---

67. Idem, *Centesimus Annus*, §46.
68. Ratzinger and Pera, *Without Roots*, 110–11.
69. Benedict XVI, *Deus Caritas Est*, §28–29.
70. Idem, *Caritas in Veritate*, §16.

people and offer them a different way of seeing things."[71] He clarifies this remark by affirming Nietzsche's claim that Christianity has been abandoned because "its model for life is apparently unconvincing."[72] What he is trying to spark, then, is a renewal of groups that pursue a form of life modeled not on Western culture but on the love of Christ. Such groups are not independent but "live naturally from the fact that the Church as a whole remains and that it lives in and stands by the faith in its divine origins."[73] They endure because they are visibly connected to a social body, giving them a location from which to critique the culture and, when necessary, the church itself. Conyers, too, notes that in the West "the Church grounded community in a comprehensive, unifying, and catholic reality; at the same time it is embodied in the local and particular."[74] The reason for the shift in tense is unclear, but the comment points to the reality that somehow the church must be local *and* universal, and "comprehensive" in each.

Benedict offers early Christianity and medieval monasticism as examples of creative minorities, to which we can add the Catholic Worker movement, New Monasticism, and many congregations who find ways to renew their neighborhoods and cities and thereby break down simple space. Creative minorities need not be idealized and do not avoid cultural engagement. On the contrary, they embrace the messiness of everyday life while cultivating practical reason. They prepare Christians for dialogue by teaching the hospitality shown by Jesus to all persons—the poor, the enemy, the non-Christian—and when agreements cannot be reached they provide the strength to be faithful. The fact that the papal meditations noted above have had little impact on average Catholics indicates that something is lost in translation, so to speak, between the hierarchy and the parish. In a word, the authority that Baptists long feared carries little weight in a culture of voluntarism. Now is the time for Baptists to re-educate their Catholic friends about the importance of the local and particular, even as they receive a truly catholic vision.

---

71. Ratzinger and Pera, *Without Roots*, 121.

72. Ibid., 125.

73. Ibid., 122–23.

74. Conyers, *Listening Heart*, 97.

Bibliography

Benedict XVI. *Caritas in Veritate.* June 29, 2009. Online: http://www.vatican.va/holy_father/benedict_xvi/encyclicals/documents/hf_ben-xvi_enc_20090629_caritas-in-veritate_en.html.

———. *Deus Caritas Est.* December 25, 2005. Online: http://www.vatican.va/holy_father/benedict_xvi/encyclicals/documents/hf_ben-xvi_enc_20051225_deus-caritas-est_en.html.

Cavanaugh, William T. "Ecclesiology and Toleration: Comments on A. J. Conyers' *The Long Truce.*" Unpublished paper presented at Baylor University, Waco, TX, April 9, 2001.

———. "'A Fire Strong Enough to Consume the House': The Wars of Religion and the Rise of the State." *Modern Theology* 11 (1995) 397–420.

———. "Killing for the Telephone Company: Why the Nation-State Is Not the Keeper of the Common Good." *Modern Theology* 20 (2004) 243–74.

Conyers, A. J. "Can Postmodernism Be Used as a Template for Christian Theology?" *Christian Scholar's Review* 33 (2004) 293–309.

———. "The Changing Face of Baptist Theology." *Review and Expositor* 95 (1998) 21–38.

———. *God, Hope, and History: Jürgen Moltmann's Christian Concept of History.* Macon, GA: Mercer University Press, 1988.

———. *The Listening Heart: Vocation and the Crisis of Modern Culture.* Dallas: Spence, 2006.

———. *The Long Truce: How Toleration Made the World Safe for Power and Profit.* Dallas: Spence, 2001.

———. "Protestant Principle, Catholic Substance." *First Things* 67 (Nov 1996) 15–17.

Eighmy, John Lee. *Churches in Cultural Captivity: A History of the Social Attitudes of Southern Baptists.* Knoxville: University of Tennessee Press, 1972.

Fannin, Coleman. "Religious Liberty and the Common Good: A Baptist Engagement with the Catholic Americanist Tradition." In *Faith in Public Life,* edited by William J. Collinge, 81–109. College Theology Society Annual Volume 53. Maryknoll, NY: Orbis, 2008.

Hankins, Barry. *Uneasy in Babylon: Southern Baptist Conservatives and American Culture.* Tuscaloosa: University of Alabama Press, 2002.

John Paul II. *Centesimus Annus.* May 1, 1991. Online: http://www.vatican.va/holy_father/john_paul_ii/encyclicals/documents/hf_jp-ii_enc_01051991_centesimus-annus_en.html.

———. *Evangelium Vitae.* March 25, 1995. Online: http://www.vatican.va/holy_father/john_paul_ii/encyclicals/documents/hf_jp-ii_enc_25031995_evangelium-vitae_en.html.

MacIntyre, Alasdair. *After Virtue: A Study in Moral Theory.* Notre Dame, IN: University of Notre Dame Press, 1981.

McClendon, James Wm., Jr. "The Believers Church in Theological Perspective." In *The Wisdom of the Cross: Essays in Honor of John Howard Yoder,* edited by Stanley Hauerwas, Harry J. Huebner, and Chris K. Huebner, 309–26. Grand Rapids: Eerdmans, 1999.

———. *Systematic Theology,* vol. 1: *Ethics.* 2nd ed. Nashville: Abingdon, 2002.

McClendon, James Wm., Jr., and John Howard Yoder. "Christian Identity in Ecumenical Perspective: A Response to David Wayne Layman." *Journal of Ecumenical Studies* 27.3 (1990) 561–80.

Murray, John Courtney. *We Hold These Truths: Catholic Reflections on the American Proposition*. Lanham, MD: Rowman & Littlefield, 2005.

Musto, Ronald G. *The Catholic Peace Tradition*. Maryknoll, NY: Orbis, 1986.

Ratzinger, Joseph, and Marcello Pera. *Without Roots: The West, Relativism, Christianity, Islam*. New York: Basic, 2006.

Spain, Rufus B. *At Ease in Zion: A Social History of Southern Baptists, 1865–1900*. Nashville: Vanderbilt University Press, 1967.

Yoder, John Howard. *Body Politics: Five Practices of the Christian Community before the Watching World*. 1992. Reprint, Scottdale, PA: Herald, 2001.

———. "A Non-Baptist View of Southern Baptists." *Review and Expositor* 67 (1970) 219–28.

———. *The Priestly Kingdom: Social Ethics as Gospel*. Notre Dame, IN: University of Notre Dame Press, 1984.

———. *The Royal Priesthood: Essays Ecclesiological and Ecumenical*. Grand Rapids: Eerdmans, 1994.

14

Passing It On

Biblical Wisdom as an Act of Love[1]

David Lyle Jeffrey

> Nothing true can be said about God from a posture of defense.
>
> —Marilynne Robinson, *Gilead*

> From cleverness shot forth on Thy behalf
> At which, while angels weep, the audience laugh;
> From all my proofs of Thy divinity,
> Thou, who wouldst give no sign, deliver me.
>
> —C. S. Lewis, "An Apologists Evening Prayer"

For many of us, a novel might not seem to be the right place to look for a deeper comprehension of biblical wisdom. Yet in the case of Marilynne Robinson's novel *Gilead* (2004)[2] we would be wrong to think so. Robinson's tale is a powerful realization of the integral relationship of wisdom to love. It thus most helpfully illuminates qualities of character without which the wisest of words are rendered vacuous or inaccessible to their hearer's understanding:

---

1. The core of this essay appeared first as an article for *Christian Reflections* (Winter 2009) 66–73, and is revised and expanded here by permission.

2 Marilynne Robinson's novel *Gilead* was published by Farrar, Strauss and Giroux in 2004. Her sequel, *Home* (2008), is the second of a diptych, focusing on the parallel life and family of the Rev. Robert Boughton, his daughter Glory, and also again son Jack, seen now from a different but complementary point of view. For Robinson's personal views on Calvinism, family, and religion in America, the reader should turn to her book of essays entitled *The Death of Adam*.

> See and see but do not perceive, hear and hear but do not understand, as the Lord says. I can't claim to understand that saying, as many times as I've heard it, and even preached on it. It simply states a deeply mysterious fact. You can know a thing to death and be for all purposes completely ignorant of it.[3]

These words of disclaimer, coming near the very beginning of the Rev. John Ames's memoir to his son, signal in their tone and tenor the deepest insight he will endeavor to pass on. In his apology there is little or no presumption of obligation, only a natural hope of communion. Ames, who knows he is dying, wants to bequeath to the son whose arrival at manhood he will never see a kind of intergenerational sense of identity. As it happens, this quite naturally includes advice born of experience, yet each such element is delivered without taint of self-righteousness or condescension. The form of this novel is a memoir, but it reads more like an extended love letter.

These same biblical words are, of course, addressed to the contemporary readers of Robinson's Pulitzer Prize-winning novel, and to a reader who still inhabits some part of the Christian culture to which Ames is a witness, they may seem to imply as much a prophetic judgment about stereotypical preacherly certitude as an admission of limited perspective in this distinctive narrative voice. This is in fact a tension that Robinson brilliantly exploits. Such a fruitful acknowledgement of limit is, paradoxically, one of the potential advantages of first person discourse over omniscient third person narration. For the potential to be realized, however, the author must first create compelling character in the speaker.

The subgenre of wisdom literature which Robinson evokes, even recreates in this novel, is distinctively biblical: "My son, hear the instruction of thy father, and forsake not the law of thy mother" (Prov 1:8, KJV[4]) is its watchword, a call to attention and recollection of family identity parallel to a larger invitation to instruction, "*Shema, Ysrael*" (Deut 6:4). Reiterations of this motif are not simply a rhetorical gambit in biblical wisdom books, but a framing device that puts biblical wisdom squarely in the context of Torah, of the obligation of parents to instruct their offspring concerning the relation of God's loving providence to

---

3. Robinson, *Gilead*, 7.

4. All biblical quotations are taken from the King James Version.

the vagaries of family history. All the *davarim* (words and deeds) of the faithful are to be kept in perpetual memory:

> And thou shalt teach them diligently unto thy children, and shalt talk of them when thou sittest in thy house, and when thou walkest by the way, and when thou liest down, and when thou risest up. (Deut 6:7)

The narrator's vocation as a pastor and his deep sense of having been called to a specific place, namely the little town of Gilead, binds his own participation to his community in such a way that he has come to understand his pastoral calling as deeply integrated with the operations of a general providence he finds in large measure inscrutable and with the explicit, only slightly more scrutable rituals of domesticity, in particular of his vocation to be a husband and a father. His late life marriage to a much younger woman is an event itself as mysterious as her appearance, as if out of nowhere, at the back of his church in the midst of a Sunday service. The son who is born to them is such another mystery, almost a miracle, yet the intensity of love he feels for them both magnifies and somehow deepens his understanding of the theological mysteries he has long loved without having ever been able to plumb their depths. Moreover, it adds focus and conscious integration to his sense of life-long vocation as a pastor; he becomes more deeply knit, by virtue of the centering power of his marriage, both to the community he has long loved and conscientiously served, and to the lineage passed down to him by his father and grandfather, which are in the light of his own fatherhood now more meaningfully to be contemplated and cherished. Community in this way becomes substantial; the remembrance of it, for himself and for the generation yet to come, invites an almost Eucharistic resonance of timeless participation on nearly every page of his journal. In this way the vocation of the narrator becomes both medium and message in the novel. As Chip Conyers in a related context has put it, someone like Ames knows and expresses his vocation as a kind of being "called together," a phenomenon that becomes artful reality "whenever communities come into being and whenever they abide, prosper, and develop, as it were, a beautiful life together."[5] A disposition to obedience to this fundamental commandment in Deuteronomy has been the way of John Ames's life in a double sense (we learn this

---

5. Conyers, *Listening Heart*, 101.

gradually), and his memory of the text, encouraged by his own father has here—entirely appropriately—been preserved in King James idiom. The task Ames has set himself in his memoir is thus doubly reflexive of the text in which he is steeped: "Your mother told you I'm writing your begats," he writes to his progeny on the page before him; the passing on of history and the bequeathing of wisdom, as in Scripture, are here also in the novel inseparable one from the other.

There is a certain audacity in writing against the grain of the modern/postmodern novel in the way that Robinson does. Yet "resisting the restlessness of modernity" (to borrow another phrase from Conyers) connects her, as a storyteller, with venerable predecessors in a near vanished heyday of the novel, when, as Walter Benjamin has memorably observed, the storyteller was one with "counsel for his readers." Benjamin, one of the greatest of European literary critics before WWII, steeped in Jewish learning, went on to say that "if today 'having counsel' is beginning to have an old-fashioned ring, this is because the communicability of experience is decreasing. In consequence," he says, "we have no counsel either for ourselves or for others."[6] If Robinson, as a kind of "sign of contradiction," in this sense has counsel, it is doubtless because she connects so naturally to the sources of communicable wisdom Benjamin's insight draws upon. But we should note also a difference of tone. In Benjamin's echo of the Deuteronomic principle there is a wistful resignation to modernity, a bittersweet overtone of nostalgia. This is an inevitable sentiment for many of Gilead's actual readers, and Robinson is certainly conscious of it. But it seems to me that she is more firmly forward looking, communicating also a sense of faith in Ames's covenant with the future that rises above somber concession to modernity's pessimism about the value of tradition.

If there is a tacit rhetorical question in much of modernist literature and critical reflection, it might perhaps be phrased, "Can anything of the past be a relevant authority for us today?" In this novel, at least, Robinson's answer is decidedly un-modern—at least to the degree that it is biblical. But I would add that it is distinctly un-modern in a closely related sense, that its purpose, again like that of Conyers, is "reversing the antipathy toward vocation."[7] In this sense, both are still of the tribe

---

6. Walter, "Storyteller."
7. Conyers, *Listening Heart*, 112.

of Walter Benjamin, whose conception of the ideal novelist is deeply inscribed with a biblical notion of vocation.

The book of Proverbs, perhaps more than any other biblical text, has for Protestant Christians been the model for this particular vein of aphoristic discourse as a means of parent-child instruction. There have been deliberate secular imitations before. One thinks of Lord Chesterfield's *Letters to his Son, Philip Stanhope* (1774), exceptionally candid written epistolary advice to his own son and his godson, born twenty-five years apart, each named Philip Stanhope after himself (it is evident that Robinson has read from this volume). Proverbs is itself, of course, far more aphoristic than Chesterfield's *Letters* or indeed than Robinson's novel, which is nonetheless richly aphoristic, with more quotations from Proverbs than any other text, including the Sermon on the Mount from Matthew and the Epistle of James. Such richness of biblical citation might well have burdened the novel with an entirely off-putting preachiness, had not Robinson's narrator and protagonist, despite his vocation, been so compellingly developed in terms of his own keenly reflective, yet surprisingly (especially in a postmodern novel) self-deprecating consciousness. One effect of such a winsome narrative voice is that the personal stories Ames tells *embody* the wisdom he wishes to convey in a fashion resistant to any reduction to aphorism merely: authentic personal transparency is the quintessence of the wisdom to be gathered.

It is because of his thoughtful self-criticism, in fact (not in spite of it), that the narrator acquires an authority altogether uncommon in contemporary fiction. This is a feature of the novel that steals in upon one almost imperceptibly in the reading, or, as it may seem, the overhearing of it. The father's authority is never asserted, as such, to his son, or even to his wayward and deeply unsettled godson. Circumspection is his manner; deferral to the opinion of others, including his own father and grandfather and even to theologians with whom in the end he does not agree, or to the sturdier Calvinism of his fellow minister and closest friend, is Ames's habitual discipline. It is not at all that he is without opinions; in fact he holds deeply considered and well-formed opinions. Rather, it is that he respects the views of others and, in the fashion suggested by the opening quotation, reckons it to be impossible for any individual to judge of a matter accountably without the aid of divergent as well as complementary perspectives.

The art of conversation is thus an integral part of the pursuit of wisdom. Just as one can read a bad book and find something to affirm in "its haplessness or pomposity or gall," Ames says, so with people: "There are pleasures to be found where you would never look for them."[8] The cultivation of deeper friendships, rooted in shared mutual affections, is nevertheless for Ames a still less dispensable anchor to reflection. In his fellow clergyman and neighbor Boughton, shepherd to another flock, he finds "a friend that sticketh closer than a brother" (Prov 18:24). This, too, has a correlative in the timbre of narrative voice; the words on Robinson's pages appear far less like prose monologue than like a conversation overheard; it might be better to say that they capture a symphony of conversations with persons in all types and categories of relationship, past and present, and with several types of books, past and present in Ames's reading, all of which still remain present to his consciousness as voices in an ongoing colloquy.

A further aspect of this remarkable diachronic and its dialogic effect of the narrative (it is given, after all, as a monologue), is the role of prayer as an undertone in the settled wisdom one "hears" in the father's voice. But an aura of prayer is also a means by which the relationship between father as teacher and any who will have eyes to see and ears to hear is established. "For me, writing has always felt like praying," Ames confesses, "even when I wasn't writing prayers, as I was often enough. You feel that you are with someone," he continues; "I feel I am with you now, whatever that can mean.... That is to say, I pray for you. And there's an intimacy in it. That's the truth."[9] Analogously, at least for the reader, Ames further admits that he does not write the way he speaks, but rather tries to write the way he thinks.[10] Thoughts can be prayers; his narrative gives the impression of being saturated with both indistinguishably. Prayer in adversity, he says at another point, brings peace, and prayer for others—often uttered through the night for his own and his friend's parishioners, each in their several needs as he understands them—brings him to identify closely with them, finding unity in the bonds of peace.[11] This too, Robinson implies, is a measure of his wisdom.

---

8. Robinson, *Gilead*, 39.
9. Ibid., 19.
10. Ibid., 28–29.
11. Ibid., 70–71.

Part of what makes Ames's character as well as his voice so appealing, then, is his candor and self-effacement. Unlike Boughton, he has always written out his sermons carefully, word for word; the attic is filled with them, he says whimsically, putting him "right up there with Augustine and Calvin for quantity. That's amazing," he continues, "I wrote almost all of it in the deepest hope and conviction. Sifting my thoughts and choosing my words. Trying to say what was true. And I'll tell you frankly, that was wonderful."[12] It is this last sentence, in its candid admission of the joy he has taken in his work, which convinces us of the authenticity of what precedes it. We are pleasantly surprised to learn later on that he is still examining his conscience regarding sermons preached long ago, as his own understanding has deepened—thinking "That's what he meant!"[13] and wishing he had put a point differently. This process, too, he interweaves with conversations long past.

It turns out that only one of his sermons has not been preserved. It was preached in a time of plague (the 1918 epidemic of Spanish influenza), as he was attempting to comfort the bereaved who would ask him "how the Lord could allow such a thing."[14] Though he still believes this sermon to have offered a persuasive biblical answer to the problem of undeserved suffering ("the only sermon I wouldn't mind answering for in the next world"), when he considered the faces of those to whom he would preach he burned it before rising to the pulpit. Instead, he preached on the parable of the lost sheep. Here too is an act of wisdom, exemplified in a fashion the author of Job might approve.

Ames's consciousness of the gap between intention and utterance is acute; his sense that truth abides beyond our judgment of it is pervasive in all he writes. Accordingly, the inner debates with self as well as those with external interlocutors—with his father, grandfather, Boughton, Feuerbach, his elder brother Edward, a seminarian who lost his faith, his wayward godson Jack Ames Boughton—all give careful respect to opposing as well as confirming positions, even on occasions when it is evidently painful for Ames. In a most poignant example, he greatly fears a corrosive influence of Jack on his wife and the young natural son for whom his memoir is being written, and he admits as much. Yet he nonetheless respects Jack's skepticism and the candor of it even when

12. Ibid., 19.
13. Ibid., 41.
14. Ibid.

he cannot but deplore some of its apparent consequences, in particular Jack's insouciant immorality.[15] This attitude reflects a much stronger virtue than tolerance. Rather, it arises from a wellspring of genuine affection that, in its application, is not dissevered from his love for truth, especially for truth about God and his love for the world. "Nothing true can be said about God from a posture of defense," he says in a remarkable passage. "In the matter of belief I have always found that defenses have the same irrelevance about them as the criticisms they are meant to answer.... There is always an inadequacy in argument about ultimate things."[16] Ames goes on to say to his son that it is possible to "assert the existence of something—Being—having not the slightest notion of what it is," an evident echo of the passage with which we began. The echo reinforces, in effect, the culminating theological wisdom Ames wishes to impart to his son, namely that in matters of faith it is seldom fruitful to look for "proofs" but always fruitful, in effect, to try to live in obedience to Christ.[17] Proofs are "never sufficient to the question, and they are always a little impertinent... because they claim to find for God a place within our conceptual grasp."[18]

Here we get a confirming insight into Ames's lifelong conversation with his Calvinist preacher friend Boughton. We see that his quiet fideism resists the reformed rationalism and strong doctrine preferred by the Presbyterian. In the course of his conversation with Boughton the character and direction of his own thinking has been sharpened (Prov 27:17). Accordingly, Ames's caution is not a reflex of anti-intellectualism, or careless pietism either, but reflects rather a deeply intellected recognition of our human incapacity fully to understand the wisdom of God. Such circumspection is itself, of course, a hallmark of biblical wisdom.

One of the most compelling aspects of Robinson's novel, and, it seems to me, an indispensable part of its wisdom for the contemporary Christian reader, is its acknowledgment of our own typical failure to transmit the wisdom of the generations even to those we most love. This is to cede a point, perhaps, to the Calvinist. The "wisdom" Jack wants

---

15. Ibid., 143–54.
16. Ibid., 177–78.
17. Cf. ibid., 139.
18. Ibid., 179.

to grasp is to know why grace does not reach him.[19] The relationship of Ames to his namesake godson and to his seven-year-old son here echoes aspects of the Abraham-Hagar-Ishmael narrative, a passage on which Ames has preached.[20] To some extent the failure of his own father as well as Ames's failure as godfather to correct Jack, or to find a way in love to understand his evident need for particular attention, is inescapably a failure of wisdom on the part of both "fathers." Ames knows it—or has come reflectively over time to know it in regret. It is evident to the reader that Jack wanted to be confronted, even as a youthful rebel, and the final conversation he has with Ames, sitting quietly in Ames's dilapidated old church, provides an irrefragable culmination to this insight. It turns out that Jack has also always wanted to be loved in such a way that, as the medieval spiritual writer William of St. Thierry puts it, *amor ipse intellectus est*—love itself embodies understanding.

Marilynne Robinson shows that wisdom comes to us in many ways; it may well be conveyed in a remembered hymn,[21] in the memorization of Scripture, which then later reveals its truths in the crucible of experience, or even in a clichéd cultural commonplace.[22] Thus Rev. Ames is pleased at the progress of his little boy, who, with his mother's help, is memorizing portions of the Scripture, including at this point the Beatitudes.[23] But he knows that the lad's present pleasure in "the magnitude of the accomplishment" will pale in comparison to the value of such wisdom later, when the meaning of these remembered words comes inwardly to life in a richer way. The boy remains as nameless as the implied son in Proverbs, that Robinson's readers might more easily become themselves the actual recipients of the wisdom taught, for the lad is yet far from the age of experience in which he can appropriate it all. Like the Christian reader of *Gilead*, he may be able to locate or even memorize the wisdom aphorisms of the Proverbs, for example, much more readily than properly to understand them: "Who among men knoweth the things of a man, save the spirit of a man, which is in

---

19. Ibid., 170–71.
20. Ibid., 128–30.
21. Ibid., 103.
22. Ibid., 60.
23. Ibid., 185.

him?"[24]; "Hope deferred makes the heart sick"[25] (Prov 13:12). Perhaps he may come to concede that "hope deferred is still hope"[26]; "There is that scattereth, and yet increaseth more"[27] (Prov 11:24); "Children' children are the crown of old men"[28] (Prov 17:6). Yet not all these elements of wisdom will come to be fully comprehended, or confirmed as one might wish in personal experience, even for Ames himself.

What then may we hope for from our efforts to pass on the wisdom of the ages—and ageless wisdom likewise—to a generation whose understanding of it we ourselves shall not live to see? Like Robinson's fading narrator, we cast our bread upon the waters in the hope that "by God's grace, of course,"[29] whatever bread returns to us will bear about it some token of our love, committed against that day which shall come to us all. The parable, tacit in Robinson's beautiful novel, is nonetheless explicit in her conclusion: the transmission of wisdom is all about a father's love. Before he dies, and his script concludes abruptly with a prayer and "sleep," Ames confers upon the renegade surrogate Jack, hand upon his head, a biblical father's blessing: "The Lord make his face to shine upon thee and be gracious unto thee: the Lord lift up his countenance upon thee, and give thee peace" (Num 6:25–26). The moment is sacramental; for Ames and his godson it is in just such a respect intimately personal. This near final act of the old pastor and father is the fruit of the wisdom which he has received, and for those who will come to have "eyes to see and ear to hear," it "simply states a deeply mysterious fact."[30] Perhaps that allusive old spiritual song hints at the good of this fact in its soothing refrain: "There is a balm in Gilead / to heal the wounded soul."

---

24. Ibid., 179.
25. Ibid., 221.
26. Ibid., 247.
27. Ibid., 198.
28. Ibid., 230.
29. Ibid., 138.
30. Ibid., 7.

Bibliography

Benjamin, Walter. *Illuminations*. Edited by Hannah Arendt. New York: Schocken, 1969.

Chesterfield, Philip Stanhope. *Letters Written by Lord Chesterfield to His Son*. New York: Kessinger, 2007.

Conyers, A. J. *The Listening Heart: Vocation and the Crisis of Modern Culture*. Dallas: Spence, 2006.

Lewis, C. S. *Poems*. Edited by Walter Hooper. New York: Harcourt Brace Jovanovich, 1964.

Robinson, Marilynne. *Gilead*. New York: Picador, 2006.

———. *The Death of Adam: Essays on Modern Thought*. New York: Picador, 2005.

15

Richard Weaver, the Gospel, and the Restoration of Culture

Bradley G. Green

MANY TWENTIETH-CENTURY PILGRIMS AT SOME POINT IN THEIR JOURney have found inspiration and insight from the pen of Richard M. Weaver (1910–1963).[1] Not a few are prone to cite Weaver's *Ideas Have Consequences* when they recount their own intellectual journey, and when they describe when and how they began really to "think." Best known as the author of *Ideas*, which was published in 1948 by the University of Chicago Press, Weaver was a Southerner who has had a significant impact on political thought in the United States in the twentieth-century.

Born and raised in North Carolina, Weaver did his undergraduate work at the University of Kentucky. A leftist-liberal during his undergraduate days in the 1920s, after a year of graduate work at Kentucky he moved on to Vanderbilt for graduate study in the early 1930s. During his time at Vanderbilt, Weaver was greatly influenced by the Nashville Agrarians (often called the Southern Agrarians, or the Vanderbilt Agrarians), which included such persons as Allen Tate, Donald Davidson, and his thesis advisor, John Crowe Ransom. Weaver would eventually do doctoral work at Louisiana State University (1940–43), where he would write his dissertation on Southern culture (eventually

---

1. When I was first asked to contribute to this *Festschrift* for Chip Conyers, my mind went immediately to this paper, which I had been working on. Those who knew Chip will recognize the ways in which the themes of this essay intersect with Chip's interests. There are three components of the essay which were all of interest to Chip: the thought of Richard Weaver, the Southern intellectual tradition, and the possibility of living faithful Christian lives in our age.

published posthumously as *The Southern Tradition at Bay*). By the time he began doctoral studies, he had become disillusioned with the Left, and had become a Southern partisan. A conservative, agrarian, Southern framework would provide the general contours within which he would work during the remainder of his life. Weaver would go on to a teaching career in English at the University of Chicago, where he taught from 1944 until his death in 1963.

Christian theological themes are found implicitly and explicitly in Weaver's work. Weaver would come to see his work as advancing a "restoration of culture," or of civilization, and he would rely extensively on Christian themes as he addressed this particular thesis. In what follows I wish to explore how distinctly Christian theological themes such as creation, the *Logos*, faith seeking understanding, eschatology and the importance of history appear consistently in Weaver's work, and how these themes serve as the necessary substructure or precondition of this intellectual program. I argue that Weaver's use of such Christian themes is both too extensive and intensive to be simply peripheral to his thought. However, I ultimately argue that there is something significant that is missing in Weaver's use of such themes—the Christian gospel— and I try to elucidate the ways in which this lacuna may weaken an otherwise very penetrating criticism of modernity, and may hamper an otherwise brilliant attempt at the restoration of a meaningful culture.

Christian Themes in the Thought of Richard Weaver

Creation

In his attempt to articulate what is necessary for civilization, or for a genuine and meaningful culture, Weaver repeatedly emphasizes the importance of a doctrine of creation. Weaver contends that a doctrine of creation is essential to an affirmation of the reality of knowledge. If this is indeed a created world, there is something outside of us, something *there* to be known.

Some of Weaver's important insights related to creation can be found in his essay "Gnostics of Education," a penetrating critique of contemporary educational theory.[2] Therein Weaver's understanding of the *necessity* of a created order is made explicit. Weaver suggests that

---

2. Weaver, "Gnostics of Education," 126.

one of the significant weaknesses of modern educational theory is that the student is being prepared "to become a member of a utopia resting on a false view of both nature and man."[3] Weaver contends that modern educational theory has abandoned centuries of tradition and insight, and that the twentieth century has witnessed a veritable revolution in the world of education—at all levels. It is common for critics to look back a few years—sometimes *very* few years—in their search for what ails us. The list of usual suspects might be Hobbes, or Descartes, or Hume, or Kant. But Weaver looks even further back—to the Gnostic heresy of the first and second centuries of the Christian era.[4] He defines Gnosticism as "an attempt to reinterpret annalistic Christianity in terms suited to the 'enlightenment' of the contemporary era."[5]

Weaver suggests that much of modern educational theory is ultimately gnostic. By his use of "Gnosticism" he means two things: (1) creation is inherently evil, the work of a demiurge limited in power; and (2) man does not require salvation from outside himself, but is already in a state of "Messianic blessedness."[6] Gnosticism, accordingly, "is a kind of irresponsibility—an irresponsibility to the past and to the structure of reality in the present."[7] Gnosticism fails because its advocates, on Weaver's understanding, "are out of line with what is."[8]

Ultimately, Gnosticism fails because it fails to deal with the world *as it truly is*. And Weaver's point is that in order for there to be true education and knowledge (both which he would affirm), our world must indeed be a created world. Significantly, Weaver links his understanding of *creation* to his understanding of *history* and *the past*. Ultimately, he contends, one's understanding of education *necessarily flows from* one's understanding of the world: "education at any level will reflect the primary assumptions that we make about reality, and for this reason no education is innocent of an attitude toward the existing world." Indeed, as he observes, "education will reveal beliefs about creation."[9]

---

3. Ibid., 117.
4. Ibid., 117–18.
5. Ibid., 118.
6. Ibid., 118ff.
7. Ibid., 120.
8. Ibid.
9. Ibid.

Weaver also criticizes this "gnostic" modern educational theory because it assumes an overly optimistic view of man. Thus, he notes, "The Gnostic belief was that man is not sinful, but divine."[10] Indeed, "The real evil in the universe cannot be imputed to him; his impulses are good, and there is no ground for restraining him from anything which he wants to do.... By divinizing man, Gnostic thinking says that what he wants to do, he should do."[11] In this Gnostic vision of things, Weaver can detect "the doctrine that human beings do not stand in need of correction, to say nothing of conversion."[12] Summarizing this modern notion, Weaver can write, "Because human nature is so good that it is not constrainable, laws and traditions are not to be respected."[13]

In the end, Weaver believes that the idea that there is a world of truth which is "worth knowing and even worth reverencing" ultimately *requires* a doctrine of creation: "Clearly this (i.e., the conviction that there is a body of data worth knowing) presumes a certain respect for the world as creation, a belief in it and a trust in its providence, rather than a view (as if out of ancient Gnosticism) positing its essential incompleteness and badness. The world is there *a priori*; the learner has the duty of familiarizing himself with its nature and its set of relations."[14] As Marion Montgomery (borrowing from Aquinas) suggests, education is concerned with coming into contact with "the truth of things."[15] In the concluding chapter of *Ideas Have Consequences*, "Distinction and Hierarchy," Weaver asserts: "Now such a look at the nature of things is imperative for our conception of everything else, and, if we feel that creation does not express purpose, it is impossible to find an authorization for purpose in our lives. Indeed, the assertion of purpose in a world we felt to be purposeless would be a form of sentimentality."[16]

---

10. Ibid., 123.
11. Ibid.
12. Ibid., 125.
13. Ibid., 124.
14. Ibid., 126
15. Historic Christianity roots the "truth of things" in the fact that we live in a good, created, and orderly world. See Montgomery, *Truth of Things*.
16. Weaver, *Ideas Have Consequences*, 51.

Logos

As a professor of English and teacher of rhetoric, Weaver was concerned with the disintegration of communication in the modern era. As such, Weaver would seem to rely on the importance of the Christian understanding of the *logos* as central to a philosophy of language and communication. Christians have long articulated a distinctively Christian understanding of language, as seen, for example, in Augustine's *On Christian Doctrine* and in a numerous Christian thinkers who were Christians influenced by Augustine.

To understand Weaver, one must recognize that although he begins *Ideas* with the line, "This is another book about the dissolution of the West," he is not simply another gloomy prophet predicting the end of Western culture. It might be more accurate to say that, according to Weaver, Western culture has in effect already crumbled, and he is more interested in the work of the *restoration* of culture. In articulating an understanding of the restoration of culture, Weaver turns to an understanding of the *logos*. He writes, "The most portentous general event of our time is the steady obliteration of those distinctions which create society. Rational society is a mirror of the logos, and this means that it has a formal structure which enables apprehension." "The preservation of society," he concludes, "is therefore directly linked with the recovery of true knowledge."[17] And part of this recovery is the recovery of the importance and nature of language. In this context, Weaver quotes John Milton with approval:

> I am inclined to believe that when the language in common use in any country becomes irregular and depraved, it is followed by their ruin and degradation. For what do terms used without skill or meaning, which are at once corrupt and misapplied, denote but a people listless, supine, and ripe for servitude? On the contrary, we have never heard of any people or state which has not flourished in some degree of prosperity as long as their language has retained its elegance and its purity?[18]

Weaver saw the recovery of language, its power, and its proper use as pivotal to a restoration of culture. He could argue: "The feeling that to

---

17. Ibid., 35.

18. Weaver, "Relativism," 389. Weaver is quoting John Milton from a correspondence with Benedetto Bonomatthai, September 10, 1638.

have power of language is to have control over things is deeply imbedded in the human mind."[19] And language has a transcendent component: "words in common human practice express something transcending the moment."[20] Noting Adam's act of naming the animals, and offering a few words on the prologue to the Gospel of John, Weaver proceeds to clarify his understanding of language. Even when Weaver's understanding of the *logos* may not have been the full-orbed christological and trinitarian affirmations on display in Augustine and the Christian tradition, he still recognizes the centrality of the *logos* as that which orders the world. And, *our* language is meaningful and powerful because of the reality of this larger and transcendent *logos*.[21]

Weaver insists that a key indicator of the health of a culture is whether it sees language as a bridge to reality, or as a transient and pragmatic combination of sounds and utterances. He observes: "Certainly one of the most important revelations about a period comes in its theory of language, for that informs us whether language is viewed as a bridge to the noumenal or as a body of fictions convenient for grappling with transitory phenomena."[22] As Weaver sees it, things went wrong with Occam, and specifically with the victory of nominalism.[23] In relation to the reality and use of language, he believes that with Occam's victory, "ontological referents were abandoned in favor of pragmatic considerations.... [I]deas become psychological figments, and words become useful signs."[24] Over against Occam, Weaver wishes to affirm and recover a type of realist ontology, an aim that appears consistently throughout his works. For example, in his essay "Language Is Sermonic," Weaver again cites a doctrine of creation as that which underlies any affirmation of the meaningfulness of language. For this reason he can suggest that "the cosmos *is* one vast system of analogy, so that our profoundest intuitions of it are made in the form of comparisons." And this, he argues, leads one back to a doctrine of creation: "To affirm that something is like something else is to begin to talk about the unitariness of creation."

19. Weaver, "Power of the Word," 148.
20. Ibid.
21. Ibid., 148–49.
22. Ibid., 150.
23. Weaver, "Language Is Sermonic," 362.
24. Weaver, "Power of the Word," 150–51.

In "Language Is Sermonic" Weaver wishes to be explicit in his understanding of where language pushes us. Referring once more to the medieval debate between realism and nominalism, he seeks to avoid a positivistic view of language—i.e., a radically empiricist (or naturalistic empiricist) understanding of language. Hence, Weaver can argue, "Language is a system of imputation, by which values and percepts are first framed in the mind and are then imputed to things."[25] But this imputation is not necessarily haphazard or simply accidental. Weaver does not want to imply that "no two people can look at the same clock face and report the same time"; rather, "The qualities or properties have to be in the things, but they are not in the things in the form in which they are framed in the mind." And Weaver explicitly admits the need for a created order as a necessary precondition of the meaningfulness of language: "Language was created by the imagination for the purposes of man, but it may have objective reference—just how we cannot say until we are in possession of a more complete metaphysics and epistemology."[26] In a fascinating turn, then, Weaver admits that a certain metaphysics and epistemology are necessary if we are to affirm the objective reference of language.

Finally, Weaver can even broach the issue of the inherently covenantal nature of language. It is clear that different cultures use different languages, and that different languages are, well, different. As he notes, "There is a difference between saying that language is relative because it is a convention and saying that because it is a convention it may be treated or used relativistically." Moreover, "If language is a more or less local convention, then its meanings are relative to those who use it. It clearly does not follow from this, however, that those who speak it may use it with unrestricted license."[27] But how does one avoid this relativistic turn that Weaver wishes to avoid? Weaver retrieves the biblical notion of covenant and suggests that "language is a covenant among those who use it. It is in the nature of a covenant to be more than a matter of simple convenience, to be departed from for light and transient causes. A covenant—and I like, in this connection, the religious overtones of the word—binds us at deeper levels and involves some

---

25. Weaver, "Language Is Sermonic," 368–69.
26. Ibid., 369.
27. Weaver, "Relativism," 403.

kind of confrontation of reality."[28] The notion of covenant receives this further qualification:

> When we covenant with one another that a word shall stand for a certain thing, we signify that it is the best available word for the thing in the present state of general understanding. The possibilities of refinement toward a more absolute correctness of meaning lie within and behind that convention. But as long as the convention is in effect, it has to be respected like any other rule, and this requires that departures from it must justify themselves.[29]

Faith Seeking Understanding

In a number of his writings, but notably in *Ideas Have Consequences*,[30] Weaver criticizes modern rationalism, comparing his own understanding to the medieval attempt to synthesize faith and reason. He speaks of "a metaphysical dream of the world," and his explication of his own view is strikingly similar to the Augustinian and Anselmian notion of "faith seeking understanding."

In the opening chapter of *Ideas*, titled "The Unsentimental Sentiment," is found perhaps the clearest allusion by Weaver to the Augustinian-Anselmian concept. Therein Weaver argues that every person evidences three levels of conscious reflection: (1) "his specific ideas about things"; (2) "his general beliefs or convictions"; and (3) "his metaphysical dream of the world." The first level is rudimentary, consisting of "the thoughts he employs in the activity of daily living." The second level consists of certain conceptions of the world around him.

But it is the third level that interests us here. This third level is what Weaver calls one's "intuitive feeling about the immanent nature of reality, and this is the sanction to which ideas (level 1) and beliefs (level 2) are ultimately referred for verification."[31] According to Weaver, the "dream carries with it an evaluation, which is the bond of spiritual community."[32] What he is suggesting is that one's basic ideas and convic-

28. Ibid., 404.
29. Ibid.
30. Weaver, "Unsentimental Sentiment."
31. Ibid., 18.
32. Ibid.

tions flow from this "metaphysical dream of the world." And the metaphysical dream is something anterior to reason, since "logic depends upon the dream, and not the dream upon it."[33] A word of explanation is in order: "We must admit this when we realize that logical processes rest ultimately on classification, that classification is by identification, and that identification is intuitive."[34] It would appear that this is Weaver's somewhat secularized way of speaking of "faith seeking understanding." It is significant that Weaver self-consciously positions himself with the medieval realists, as opposed to the nominalists, in his assertion that universals exist *before*, not *after*, the particulars. And at the end of his chapter on "the unsentimental sentiment," Weaver can write, "The only redemption lies in restraint imposed by idea; but our ideas, if they are not to worsen the confusion, must be harmonized by some vision. Our task is much like finding the relationship between faith and reason for an age that does not know the meaning of faith."[35]

Past and Future: History and Eschatology

Weaver sees himself as essentially a premodern thinker, in that whereas the modern age has largely abandoned the affirmation of first and final causes, Weaver wishes to recover the importance of such causes. In particular, Weaver wishes to affirm the importance of history, or of the past, as well as to affirm the importance of the notion that history is indeed *going* somewhere (eschatology). He explicitly relies on a Christian versus a "gnostic" understanding of the world to make his argument.

Why the Past Matters: The Importance of History

What Weaver saw, and sadly many contemporary Christians fail to see, was the importance of history. As noted above, Weaver saw Gnosticism as being fundamentally *anti*-historical, given its overriding assumption that knowledge need not be mediated over time. Rather, what is important for the Gnostic is the immediate—i.e., that which is *not* mediated. Thus, in Gnostic thinking there is a disinterest in the flow of events, the events of history, and how these events culminate in the present. This

---

33. Ibid., 21.
34. Ibid.
35. Ibid., 34.

forces Weaver to conclude that "the essence of Gnosticism is a kind of irresponsibility—an irresponsibility to the past and to the structure of reality in the present."[36]

Significantly, Weaver is explicit in connecting a proper understanding of *history* with *creation*. This leads him to conclude that history is the "memory of all the past with all its uniqueness, as they were expressed in the concrete matter which is creation."[37]

Central to Weaver's argument is the function of memory, the ability to recall the past, and the possibility of knowledge and understanding. Could it be, Weaver wonders, that an age that lacks memory *ipso facto* will be an age lacking in understanding? "Intelligence," he observes, "is the power to associate remembered potencies with things seen simply."[38] Indeed, "In general all intellectuality rests upon our power to associate things not present or only suggested by what is present. Thus the intellectual value of anything depends upon our ability to retrieve from memory."[39] Since our age sees little value in the past, there will be little emphasis on memory. And if Weaver is right, to lack memory is to lack understanding. "It is therefore impossible," as he views it, "to imagine a high-grade or effective intelligence without things supplied by the remembering process." Therefore, "It seems beyond question then that any attack upon memory, insofar as this metaphor expresses real facts, is an attack upon mind."[40] This leads Weaver to conclude, "The preservation of society is therefore directly linked with the recovery of true knowledge."[41]

If Weaver is correct, on the whole, it is almost as if man is intent on destroying himself. And indeed, more than one twentieth-century writer has commented that modern man seems to have a sort of death-wish. Malcolm Muggereridge, commenting on his travels in the Soviet Union (see, for example, his *Chronicles of Wasted Time* and his novel *Winter in Moscow*), spoke of his "fellow-travelers," by which he was referring to those Western journalists, academics, union leaders, etc., who were enthralled with Stalin and his regime. Muggeridge was convinced

36. Weaver, "Gnostics of Education," 120.
37. Weaver, "Attack upon Memory," 52.
38. Ibid., 42.
39. Ibid., 43.
40. Ibid.
41. Ibid., 35.

that these visitors to Stalin's "paradise" must have had a "death-wish." Weaver, likewise, can wonder if modern man does not often seem to have a "suicidal impulse," or at least an "impulse of self-hatred."

But surely, we might object, Weaver overstates his point. Or does he? Weaver laments that modern man seems to have no memory, no historical consciousness. He goes on to suggest that memory, a sense of history, is central to one's identity. If it really is the case—that memory is central to who we are as humans—then to reject, or jettison memory is to a large extent to manifest a "suicidal impulse," or to manifest an "impulse of self-hatred." As Weaver argues, "no man exists really except through that mysterious storehouse of his remembered acts and his formed personality." Indeed, his very reality "depends upon his carrying the past into the present through the power of memory." One can only conclude: "If he does not want identity, if he has actually come to hate himself, it is natural for him to try to get rid of memory's baggage. He will travel light." Whereas modern thinkers like David Hume, in his *Treatise of Human Nature* (1739–1740), can write that his own system of philosophy intends to be "built on a foundation almost entirely new," Weaver suggests that knowledge is virtually impossible without attention to the past, without the reality of memory.[42]

One of the central traits of modernity is this "attack" on memory, as Weaver saw. Sadly, this animus toward memory is even dominant in the contemporary academy. Whereas in the not-too distant past it would have been taken as a *given* that to be educated is to be grounded in the central texts, ideas, and figures of one's own intellectual inheritance, it is probably *more* common (than not) for someone to graduate from a prominent university with *no real immersion* in one's own intellectual tradition. This hostility to the past can be seen in myriad examples, and—in a southern context—has manifested itself in the quite adamant insistence that all vestiges of southern culture be removed from public places. This hostility toward the past is ultimately rooted in a certain kind of contemporary Gnosticism, since this hostility toward the past is due to a gnostic obsession with the immediate. Weaver saw this gnostic error as insidious and dangerous. He writes: "in the way they have cut the young people off from knowledge of the excellencies achieved in the past, and in the way they have turned attention toward transient externals and away from the central problem of man, they have no

---

42. Hume, *Treatise of Human Nature*, 43.

equal as an agency of subversion."[43] One of the ways to help persons (particularly students) avoid being caught up in such a "gnostic" error is through attention to the past, and through encouraging students (and ourselves) to attend to the central texts and persons and artifacts of our own cultural and intellectual inheritance.

Where Are We Headed? The Importance of Eschatology

In his attempt at a restoration of culture, Weaver wishes to recover an affirmation of transcendent goals. This can be seen in the fact that Weaver's critique of the demise of Western culture often returns to the loss of ultimate, transcendent goals or ends. Thus, in A. J. Conyers' words, we witness in contemporary culture the "eclipse of heaven."[44] In explaining the vacuous nature of most modern educational institutions, Weaver can write, "if the primary need of man is to perfect his spiritual being and prepare for immortality, then education of the mind and the passions will take precedence over all else.... Those who maintain that education should prepare one for living successfully in this world have won a practically complete victory."[45] When we think of eschatology in terms of an understanding of the nature and purposes of history—indeed, the question of where we are headed—we see that Weaver is here arguing for a certain kind of eschatological vision of the world. Man is supposed to do more than simply get a "job," and man—contra John Dewey—is to be more than simply a cog in the economy.

Weaver does not speak to eschatology in terms of end-times schemes or timelines. I use the term "eschatology" here in the sense that Weaver is highly interested in recovering the reality of ultimate and final causes. He posits that one way of understanding modernity is in terms of the *loss* of ultimate and final causes. Whereas in the premodern world there was often an affirmation of multiple levels of causality, in the modern world there is often a reduction of causes to simply efficient and material causes. Thus, Weaver can write, "The nature and proper end of man are central to any discussion not only of whether a certain culture is weakening, but also of whether such a culture is

---

43. Weaver, "Gnostics of Education," 132–33.
44. Conyers, *Eclipse of Heaven*.
45. Weaver, *Ideas Have Consequences*, 49.

worth preserving."[46] Similarly, in an essay on the nature and purpose of education, he can insist, "Man has an irresistible desire to relate himself somehow to the totality, to ask what is the meaning of his presence here amid the great empirical fact of the universe."[47]

In short, Weaver argues consistently in his writings for the centrality and importance of history, and for the centrality of importance of seeing man and his purposes in the light of transcendent and ultimate ends and goals. These appeals to the importance of history and such transcendent and ultimate goals, at the very least, might be said to draw their inspiration from fundamental Christian themes and convictions.

Richard Weaver and the Gospel

What are we to make of Weaver's repeated use of Christian themes in his writing? This essay does not try to make a case for or against Weaver's personal faith commitment. It does appear that Weaver's own intellectual program is essentially, and not peripherally, tied to certain Christian theological themes that provide the necessary substructure and precondition to that program. Additionally, I would argue that the use of these Christian themes is thoroughly intentional.

There are, however, some striking omissions in Weaver's use of Christian themes. While Weaver appropriates utilizes a doctrine of creation, the idea of the *logos*, a type of faith seeking understanding, and an affirmation of the importance of history and eschatology, a notable omission is, of course, the gospel itself. Absent from his thought is any reference to the death, burial, and resurrection of Jesus or the implications thereof. While his presuppositions consistently pushed him to affirm a created order, to combat Gnosticism, to maintain a realist view of the universe, and to affirm the possibility of knowledge grounded in metaphysics, the centrality of history, and the attention to a sense of ultimate goals and aims (i.e., eschatology), he stopped short—at least publicly—of a more full-orbed affirmation of historic Christian orthodoxy. It is striking, given his repeated reference to other prominent Christian themes, that the gospel itself is conspicuously absent from his written work.

---

46. Weaver, "Image of Culture," 4.
47. Weaver, "Education and the Individual," 187.

This omission represents the major divide between Weaver and more explicitly Christian thinkers who have sought to articulate a more explicitly Christian understanding of intellectual and cultural life. And my critique is similar to that offered by Marion Montgomery, who in approvingly summarizing T. S. Eliot's critique of the agrarians, can write that Eliot "has as his initial fear that these (somewhat) younger poets, those Fugitives turned Agrarian turned polemicists, might not be sufficiently oriented, under the pressure of their concerns, to the necessity that *tradition* be recovered through *orthodoxy*."[48] Indeed, Montgomery echoes my own concerns (or I echo his!) when he writes, "without some metaphysical purchase in the nature of reality, the life of the mind can only *ad hoc*, in response to the present moment's circumstances."[49] Montgomery is clearly sympathetic to Weaver's attempt to resist the pressures and pitfalls of modernity, although he fears that Weaver's resistance to modernity was rather impromptu, and not sufficiently rooted in an understanding of, and commitment to, the "truth of things." Montgomery writes: "It was a valiant resistance nonetheless, and it gained for us some advantage to the continuing resistance, though we may ourselves at the close of our century feel so hard pressed as not to appreciate or take possession of a possible position beyond those *ad hoc* weaknesses we may ourselves discover."[50]

Montgomery expresses serious concerns both about Weaver's understanding of modernity and about Weaver's scheme for some sort of "restoration of culture." He faults Weaver for a misunderstanding of Aristotle, and of failing to appropriate "the Teacher's" insights. But more significantly, Weaver is not sufficiently Thomist for Montgomery, particularly for his supposed failure—on Montgomery's view—to appreciate the goodness of creation, a creation whose reality is structured and oriented by God. One can appreciate Montgomery's skittishness concerning Weaver on these issues, even if one does not walk down the Thomist road all the way with Montgomery.

But Montgomery makes a particularly pointed criticism of Weaver when he suggests that Weaver is avoiding a central issue—the question of atonement. He writes: "As a Christian apologist against Modernist secularism, therefore, Weaver avoids (it seems to me) the Christian mys-

48. Montgomery, "Consequences in the Provinces," 177.
49. Ibid., 183.
50. Ibid., 190.

tery which declares that through Christ there is both anticipated and provided to man a rescuing propitiation. And through that rescue lies a hope of the resurrection of body and soul in a perfected simplicity."[51] Here Montgomery is moving in the direction I wish to pursue. The fundamental reality missing in Weaver is of course the gospel itself—any attention to the death, burial, and resurrection of Jesus. Weaver continually utilizes various Christian insights and resources, but he never quite reaches for the heart of the matter—the gospel. While Montgomery does not linger long on this issue of atonement, he does register his doubts about Weaver's effort to restore culture apart from a more explicit and robust theological matrix. In short, in Weaver's proposal Montgomery finds "little hope of new cathedrals."[52]

While Montgomery's analysis is illuminating, in the end it may not go far enough. Weaver consistently utilized Christian themes in explicating his understanding of our culture's dilemma, particularly in his scheme for the "restoration of culture." But to borrow numerous insights and themes from the Christian tradition yet pull up short of the heart and soul of historic Christianity cannot but help draw attention as well as criticism. From a Christian vantage point, it is understandable (perhaps inevitable?) that a thoughtful person would "stumble" into the insights of the Christian tradition when attempting to chart the road ahead in our attempt to restore culture. But to fail to deal fully with the problem of human sin and the historic Christian response to this dilemma is really to fail to come to terms with why a culture disintegrates in the first place.

Montgomery also properly locates a weakness—at least on Christian terms—in Weaver's diagnosis of our malaise, and therefore in his diagnosis of a possible way ahead. He is concerned that Weaver's understanding of creation—and hence of that "last metaphysical right," property—is inadequate. Weaver properly affirms the importance of property, but because his construal is not sufficiently theologically oriented, it fails. Montgomery suggests that what is missing is "the metaphysical vision which orients intellect to nature."[53] Indeed, Montgomery notes, what is needed is "a vision of the person as created intellectual soul incarnate who must recover and maintain himself in responsibili-

---

51. Ibid., 231.
52. Ibid., 233.
53. Ibid., 242.

ties as steward." For, "it becomes lost in the rejection of the law of nature as under the law of God, a law available to the discrete intellect through a grace to that intellect called natural law."[54] In short, property indeed should be affirmed as a "right," but it is only a more robustly Christian theological framework—wherein creation as seen as *fundamentally good*, nature is oriented toward a *telos*, and man is seen as steward over creation (but *under* God)—that can provide the proper and necessary substructure for, or justification of, such an understanding and affirmation of property as a "right."

Why so little attention to the gospel in Weaver's writings? There is a certain interpretation of the differences between North and South that suggests that the North was overly concerned with doctrinal precision and details, while the South was less concerned with these issues. To wit, Weaver can write that "although the South was heavily Protestant, its attitude toward religion was essentially the attitude of orthodoxy: it was a simple acceptance of a body of belief, an innocence of protest and schism by which religion was left one of the unquestioned and unquestionable supports of the general settlement under which men live."[55]

Weaver also summarizes Southern religion by speaking of a "doctrinal innocence, for the average Southerner knew little and probably cared less about casuistical theology." Indeed, what the Southerner held as central was "the acknowledgement, the submissiveness of the will, and that *general respect for* order, natural and institutional, which is piety."[56] And I suspect that when Weaver speaks of this "general respect for order, natural and institutional," we are given a window into Weaver's own religious or theological disposition. Weaver's summary of religion is rather vague and lacks the robustness and fullness that has traditionally and historically marked the best of Christian theological affirmations and conviction. In fact, for a person to be religious in the south "did not obligate him to examine the foundations of belief or to assail the professions of others."[57] Weaver can even write that the Southerner "did not want a reasoned belief, but a satisfying dogma."[58] Whereas the Southerner possesses "a sense of restraint, and a willingness to abide by

54. Ibid., 242.
55. Weaver, "Older Religiousness," 135.
56. Ibid., 135.
57. Ibid.
58. Ibid.

the tradition," of the Northerner he could write, "the spirit of discontent, of aggressiveness, and of inquisitiveness was associated with those who had something to gain by overturning the established order."[59] Some of this is admirable, particularly the emphasis on the receiving of tradition. But, on the other hand, is it really necessary to believe that in the South, Christians did not—for example—desire to examine the foundations of belief? Weaver recounts the testimony of a minister, whose only lament after ministering for some time in the South was that "no token had reached him that he had religiously impressed their minds, more or less. They met regularly and decorously on Sundays, and departed quietly, and there was an end."[60] That is, the minister's complaint (not Weaver's) was that corporate worship—and church life more general—did not seem to have a noticeable or discernible impact on those involved.

According to Weaver, "What the Southerner desired above all else in religion was a fine set of images to contemplate . . ."[61] Again, if this is what Southerners *really* desired, then Southern Christianity is a Christianity of a rather unique sort. For Weaver, the Southerner has inherited a certain tradition, and is happy pretty much to leave the tradition alone. The Northerner on the other hand is marked by some level of discontent and aggressiveness.[62] Toward the end of his essay "The Older Religiousness of the South," Weaver comments that "in the sphere of religion the Southerner has always been hostile to the spirit of inquiry."[63] One is tempted to tease this out a bit, for if Weaver's understanding of Southern religion is on the whole accurate, this may go a long way to explaining why the South—like virtually all other regions and peoples—has had such a difficult time resisting antipathy to traditional revealed religion. If the Southerner typically did *not* feel compelled to trace out the implications of the Christian vision of God, man, and the world (to paraphrase Scottish divine James Orr), and to attempt to think through the implications of the Christian understanding of things to every facet of reality and to every area of human concern and life, it is certainly understandable (inevitable?) that "religion" would—over time—cease to satisfy and persuade and compel.

59. Ibid., 141.
60. Ibid., 140.
61. Ibid., 141. He here references Tate, "Religion and the Old South."
62. Weaver, "Older Religiousness," 141.
63. Ibid., 146.

When Weaver speaks like this, one is led perhaps to recall Walker Percy's essay "Stoicism in the South," wherein Percy suggests that the South has always had a dual allegiance to stoicism and Christianity.[64] Percy summarizes what a Stoic does when civilization is crumbling: "For the Stoic there is no real hope. His finest hour is to sit tight-lipped and ironic while the world comes crashing down around him."[65] If Percy is fair to the Stoic here, perhaps we should be hesitant to see Weaver as such a Stoic figure. For if the Stoic can simply sit tight-lipped without hope, at the heart of Weaver's writings lies a certain hope of cultural renewal. And again, perhaps Weaver has been influenced by an important Christian tenet—the resurrection; for no one who believes in the resurrection can be satisfied to sit hopelessly and tight-lipped. And Weaver *does* hold forth the hope of cultural restoration and renewal. I suspect the reality of cultural restoration and renewal is one that requires the gospel itself as a necessary precondition. And while Weaver does not state things quite *that* way, he does hold out hope for the restoration of culture. Unless one is a Gnostic—in which case one has to sequester the reality of the resurrection from any notion of cultural renewal—then one believes that the resurrection lies at the heart of the transformation of all things. And this is Percy's point as well: "The Christian is optimistic precisely where the Stoic is pessimistic."[66]

One might also be inclined to think of Allen Tate's essay "A Southern Mode of Imagination," wherein Tate argues that the Southern "mode of discourse" has traditionally been *rhetoric*, and not *dialectic*.[67] Indeed, writes Tate, "The Southerner has never been a dialectician."[68] Tate can also speak of the "notorious lack of self-consciousness of the ante-bellum Southerner,"[69] positing that "the failure of the old Southern

64. Percy, "Stoicism in the South," 83–88.
65. Ibid., 86.
66. Ibid.
67. Tate, "Southern Mode of Imagination."
68. Ibid., 583. Tate's words on Southern conversation (p. 584) are worth quoting in full: "The Southerner always talks to somebody else, and this somebody else, after varying intervals, is given his turn; but the conversation is always among rhetoricians; that is to say, the typical Southern conversation is not going anywhere; it is not about anything. *It is about the people who are talking,* even if they never refer to themselves, which they usually don't, since conversation is only an expression of manners, the purpose of which is to make everybody happy."
69. Ibid., 585.

leaders to understand the Northern mind (which was then almost entirely the New England mind) was a failure of intelligence."[70] In short, it is suggested that in the South there is a generally antipathy to theological exactness or theological inquiry.

Perhaps there is no gospel in Weaver's work because there is ultimately no vision of man as sinner. To be sure, Weaver does hold forth the necessity of the "tragic vision." But the "tragic vision" does not appear to flow from a Pauline or Augustinian vision of man as fallen and in dire need. Weaver does speak of the "tragic vision" that man must face if he is to be able to respond rightly to the world in which he lives. But it may be that Weaver's "tragic vision" is simply not "tragic" enough. Christian orthodoxy has historically held that man's dilemma is due to an act of human willing, indeed of human rebellion. While Christian theologians have debated the exact nature and origin of human sinfulness, virtually all orthodox Christians have rooted our dilemma in a fundamental rebellion which extends to all of us.

What is intriguing is Weaver's use of "tragic *vision*," for it is exactly at that point—at the point of human *vision*—that historic Christian theology has so much to say. For Weaver, man—as far back as Ockham and nominalism—began to cultivate an inferior and mistaken vision of things. Part of the genius of *Ideas Have Consequences* is the way in which Weaver traces the consequences of nominalism over time. This nominalist move initiated a trajectory leading to and culminating in modernism, and only an intentional recovery of something like realism, as well as an openness to transcendentals, bolstered by (1) the recovery of property rights, (2) a recovery of the nature and meaningfulness of language, and (3) and an appropriate understanding of piety and justice, can lead the way in the restoration of culture.

But again, perhaps Weaver is not tragic enough. For the tragedy of our human situation is that we have enslaved ourselves because we have *wanted* to be slaves. We did not simply make a wrong turn in the Middle Ages with the trajectory of nominalism. We have loved wrong things, and we have loved the right things in the wrong way. We are fundamentally disordered because we *want* to be disordered. This is a tragic situation indeed. And we lack *vision* because of our spiritual state.

To illustrate, Augustine could write that creation is objectively beautiful. Beauty is not an "imposition" on the created order. Creation

---

70. Ibid., 587.

really *is* beautiful. But then Augustine asks the obvious question: if creation really *is* beautiful, why do not all persons see this beauty? His answer is that persons do not *see* the beauty that is *there* because of disordered loves. We love the created order in an inordinate way, and because of our disordered loves we do not see what is *there*. In short, for Augustine the ability to *know* is linked to our spiritual state—to the nature of our loves. In this realm at least, Pascal is a thoroughgoing Augustinian.

Pascal, like Augustine, understood the way our desires, loves, and affections—the state of our hearts—effected our ability to know the truth, our ability to "see" things. A heart must be changed if one is truly going to be able to understand reality. Thus, Pascal at one point could write:

> Not only do we only know God through Jesus Christ, but we only know ourselves through Jesus Christ; we only know life and death through Jesus Christ. Apart from Jesus Christ we cannot know the meaning of our life or our death, of God or of ourselves. Thus without Scripture, whose only object is Christ, we know nothing, and can see nothing but obscurity and confusion in the nature of God and in nature itself.[71]

Nietzsche quotes Pascal: "Without the Christian faith, you, no less than nature and history, will become for yourselves *un monstre et un chaos*." Indeed, "Our inability to know the truth is the consequence of our corruption, our moral decay."[72]

What Weaver does not explore at great length—as far as I know—are the themes of sin and redemption. In fairness to Weaver, I should note that in the closing chapter of *Ideas Have Consequences*, "Piety and Justice," he does in fact begin to use some of the language and concepts that strike me as essential for understanding a more thoroughly Christian way of thinking about the modern era. He can assert that modernity is a "rebellion"; however, it is a rebellion primarily against nature.[73] He can also speak of modern man's problem as a "disease" of sorts, approximating in such language one way in which historic Christianity has spoken of the reality of sin.[74] Particularly interesting,

71. Pascal, *Pensées*, 308.
72. Nietzsche, *Will to Power*, 1.83.
73. Weaver, *Ideas Have Consequences*, 182.
74. Ibid., 184.

as well, is the fact that in this final chapter Weaver can again speak of modern man's apparent "suicidal impulse."[75] Indeed, man's problem—and here Weaver sounds a bit more Augustinian—is that perhaps he simply does not *want* to get better.[76]

Nonetheless, this more Augustinian way of speaking seems to be more the exception than the rule. Such typifies the serious lacunae in Weaver's utilization of Christian themes. Perhaps if Weaver had explored the themes of sin and redemption in more depth, he may have been led to ask *why* nominalism became attractive to many persons in the West. But as far as I can tell, this is precisely the question he does not ask—*why* nominalism became attractive in later Middle Ages, and *why* something like "nominalism" continues to be persuasive today. For Weaver, it is essentially a misstep in relation to *ontology*—the misstep of denying the centrality of universals in favor of the primacy of particulars—which is the fatal wrong turn in the Western intellectual tradition. Thus, modernity is fundamentally rooted in an *ontological* misstep.

Others—in attempting to understand modernity—have emphasized the importance of *epistemology*. That is, modernity is understood as fundamentally flowing from, or rooted in, certain epistemological shifts that occurred in say, the seventeenth and eighteenth centuries. To be sure, an analysis of different understandings of of modernity is beyond the scope of this essay. Nevertheless, Weaver's assumptions about modernity need scrutinizing. Weaver clearly sees modernity as rooted in a wrong understanding of the nature of universals. Modernity, for him, is fundamentally rooted in a certain *ontological* shift. Others stress that modernity is fundamentally rooted in a certain *epistemological* shift. But it may well be that both the ontological and epistemological emphases miss the point, or at least are simply a part of a larger problem, and to that potential problem I now turn.

In his penetrating analysis of the origin and nature of modernity, Stephen Williams suggests that whereas many persons point to epistemology as the watershed issue that is central to modernity and the Enlightenment, in fact there is a deeper problem. That is, Williams argues, modernity was about more than simply an epistemological issue whereby different persons debated whether knowledge of the supernatural was possible, or indeed, whether knowledge was possible at all.

75. Ibid., 185.
76. Ibid., 186.

Williams suggests—and here I suspect he has Scripture and much of the Christian tradition in his corner—that at the heart of the modern malaise lays a problem of the *will*. Neither ontology nor epistemology are the root problem; rather, the dilemma is volitional and moral. That is to say, modernity was resistance to (and rejecting of) the fact that we are fallen creatures in need of *reconciliation*. In Augustinian fashion, Williams suggests that the problem is not simply a particular intellectual conundrum—i.e., a misunderstanding about universals—but a deeper problem of the human will. Williams quotes Kierkegaard approvingly:

> People try to persuade us that the objections against Christianity spring from doubt. The objections against Christianity spring from insubordination, the dislike of obedience, rebellion against all authority. As a result people have hitherto been beating the air in their struggle against objections, because they have fought intellectually with doubt instead of fighting morally with rebellion.[77]

In short, the problems of modernity center—at least to a large degree—on the human *will*. As Williams observes, "Western atheism may be understood as a spiritual movement of the soul as well as intellectual movement of the mind."[78]

While there is not time to trace how such a construal might be justified historically (and here I would point readers to the work of Williams), it does seem that Williams has both Scripture and the Christian tradition on his side. When Paul says in the first chapter of Romans that all persons know God, yet suppress the knowledge of God, we see that this suppression of the knowledge of God is not rooted in an epistemological misstep, or ignorance, but that it is a willful act for which man is culpable. Indeed, this suppression—as Paul understands it—leads to such things as futile thinking and foolish, darkened hearts (Rom 1:22). If we turn to Proverbs we see that fools actually *hate* knowledge (Prov 1:22), and that "evil men do not *understand* justice" (Prov 28:5).

Karl Barth could speak of the modern dilemma in similar terms as found in Augustine, Pascal, and Kierkegaard. In his *Protestant Theology in the Nineteenth Century*, Barth writes:

---

77. Williams, *Revelation and Reconciliation*, 6. Williams is quoting Kierkegaard, *Works of Love*, eds., H. and E. Hong (New York: Harper & Row, 1962), 11.

78. Williams, *Revelation and Reconciliation*, 8.

> Fine and impressive reasons are given so that men in the modern world *can* no longer believe the teaching of Christianity in its traditional form, without a deliberate intention to deceive, but in fact because people no longer *want* to believe it. Man makes the opposition to older Christianity which had come about through his new moralism into a contrast between the modern and the obsolete presuppositions for cosmology and epistemology—in order to justify himself.[79]

And Barth sees this same trend in Friedrich Nietzsche himself:

> [That] everything should finally become a formal crusade against the cross, is not immediately apparent, but has to be learned and noted from a reading of Nietzsche. Yet it must be learned and noted if we are to understand him.[80]

As Williams views it, modernity is less a battle of "reason versus revelation" than a "moral-religious sufficiency versus reconciliation."[81]

If Williams is right, and modernity is more about a problem of the *will*—i.e., a *moral* problem rather than an *ontological* or *epistemological* problem—then we find ourselves inching toward an understanding of the strengths and weaknesses of Weaver's attempt to restore culture, and more particularly, the nature of his utilization of Christian themes. Weaver appropriately sees the centrality of certain important Christian themes: creation, the *logos*, faith seeking understanding, and eschatology and the importance of history. But he does not—as least as far as I can tell—see the problem as a problem of "disordered loves," or as an issue of moral *rebellion*, or as a willful suppression of the truth, a situation which can only be set right through atonement. We might gain insight by turning to a certain medieval thinker, Hugh of St. Victor (d. 1141), who wrote: "the eye of the heart must be cleansed by the study of virtue, so that it may thereafter see clearly for the investigation of truth in the theoretical arts."[82] The "eye of the heart" indeed must be cleansed, and this only happens through atonement—through the gospel of a very particular first-century Jew who was crucified and risen.

---

79. Barth, *Protestant Theology*, 94.

80. Quoted in Williams, *Revelation and Reconciliation*, 80.

81. Ibid., 81.

82. Hugh of St. Victor, *Didascalicon*, 154. Hugh of St. Victor could also write, "The subject matter of all the Divine Scriptures is the work of man's restoration" (3). See his *De Sacramentis* (On the Sacraments of the Christian Faith), prologue.1 (p. 3).

Some seven hundred years earlier Augustine could argue in *De Trinitate* that in order to see God face-to-face, one must be cleansed by the cross of Christ. And even to truly "see" beauty in *this* life requires that one's loves be ordered correctly—and this, of course, also requires the type of transformation brought about by atonement.

Richard Weaver desired to "restore culture," and countless twentieth- and twenty-first-century pilgrims have been helped by the wisdom of Weaver, particularly as expressed in his *Ideas Have Consequences*. Many have certainly moved from despair to hope (or from naïve utopianism to a more profound hopefulness) because of his writings. But to restore "culture" means, of course, to restore persons. And not just "persons" in the abstract, but *particular* persons. *My* neighbor, and *your* neighbor. *You* and *me*. What's more, the restoration of persons is serious—and hard—business. We *should* desire the restoration of "culture." Jonah was indeed rebuked, for example, for not caring for "the city." But he was rebuked for not caring for a *particular* city—Nineveh. The restoration of culture begins with the restoration of persons. And to be restored means having to understand something of how and why we have been deformed. The Christian tradition—upon which Weaver depended so heavily—has always taught that restoration begins with a particular person—the risen Jesus. Through faith in (and union with) him, restoration has begun. Without question, this restoration entails a proper construal and understanding of such things as creation, the *logos*, faith seeking understanding, and eschatology and the importance of history. But one must begin with the restoration of *persons*—this person and that person. Your unpleasant neighbor and my unpleasant neighbor.

Weaver was spot-on to recognize—even if he never quite said it this way—that the verities of the Christian tradition are the necessary "first things" in his own hopes of restoring culture. He appears to have perhaps stumbled over the rock of offense, for indeed the gospel is at its heart offensive, and strikes at our pride. Perhaps it was simply too difficult to think that a fleshly, first-century Jew from the backwater town of Nazareth—a *particular* man, of a *particular* race, in a *particular* time—was, and is, the key to the restoration of culture. Weaver's own Southern tradition—at its best—has admirably paid attention to particulars, and appropriately so. In his attempt to outline the possibility of a restoration of culture, I suspect that Weaver ignored the central particularity which is the key to the whole affair—a particular first-century Jew. Ideas indeed do have consequences, but sometimes the solution is found by giving attention to the particulars, and it is by giving attention to a particular first-century carpenter's son that we find the solution to the restoration of persons—and of culture.

Bibliography

Barth, Karl. *Protestant Theology in the Nineteenth Century: Its Background and History.* Translated by Brian Cozens and John Bowden. New York: Harper & Row, 1962.

Bradford, Mel. "Against the Barbarians." In *Against the Barbarians and Other Reflections on Familiar Themes*, 7–16. Columbia: University of Missouri Press, 1992.

Conyers, A. J. *The Eclipse of Heaven: Rediscovering the Hope of a World Beyond.* Downers Grove, IL: InterVarsity, 1992.

———. *The Listening Heart: Vocation and the Crisis of Modern Culture.* Dallas: Spence, 2006.

Curtis, George M., III, and James J. Thompson Jr., editors. *The Southern Essays of Richard Weaver.* Indianapolis: Liberty Fund, 1987.

Hugh of St. Victor. *De Sacramentis.* Edited by Roy J. Deferrari. Eugene, OR: Wipf & Stock, 2007.

———. *Didascalicon.* Translated by Jerome Taylor. New York: Columbia University Press, 1961.

Hume, David. *A Treatise of Human Nature.* London: Penguin, 1985.

Montgomery, Marion. "Consequences in the Provinces: *Ideas Have Consequences* Fifty Years After." In *Steps Toward Restoration: The Consequences of Richard Weaver's Ideas*, edited by Ted J. Smith III. Delaware, IN: Intercollegiate Studies Institute, 1998.

———. *The Truth of Things: Liberal Arts and the Recovery of Reality.* Dallas: Spence, 1999.

Nietzsche, Friedrich. *The Will to Power.* Translated by Walter Kaufmann and R. J. Hollingdale. New York: Vintage, 1968.

Pascal, Blaise. *Pensees.* Translated by A. J. Krailsheimer. Harmondsworth, UK: Penguin, 1966.

Percy, Walker. "Stoicism in the South." In *Signposts in a Strange Land*, edited by Patrick Samway. New York: Picador, 1991.

Smith, Ted, III, editor. *Steps toward Restoration: The Consequences of Richard Weaver's Ideas.* Delaware, IN: Intercollegiate Studies Institute, 1998.

Tate, Allen. "Religion and the Old South." In *I'll Take My Stand: The South and the Agrarian Tradition*, by Twelve Southerners, 155–75. Baton Rouge: Louisiana State University Press, 1977.

———. "A Southern Mode of Imagination." In *Essays of Four Decades*, 577–92. Chicago: Swallos, 1968.

Weaver, Richard M. "The Attack upon Memory." In *Visions of Order: The Cultural Crisis of Our Time*, 40–54. Wilmington, DE: Intercollegiate Studies Institute, 1995.

———. "Education and the Individual." In *Visions of Order: The Cultural Crisis of Our Time*, 184–99. Wilmington, DE: Intercollegiate Studies Institute, 1995.

———. "Gnostics of Education." In *Visions of Order: The Cultural Crisis of Our Time*, 113–33. Wilmington, DE: Intercollegiate Studies Institute, 1995.

———. *Ideas Have Consequences.* Chicago: University of Chicago Press, 1948.

———. "The Image of Culture." In *Visions of Order: The Cultural Crisis of Our Time*, 3–21. Wilmington, DE: Intercollegiate Studies Institute, 1995.

———. "Language Is Sermonic." In *In Defense of Tradition: Collected Shorter Writings of Richard M. Weaver 1929–1963*, edited by Ted J. Smith III, 353–70. Indianapolis: Liberty Fund, 2000.

———. "The Older Religiousness of the South." In *The Southern Essays of Richard Weaver*, edited by George M. Curtis III and James J. Thompson Jr., 134–46. Indianapolis: Liberty Fund, 1987.

———. "Relativism and the Use of Language." In *In Defense of Tradition: Collected Shorter Writings of Richard M. Weaver 1929–1963*, edited by Ted J. Smith III, 389–404. Indianapolis: Liberty Fund, 2000.

———. The Unsentimental Sentiment." In *Ideas Have Consequences*, 18–34. Chicago: University of Chicago Press, 1948.

———. *Visions of Order: The Cultural Crisis of Our Time*. Wilmington, DE: Intercollegiate Studies Institute, 1995.

Williams, Stephen N. *Revelation and Reconciliation: A Window on Modernity*. Cambridge: Cambridge University Press, 1995.

16

Preserving the Church's Story

D. H. Williams

Toward the end of Tolkien's *The Fellowship of the Ring*, Frodo Baggins and his company, exhausted and discouraged from their journey, come to the forest of the elves where Galadriel the elven queen gives to Frodo a special gift:

> She held up a small crystal phial: it glittered as she moved it, and rays of white light sprang from her hand. "In this phial," she said, "is caught the light of Earendil's star [Venus], set amid the waters of my fountain. *It will shine still brighter when night is about you. May it be a light to you in dark places, when all other lights go out.*"

The implication of this light's singular and unique value establishes an ideal that is not easily grasped by most readers (or viewers) within our current cultural climate. This light offered to Frodo is not a flashlight or torch for illuminating his path when it becomes too dark. It is, rather, an enlightenment of what is good from that darkness which harbors dangerous evil. The problem for contemporary readers is that this kind of illumination carries with it a notion that may seem too exclusive since it is supposed to be "a light ... when all other lights go out." If one accepts this light for what it purports to be, it threatens to nullify the value of other lights that are just as useful for one's journey. Today we are taught by various forms of media that there are always alternative roads, ideas, methods, etc., because there is no ultimate standard or transcendent reference point that is independent of our experience and preferences. Indeed, the positing of alternatives to a seemingly vague and universal truth have become the staple of intellectual, and not-so-intellectual, discourse. According to this understanding there can be no one light in the darkness; only various lights according to your gender, race, cultural context or sexual orientation. The very suggestion to the contrary smacks of naiveté, arrogance, or worse, intolerance.

Such a view has put a particular strain on learning in academic circles, since no core tradition should be preferred over others. Whereas drawing upon a canon of western literary thought was once generally considered necessary for teaching young minds, this is no longer the case. It is quite the reverse, actually. Diversity and multiculturalism have become the new mandate of higher education, which, if pushed to the extreme, can have a debilitating effect on any idea of a core of knowledge. It is the perspective that demands alternatives to any absolute or ideal, whether philosophical, religious or literary.[1] Such a view is not denying the existence of absolutes *per se*; rather, it is the demand that every claim for an absolute be grounded within a time and place and social circumstance. While this latter claim is important for giving a historic particularity to universalist assertions, there is an accompanying epistemology that ignores its own implicit universalism. Also behind this perspective, my former colleague, Chip Conyers, has reminded us, is the commonly accepted notion that every point of view is as valid as every other. This is part of modernity's mistaken understanding of ideological toleration. The complete loss of transcendence, truth, or universals will most likely produce an illusory idea of diversity that tends toward reducing all ideals to preferred practices. To quote Conyers directly, modernity has replaced the value of ends with means: the "[t]alk of ultimate ends becomes meaningless, for the horizon beyond the limited self has disappeared. We can only speak of operations, of practice, of techniques."[2]

A report issued in 2004 by the American Council of Trustees and Alumni entitled "The Hollow Core: Failure of the General Education Curriculum" is symptomatic of the above ideological trends. The report is a stinging rebuke to the top-rated fifty universities and colleges for utterly failing to ensure that their graduates become familiar with essential fields of knowledge such as American history, the best of English literature, economics, foreign languages, philosophy, and natural or

---

1. While one might expect this attitude within public universities, the same can be said for most private or Roman Catholic universities in the United States.

2. Conyers, "Three Sources of the Secular Mind," 321. Cf. idem, "Rescuing Tolerance," 43–46.

physical science. "[P]restige is not a guarantee of a solid general education curriculum. Time and again we ensure that their graduates are familiar with major fields of knowledge."[3]

The schools surveyed presented a smorgasbord of wide-varying elective courses, the majority of which represented cultural fads or material of questionable scholarly merit. A few examples are "History of Comic Book Art," "History and Philosophy of Dress," "Love and Money," "Survey of World Cinema," "Ghosts, Demons and Monsters," and "Rock Music from 1970 to Present." This cafeteria-style approach to learning "is a poor substitute for an informed, carefully designed core curriculum." It allows students to select almost any combination of courses, resulting in a "patchwork" that reflects youthful interests, but not lifelong educational needs. Some schools are paying attention to this serious problem. But relying upon a foundation of learning seems to matter little in the world of alternatives, especially if many aspects of this foundation lack utilitarian purposes. It is not without interest that the previous publication by the ACTA was entitled *Losing America's Memory: Historical Illiteracy in the 21st Century* (2000).

Believing that a core of knowledge carries significant meaning assumes that there exists a ground or a canonical understanding upon which a core may be built. As a new faculty member[4] I remember being assigned to a university committee that was charged with developing a basic core of courses that would be required of every student. After debating all semester, we could agree only on a vague menu of possibilities from which students could choose. Chiefly, the problem had to do with the committee's inability to concur upon a common intellectual tradition. Worrying that the students wouldn't be exposed to enough diversity, we failed to find a sufficient common ground of unity because no one literary or philosophical or religious body had greater relevance (so it was thought) to American students than any other.

We should not be surprised when our peers think that all statements are so culturally and historically conditioned, thus constituting equal value, and that they cannot be transferred from one age or one cultural region to another. Nor is the Christian mind immune from this defective idea of toleration. Avery Dulles commented, it is not

---

3. The text of "The Hollow Core" is accessible at www.goacta.org/publications/downloads/TheHollowCore.

4. I was not at my present university during this time.

uncommon to find the notion among church leadership, Roman Catholic and Protestant, that maintaining a doctrinal consensus in the Church is an obstacle to the creativity of local churches.[5] Practices may be acceptable, but doctrine serves only to divide.

Seeing that the Christian churches in North America have no less been affected by the above-mentioned cultural attitudes, we need to reexamine how the Church has responded to religious and philosophical pluralism[6] in the past when it comes to educating Christians in understanding and articulating their faith. Too often self-proclaimed Christians have a very limited grasp of their faith beyond that of their own religious experiences. We should not wonder when believers minimize the importance of Christian teaching for the practicalities of a pseudo-unanimity. This is not because they are dull of learning. It is rather because the Church does not expect more of them than the surrounding culture. When the "bar" for Christian ethics and doctrinal comprehension is set low, congregational members will follow suit. When necessity of basic theology becomes replaced with platitudes of "story," the lower common denominator will win over. But the greater problem, however, is when faith communities remain ignorant of those solutions for teaching its believers that have been used in the Church's own history with great benefit.

. . .

Christianity began with the promise of "one Lord, one faith, one baptism" (Eph 4:5) and perceived itself implicitly to be opposing a vast number of religious alternatives available in the ancient Roman world. Some Graeco-Roman religions were lively and colorful, others hidden and mysterious; almost all sought to keep the wrath of the gods at bay. Too much specification of one's belief was unnecessary provided that the proper practices were observed. The lack of a unified tradition or set of principles was not regarded as a problem. Indeed, philosophies that acknowledged a singular path which led to truth or the absolute were not welcome since the mere existence of religious multiplicity served as a kind of insulation between capricious divine powers and society. The ancient Pagan ideal is summed up in a state

---

5. Dulles, "Saving Ecumenism from Itself," 23–27.

6. Of course, social and religious pluralism is nothing new, nor is it an inherently negative condition. Herein lies both opportunity for easily creating new associations and dangers of creating a culture that is fundamentally intolerant while enforcing its own definition of tolerance. This two-fold character serves as a good description of the Roman Empire especially as it concerns religion.

paper written in the fourth century by Quintus Aurelius Symmachus, one-time mayor of the city of Rome:[7]

> Everyone has their own custom, their own ritual. The divine purpose assigned different cults[8] to different cities in order to protect them. Just as souls are given to each person at birth, so nations are allotted a genius[9] to preside over their destiny. There is also the matter of the benefits which the gods render, which is man's strongest argument for their existence.
>
> What does it matter what scheme of thought a person uses in the search for the truth. Man cannot come to so profound a mystery by one road alone.[10]

The formation of new believers coming into the church, therefore, would have to be re-oriented to monotheism and its crucial implication: you could not simply add the God of Abraham and Moses and Christ to your menu of religious options. Converting to the Christian faith meant rejecting all previous religious attachments and allegiances in order to embrace a singular and exclusive core of doctrinal and moral directions. There may be many different churches in many different ethnic and cultural settings, but as Tertullian of Carthage argued in the early third century, "they are all primitive and all are apostolic, while they are all proved to be one, in (unbroken) unity, by their peaceful communion, and title of brotherhood, and bond of hospitality, and privileges. No other rule directs than the one tradition of the selfsame mystery."[11] While Tertullian's expression is typically hyperbolic, in comparison to the kaleidoscopic phenomenon of Gnosticism, his point carries validity.

Because of its original basis in doctrines (and practices) that were sufficiently shared, the Church from the earliest moments of its existence was a teaching church. Biblical commentary, credal instruction, doctrinal explanations, recounting the lives of holy men worthy of imitation, and theological poetry all served to articulate a uniquely Christian un-

---

7. Praefectus urbis.

8. "Cultus" is the practice and rites involved in religious acts.

9. A guardian spirit of a person or a place.

10. *Relatio* III. 8, 10. This is the same Symmachus who appointed Augustine to the position of rhetor in Milan partly because Augustine, at the time, was not a Christian.

11. *De praescriptione haereticorum* 20.

derstanding of Scripture and of the life of faith.[12] The Christian regarded the faith as a body of understanding that transcended him, directing the believer to that which was beyond the self.

This form of "the faith" had a particular substance that must be taught. We should observe that the Apostle Paul, who was given the truths of God through special revelation, also (and more often) talks about this faith in the form of the Church's tradition. Specifically, he describes the faith as something "handed over" and "received" by those who would rightly understand the gospel (e.g., 1 Cor 11:23–24). After returning from the desert, Paul himself tells us that he spent time with Peter and James, the Lord's brother, where further confirmation and impartation was made to him about the Gospel "received" by the original apostles (Galatians 1–2).

• • •

The earliest developments in educating Christians to think and live as Christians emerged out of situations of need. On one hand, the early Fathers speak most directly of the Church's tradition in apologetic contexts when they are defending catholic faith against its detractors. On the other hand, succinct summaries of faith were also drawn up for the purpose of instructing new converts. It is difficult to draw a hard line between the two purposes. In both cases, the reception and transmission of a core of the Church's faith as expressed in its life reveal the importance which the preservation of the apostolic memory had for the churches of the post-apostolic period. The oral impartation of Christian teaching to serious inquirers and learners was a constant and central feature in the life of these churches that extended beyond Sunday sermons.

The fact that most believers were functionally illiterate meant that auditory and visual means of transmitting the faith were necessary. Most learning would have to occur through short formulae and repetition, as found in the liturgies, but also through intensive instruction: periods of fasting, prayer, and closely observing the lives of those who taught them. In particular, I refer to that period known as the *scrutinies*,[13] i.e., that period which immediately preceded baptism and was meant to usher the

---

12. "Faith" was usually regarded as a noun rather than a personal religious experience. It was a standard to which the believer was joined.

13. At this stage, pre-baptismal candidates were called *competentes*.

new believer into the thought-world and life practice of Christianity. Upon entering this stage, one was no longer a mere catechumen, a stage which could last indefinitely.

Allusions to this process of baptismal instruction in the ethical and intellectual life demonstrate that it "served as a control with considerable effect on the understanding of the Christian faith." We should bear in mind, however, that there is very little evidence for how pre- and post-baptismal instruction was handled in the first three centuries. We know of no theological textbooks or "Sunday school" type of materials offering a rudimentary outline of Christian belief and practice before the mid-fourth century. The practice of *catechesis*—a series of steps that leads the new believer to baptism and a deeper knowledge of the faith—was created by the early Fathers, but hardly any texts that address the mechanics of the subject are extant until the middle of the fourth century. Reasons for this silence vary from the relative secrecy with which the Church had to live, to the understanding that the Church's deposit of faith was not to be taken lightly by allowing anyone to know it.[14] It was also regarded as one of the church's mysteries (1 Tim 3:6) that should only be written in the Christian's heart. Perhaps the reason that we possess very little evidence about pre-Nicene teaching practices is simply because there never existed much to begin with.

Still, there is an important lesson here for the church of today, which is almost frantic to embrace all and any who come through the doors. The early Church's leaders used a method—if we may call it such—of what may be called paradoxically an *inclusivist exclusivism* that was more interested to preserve the faith's unique identity and the church's holiness than swell the size of its congregations. At least one document from the third century provides the details of which lifestyles and employment positions were unacceptable for those who wished to be baptized. At first, applicants for baptism are examined why they are seeking to enter the church. "Then they will be questioned concerning the reason that they have come forward to the faith. Those who bring them will bear witness concerning them as to whether they are able to hear. They shall be questioned concerning their life and occupation, marriage status, and whether they are slave or free."[15] The process

---

14. See Ferguson, *Baptism in the Early Church*.

15 *Apostolic Tradition* 15.2–3. This text has been long attributed to Hippolytus of Rome, though see Baldovin, "Hippolytus and the *Apostolic Tradition*: Recent Research and Commentary," 520–42.

continues with inquiry into their occupations. Gladiators (or teachers of gladiators), those who arrange public games, prostitutes, makers of amulets or other materials used in divination, pagan priests, astrologers, soldiers or military governors who participate in killing—to name several—are not accepted into baptismal instruction until they abandon these pursuits.[16]

The little we do know about the mechanics of the process of educating new Christians in the earliest centuries is that the actual teaching was accomplished by those who were specially appointed to serve as catechists. Given that most "congregations" were house churches, the work of catechizing new believers took place in the catechist's own dwelling or some designated spot. When Justin (the Martyr) was arrested in his apartment in Rome, it turns out that there were with him six others whom he was teaching, presumably preparing them for baptism. All seven were executed shortly thereafter for their confession of faith. Likewise, the arrest of Perpetua of Carthage took place when the authorities suddenly burst into a catechetical "class." Perpetua was imprisoned and later martyred with four other catechumens and their catechist, Saturus, in the amphitheater at Carthage on 7 March 203. Obviously, being taught the Christian faith was no less hazardous than outwardly professing it.

Other well-known Christian intellectuals of the era were catechists. Clement of Alexandria was a leading teacher for catechumens in the church of Alexandria, as would be his most famous pupil, Origen. Almost as renowned was Didymus, the chief catechist of Alexandria in the early fourth century, who was made blind by disease at the age of four. Probably the otherwise unknown Marcianus, to whom Irenaeus wrote his *Proof of the Apostolic Preaching*, was a catechist.[17] This early practice of "farming out" the training of new Christians to local Christian philosophers differs from later practices when bishops usually handled this task, or at least the last stages of it.

While the ancient evidence for the process indicates that it differed from place to place, a basic structure seems to run throughout the origins of catechetical instruction. For the early Christians, theological instruction (or what the ancients often called "the true philosophy") was not a metaphysical exercise detached from the spiritual, liturgical, and

---

16. Ibid., 16. 1–16.
17. Williams, *Retrieving the Tradition and Renewing Evangelicalism*, 79.

ethical needs of congregations. Nor was it a menu of religious options that the believer could merely take or leave. Let me illustrate.

The earliest known document that bears resemblance to what we later recognize as a "catechism"—to use the word anachronistically—is a Jewish-Christian guideline for ethics and regulating internal church practice known as the "Two Ways." Jewish in origin, it was immediately adopted in Christian circles by the early second century.[18] It begins with the words, "There are two ways, one of life (or light) and one of death (or darkness); and between the two ways there is a great difference." What follows is a series of moral injunctions from Deuteronomy and the Sermon on the Mount, quoting directly from Matthew 5 and Luke 6. Jesus' teaching on the lifestyle for the Kingdom of God is taken at face value and embraced as authentic Christian living. The didactic nature of these injunctions is made clear from the fact that they are issued within the context of a congregation: among other things the reader is urged to honor those "who preach God's word to you" (*Didache* 4.1), all forms of schism among believers are condemned (4.3), and the confession of sins in the church assembly before offering prayer is said to be "the way of life" (4.14). That the "Two Ways" pattern is immediately followed by baptismal instructions in both the *Didache* and two other later documents that cite the "Two Ways" underscores its adaptation by churches as part of a catechism. We must, however, be careful in broadly construing the evidence of the *Didache* since it has features which are idiosyncratic to the region of northern Syria and not found elsewhere.

An acknowledged handbook of catechetical instruction from the later second century is Irenaeus' *Proof of the Apostolic Preaching*, a late second-century work that survives today only in a sixth-century Armenian translation. The addressee of the work, the same Marcianus mentioned above, is told that its aim is to "set forth in brief the preaching of the truth" by providing "in brief the proof (or exposition) of the things of God," i.e., a concentrated explanation of God's unfolding plan for salvation. This condensed narration of God's redemptive activity was in keeping with a didactic format that naturally lent itself to catechetical purposes.

---

18. Almost certainly, this instruction existed independently of its later textual manifestations. Three versions of it have come down to us in the *Epistle of Barnabas* 18–19, the *Didache*, and much later in book VII of the *Apostolic Constitutions*. Allusions to it abound throughout patristic writings.

Irenaeus begins by declaring that our faith "admonishes us to remember that we have received baptism for the remission of sins in the name of God the Father, and in the name of Jesus Christ, the Son of God, who became incarnate and died and was raised, and in the Holy Spirit of God" (c. 3). Doctrinal elaboration immediately follows this baptismal formula, evidently drawing on the profession of faith that was accepted in the Gallic churches. Irenaeus here lays out the basis "of our faith, the foundation of the building, and the consolidation of a way of life":

> God the Father, uncreated, beyond grasp, invisible, one God the maker of all; this is the first and foremost article of our faith. But the second article is the Word of God, the Son of God, Christ Jesus our Lord, who was shown forth by the prophets according to the design of their prophecy and according to the manner in which the Father disposed; and through Him were made all things whatsoever. He also, in the end of times . . . became a man among men, visible and tangible, in order to abolish death and bring to light life, and bring about the communion of God and man. And the third article is the Holy Spirit, through whom the prophets prophesied and the patriarchs were taught about God . . . and who in the end of times has been poured forth in a new manner upon humanity over all the earth renewing man to God. (c. 6)

The Trinitarian pattern, or "three articles," exhibited here is not fashioned by Irenaeus, but likely comes from baptismal confession of faith already used in the West before his time. The pattern becomes the doctrinal anchor for the rest of the profession as it will for the next several centuries. Thus, the beginning of Christian learning was to focus the believer on the centrality of God rather than become absorbed with the personal response to God. Were not the believer's spiritual experiences of importance in the early church? Certainly. Hilary of Poitiers' preface to his *De trinitate* or Augustine's *Confessiones* 8–9 offer sufficient demonstration of this. But it is the same Augustine who directs Christian leaders in *De doctrina Christiana* to the greater truth that we are to love the Trinitarian God as our first and highest good. The truth of God places all our other loves of our neighbor, of ourselves, etc., into their proper balance. Benedict XVI makes a related point in his recent encyclical *Caritas in Veritate*: "Only in truth does charity shine forth, only in truth can charity be authentically lived. Truth is the light that gives meaning and value to charity."[19]

An anonymous and composite work edited in the later fourth century containing elements from earlier periods known as the *Apostolic Constitutions* sets forth the goal of baptismal instruction very succinctly. Such instruction likely carries material from the pre-Nicene period:

> Let him, therefore, who is to be taught the truth in regard to piety be instructed before his baptism in the knowledge of the Unbegotten God, in the understanding of His Only-begotten Son, in the assured acknowledgement of the Holy Spirit. Let him learn the order of the several parts of the creation, the series of providential acts, the different workings of God's laws.
>
> Let him be instructed about why the world was made, and why man was appointed to be a citizen in it; let him also know about his own human nature, of what sort of creature he is; let him be taught how God punished the wicked with water and fire, and glorified the saints in every generation . . . and how God did not reject mankind, but called them from their error and vanity to acknowledge the truth in various stages of history, leading them from bondage and impiety to liberty and piety, from injustice to justice, from death eternal to everlasting life.[20]

• • •

The instruction of new believers became more sophisticated in the fourth century with the convergence of several trends: greater doctrinal sophistication due to the Trinitarian and Christological debates, the rise of highly educated and erudite Christian thinkers entering the church, and the influx of very many new Christians now that the persecutions were mostly over. The result was that the structures for Christianizing converts were becoming more carefully and consistently defined.[21]

A new stage was added in the catechetical process. "Catechumen" became the term for anyone who had enrolled for baptism but had not yet begun the actual period of instruction. In theory and in practice persons could be regarded as catechumens for years before they took the next step. Many Christians in military or imperial positions took this route, putting off their actual baptism until they were near death

---

19. *Caritas in Veritate*, pref. 3.
20. *Apostolic Constitutions* VII. 39, 1–4; ANF VII. 475–76 (slightly altered).
21. Harmless, *Augustine and the Catechumenate*, 51–56.

because the demands of their offices required acts of killing, torture, limited participation in old pagan rites, and so on, that were inconsistent with the life of the baptized believer. Emperor Constantine availed himself of this flexibility. Once catechumens proved the intentional sanctity of their life and began to attend the weekly and then daily meetings of instruction (usually held in the period before Easter), they became *competentes*, that is, they were qualified to go on to the next stage.[22] This would be a shorter and more intense period of training, usually during Lent, in which the candidates would receive the Church's creed for the first time and have it explained to them. Not unexpectedly, this part of the process was called the *traditio*. The candidates would commit the creed to memory and recite it before the congregation on the day of their baptism—a moment called the *redditio*, the giving back of the church's faith.

The most the memorable *redditio* seems to have been the great Pagan rhetor of Rome, Marius Victorinus, who converted to Christianity (c. 350). Because of his renown, a statue was erected in his honor in the Roman forum—while he was still living(!). It was as if a famous actor or eminent scientist had suddenly come to Christ and was baptized on public television. But now having been converted, Victorinus was reluctant to come to the church and be baptized. Nonetheless, on an Easter Sunday, he publicly recited the Roman creed (which is a forerunner of the Apostles' Creed) while the congregation chanted in the background "Victorinus, Victorinus, Victorinus."

Besides learning the creed, candidates were also taught how to distinguish the truths behind the creed and (to a smaller extent) those distortions of the tradition manifested through various heresies of the time. The Beatitudes and the Lord's Prayer were often included as part of the instruction because no one could pray "Our Father" until he had been made a son of God and received the gift of adoption.

The seriousness with which Christian leaders took pre- and post-baptismal instruction is evident in how meticulously they formulated and taught the faith. Gregory of Nyssa (ca. 335–ca. 394) manifests its significance in his *Address on Catechetical Instruction*. Without ever mentioning the creed, Gregory presents a theological narrative of

---

22. This period of instruction was called the *Quadragesima*, or the "fortieth," because it occurred in the forty days before Holy Week (though some areas took a longer period of time for instruction and others much shorter).

salvation history, supported by scriptural references and allusions, defending a pro-Nicene/Constantinopolitan position on the Trinity. He calls this narrative the "gospel revelation," and its overall end is to show both how "[God] is united to us in so far as he sustains existing things [as creator]" and that "he united himself with our nature in order that by its union with the Divine, it might become divine."[23] Judging from Gregory's address, one may reasonably conclude there is no doubt that he expected his listeners to become well-versed in the basics of good theology, which stands as an important model for us.

A number of sermons and addresses from this period show that the catechizing process was becoming more formalized and unified as the Church received an ever larger number of converts. It is commonplace to hear that church discipline and doctrine became lax after Constantine, and so many were turning to Christianity; but this is not the case. A female pilgrim to Jerusalem named Egeria who lived a generation after Constantine alludes to the elaborate preparatory steps which catechumens had to undergo during the forty-day period before Easter.[24] She observes that not only the creed but also instruction on doctrinal and moral issues was imparted to the new believers before they could be full-fledged members of the church.

The actual course of instruction is outlined in a set of addresses delivered by Cyril, the Bishop of Jerusalem, to baptismal candidates during Lent (probably around AD 350). It is worth reading his introduction to the *competentes* at length:

> Now the one and only faith that you are to take and preserve in the way of learning and professing is being committed to you by the Church as confirmed throughout the Scriptures. For seeing that not everyone can read the Scriptures, some because they lack the learning and others because, for one reason or another, they find no opportunity to get to know them, we can acquire the whole doctrine of the Christian faith in a few articles and so prevent any soul from being lost by not learning the faith. At this stage listen to the exact form of words [i.e., the Jerusalem creed] and memorize this faith, leaving it to the appropriate time when each article it contains may be built up from Holy Scripture. For these articles of our faith were not composed out of human

---

23. *Address on Catechetical Instruction*, 25.

24. For the specific passage where she describes the details of how the church applied the process, see Williams, *Tradition, Scripture and Interpretation*, 85–88.

> opinion, but are the principal points collected out of the whole of Scripture to complete a single doctrinal formulation of the faith. And just as the mustard seed contains many future tree branches within its tiny grain, so also this faith embraces in a few phrases all the religious knowledge contained in the Old and New Testaments together. Be sure, brothers, to "hold the traditions" [2 Thess 2:15] which are being imparted to you, and "write them on the table of your hearts" [Prov 7:3].[25]

Being schooled in the creed's particularities was the first step not only in learning what the Bible means, but also in preparing to read Scripture with insight. Cyril urges his listeners to persevere with the intensive classes of instruction because the goal is to arm them against error and provide a solid foundation for the Christian life. He proceeds to lay forth "indispensable teachings" on God, on Christ's divinity, incarnation and passion, on the Holy Spirit, on the soul and body, on bodily resurrection, on the centrality of Scripture, and on the catholic church. Besides the sessions of instruction, the catechumens were required to renew their repentance, show the purity of their intention, and undertake fasting, thus preparing them for a baptism that would lead them out of one dominion into another. I use the word "dominion" intentionally because part of the profession of baptism was the public renunciation of Satan and all his works. Baptism was nothing less than the release of the believer from the captivity of the devil and sin.

• • •

We should take note of the ancient church's focus on catechesis, that is, on its methods of carefully instructing recent converts or those preparing for baptism about the biblical and doctrinal fundamentals of the Christian faith. Expressing one's experience of the grace of God does not make for strong or spiritually discerning Christians, which is partly the reason for Clement of Alexandria's comment that "[i]t is impossible to believe without instruction."[26] Within its original context of social and religious plurality, the early Christians had to create for themselves a culture of learning not as an alternative to their surrounding environment, but as a culture that enabled them to interpret and discern. It follows that there were high expectations of each believer, as well as of the shepherds. In the preface to his manual of Christian instruction,

25. *Catechetical Addresses*, 5.12.
26. *Eclogues* 28. 3.

Gregory of Nyssa declared that "religious catechism is an essential duty of the leaders 'of the mystery of our religion'" (1 Tim 3:16).[27] If it is the case that the Church "is the pillar and foundation of the truth" (1 Tim 3:15), then ecclesiastical leadership must not shirk the critical and time-consuming job of imparting Christian truth or catechizing those who profess to be Christian.

We are acting in accord with Gregory's remarks when we insist that new Christians or new members be taught much more than the congregation's leadership structure and polity, stewardship plan, and mission statement, or be given a brief denominational summary. Too often we assume potential church members already know the fundamentals of their faith, whereas in reality they are incapable of explaining even the basics of "the pattern of sound teaching" (2 Tim 1:13). When we introduce new or "old" believers to the truths that exceed their own experiences we are, as Augustine said, "distributing the treasure of the Lord."[28] Such treasures are the central points of the apostolic faith and practice—a faith that is larger than any one denomination's or church's claims upon it—sharpened and transmitted through the ages, within a doctrinal and moral community.

In sum, Christians should in no way abandon the reality and potential for teaching truth, or relegate themselves to the realm where practices and preferences are more acceptable. One does not need to be an advocate of propositional revelation in order to stand upon the witness of Scripture and the Church's tradition. Likewise, religious tolerance is not necessitated by swallowing the assertion that any religion is as good as any other, or that truth about religious matters is virtually impossible to attain. "Without a conviction about the first things, tolerance becomes apathy, pluralism becomes ignorance, and dialogue becomes cacophony."[29] All the manuals of catechism in the world are of no value if the quest for what is truly good, just, and beautiful has been made ephemeral. The Church and its message are not about inventing alternatives to ethical purity or intellectual fidelity in order to accommodate the greatest number of people. We should rather seek for the conscious construction of the "school of the Lord" which creates the best context for toleration when Christians are taught "Blessed are the poor in spirit . . . the meek . . . the peacemakers . . . the pure in heart."

27. *Address on Catechetical Instruction*, preface.
28. *On Catechizing the Unlearned* I. 1.
29. Graebe, "Tolerance and Charity."

Bibliography

Baldovin, John F. "Hippolytus and the Apostolic Tradition." *Theological Studies* 64, no. 3 (2003) 520-42.

Bauckham, Richard and Benjamin Dewey, eds., *Scripture, Tradition and Reason: A Study in the Criteria of Christian Doctrine*. Edinburgh: T. & T. Clark, 1988.

Benedict XVI, *Caritas in Veritate*. Online: www.vatican.va/holy_father/benedict_xvi/encyclicals/documents/hf_ben-xvi_enc_20090629_caritas-in-veritate_en.html.

Conyers, A. J. "Rescuing Tolerance." *First Things* (August/ September 2001) 43-46.

———. "Three Sources of the Secular Mind." *Journal of the Evangelical Theological Society* 41 (1998) 313–21.

Dulles, Avery. "Saving Ecumenism from Itself." *First Things* (December 2007). Online: www.firstthings.com/article/2007/11/001-saving-ecumenism-from-itself-36.

Ferguson, Everett, *Baptism in the Early Church*. Grand Rapids: Eerdmans, 2009.

Finn, Thomas M. *Early Christian Baptism and the Catechumenate: West and East Syria*. Collegeville, MN: Liturgical Press, 1992.

Graebe, Brian A. "Tolerance and Charity." *First Things* (July 30, 2009). Online: http://www.firstthings.com/onthesquare/2009/07/tolerance-and-charity.

Harmless, William. *Augustine and the Catechumenate*. Collegeville, MN: Liturgical Press, 1995.

"The Hollow Core." Online: www.goacta.org/publications/downloads/TheHollowCore.

Kelly, J. N. D. *Early Christian Creeds*. London: Longman, 1978; rev. ed., 1956.

Norris, Frederick. *The Apostolic Faith: Protestants and Roman Catholics*. Collegeville, MN: Liturgical, 1992.

Williams, D. H. *Retrieving the Tradition and Renewing Evangelicalism: A Primer for Suspicious Protestants*. Grand Rapids: Eerdmans, 1999.

———. *Tradition, Scripture and Interpretation: A Sourcebook of the Ancient Church*. Grand Rapids: Baker Academic Books, 2006.

Wood, Ralph, *Contending for the Faith: The Church's Engagement with Culture*. Waco, TX: Baylor University Press, 2003.

Selected Bibliography of A. J. Conyers

Books

How to Read the Bible. Downers Grove, IL: InterVarsity, 1986. Korean ed.: Korean InterVarsity, 1990.

God, Hope and History: Jürgen Moltmann's Christian Concept of History. Macon, GA: Mercer University Press, 1988.

The Eclipse of Heaven. Downers Grove, IL: InterVarsity, 1992. Reprint, St. Augustine's Press, 1999.

The End: What the Gospels Say about the Last Things. Downers Grove, IL: InterVarsity, 1995. Portuguese ed.: *O Fim Do Mundo.* Sao Paulo, Brazil: Editora Mundo Christão, 2000.

A Basic Christian Theology. Nashville: Broadman & Holman, 1995.

The Long Truce: How Toleration Made the World Safe for Power and Profit. Dallas: Spence, 2000. Reprint, Waco, TX: Baylor University Press, 2009.

The Listening Heart: Vocation and the Crisis of Modern Culture. Dallas: Spence, 2006. Reprint, Waco, TX: Baylor University Press, 2009.

Articles

"God and Man in Dialogue with Marxism." *Christianity Today* (July 2, 1971).

"Is Patriotism Christian?" *Christian Heritage* (June 1972).

"Teaching the Holocaust: The Role of Theology." *Perspectives in Religious Studies* (Summer 1981).

"Liberation Theology: Whom Does It Liberate?" *Modern Age* (Spring 1983).

"When Doubt Can Help You." *Christianity Today* (February 4, 1984).

"The Revival of Joachite Apocalyptic Speculation in Contemporary Theology." *Perspectives in Religious Studies* (Fall 1985).

"Interview with Jürgen Moltmann." *Christianity Today*, (March 10, 1987).

"James: A Pillar of the Church." *Biblical Illustrator* (Fall 1988).

"Communism's Collapse: The Receding Shadow of Transcendence." *Christian Century* (May 2, 1990).

"Mount Ararat." *Broadman Dictionary of the Bible.* Nashville: Broadman, 1991.

"After the Hurricane." *Christianity Today*, (November 9, 1992).

"A Profile of Levi." *Biblical Illustrator* (Spring 1995).

"Protestant Principle/ Catholic Substance." *First Things* (November 1996).

"Cloning and the Moral Imagination." *Touchstone* (Summer 1997).

"The Changing Face of Baptist Theology." *Review and Expositor* (Winter 1998).

"Beyond Walden Pond: Illusion and Reality in the Pursuit of the Simple Life." *Touchstone* (November/December 1998).

"Three Sources of the Secular Mind." *Journal of the Evangelical Theological Society* (June 1998).

"Simms' Sabbath Lyrics and the Reclaiming of Sacred Time in the Religious Imagination." *Simms Review* (Summer 2000).

"History as Problem and Hope." *Asbury Theological Journal* (Spring 2000).

"Why the Chattahoochee Sings: Notes on a Theory of 'Place.'" *Modern Age* (Spring 2001).

"Rescuing Tolerance," *First Things* (August/September 2001).

"Living under Vacant Skies." *Christian Reflection* (Spring 2002).

"Vocation and the Liberal Arts." *Modern Age* (Spring 2003).

"Can Postmodernism Be Used as a Template for Christian Theology?" *Christian Scholar's Review* (Spring 2004).